GLOBAL  STUDIES

CHINA

SEVENTH EDITION

Dr. Suzanne Ogden

Northeastern University

Dushkin/McGraw-Hill
Sluice Dock, Guilford, Connecticut 06437

Visit us on the Internet—http://www.dushkin.com/

China

OTHER BOOKS IN THE GLOBAL STUDIES SERIES

- Africa
- India and South Asia
- Japan and the Pacific Rim
- Latin America
- The Middle East
- Russia, the Eurasian Republics, and Central/Eastern Europe
- Western Europe

Cataloging in Publication Data
Main Entry under title: Global Studies: China. 7th ed.
    1. China—History—1976–. 2. Taiwan—History—1945–. I. Title: China. II. Ogden, Suzanne, *comp.*
ISBN 0–697–37421–1

Seventh Edition

Printed in the United States of America

China

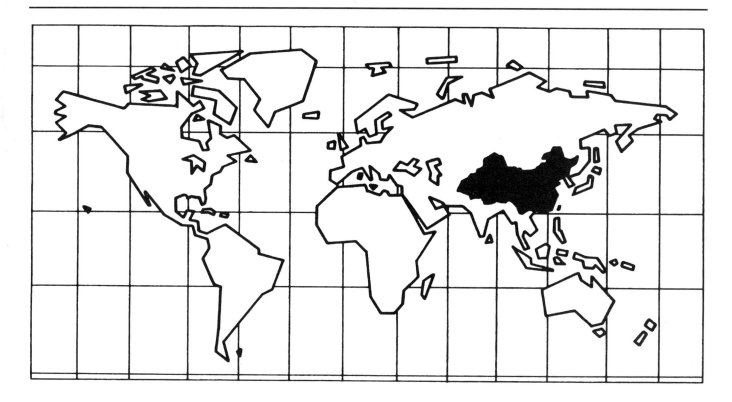

AUTHOR/EDITOR

Dr. Suzanne Ogden

Dr. Suzanne Ogden is professor and chair of the Political Science Department at Northeastern University and research associate at the Fairbank Center for East Asian Research, Harvard University. She has lived in both Taiwan and Hong Kong and has traveled frequently to the People's Republic of China. Dr. Ogden is the author of *China's Unresolved Issues: Politics, Development, and Culture* (Prentice Hall, 1989, 1992, 1995); and chief editor and project director of *China's Search for Democracy: The Student and Mass Movement of 1989* (M. E. Sharpe, 1992). Dr. Ogden's current research is focused on democratization in the P.R.C.

SERIES CONSULTANT

H. Thomas Collins
PROJECT LINKS
George Washington University

STAFF

Ian A. Nielsen	Publisher
Brenda S. Filley	Production Manager
Lisa M. Clyde	Developmental Editor
Roberta Monaco	Editor
Charles Vitelli	Designer
Cheryl Greenleaf	Permissions Coordinator
Shawn Callahan	Graphics Coordinator
Lara M. Johnson	Graphics Coordinator
Laura Levine	Graphics Coordinator
Michael Campbell	Graphics Coordinator
Joseph Offredi	Graphics Coordinator
Juliana Arbo	Typesetting Supervisor

Selected World Wide Web Sites for Global Studies: China

(Some Web sites continually change their structure and content, so the information listed here may not always be available.—Ed.)

GENERAL SITES

CNN Online Page—**http://www.cnn.com/**—U.S. 24-hour video news channel. News, updated every few hours, includes text, pictures, and film. Good external links.

C-SPAN ONLINE—**http://www.c-span.org/**—See especially C-SPAN International on the Web for International Programming Highlights and archived C-Span programs.

International Network Information Center at University of Texas—**http://inic.utexas.edu/**—Gateway has pointers to international sites, including China, Hong Kong, and Taiwan.

I-Trade International Trade Resources & Data Exchange—**http://www.i-trade.com/**—Monthly exchange-rate data, U.S. Document Export Market Information (GEMS), U.S. Global Trade Outlook, and World Fact Book 1995 statistical demographic and geographic data for 180+ countries.

Political Science RESOURCES—**http://www.keele.ac.uk:80/depts/po/psr.htm/**—Dynamic gateway to sources available via European addresses. Listed by country name. Include official government pages, official documents, speeches, elections, political events.

ReliefWeb—**http://www.reliefweb.int/**—UN's Department of Humanitarian Affairs clearinghouse for international humanitarian emergencies. Has daily updates, including Reuters, VOA, PANA.

Social Science Information Gateway (SOSIG)—**http://sosig.esrc.bris.ac.uk/**—Project of the Economic and Social Research Council (ESRC). It catalogs 22 subjects and lists developing countries' URL addresses.

United Nations System—**http://www.unsystem.org/**—This is the official Web site for the United Nations system of organizations. Everything is listed alphabetically. Offers: UNICC; Food and Agriculture Organization.

UN Development Programme (UNDP)—**http://www.undp.org/**—Publications and current information on world poverty, Mission Statement, UN Development Fund for Women, and more. Be sure to see Poverty Clock.

UN Environmental Programme (UNEP)—**http://www.unchs.unon.org/**—Official site of UNEP. Information on UN environmental programs 1996/97, products, services, events, search engine.

U.S. Agency for International Development (USAID)—**http://www. info.usaid.gov/**—U.S. trade statistics with China, Hong Kong, and Taiwan in graphic form are available at this site.

U.S. Central Intelligence Agency Home Page—**http://www.odci.gov/cia**—This site includes publications of the CIA, such as the 1996 World Fact Book, 1995 Fact Book on Intelligence, Handbook of International Economic Statistics, 1996, and CIA maps.

U.S. Department of State Home Page—**http://www.state.gov/index.html/**—Organized by categories: Hot Topics (i.e., 1996 Country Reports on Human Rights Practices), International Policy, Business Services.

World Bank Group—**www.worldbank.org/html/Welcome.html/**—News (i.e., press releases, summary of new projects, speeches), publications, topics in development, countries and regions. Links to other financial organizations, including IBRD, IDA, IFC, MIGA. There are links to many special-interest subjects.

World Health Organization (WHO)—**http://www.who.ch/**—Maintained by WHO's headquarters in Geneva, Switzerland, uses Excite search engine to conduct keyword searches.

World Trade Organization—**http://www.wto.org/**—Topics include foundation of world trade systems, data on textiles, intellectual property rights, legal frameworks, trade and environmental policies, recent agreements, etc.

CHINA

Asia-Yahoo—**http://www.yahoo.com/Regional/Regions/Asia/**—Specialized Yahoo search site permits key-word search on Asian events, countries, or topics.

Chinese Society Home Page—**http://members.aol.com/mehampton/ chinasec.html/**—Information is listed under Chinese Military Links, Data Sources on Chinese Security Issues, Key Newspapers and News Services, and Key Scholarly Journals and Magazines. Several links to other security-related sites.

CRLP: Women of the World—**http://www.echonyc.com/~jmkm/wotw/html/** —Click on China at this Web site and view by Topic by clicking on Health, Contraception, Population, and Family Planning, etc., for information on issues relating to women in China.

Information Office of State Council of People's Republic of China—**hhtp://www.cityu.edu.hk/HumanRights/index.htm/**—Official site of China's government contains policy statements by the government related to Human Rights.

Inside China Today—**http://www.insidechina.com/**—This Web site is part of the European Information Network. Recent information on China is organized under Headline News, Government, and Related Sites, Mainland China, Hong Kong, Macao, and Taiwan.

HONG KONG

Hong Kong Internet & Gateway Services—**http://www. hk.net/**—This gateway has up-to-date information about Hong Kong past and present and also contains a search engine.

Hong Kong World Wide Web Virtual Library—**http://www.asiawind.com/hkwwwvl/**—This is another excellent set of links to historical and topical information about Hong Kong.

We recommend that you check out our Web site, which can be reached at *http://www.dushkin.com/*

Contents

Global Studies: China, Seventh Edition

People's Republic of China Page 13

Taiwan Page 58

Hong Kong Page 78

Introduction

(United Nations photo/John Isaac)

Understanding the problems and lifestyles of other countries will help make us literate in global matters.

THE GLOBAL AGE

As we approach the end of the twentieth century, it is clear that the future we face will be considerably more international in nature than was ever believed attainable in the past. Each day, print and broadcast journalists make us aware that our world is becoming increasingly smaller and substantially more interdependent.

The environmental crisis, world food shortages, nuclear weaponry, and regional conflicts that threaten to involve us all make it clear that the distinctions between domestic and foreign problems are often artificial—that many seemingly domestic problems no longer stop at national boundaries. As Rene Dubos, the 1969 Pulitzer Prize recipient, stated: "[I]t becomes obvious that each [of us] has two countries, [our] own and planet Earth." Global interdependence having become a reality, it is now vital for the citizens of our planet to develop literacy in global matters.

THE GLOBAL STUDIES SERIES

The Global Studies series aims to help readers acquire a basic knowledge and understanding of the regions and countries in the world. Each volume provides a foundation of varied information—geographic, cultural, economic, political, historical, artistic, and religious—that will allow readers to com-

prehend better the current and future problems within these countries and regions and to understand how events there might affect their own well-being. In short, these volumes attempt to provide the background information necessary to respond to the realities of our global age.

Author/Editor
Each of the volumes in the Global Studies series is crafted under the careful direction of an author/editor—an expert in the area under study. These authors/editors teach and conduct research and have traveled extensively through the regions about which they are writing.

The author/editor for this volume has written the essays on each of the areas within the region being studied and has been instrumental in the selection of the world press articles.

Contents and Features
The Global Studies volumes are organized to provide concise information and current world press articles on the regions and countries within those areas under study.

Country Reports
Global Studies: China, Seventh Edition, covers the People's Republic of China, Hong Kong, and Taiwan. For each of these areas, the author/editor has written a report focusing on the geographical, cultural, sociopolitical, and economic differ-

(Xinhua News Agency)

The global age is making all countries and all peoples more interdependent.

ences and similarities of the peoples in the region. The purpose of the reports is to provide the reader with an effective sense of the diversity of the areas and an understanding of China's cultural and historical background. Each report contains a detailed map, a brief "wild card" highlighting an interesting facet of the country, and a summary of statistical information. In the essay on the People's Republic of China, a historical timeline provides a convenient visual survey of the key historical events that have shaped this important area of the world.

A Note on the Statistical Summaries

The statistical information provided for each country has been drawn from a wide range of sources. The most frequently referenced are listed on page 200. Every effort has been made to provide the most current and accurate information available. However, occasionally the information cited by these sources differs significantly; and, all too often, the most current information available for some countries is quite dated. Aside from these difficulties, the statistical summary for each country is generally quite complete and reasonably current, but care should be taken in using these statistics (or, for that matter, any published statistics) in making hard comparisons among countries. However, as a point of reference, we have also included comparable statistics on Canada and the United States, which follow on the next two pages.

World Press Articles

Within each Global Studies volume is reprinted a large number of articles carefully selected by our editorial staff and the author/editor from a broad range of international periodicals and newspapers. The articles have been chosen for currency, interest, and their differing perspectives on the region. There are 30 articles in *Global Studies: China, Seventh Edition*—24 addressing the People's Republic of China, three dealing with Taiwan, and three on Hong Kong. The articles section is preceded by an annotated table of contents and a topic guide. The annotated table of contents offers a brief summary of each article, while the topic guide indicates the main theme(s) of each article. Thus, readers desiring to focus on articles dealing with a particular theme, say, economics, may refer to the topic guide to find those articles.

WWW Sites, Glossary, Bibliography, Index, Charts

An annotated list of selected World Wide Web sites can be found on page v in this edition of *Global Studies: China*.

At the back of each Global Studies volume is a glossary of terms and abbreviations, which provides a quick reference to the specialized vocabulary of the area under study and to the standard acronyms (P.R.C., R.O.C., etc.) used throughout the volume.

Following the glossary is a bibliography, which is organized into general-reference volumes, national and regional histories, and books on politics and society as well as on economic and foreign policy. There are separate bibliographic sections for the People's Republic of China, Hong Kong, and Taiwan.

The index at the end of the volume is an accurate reference to the contents of the volume. Readers seeking specific information and citations should consult this standard index.

Currency and Usefulness

This seventh edition of *Global Studies: China*, like other Global Studies volumes, is intended to provide the most current and useful information available necessary to understanding the events that are shaping China today.

We plan to issue this volume on a continuing basis. The statistics will be updated, essays rewritten, country reports revised, and articles completely replaced as new and current information becomes available. In order to accomplish this task we will turn to our author/editor, our advisory board and—hopefully—to you, the users of this volume. Your comments are more than welcome. If you have an idea that you think will make the volume more useful, an article or bit of information that will make it more current, or a general comment on its organization, content, or features that you would like to share with us, please send it in for serious consideration for the next edition.

Canada

GEOGRAPHY

Area in Square Kilometers (Miles):
9,976,140 (3,850,790) (slightly larger than the United States)
Capital (Population): Ottawa (980,000)
Climate: from temperate in south to subarctic and arctic in north

PEOPLE

Population
Total: 28,820,670
Annual Growth Rate: 1.09%
Rural/Urban Population Ratio: 23/77
Major Languages: English; French
Ethnic Makeup: 40% British Isles origin; 27% French origin; 20% other European; 1.5% indigenous Indian and Eskimo; 11.5% mixed

Health
Life Expectancy at Birth: 76 years (male); 83 years (female)
Infant Mortality Rate (Ratio): 6.8/1,000
Average Caloric Intake: 127% of FAO minimum
Physicians Available (Ratio): 1/464

Religions
46% Roman Catholic; 16% United Church; 10% Anglican; 28% others

Education
Adult Literacy Rate: 97%

COMMUNICATION

Telephones: 18,000,000
Newspapers: 96 in English; 11 in French

TRANSPORTATION

Highways—Kilometers (Miles): 849,404 (530,028)
Railroads—Kilometers (Miles): 78,148 (48,764)
Usable Airfields: 1,386

GOVERNMENT

Type: confederation with parliamentary democracy
Independence Date: July 1, 1867
Head of State/Government: Queen Elizabeth II; Prime Minister Jean Chrétien
Political Parties: Progressive Conservative Party; Liberal Party; New Democratic Party; Reform Party; Bloc Québécois
Suffrage: universal at 18

MILITARY

Number of Armed Forces: 88,000
Military Expenditures (% of Central Government Expenditures): 1.6%
Current Hostilities: none

ECONOMY

Currency ($U.S. Equivalent): 1.35 Canadian dollars = $1
Per Capita Income/GDP: $22,760/$639.8 billion
Inflation Rate: 0.2%
Natural Resources: petroleum; natural gas; fish; minerals; cement; forestry products; fur
Agriculture: grains; livestock; dairy products; potatoes; hogs; poultry and eggs; tobacco
Industry: oil production and refining; natural-gas development; fish products; wood and paper products; chemicals; transportation equipment

FOREIGN TRADE

Exports: $164.3 billion
Imports: $151.5 billion

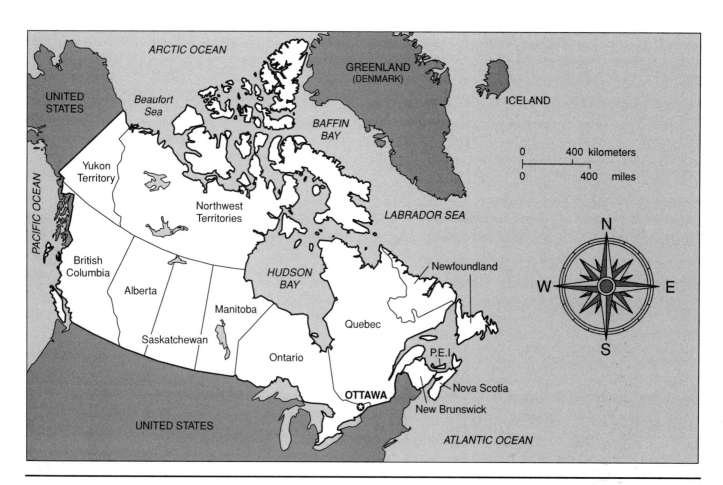

The United States

GEOGRAPHY

Area in Square Kilometers (Miles):
9,578,626 (3,618,770)
Capital (Population): Washington,
D.C. (567,100)
Climate: temperate

PEOPLE

Population
Total: 265,562,700
Annual Growth Rate: 1.02%
Rural/Urban Population Ratio: 25/75
Major Languages: English; Spanish;
others
Ethnic Makeup: 80% white; 12%
black; 6% Hispanic; 2% Asian,
Pacific Islander, American Indian,
Eskimo, and Aleut

Health
Life Expectancy at Birth: 73 years
(male); 80 years (female)
Infant Mortality Rate (Ratio):
7.8/1,000
Average Caloric Intake: 138% of
FAO minimum
Physicians Available (Ratio): 1/391

Religions
55% Protestant; 36% Roman
Catholic; 4% Jewish; 5% Muslim
and others

Education
Adult Literacy Rate: 97.9% (official)
(estimates vary widely)

COMMUNICATION

Telephones: 182,558,000
Newspapers: 1,679 dailies;
approximately 63,000,000 circulation

TRANSPORTATION

Highways—Kilometers (Miles):
6,243,163 (3,895,733)
Railroads—Kilometers (Miles):
240,000 (149,161)
Usable Airfields: 15,032

GOVERNMENT

Type: federal republic
Independence Date: July 4, 1776
Head of State: President William
("Bill") Jefferson Clinton
Political Parties: Democratic Party;
Republican Party; others of minor
political significance
Suffrage: universal at 18

MILITARY

Number of Armed Forces: 1,807,177
*Military Expenditures (% of Central
Government Expenditures):* 4.2%
Current Hostilities: none

ECONOMY

Per Capita Income/GDP:
$25,800/$6.738 trillion
Inflation Rate: 2.6%
Natural Resources: metallic and
nonmetallic minerals; petroleum;
arable land
Agriculture: food grains; feed crops;
oil-bearing crops; livestock; dairy
products
Industry: diversified in both capital-
and consumer-goods industries

FOREIGN TRADE

Exports: $513 billion
Imports: $664 billion

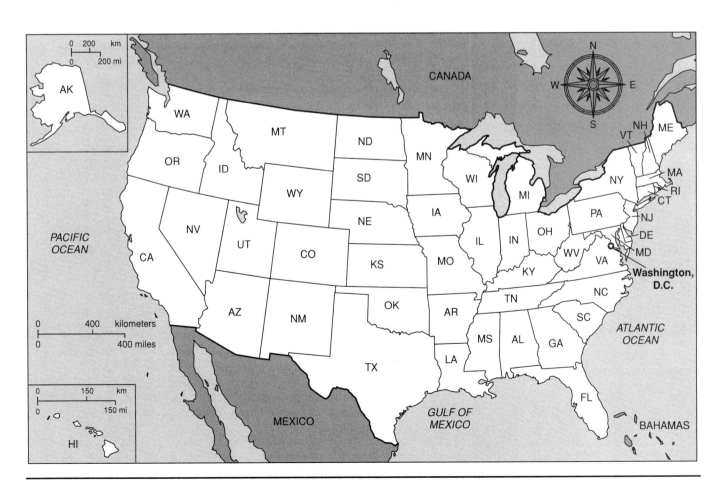

This map of the world highlights the People's Republic of China, Hong Kong, and Taiwan. The following reports are written from a perspective that will give readers a sense of what life is like in the region today. The essays are designed to present the most current and useful information available. Other books in the Global Studies series cover different global areas and examine the current state of affairs of the countries within those regions.

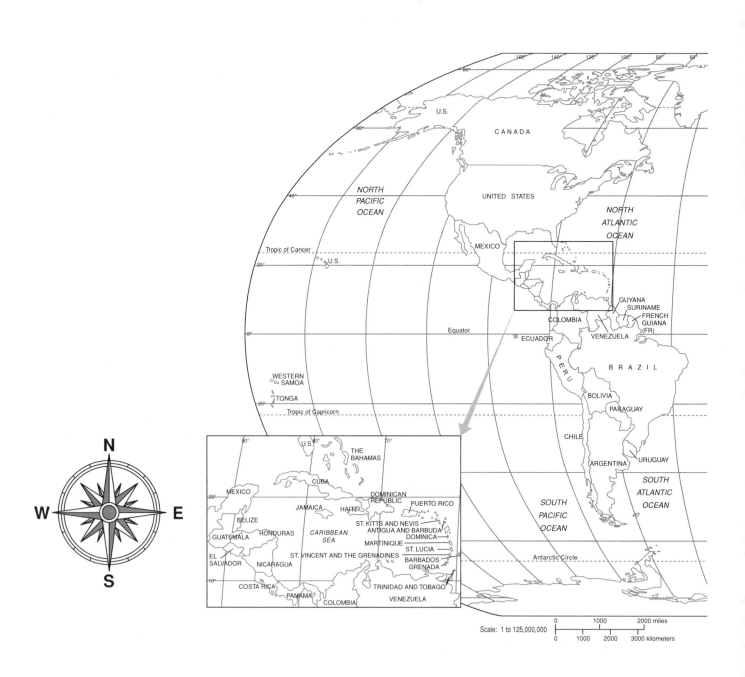

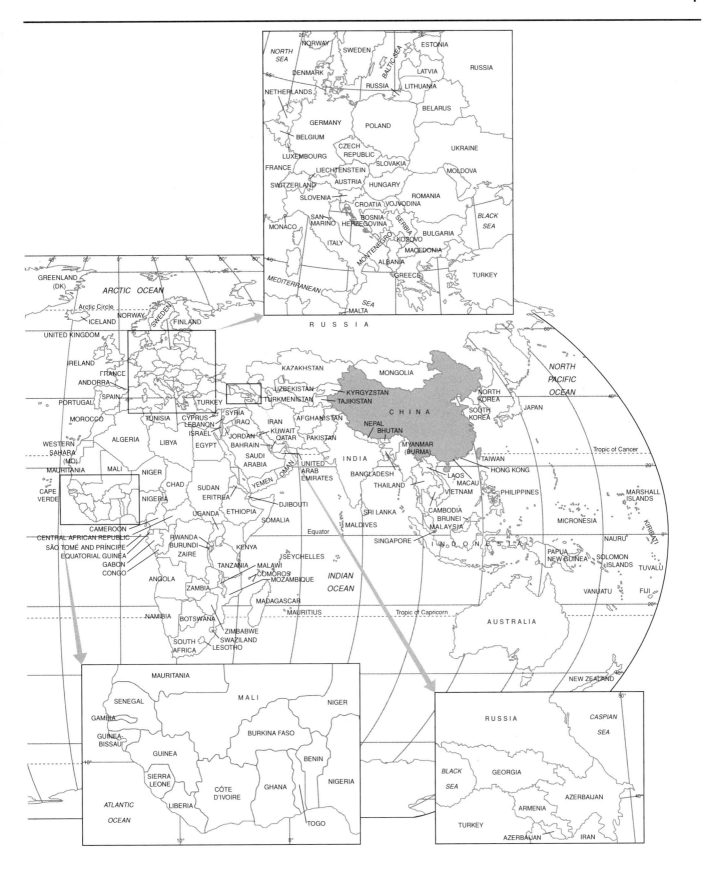

China

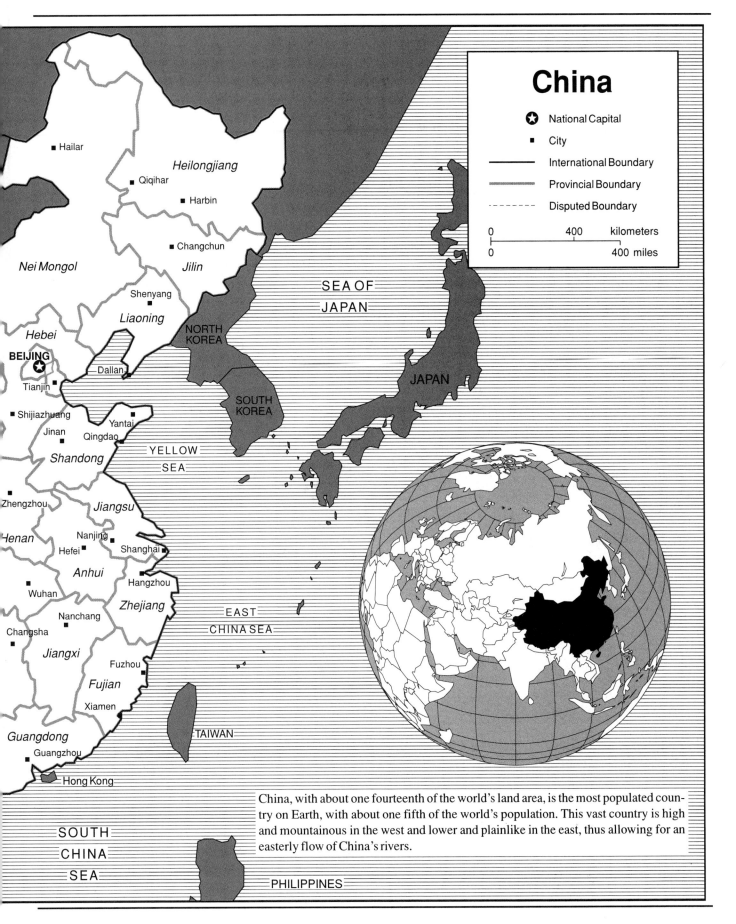

China

★ National Capital

■ City

—— International Boundary

══ Provincial Boundary

- - - - Disputed Boundary

0 ____ 400 ____ kilometers

0 ____ 400 miles

■ Hailar

Heilongjiang

■ Qiqihar

■ Harbin

■ Changchun

Nei Mongol

Jilin

■ Shenyang

Liaoning

Hebei

BEIJING ★

■ Dalian

■ Tianjin

SEA OF JAPAN

NORTH KOREA

JAPAN

SOUTH KOREA

■ Shijiazhuang

■ Yantai

■ Jinan

■ Qingdao

Shandong

YELLOW SEA

■ Zhengzhou

Jiangsu

Henan

■ Nanjing

■ Shanghai

■ Hefei

Anhui

■ Hangzhou

■ Wuhan

Zhejiang

■ Nanchang

EAST CHINA SEA

■ Changsha

Jiangxi

■ Fuzhou

Fujian

■ Xiamen

Guangdong

■ Guangzhou

■ Hong Kong

SOUTH CHINA SEA

TAIWAN

PHILIPPINES

China, with about one fourteenth of the world's land area, is the most populated country on Earth, with about one fifth of the world's population. This vast country is high and mountainous in the west and lower and plainlike in the east, thus allowing for an easterly flow of China's rivers.

China (People's Republic of China)

GEOGRAPHY

Area in Square Kilometers (Miles):
9,572,900 (3,696,100) (slightly larger
than the contiguous United States)
Capital (Population): Beijing (6,900,000)
Climate: extremely diverse

PEOPLE

Population
Total: 1,203,097,000
Annual Growth Rate: 1.04%
Rural/Urban Population Ratio: 73/27
Ethnic Makeup: 92% Han Chinese; 8%
minority groups (the largest being
Chuang, Hui, Uighur, Yi, and Miao)
Major Languages: Standard Chinese
(Putonghua) or Mandarin; Yue
(Cantonese); Wu (Shanghainese);
Minbei (Fuzhou); Minuan (Hokkien-
Taiwanese); Xiang; Gan; Hahka

Health
Life Expectancy at Birth: 67 years
(male); 69 years (female)
Infant Mortality Rate (Ratio): 52.1/1,000
Average Caloric Intake: 104% of FAO
minimum
Physicians Available (Ratio): 1/646

Religions
officially atheist; but Taoism,
Buddhism, Islam, Christianity, ancestor
worship, and animism do exist

Education
Adult Literacy Rate: 73%

COMMUNICATION

Telephones: 20,000,000
Newspapers: 852

THE FIRST CHINESE EMPEROR

By 221 B.C., Qin Shi Huang Di had conquered the last of the independent
states that had been fighting one another for the previous 500 years. He
thereby unified China and founded the Chinese Empire. The system of
governmental institutions and social organization that he enforced
throughout the country was intended to ensure that China would hence-
forth be ruled by a single emperor. All peoples, whether native Chinese or
"barbarian" foreigners, were expected to acknowledge him as the rightful
"Son of Heaven."

TRANSPORTATION

Highways—Kilometers (Miles):
1,029,000 (639,009)
Railroads—Kilometers (Miles): 65,780
(41,047)
Usable Airfields: 204

GOVERNMENT

Type: one-party Communist state
Independence Date: October 1, 1949
Head of State/Government: President
Jiang Zemin; Premier Li Peng
Political Parties: Chinese Communist
Party; several small and politically
insignificant non-Communist parties
Suffrage: universal at 18

MILITARY

Number of Armed Forces: n/a
*Military Expenditures (% of Central
Government Expenditures):* n/a
Current Hostilities: none

ECONOMY

Currency ($ U.S. Equivalent): 8.32
yuan = $1
Per Capita Income/GDP: $2,500/$2.97
trillion (est.)
Inflation Rate: 9% (est.)
Natural Resources: coal; oil;
hydroelectric sites; natural gas; iron
ores; tin; tungsten
Agriculture: food grains; cotton; oil
seeds; pigs; tea
Industry: iron and steel; coal;
machinery; light industry; armaments

FOREIGN TRADE

Exports: $121.0 billion
Imports: $115.7 billion

China

National Capital
International Boundary
Provincial Boundary
Disputed Boundary

People's Republic of China

Tensions between
Modernization and Ideology

HISTORY

The history and achievements of Chinese civilization rival those of the Greek and Roman Empires at their height. Chinese civilization began in the Neolithic Period (beginning roughly in 5000 B.C.), but scholars know more about its exact nature during the Shang Dynasty (dating approximately from the second millennium B.C.). By that time, the Chinese had developed their sophisticated ideograph system of writing—in which words are portrayed as picturelike characters, a system that continues to be used today—and they had already developed the technology and art of bronze casting to a high standard.

From the fifth to the third centuries B.C., the level of literature and the arts was comparable to that of Greece in the Classical Period, which occurred at the same time. Science flourished, and the philosopher Confucius developed a highly sophisticated system of ethics for government and moral codes for society. These were dominant until the early twentieth century, and they influence Chinese thought and behavior even today, not only in the People's Republic of China (China, or the P.R.C.), but also in Taiwan, Hong Kong, and Singapore.

THE CHINESE EMPIRE

By 221 B.C., the many feudal states ruled by independent princes had been conquered by Qin (or Ch'in) Shi Huang Di, the first ruler of a unified Chinese Empire. He established a system of governmental institutions and a concept of empire that continued in China until A.D. 1911. Although China was unified from the Qin Dynasty on, it was far less concrete than the term *empire* might indicate. China's borders really reached only as far as its cultural influence did. Thus China contracted and expanded according to whether or not other groups of people accepted the Chinese ruler and culture as their own.

Those peoples outside "China" who refused to acknowledge the Chinese ruler as the "Son of Heaven" or pay tribute to him were called "barbarians." In fact, the Great Wall, which stretches more than 2,000 miles across north China and was built in stages between the third century B.C. and the seventeenth century A.D., was constructed in order to keep marauding "barbarians" out of China. Nevertheless, they frequently invaded China and occasionally even succeeded in subduing the Chinese—as in the Yuan (Mongol) Dynasty

(1279–1368) and, later, the Qing (Ch'ing, or Manchu) Dynasty (1644–1911).

However, the customs and institutions of the invaders eventually yielded to the powerful cultural influence of the Chinese. Indeed, in the case of the Manchus, who seized control of the Chinese Empire in 1644 and ruled until 1911, their success in holding onto the throne for so long may in part be due to their willingness to assimilate Chinese ways and to rule through existing Chinese institutions, such as the Confucian-ordered bureaucracy. By the time of their overthrow, the Manchu rulers were hardly distinguishable from the pure (Han) Chinese in their customs, habits, and beliefs. When considering today's policies toward the numerous minorities who inhabit such a large expanse of the People's Republic of China, it should be remembered that the central Chinese government's ability to absorb minorities was the key to its success in maintaining a unified entity called *China* for more than 2,000 years.

THE IMPERIAL BUREAUCRACY

A distinguishing feature of the political system of imperial China was the civil-service examinations through which government officials were chosen. These examinations tested knowledge of the moral principles embodied in the classical Confucian texts. Although the exams were, in theory, open to all males in the Chinese Empire, the lengthy and rigorous preparation required meant that, in practice, the sons of the wealthy and powerful with access to a good education had an enormous advantage. Only a small percentage of those who began the process actually passed the examinations and received an appointment in the imperial bureaucracy. Those who were successful were sent as the emperor's agents to govern throughout the far-flung realm.

The Decline of the Manchus
The vitality of Chinese institutions and their ability to respond creatively to new problems came to an end during the Manchu Dynasty (1644–1911). This was due in part to internal rebellions, caused by a stagnant agriculture incapable of supporting the growing population and by increasing exploitation of the poor peasants who made up the vast majority of Chinese society. As the imperial bureaucracy and the emperor's court itself became increasingly corrupt and incompetent, they gradually lost the ability to govern the empire

effectively. Furthermore, the social-class structure rewarded those who could pass the archaic, morality-based civil-service examination rather than scientists and others who could make contributions to China's material advancement.

China's decline in the nineteenth century was exacerbated by cultural "blinders" that prevented the Chinese from understanding the dynamism of the Industrial Revolution then taking place in the West. Gradually the barriers erected by the Manchu rulers to prevent Western culture and technology from polluting the ancient beauty of Chinese civilization were knocked down.

The Opium War

The British began importing opium into China in the nineteenth century. Eventually they used the Chinese attack on British ships carrying opium as an excuse for declaring war on the decaying and decrepit Chinese Empire. The Opium War (1839–1842) ended with defeat for the Chinese and the forcible entry of European merchants and missionaries into China.

Other wars brought further concessions—the most important of which was the Chinese granting of "treaty ports" to Europeans. These ports inevitably led to the spread of Western values that challenged the stagnant, and by then morally impotent, Chinese Empire. As the West and Japan nibbled away at China, the Manchu rulers made a last-ditch effort at reform, so as to strengthen and enrich China. But the combination of internal decay, provincialism, revolution, and foreign imperialism finally toppled the Manchu Dynasty. Thus ended more than 2,000 years of imperial rule in China.

REPUBLICAN CHINA

The 1911 Revolution, which derived its greatest inspiration from Sun Yat-sen (even though he was on a political fund-raising trip in the United States when it happened), led to the establishment of the Republic of China (R.O.C.)—in name, if not in fact. China was briefly united under the control of the dominant warlord of the time, Yuan Shih-kai. But with his death in 1916, China was again torn apart by the resurgence of contending warlords, internal political decay, and further attempts at territorial expansion, especially by the militant Japanese, who were searching for an East Asian empire of their own. Attempts at reform failed because China was so divided and weak.

Chinese intellectuals searched for new ideas from abroad to strengthen their nation in the vibrant May Fourth period, spanning from roughly 1917 through the early 1920s. In the process, influential foreigners such as English mathematician and philosopher Bertrand Russell, American philosopher and educator John Dewey, and renowned Indian poet Rabindranath Tagore came to lecture in China. Thousands of Chinese students traveled and studied abroad. Ideas such as liberal democracy, syndicalism, guild socialism, and commu-

(New York Public Library)

CONFUCIUS: CHINA'S FIRST "TEACHER"

Confucius (551–479 B.C.), whose efforts to teach the various central governments of China how to govern well were spurned, spent most of his life teaching his own disciples. Yet 300 years later, Confucianism, as taught by descendants of his own disciples, was adopted as the official state philosophy. The basic principles of Confucianism include hierarchical principles of obedience and loyalty to one's superiors, respect for one's elders, and filial piety; how to maintain social order and harmony; and the responsibility of rulers to exercise their power benevolently.

nism were contemplated as possible solutions to China's many problems.

The Founding of the Chinese Communist Party

In 1921, a small Marxist study group founded the Chinese Communist Party (CCP). The Moscow-based Comintern (Communist International) advised this highly intellectual but politically impotent group to link up with the more promising and militarily powerful Kuomintang (KMT, or Nationalist Party, led first by Sun Yat-sen and, after his death in 1925, by Chiang Kai-shek), in order to reunify China under one central government. Without adequate support from the Soviets or from forces within China—because there were so few capitalists in China, there was no urban proletariat, and therefore the Marxist aim of "overthrowing the capitalist class"

THE OPIUM WAR: NARCOTICS SMUGGLING JUST A PRETEXT FOR WAR

Although the opium poppy is native to China, large amounts of opium were shipped to China by the English-owned East India Company from the British colony of India. Eventually India exported so much opium to China that 5 to 10 percent of its revenues derived from its sale.

By the late 1700s, the Chinese government had officially prohibited first the smoking and selling of opium, and later its importation or domestic production. But because the sale of opium was so profitable—and also because so many Chinese officials were addicted to it—the Chinese officials themselves illegally engaged in the opium trade. As the number of addicts grew and the Chinese government became more corrupted by its own unacknowledged participation in opium smuggling, so grew the interest of enterprising Englishmen in smuggling it into China for financial gain.

But the British government was primarily interested in establishing an equal diplomatic and trade relationship with the Chinese to supplant the existing one, in which the Chinese court demanded that the English kowtow to the Chinese emperor. Great Britain was interested in expanded trade with China. But, it also wanted to secure legal jurisdiction over its nationals residing in China to protect them against Chinese prac-

(New York Public Library)

tices of torture of those suspected of having committed a crime.

Chinese efforts to curb the smuggling of opium and refusal to recognize the British as equals reached a climax in 1839, when the Chinese destroyed thousands of chests of opium aboard a British ship. This served as an ideal pretext for the British to attack China with their sophisticated gun-

boats (pictured above destroying a junk in Canton's harbor). Ultimately their superior firepower gave victory to the British.

Thus the so-called Opium War (1839–1842) ended with defeat for the Chinese and the signing of the Treaty of Nanking, which ceded the island of Hong Kong to the British and allowed them to establish trading posts on the Chinese mainland.

---

was irrelevant—the Chinese Communists agreed to form a united front with the KMT. They hoped that once they had built up their own organization while cooperating with the KMT, they could break away to establish themselves as an independent political party. Thus, it was with Communist support that Chiang Kai-shek successfully united China under his control during the Northern Expedition. Then, in 1927, he brutally quashed the Communist Party.

The Long March

The Chinese Communist Party's ranks were decimated two more times by the KMT's superior police and military forces, largely because the CCP had obeyed Moscow's advice to organize an orthodox Marxist urban-based movement in the cities. The cities, however, were completely controlled by the KMT. It is a testimony to the strength of the appeal of

Communist ideas in that era that the CCP managed to recover its strength each time. Indeed, the growing power of the CCP was such that Chiang considered it, even more than the invading Japanese, the main threat to his complete control of China. Eventually the Chinese Communist leaders agreed that an urban strategy was doomed, yet they lacked adequate military power to confront the KMT head-on. They retreated in the famous Long March (1934–1935), traveling 6,000 miles from the southeast through the rugged interior, to the windswept plains of Yanan in northern China.

It was during this retreat, in which as many as 100,000 people perished, that Mao Zedong (Mao Tse-tung) staged his contest for power within the CCP. With his victory, the Chinese Communist Party reoriented itself toward a rural strategy and attempted to capture the loyalty of the peasants, then comprising some 85 percent of China's total population. Mao

MAO ZEDONG: CHINA'S REVOLUTIONARY LEADER

(New York Public Library)

appeared to be right: "Political power grows out of the barrel of a gun."

The Communists' retreat to Yanan on the Long March was not only for the purpose of survival but also for regrouping and forming a stronger "Red Army." There the followers of the Chinese Communist Party were taught Mao's ideas about guerrilla warfare, the importance of winning the support of the people, principles of party leadership, and socialist values. Mao consolidated his control over the leadership of the CCP during the Yanan period and led it to victory over the Nationalists in 1949.

From that time onward, Mao became a symbol of the new Chinese government, of national unity, and of the strength of China against foreign humiliation. In later years, although his real power was eclipsed, the party maintained the illusion that Mao was the undisputed leader of China.

In his declining years, Mao waged a struggle, in the form of the "Cultural Revolution," against those who followed policies antagonistic to his own, a struggle that brought the country to the brink of civil war and turned the Chinese against one another. The symbol of Mao as China's "great leader" and "great teacher" was used by those who hoped to seize power after him: first the minister of defense, Lin Biao, and then the "Gang of Four," which included Mao's wife.

Mao's death in 1976 ended the control of policy by the Gang of Four. Within a few years, questions were being raised about the legacy that Mao had left China. By the 1980s, it was broadly accepted throughout China that Mao had been responsible for a full 20 years of misguided policies. Since the Tiananmen protests of 1989, however, there has been a resurgence of nostalgia for Mao. This nostalgia is captured in such aspects of popular culture as a tape of songs about Mao entitled "The Red Sun"—an all-time best-selling tape in China, at 5 million copies—that encapsulates the Mao cult and Mao mania of the Cultural Revolution; and in a small portrait of Mao that virtually all car owners and taxi drivers hang over their rear-view mirrors for "good luck." Many Chinese long for the "good old days" of Mao's rule, when crime and corruption were at far lower levels than today and when there was a sense of collective commitment to China's future. But they do not long for a return to the mass terror of the Cultural Revolution, for which Mao also bears responsibility.

Mao Zedong (1893–1976) came from a moderately well-to-do peasant family and, as a result, received a very good education, as compared to the vast majority of the Chinese. Mao (pictured above) was one of the founders of the Chinese Communist Party in 1921, but his views on the need to switch from an orthodox Marxist strategy, which called for the party to seek roots among the urban working class, to a rural strategy centered on the exploited peasants were spurned by the leadership of the CCP and its sponsors in Moscow.

Later, it became evident that the CCP could not flourish in the Nationalist-controlled cities, as time and again the KMT quashed the idealistic but militarily weak CCP. Mao

saw the peasants as the major source of support for revolution. In most areas of China, the peasants were suffering from an oppressive and brutal system of landlord control; they were the discontented masses who had "nothing to lose but [their] chains." Appealing to the peasants' desire to own their own land as well as to their disillusionment with KMT rule, the CCP slowly started to gain control over the countryside.

"United" against the Japanese

The Japanese invasion of 1937 and their subsequent occupation of the north and east coasts of China caused the CCP once

again to agree to a unified front with the KMT, in order to halt Japanese aggression. Both the KMT and the CCP had ulterior motives, but, according to most accounts, the Communists contributed more to the national wartime efforts. The Communists organized guerrilla efforts to peck away at the fringes of Japanese-controlled areas while Chiang Kai-shek, head of the KMT, holed up with his elite corps in the wartime capital of Chungking, taking the best of the American supplies for themselves and leaving the rank-and-file to fight bootless against the Japanese. Once the Americans and the brave, self-sacrificing Chinese masses had won the war for him,

Chiang Kai-shek believed his army would have the strength to defeat the Communists.

The Communists Oust the KMT

However, when World War II was over in 1945, it seemed as if hard fighting had actually strengthened the Chinese Communists, while the soft life of the KMT military elite had weakened them. Moving quickly to annihilate the Communists, Chiang pursued his old strategy of taking the cities. But the Communists, who had gained control over the countryside, surrounded the cities, which, like besieged fortresses, eventually fell. By October 1949, the CCP could claim control over all of China—except for Taiwan, where the KMT's political, economic, and military elite who were loyal to Chiang had fled, with American support.

Scholars still dispute why the CCP ultimately defeated the KMT, citing as probable reasons the Communist Party's appeal to the Chinese people, the Communists' higher moral standards in comparison to those of the KMT soldiers, the party's more successful appeal to the Chinese sense of nationalism, and Chiang's unwillingness to undertake significant reforms. Certainly, any wartime government confronted with the demoralization within its own ranks resulting from inflation, economic destruction, and the humiliation caused by a foreign occupation would have had a hard time maintaining the loyal support of the populace. Even the middle class eventually deserted the KMT. Those industrial and commercial capitalists who stayed behind in the cities hoped to join in a patriotic effort with the CCP to rebuild China.

THE PEOPLE'S REPUBLIC OF CHINA

The Chinese Communists' final victory came rapidly, far faster than anticipated. Suddenly they were in control of a nation of more than 600 million people and had to make important decisions about how to unify and rebuild the country. They were obligated, of course, to fulfill their promise to redistribute land to the poor and landless peasants. However, the CCP leaders, largely recruited from the peasantry, had a profound understanding of how to create revolution but little knowledge of how to govern. So, rejected by the Western democratic–capitalist countries because of their embrace of communism, they turned to the Soviet Union for support—this in spite of the Soviet leader Joseph Stalin's lackluster and fickle support for the Chinese Communists throughout the 1930s and 1940s.

The Soviet Model

Desperate for aid and advice, the CCP "leaned to one side" in the early 1950s and followed the Soviet model of development. This model favored capital-intensive industrialization and a high degree of centralized control. Such an approach to solving China's problems had some harmful long-term effects; but without Soviet support in the beginning, it is questionable whether the Chinese Communist Party would have been as successful as it was in the 1950s.

The Chinese Approach

The CCP leaders soon became exasperated with the inapplicability of the Soviet model to Chinese circumstances and with the limits of Soviet aid. Because China was unable to afford the extensive capital investments called for by the Soviet model of rapid industrialization through the development of heavy industry, Mao Zedong formulated a Chinese approach to the problem of development. He hoped to substitute China's enormous manpower for expensive capital equipment by organizing people into ever larger working units.

In 1958, in an attempt to catch up with the industrialized states through a spurt of energy, Mao announced a policy termed the *Great Leap Forward*. This bold scheme to increase production by moving peasants into still larger collective units, called *communes* (the CCP had already moved most peasants into cooperatives by 1955 and taken away almost all their land), and to accelerate industrial production in the cities and countryside was a direct rejection of the Soviet model.

Sino–Soviet Relations Sour

The Soviet leader Nikita Khrushchev denounced the Great Leap Forward as "irrational." He was also distressed at what seemed an adventurist scheme by Mao to bring the Soviets and Americans into direct conflict over the Nationalist-controlled Offshore Islands. In 1959, the Soviets picked up their bags—as well as their blueprints for unfinished factories and spare parts—and left. The Soviets' action, combined with the disastrous decline in production resulting from the policies of the Great Leap Forward and several years of bad weather, set China's economic development back many years. Population figures now available indicate that somewhere between 20 million and 30 million people died in the years from 1959 to 1962, mostly from starvation and diseases caused by malnutrition. Within the party, Mao's ideas were paid only lip service. Not until 1962 did the Chinese start to recover their productivity gains of the 1950s and to move forward.

The Sino–Soviet split became public in 1963, as the two Communist powers found themselves in profound disagreement over a wide range of issues: what methods socialist countries could use to develop; policy toward the United States; and whether China or the Soviet Union followed Marxism-Leninism more faithfully and, hence, was entitled to lead the Communist world. This split was not healed until the late 1980s. By then, neither country was interested in claiming Communist orthodoxy.

(New York Public Library)

RED GUARDS: ROOTING OUT THOSE "ON THE CAPITALIST ROAD"

During the Cultural Revolution, Mao Zedong called upon the country's young people to "make revolution." Called Mao's Red Guards, these youngsters' ages varied, but for the most part they were teenagers.

Within each class and school, various youths would band together in a Red Guard group that would take on a revolutionary-sounding name and would then carry out the objective of challenging people in authority. But the people in authority, especially schoolteachers, school principals, bureaucrats, and local leaders of the Communist Party, initially ignored the demands of the Red Guards that they reform their "reactionary thoughts" or eliminate their "feudal" habits.

Since the Red Guards initially had no real weapons and could only threaten, and since they were considered just misdirected children by those under attack, their initial assaults had little effect. But soon, the frustrated Red Guards took to physically beating and publicly humiliating those who stubbornly refused to obey them. Since Mao had not clearly defined precisely what should be their objectives or methods, the Red Guards were free to believe that the ends justified extreme and often violent means. Moreover, many Red Guards took the opportunity to take revenge against authorities, such as teachers who had given them bad grades. Others (like those pictured above wearing masks to guard against the influenza virus while simultaneously concealing their identities) would harangue crowds on the benefits of Maoism and the evils of foreign influence.

Mao eventually called on the army to support the Red Guards in their effort to challenge "those in authority taking the capitalist road." This created even more confusion, as many of the Red Guard groups actually supported the people they were supposed to be attacking. But their revolutionary-sounding names and their pretenses at being "Red" (Communist) confused the army. Moreover, the army was divided within itself and did not particularly wish to overthrow the Chinese Communist Party authorities, the main supporters of the military in their respective areas of jurisdiction.

The Red Guards began to go on rampages throughout the country, breaking into people's houses and stealing or destroying their property, harassing people in their homes in the middle of the night, stopping girls with long hair and cutting it off on the spot, destroying the files of ministries and industrial enterprises, and clogging up the transportation system by their travels throughout the country to "make revolution." Different Red Guard factions began to fight with one another, each claiming to be the most revolutionary.

Since the schools had been closed, the youth of China were not receiving any formal education during this period. Finally, in 1969, Mao called a halt to the excesses of the Red Guards. They were disbanded and sent home or out to the countryside to labor in the fields with the peasants. But the chaos set in motion during the Cultural Revolution did not come to a halt until the arrest of the Gang of Four, some 10 years after the Cultural Revolution had begun.

Children of school age during the "10 bad years," when schools were either closed or operating with a minimal program, received virtually no formal education beyond an elementary-school level. Although this meant that China's development of an educated elite in most fields came to a halt, nevertheless it resulted in well over a 90 percent basic literacy rate among the Chinese raised in that generation.

THE CULTURAL REVOLUTION

In 1966, whether Mao hoped to provoke an internal party struggle in order to regain control over policy or (as he alleged) to rid China of its repressive bureaucracy in order to restore a revolutionary spirit to the Chinese people and to prevent China from abandoning socialism, Mao launched what was termed the *Great Proletarian Cultural Revolution.* He called on the youth of China to "challenge authority"—particularly "those revisionists in authority who are taking the capitalist road"—and to "make revolution."

Such vague objectives invited abuse, including personal feuds and retribution for alleged past wrongs, and led to murders, suicides, ruined careers, and broken families. Determining just who was "Red" (Communist) and who was "reactionary" itself became the basis for chaos, as people tried to protect themselves by attacking others, even friends and relatives. The major targets were intellectuals, experts, bureaucrats, and people with foreign connections of even the most remote sort. It is estimated that 10 percent of the population—that is, *100 million people*—became targets of the Cultural Revolution and that tens of thousands lost their lives during the decade of political chaos.

Ultimately, the Chinese Communist Party was itself the victim of the Cultural Revolution. When the smoke cleared, there was little left for the people to believe in or respect. The Cultural Revolution attacked as feudal and outmoded the traditions and customs revered by the Chinese people; then the authority of the party itself was irretrievably damaged by the attacks on many of its leaders. By 1976, there was a nearly total breakdown of both traditional Chinese morality and Marxist-Leninist values. Policies had changed frequently in those "10 bad years" from 1966 to 1976, as first one faction and then another gained the upper hand.

"Pragmatic" Policies

In September 1976, the aged Mao died. In October, the so-called Gang of Four (including Mao's wife), who had been the most radical leaders of the Cultural Revolution, were arrested and removed from power. Deng Xiaoping, a veteran leader of the Chinese Communist Party who had been purged twice during the "10 bad years," was "rehabilitated" in 1977.

Once again China set off on the road of construction and put to an end the radical policies of "continuous revolution" and the idea that it was more important to be "Red" than "expert." Under Deng's "pragmatic" policies, China has, in spite of readjustments and setbacks, put its major effort into modernization in four areas: science and technology, industry, agriculture, and the military.

The issue of de-Maoification has been a thorny one, as to defrock Mao would raise serious issues about the CCP's right to rule. The CCP has already admitted that, after 1957, Mao made many "serious mistakes," but it insists that these errors should be seen within the context of his many accomplishments and the fact that he was a committed, if sometimes misdirected, Marxist and revolutionary.

The Challenge of Reform

The inevitable result of this endless questioning and rejection—first of traditional Chinese values, next of Marxism-Leninism and its concept of the infallibility of the party, and finally of "Mao Thought" (the Chinese adaptation of Marxism-Leninism to Chinese conditions)—was to leave China without any strong belief system. Such Western values as materialism, capitalism, individualism, and freedom have flowed into this vacuum to challenge both Communist ideology and traditional Chinese values.

Had their ideology and values remained intact, these foreign values would appear less threatening. But, as indicated by the campaign in the 1980s against "spiritual pollution" and then the crackdown on those calling for greater democracy during the spring of 1989, the "screen door" that Deng Xiaoping thought would permit Western science and technology to flow into China while keeping out the annoying insects of Western values appeared to have many large holes in it. The less "pragmatic," more ideologically oriented "conservative" or "hard-line" leadership used these problems as a rationale to challenge the economic reforms aimed at liberalization and to reverse the trend away from ideological education in the schools and propaganda in the workplace.

By 1992, policy had again shifted in favor of the more liberal reformers, with Deng Xiaoping, "retired" but still very much in control, successfully manuvering first to bypass, and then to replace, those in the central leadership resisting reform. Again he encouraged the people to do "whatever works," regardless of ideology, to experiment until they succeeded. At the 14th Party Congress, in October 1992, the balance within the Standing Committee of the Politburo and the Politburo itself shifted in favor of those promoting reform. Although these reforms are in theory restricted to the economic realm, in practice they spill over into the political, social, and cultural realms as well.

THE PEOPLE OF CHINA

Population

China's population exceeded 1.2 billion by 1996. In the 1950s, Mao had encouraged population growth, as he considered a large population to be a major source of strength. No sustained attempts to limit Chinese population occurred until the mid-1970s. Even then, population-control programs were only marginally successful, because there were no penalties for those Chinese who ignored them.

In 1979, the government launched a serious birth-control campaign, rewarding couples giving birth to only one child with work bonuses and priority in housing. The only child was later to receive preferential treatment in university admissions and job assignments (a policy later abandoned). Cou-

(China Pictorial)

The radical leaders of China's Cultural Revolution, who came to be known as the Gang of Four, were brought to trial in late 1980. Here they are pictured (along with another radical who was not part of the Gang) in a Beijing courtroom, listening to the judge pass sentence. The Gang of Four are the first four (from right to left) standing in the prisoners' dock: Jiang Qing, Yao Wenyuan, Wang Hongwen, and Zhang Chunqiao.

THE GANG OF FOUR

The current leadership of the Chinese Communist Party views the Cultural Revolution of 1966–1976 as having been a period of total chaos that brought the People's Republic of China to the brink of political and economic ruin. While Mao Zedong is criticized for having begun the Cultural Revolution with his mistaken ideas about the danger of China turning "capitalist," the major blame for the turmoil of those years is placed on a group of extreme radicals labeled the Gang of Four.

The Gang of Four consisted of Jiang Qing, Mao's wife, who began playing a key role in P.R.C. cultural affairs during the early 1960s; Zhang Chunqiao, a veteran party leader in Shanghai; Yao Wenyuan, a literary critic and ideologue; and Wang Hongwen, a factory worker catapulted into national prominence by his leadership of rebel workers during the Cultural Revolution. By the late 1960s, these four individuals were among the most powerful leaders in China. Drawn together by common political interests and a shared belief that the Communist Party should be relentless in ridding China of suspected "capitalist roaders," they worked together to keep the Cultural Revolution on a radical course. One of their arch enemies was Deng Xiaoping, who emerged as China's paramount leader in 1978, after the Gang of Four was arrested.

Although they had close political and personal ties to Mao and derived many of their ideas from him, Mao became quite disenchanted with the radicals in the last few years of his life. He was particularly displeased with the unscrupulous and secretive way in which they behaved as a faction within the top levels of the party. Indeed, it was Mao who coined the phrase Gang of Four, as part of a written warning to the radicals to cease their conspiracies and obey established party procedures.

The Gang of Four hoped to be able to take over supreme power in China following Mao's death on September 9, 1976. However, their plans were upset less than a month later, when other party and army leaders had them arrested—an event that is now said to mark the formal end of the Cultural Revolution. By removing from power the party's most influential radicals, the arrest of the Gang of Four set the stage for the dramatic reforms that have become the hallmark of the post-Mao era in China.

In November 1980, the Gang of Four were put on trial in Beijing. They were charged with having committed serious crimes against the Chinese people and accused of having had a hand in "persecuting to death" tens of thousands of officials and intellectuals whom they perceived as their political enemies. All four were convicted and sentenced to long terms in prison.

ples who had more than one child, on the other hand, were to be penalized by a 10 percent decrease in their annual wages, and their children would not be eligible for free education and health care benefits.

In China's major cities, the one-child policy has been rigorously enforced, to the point where it is almost impossible for a woman to get away with a second pregnancy. Who is allowed to have a child and when she may give birth are rigidly controlled by the woman's work unit. With so many enterprises now paying close to half of their workers' annual wages as "bonuses," authorities have come up with further sanctions to ensure compliance. For example, workers are

(United Nations photo/John Isaac)

The Chinese government has made great efforts to curb the country's population growth by promoting the merits of the one-child family. Today, China has an average annual population growth rate of 1.1 percent.

usually organized in groups of 10 to 30 individuals. If any woman in the group gives birth to more than one child, *the entire group* will lose its annual bonus. With such overwhelming penalties for the group as a whole, pressures not to give birth to a second child are enormous.

To ensure that any unauthorized pregnancy does not occur, women who have already given birth are required to stand in front of x-ray machines (fluoroscopes) to make sure that their IUDs are still in place. Abortions can and will be performed throughout a woman's unsanctioned pregnancy. (The moral issues that surround abortions concerning the rights of the unborn fetus in the West are not issues for the Chinese.)

The effectiveness of China's birth-control policy in the cities is not merely attributable to the surveillance by work units, the neighborhood committees, and "granny police" who watch over the families in their locales—changed social attitudes also play a critical role. Urban Chinese now accept the absolute necessity of population control in their overcrowded cities.

The success of the one-child policy in the cities has led to a serious social problem: spoiled children. Known as "little emperors," these only children are the center of attention of six anxious adults (two sets of grandparents and the parents), who carefully scrutinize their every movement. It has led to

the overuse of medical services by these parents and grandparents, who rush their only child/grandchild to the doctor at the first signs of a sniffle or sore throat. It has also led to children who are overfed. Being overweight used to be considered a hedge against bad times in China, and the Chinese were initially pleased that their children were becoming heavier. A common greeting showing admiration has been "You have become fat!" As the urban Chinese adopt many of the values associated with becoming wealthier in the developed world, however, they are changing their perspective on weight. (So far, though, salad bars do not loom on the horizon, and the major purpose of physical exercise is still to keep China a strong nation, not to look more attractive.) Another serious implication of the one-child policy is demographic: In the future, there may be too few young people to support the large number of elderly people.

In the vast rural areas of China, where approximately three quarters of the population still live, the one-child policy has been less successful. The benefits and punishments of the policy are not as relevant for peasants as for city dwellers. However, the policy has led to female infanticide as couples try to produce a male child. This practice still continues despite governmental efforts to stop it.

Under the "contract responsibility system" initiated in the 1980s, communes were disbanded and families given their own land to till. As a result, peasants wanted sons to help with farming because they were physically more able to do heavy farm labor. Today, for a substantial fee, peasants can pay the local government for the right to have a second, male, child. Yet, ironically, it is the men who are given the relatively easy factory jobs now available in rural towns, thereby leaving the daughters to work in the fields.

A result of the one-child policy has been a decline in the ratio of women to men. This, in turn, has led to another demographic crisis: an insufficient number of women to marry men. This has brought a sharp increase in the kidnapping of young women and the practice of selling girls as brides in rural marketplaces as the age group affected by the birth-control policy has come of marriageable age.[1]

In the countryside, it is estimated that at least several million peasants have taken steps to ensure that their female offspring are not counted toward their one-child (and now, in some places, two-child) limit: a pregnant woman simply moves to another village to have her child. Since the local village leaders are not responsible for women's reproduction when they are not their own villagers, women are not harassed into getting an abortion in other villages. If the child is a boy, she can simply return to her native village and register him; if a girl, she can return and *not* register her. Thus, a whole generation of young girls is growing up in the countryside without ever having been registered. Since, except for schooling, peasants have few claims to state-supplied benefits anyway, they may consider this official nonexistence of their daughters a small price to pay for having as many children as necessary until giving birth to a boy. If this practice is as common as believed, moreover, it may mean that China will not face quite such a large demographic crisis in the ratio between males and females as some have suggested.

One important reason why males continue to be more valued than females in Chinese culture is that only sons have been permitted to carry on traditional Chinese family rituals and ancestor worship. A few villages, realizing this is unbearably painful, even unacceptable, for families without sons—who feel their entire ancestral history, often recorded for hundreds of years on village temple tablets is coming to an end—have changed the very foundations of ancestral worship: They now permit daughters to continue the family lineage down the female line.

The government itself is encouraging this practice. It is also changing certain government policies, such as who is responsible under the law for taking care of their parents. It used to be the son, meaning that parents who only had a daughter could not expect to be supported in their old age. Now both sons and daughters are responsible. Furthermore, through a new system of social security and pensions for the retired, the responsibility for caring for the elderly is gradually being absorbed by the state and employers.

Despite the problems enumerated above, China's strict population-control policies have been effective: Since 1977, the population has grown at an average annual rate of 1.1 percent, one of the lowest growth rates in the developing world. Unfortunately, even this relatively low rate means an average annual increase of China's population of more than 12 million people. This poses a challenge—and perhaps a threat—to future economic development and, therefore, to political stability.

Women

It is hardly surprising that overlaying (but never eradicating) China's traditional culture with a Communist system in which men and women are supposed to be equal has generated a bundle of contradictions. Under Chinese Communist Party rule, women have long had more rights and opportunities than women in almost any other developing country and, in some respects, have outpaced the rights of women in some of the developed countries.[2] Although Chinese women have rarely broken through the "glass ceiling" to the highest levels of the CCP or management and have often been given "women's work," they have received pay fairly equivalent to that of men (in an economy where the gap between the highest and lowest paid, whether male or female, was small as well). Furthermore, an ideological morality that insisted on respect for women as equals (with both men and women being addressed as "comrades"), combined with a de-emphasis on the importance of sexuality, resulted in at least a superficial respect for women that was rare before the Communist period.

The economic reforms that began in 1979 have, however, precipitated changes in the manner in which women are treated and how women act. While many women entrepreneurs and workers are benefiting as much as the men from economic reforms, there have also been certain throwbacks to earlier times that have undercut women's equality. Women are now treated much more as sex objects than they used to be. Some women revel in their new freedom to beautify themselves, but some companies will hire only women who are attractive, and many enterprises are now using women as "window dressing." The emphasis on profits and efficiency since the reforms has also made state-run corporations reluctant to hire women because of the costs in maternity benefits (including 3 to 12 months of maternity leave at partial or full pay) and because mothers are still more likely than fathers to be in charge of sick children and the household.

National Minorities

Ninety-four percent of the population are Han Chinese. Although only 6 percent are "national minorities," they occupy more than 60 percent of China's geographical expanse. These minorities inhabit almost the entire border area, including Tibet, Inner Mongolia, and Xinjiang, the security of which is important for China's defense. China's borders with the many

This one-child family lives in a commune in Inner Mongolia. China's central government has long attempted to undermine distinctive national identifies on and around its borders.

countries on its national borders are poorly defined, and members of the same minority usually live on both sides of the borders.

To address this issue, China's central government pursued policies designed to get the minorities on the Chinese side of the border to identify with the Han Chinese majority. Rather than admitting to this objective of undermining distinctive national identities, the CCP leaders phrased the policies in terms of getting rid of the minorities' "feudal" customs, such as religious practices, which are contrary to the "scientific" values of socialism. At times, these policies have been brutal and have caused extreme bitterness among the minorities, particularly the Tibetans and the large number of minority peoples who practice Islam.

In the 1980s, the Deng Xiaoping leadership conceded that Beijing's harsh assimilation policies had been ill conceived, and it tried to gain the loyalty of the national minorities through more sensitive policies. By late in the decade, however, the loosening of controls had led to further challenges to Beijing's control. For example, the central government reimposed martial law in Tibet to quell protests and riots against

Beijing's repressive policies toward Tibetans. Martial law was lifted in 1990, but security has remained tight.

In 1995–1996, there was a surge of demonstrations for a more autonomous, and even an independent, Tibet. The Dalai Lama, the most important spiritual leader of the Tibetans but living in exile in India, stepped up his efforts to reach some form of accommodation with Beijing. He insists that, as long as he is in charge, Tibetans will use only nonviolent methods to gain greater autonomy for Tibet. The Dalai Lama also asserts that he wants greater autonomy for Tibet but not independence and that more control over their own affairs is necessary to protect the Tibetans' culture from extinction. The threat to Tibetan culture at this point comes not from efforts by China's government to assimilate Tibetans into Han culture but, rather from highly successful Chinese entrepreneurs who, under economic liberalization policies, have taken over many of the commercial and entrepreneurial activities in Tibet.

Not all Tibetans accept the path of nonviolence, and many even challenge the Dalai Lama's leadership. In 1996, for the first time in decades, the government admitted that there were isolated bombing incidents and violent clashes between anti-Chinese Tibetans (reportedly armed) and Chinese authorities. In response, the government sealed off most monasteries in Lhasa, the capital of Tibet.[3] Nevertheless, thus far, most actions have been confined to peaceful demonstrations against China's control over Tibet.

Much of the anger in Tibet against China's central government arose from Beijing's decision in 1995 not to accept the Tibetan Buddhists' choice of a young boy as the reincarnation of the former Panchen Lama,[4] the second most important spiritual leader of the Tibetans. Instead of accepting the Tibetans' recommendation of the boy to be their next Panchen Lama, chosen according to traditional Tibetan Buddhist ritual, Beijing substituted their own 6-year-old candidate. The Tibetans choice, meanwhile, is living in seclusion somewhere in Beijing under the watchful eye of the Chinese. China's concern is that any new spiritual leader could become a focus for a new push for Tibetan independence, an eventuality it wishes to avoid.

In the far northwest, the predominantly Muslim population of Xinjiang province continues to challenge the authority of China's central leadership. The loosening of policies aimed at assimilating the minority populations into the Han (Chinese) culture has given a rebirth to Islamic culture and practices, including prayer five times a day, architecture in the Islamic style, traditional Islamic medicine, and teaching Islam in the schools. With the dissolution of the Soviet Union into 15 independent states, the ties between the Islamic states on China's borders (Kazakhstan and Kyrgyzstan, as well as Afghanistan and Pakistan) are accelerating rapidly.

Beijing is certainly concerned that China's Islamic minorities may find that they have more in common with these neighboring Islamic nations than with the Chinese Han majority and may attempt to secede from China. Signs of a growing worldwide Islamic movement have exacerbated Beijing's anxieties. Since 1995, there has been a growing number of demonstrations for greater autonomy, and even independence, in Xinjiang. Several thousand people were arrested for separatist activities in the 1996 "Strike Hard" campaign against crime. Officials in Xinjiang have also at least temporarily banned the construction of new mosques, tightened existing controls on religious practices, and intensified the search for weapons hidden in goods arriving in Xinjiang.[5] And in 1997, a number of terrorist bombings occurred in Ürümqi, the capital of Xinjiang, as well as in Beijing where a large number of Muslims from Xinjiang live.

Events in (Outer) Mongolia have also led China's central leadership to keep a watchful eye on Inner Mongolia, an autonomous region under Beijing's control. In 1989, Mongolia's government, theoretically independent but in fact under Soviet tutelage, decided to permit multiparty rule at the expense of the Communist Party's complete control; and in democratic elections held in 1996, the Mongolian Communist Party was ousted from power.

Beijing has grown increasingly anxious that these democratic leanings might spread to Inner Mongolia, with a resulting challenge to one-party CCP rule. As with the Islamic minorities, China's leadership is concerned that the Mongols in Inner Mongolia may try to secede from China and join with the independent state of Mongolia because of a shared culture. So far, however, those Inner Mongolians who have traveled to Mongolia have been surprised by the relative lack of development there, to the point that they have been fairly quiet about seceding from China.

Religion

Confucianism is the "religion" most closely associated with China. It is not, however, a religion in Western terms, as there is no place for gods, the afterlife, or most other beliefs associated with formal religions. But, like most religions, it does have a system of ethics for governing human relationships; and it adds to this what most religions do not have—namely, ethics and principles for good governance. The Chinese Communists rejected Confucianism until the 1980s, but not because it was an "opiate of the masses." (This was Karl Marx's view of religion, which he viewed as a way of trapping people in a web of superstitions, robbing them of their money, and causing them to endure their miserable lives passively.) Instead, they denounced Confucianism for providing the ethical rationale for a system of patriarchy that allowed officials to insist on obedience from subordinates. During the years in which "leftists" set the agenda, moreover, the CCP rejected Confucianism for its emphasis on education as essential for those who would join the ruling elite. Instead, the Communist Party favored ideological commitment as the primary criterion for ruling. The series of reforms that began in 1979, however, have generally supported an emphasis on an educated elite, and some Confucian values are now referred to in support of the CCP's pragmatic policies.

Buddhism and Islam have remained important among some of the largest of the national minorities, notably the Tibetans (for Buddhism) and the Uiqhurs and Mongols (for Islam). The CCP's efforts to eradicate these religious influences have been interpreted by the minorities as national oppression by the Han Chinese majority. As a result, the revival of Islam and Buddhism in the 1980s was associated with efforts by the national minorities to assert their national identities and to gain greater autonomy in formulating their own policies.

For most Chinese, however, folk religions are far more important than any organized religion.[6] The CCP's best efforts to eradicate folk religions and to impart in their place an educated "scientific" viewpoint have failed. Animism, the belief that nonliving things have spirits that should be respected through worship, continues to be practiced by China's vast peasantry. Ancestor worship, based on the belief that the living can communicate with the dead and that the dead spirits to whom sacrifices are ritually made have the ability to bring a better (or worse) life to the living, absorbs much of the excess income of China's peasants. The costs of burning paper money, offerings, and of using shamans and priests to perform rituals that will heal the sick, appease the ancestors, and exorcise ghosts (who are often those poorly treated ancestors returned to haunt their descendants) at times of birth, marriage, and death, can be burdensome. But peasants are once again spending money on traditional religious folk practices, thereby contributing to the reconstruction of practices prohibited in earlier decades of Communist rule.

Taoism, which requires its disciples to renounce the secular world, has had few adherents in China since the early twentieth century. But, during the repression that followed the crackdown on Tiananmen Square's prodemocracy movement in 1989, many Chinese who felt unable to speak freely turned to mysticism and Taoism. *Qigong,* the ancient Taoist art of deep breathing, had by 1990 become a national pastime. Some 30 Taoist priests in China took on the role of national soothsayers, portending the future of everything from the weather to China's political leadership. What these priests said—or were believed to have said—quickly spread through a vast rumor network in the cities. Meanwhile, on Chinese Communist Party–controlled television, *qigong* experts swallow needles and thread, only to have the needles subsequently come out of their noses, perfectly threaded. It is widely believed that, with a sufficient concentration of *qi* (vital energy or breath), a practitioner may literally knock a person to the ground.[7] The revival of Taoist mysticism and meditation, folk religion, and formal religions suggests a need to find meaning from religion to fill the moral and ideological vacuum created by the near collapse of Communist values.

In the 1980s, under the influence of the more moderate policies of the Deng Xiaoping reformist leadership, the CCP reconsidered its efforts to eliminate religion. The 1982 State Constitution permits religious freedom, whereas previously only atheism was allowed. Until 1996–1997, when the separatists movements in Tibet and Xinjiang began to gather force, the state had actually encouraged the restoration of Buddhist temples and Islamic mosques. This occurred in part because of Beijing's awareness of the tensions caused by its efforts to deny minorities their respective religious practices, and in part because of a desire to attract both tourists and money to the minority areas.

Christianity, which was introduced in the 1800s and early 1900s by European missionaries, has several million known adherents. Its churches, which were often used as warehouses or public offices after the Communist victory in 1949, have in recent years been reopened for religious practice. A steady stream of Christian proselytizers flows to China in search of new converts. Today's churches are attended as much by the curious as by the devout. As with eating Western food in places such as McDonald's and Kentucky Fried Chicken,

attending Christian churches is a way some Chinese feel they can participate in Western culture.

While in general the government permits mainstream Christian churches to practice in China, it does have one major control over Roman Catholics: Their loyalty must be declared to the state, not to the pope. The Vatican is not permitted to be involved in China's practice of Catholicism, and Beijing does not recognize the Vatican's appointment of bishops or cardinals for China as valid.

In 1996, the government began to clamp down on a number of religious sects, arresting and even jailing some of their leaders. They justified their actions on the grounds that, as in the West, some of these religious cults were involved in practices that endangered their adherents; some were actually involved in seditious activities against the state; and some were set up as fronts for illegal activities, including gambling, prostitution, and drugs.

Marxism-Leninism-Mao Zedong Thought

Unlike religions, which the CCP leadership believes hinder the development of "rational" behavior and values that are so important to modernization, "Marxism-Leninism-Mao Zedong Thought" has been considered an integrated, rational thought system. Nevertheless, this core of China's Communist political ideology has exhibited many of the trappings of religions. These include scriptures (the works of Marx, Lenin, and Mao, as well as party doctrine); a spiritual head (Mao); and ritual observances (particularly during the Cultural Revolution, when Chinese were forced to participate in the political equivalent of Bible study each day).

In the 1980s, as the more pragmatic leadership focused on liberalizing reforms, people were encouraged to "seek truth from facts" rather than from Marxism-Leninism-Mao Zedong Thought. Thus, the role of this political ideology declined. More conservative elements in the political leadership, however, attempted to keep it as a guiding moral and political force. They were successful in returning the country to ideological study and control in both the schools and the workplace in the immediate aftermath of the Tiananmen Square protests of 1989; but by 1992, the reform group within the leadership reasserted dominance and once again directed the people's attention away from ideology. The required Friday afternoon "political study" sessions in all urban work units abandoned any pretense of interest in politics. Instead, they focused on such issues as "how to do our work better" (i.e., how to become more efficient and make a profit) that were in line with the more pragmatic approach to the workplace.

This is not to suggest that ideology has been entirely abandoned. In the context of modernizing the economy and raising the standard of living, the current leadership is still committed to building "socialism with Chinese characteristics." Marxist-Leninist ideology is still being reformulated in China; however, it is increasingly evident that there

DENG XIAOPING = TENG HSIAO-P'ING. WHAT IS PINYIN?

Chinese is the oldest of the world's active languages and is now spoken and written by more people than any other modern language. Chinese is written in the form of characters, which have evolved over several thousand years from picture symbols (like ancient Egyptian hieroglyphics) to the more abstract forms now in use. Although spoken Chinese varies greatly from dialect to dialect (for example, Mandarin, Cantonese, Shanghai-ese), the characters used to represent the language remain the same throughout China. Dialects are really just different ways of pronouncing the same characters.

There are more than 50,000 different Chinese characters. A well-educated person may be able to recognize as many as 25,000 characters, but basic literacy requires familiarity with only a few thousand.

Since Chinese is written in the form of characters rather than by a phonetic alphabet, Chinese words must be transliterated so that foreigners can pronounce them. This means that the sound of the character must be put into an alphabetic approximation.

Since English uses the Roman alphabet, Chinese characters are Romanized. (We do the same thing with other languages that are based on non-Roman alphabets, such as Russian, Greek, Hebrew, and Arabic.) Over the years, a number of methods have been developed to Romanize the Chinese language. Each method presents what the linguists who developed it believe to be the best way of approximating the sound of Chinese characters. Pinyin (literally, "spell sounds"), the system developed in the People's Republic of China, has gradually become the most commonly accepted system of Romanizing Chinese.

⊙	⊖	⊟	日	rì sun
☽	☾	⼣	月	yuè moon
𠂉	𠂊	儿	人	rén person
𣎳	𣎴	𣏐	木	mù tree

Chinese characters are the symbols used to write Chinese. Modern Chinese characters fall into two categories: one with a phonetic component, the other without it. Most of those without a phonetic component developed from pictographs. From ancient writing on archaeological relics we can see their evolution, as in the examples shown (from left to right) above.

However, other systems are still used outside China, such as in Taiwan. This can cause some confusion, since the differences between Romanization systems can be quite significant. For example, in pinyin, the name of China's dominant leader is spelled Deng Xiaoping. But the Wade-Giles system, which was until recently the Romanization method most widely used by Westerners, transliterates his name as Teng Hsiao-p'ing. Same person, same characters, but a difference in how to spell his name in Roman letters.

are few true believers in communism left. In its place is an evolving mixture of Maoism, Confucianism, and nationalism. ". . . [C]ontemporary Communist leaders have gone to new lengths to wrap themselves in the flag and identify the party with the nation—and thus make criticism of the party line an unpatriotic act. . . . Nationalist day celebrations no longer include large portraits of Communist philosophers Marx and Engels; instead, a giant portrait of the non-Communist Chinese nationalist Sun Yat-Sen stands alone in [Tiananmen] Square."[8] Much of China's nationalism is fired, as it almost always has been, by antiforeign sentiments. These sentiments derive from the belief that foreign countries are (either militarily, economically, or through insidious cultural invasion) attempting somehow to hurt China or to tell China's rulers how to govern properly. But undergirding it all is a fierce pride in China's history, civilization, and people. Insult, snub, slight, or challenge the Chinese, and the result is certain to be a country united behind its leadership against the offender.

Language
The Chinese had a written language by the time of the Shang Dynasty, which ruled in the second millennium B.C. It has evolved through 4,000 years into its present-day form, which is still ideographic. Each Chinese character, or *ideograph,* originally represented both a picture and/or a sound of a word. Before the May Fourth Movement of the 1920s, only a tiny elite of highly educated men could read these ideographs in the difficult grammar of the classical style, a style that in no way reflected the spoken language. All this changed with language reform in the 1920s: The classical style was abandoned, and the written language became almost identical in its structure to the spoken language.

Increasing Literacy
When the Chinese Communists came to power in 1949, they decided to facilitate the process of becoming literate by allowing only a few thousand of the more than 50,000 Chinese characters in existence to be used in printing newspapers, official documents, and educational materials. However, since a word is usually comprised of a combination of two characters, these few thousand characters form the basis of a very rich vocabulary; any single character may be used in numerous combinations in order to form many different words. The Chinese Communists have gone even further in facilitating literacy by simplifying thousands of characters,

often reducing a character from more than 20 strokes to 10 strokes or even fewer.

In 1979, China adopted a new system, *pinyin,* for spelling Chinese words and names. This system, which uses the Latin alphabet of 26 letters, is still largely for foreign consumption; it is not commonly used within China. The fact that so many characters have the same Romanization (and pronunciation), plus cultural resistance, has thus far resulted in ideographs remaining the basis for Chinese writing. There are, as an example, at least 70 different Chinese ideographs that are pronounced *zhu,* but each means something different. Usually the context is adequate to indicate which word is being used, but Chinese often use their fingers to draw a particular character in the air so that those listening to them will know which of the many characters that sound the same is meant.

Spoken Chinese

To facilitate national unity, the government decided that all Chinese would speak the same dialect. Although the Chinese have shared the same written language over the last 2,000 years, regardless of which dialect of Chinese they spoke (the same written characters were simply pronounced in different ways depending on the dialect), a sense of national unity was difficult—people often needed interpreters to speak with someone even a few miles away. After the Communist victory in 1949, a majority of the delegates to the National People's Congress voted to adopt the northern dialect, Mandarin (standard Chinese), as the national language, and required all schools to teach in Mandarin.

The reality in the countryside, however, was that it was difficult to find teachers capable of speaking Mandarin; and at home, whether in the countryside or the cities, the people continued to speak their local dialects. The liberalization policies of the 1980s and 1990s have had as their by-product a discernible trend back to speaking local dialects even in the workplace and on the streets. Whereas 10 years ago a person could count on most people speaking Mandarin in the major cities, this is no longer the case. As a unified language is an important factor in supporting national cohesion, the reemergence of local dialects at the expense of standard Chinese threatens China's fragile unity.

One force that is slowing this disintegration is television, for programs are broadcast almost entirely in standard Chinese. As there is now a wide variety of interesting programming available on Chinese television, it may be that most Chinese will make an effort to acquire at least the ability to understand, if not speak, standard Chinese.

Education

The People's Republic of China can be proud of its success in educating its people. Before 1949, fewer than 20 percent of the population could read and write. Today, almost all school-age children in the cities attend the 5-year program at the primary level, and close to 90 percent of those children living in rural areas do. In larger cities, 12 years of schooling is becoming the norm, with children attending either a vocational middle school or a college-preparatory school; but in the countryside, few children receive an education beyond the primary level. Not only are they needed to help in the fields, but even the very low school tuition is too expensive for a poor peasant family. Rural education also suffers from a lack of qualified teachers, as any person educated enough to teach can probably get a better-paying job in the industrial or commercial sector.

Overeducated Students

As in the West, there is concern in China that too many students are now preparing to go on to a university. The reason for the concern, however, is different. In the United States, for example, college graduates who lack vocational training often find themselves poorly prepared to get a good job. In China, only about 5 percent of the senior middle-school graduates will pass the university entrance examinations and be admitted; but far more people than this pursue a college-oriented curriculum. Thus, in China, it is high school graduates who find themselves inappropriately educated for the workplace. As a result, the government is attempting to augment vocational training at the high school level as well as to increase the number of slots available in colleges and universities. Some private high schools and colleges are also being established to address these needs.

In the context of the freewheeling small-enterprise capitalist economy that has thrived since the early 1980s, many Chinese have grown cynical about the value of a college education. Those making the most money have not, in most cases, been those with a college education but, rather, those successful at entrepreneurship. A college graduate, who is usually assigned to the low-paying state sector, still makes a mere $60 to $200 per month. An uneducated individual selling noodle soup out of his back door can often make at least that much in just a week. And workers in the state industrial sector have always earned far more money than have China's "intellectuals." At a time when moonlighting is permitted, ordinary workers often move on to a second job at the end of the day. There are few such opportunities available, however, to those with a "liberal arts" college education.

Political Education

Until the reforms that began in 1979, the content of Chinese education was suffused with political values and objectives. A considerable amount of school time—as much as 100 percent during political campaigns—was devoted to political education. Often this amounted to nothing more than learning by rote the favorite axioms and policies of the leading faction in power. When that faction lost power, the students' political thought had to be reoriented in the direction of the new policies and values. History, philosophy, literature, and even foreign language and science were laced with a political vocabulary.

The prevailing political line has affected the balance in the curriculum between political study and the learning of skills and scientific knowledge. Beginning in the 1960s, the political content of education increased dramatically until, during the Cultural Revolution, schools were shut down. When they reopened in the early 1970s, politics dominated the curriculum. When Deng Xiaoping and the "modernizers" consolidated their power in the late 1970s, this tendency was reversed. During the 1980s, in fact, schools jettisoned the study of political theory—both administrators and teachers wanted their students to do well on college-entrance examinations, which by then focused on academic subjects. As a result, students refused to clog their schedules with the study of political theory and the CCP's history. The study of Marxism and party history was revived in the wake of the events of Tiananmen Square in 1989, with the entering classes for many universities required to spend the first year in political study and indoctrination, sometimes under military supervision; but this practice was abandoned after 2 years. Today, political study has again been confined to a narrow part of the curriculum, in the interest of giving students an education that will help advance China's modernization.

Study Abroad

Since 1979, when China began to promote an "open door" policy, more than 100,000 P.R.C. students have been sent for a university education to the United States, and thousands more have gone to Europe and Japan; for although China does have universities, it only has space for a small percentage of all high school graduates. Furthermore, until the late 1980s, Chinese universities were unable to offer graduate training. Those trained abroad were expected to return to China to establish graduate education in Chinese universities.

The fate of P.R.C. students educated abroad who return to China has not always been a happy one. The elite educated in Western universities who were in China in 1949 or who returned to China thereafter were not permitted to hold leadership positions within their fields. Ultimately, they were the targets of class-struggle campaigns and purges in the 1950s, 1960s, and 1970s—precisely because of their Western educations. For the most part, those students who returned to China in the 1980s after studying abroad were given the same positions that they occupied before they received advanced education abroad. This was in part because their less-well-educated seniors who had not been able to study abroad held a jealous regard for their own positions. These individuals still have the power to make arbitrary decisions about their subordinates, and they ignore the mandate from the central authorities to promote the returned students to appropriate positions. In those places where the seniority system is still the basis for promotion, however, it may be difficult for returned students to get satisfactory jobs in China.

What is more, while studying abroad, Chinese students and older "visiting scholars" also learn much about liberal democratic societies. When they return to China—and to date, only a small percentage of students have—they bring with them the theories, values, and concepts at the heart of liberal democratic societies. The central CCP leadership saw the danger signs of this in 1986, when student demonstrations erupted, and later, in 1989, when the student-led movement took on massive proportions in demonstrations in Beijing and other cities. The conservative members of the party leadership placed the blame for these efforts to push for democratic political reform in China squarely on the liberalization policies that permitted an opening to the West, including the education of Chinese students abroad.

Nevertheless, much has changed since 1992, when Deng Xiaoping announced a major shift in government economic and commercial policy to support just about anything that would help China become strong and powerful. The impact of this on students who have studied abroad is that the government is offering them significant incentives to come back, including excellent jobs, good salaries, and even the chance to start up new companies. Chinese students who have graduated from foreign universities are also being recruited for both their expertise and their understanding of the outside world by the rapidly multiplying number of joint ventures in China.

The flow of Chinese students to study in foreign countries continues unabated, even though further hurdles must now be negotiated before any university student can leave China. Students who have received a university education in China must work for 5 years after college before going abroad for graduate study; otherwise, they must repay the state government for the university education they received at state expense before they leave China. Yet this requirement has seemingly done little to stem the outward flow of China's college students, as the rapid accumulation of wealth by many Chinese in recent years has made it possible to repay what used to be considered extraordinary debts.

THE ECONOMIC SYSTEM

A Command Economy

Until 1979, the Chinese had what is known as a centrally controlled command economy. That is, the central leadership determined the economic policies to be followed and allocated all of the country's resources—labor, capital, and raw materials. Once the Communist Party leadership determined the country's political goals and the correct ideology to follow, the State Planning Commission and the State Economic Commission decided how to implement these objectives through specific policies for agriculture and industry and the allocation of resources. This is in striking contrast to a capitalist laissez faire economy, in which there is a minimum of government control and market forces of supply and demand are the primary determinants of what is produced.

The CCP leadership adopted the model of a centralized economy from the Soviet Union. Such a system was not only

(United Nations photo)
Communes had been disbanded by the early 1980s. In some areas, however, farmers have continued to work their now privatized land as a single unit to benefit from the economies of scale of large tracts of land.

bution to development, regardless of whether or not there was a market for the products manufactured.

The state planning agencies, without the benefit of market research, determined which products should be manufactured and in what quantity. For example, the central government might set a goal for a factory to manufacture 5 million springs per year, without knowing whether or not there was a market for them. The factory management did not care, since the state was responsible for marketing the products and paying the factory's bills. If the state had no buyer, the springs would pile up in warehouses. But rarely would production be cut back, much less a factory be closed, because jobs would have to be found for the workers cut from the payroll. Economic inefficiencies of this sort were often justified because socialist political objectives were being met. Thus, even today, the state worries about shutting down an inefficient factory, because it would create unemployment.

Quality control was not as important an issue as it should have been for state-run industries as, until market reforms occurred after 1979, the state itself allocated all finished products to other industries that needed them. If a state-controlled factory made defective parts, the industry using them had no recourse against the supplier—each factory had a contract with the state, not with each other.

As a result, China's economic development under the centralized political leadership of the CCP occurred by fits and starts. Much waste resulted from planning that did not take into account market factors of supply and demand. Centrally set production quotas took the place of profit-and-loss issues in the allocation of resources. Although China's command economy was able to meet the country's most important industrial needs, problems like these took their toll over time. Enterprises had little incentive to raise productivity, quality, or efficiency when doing so did not affect their budgets, wages, or funds for expansion.

Unrealistic Agricultural Programs
The agricultural sector suffered most from centralized planning. Regardless of geography or climate, China's economic planners repeatedly ordered the peasants to restructure their economic production units according to one centralized plan. China's peasants, who had supported the CCP in its rise to power before 1949 in order to acquire their own land, had enthusiastically embraced the CCP's fulfillment of its pledge of "land to the tillers" after the Communists took over in 1949. But in 1953, the leadership, motivated by a belief that small-scale agricultural production could not meet the production goals of socialist development, ordered all but 15 percent of the arable land to be pooled into "lower-level agricultural producer cooperatives" of between 300 and 700 workers. The remaining 15 percent of land was to be set aside as private plots for the peasants, and they could market the produce from these plots in private markets throughout the countryside. Then, in 1956, the peasants throughout the coun-

in accord with the Leninist model of centralized state governance but also made sense for a government desperate to unify China after more than 100 years of internal division, instability, and economic collapse. Historically, China suffered from large regions evading the grasp of central control over such matters as currency and the payment of taxes. The inability of the Kuomintang government to gain control over the country's economy in the 1930s and early 1940s undercut its power and contributed to its failure to win control over China. Thus, the Chinese Communist Party's decision to centralize economic decision making after 1949 contributed to the state functioning as an integrated whole.

Over time, however, China's highly centralized economy became inefficient and inadequately flexible to address the complexity of the country's needs. Although China possesses a large and diverse economy and has a broad range of resources, topography, and climate, the P.R.C.'s economic planners made policy as if it were a uniform, homogeneous whole. Merely increasing production was itself considered a contri-

(United Nations photo)

COMMUNES: PEASANTS WORK OVERTIME DURING THE GREAT LEAP FORWARD

In the socialist scheme of things, communes are considered ideal forms of organization for agriculture. They are supposed to increase productivity and equality, reduce inefficiencies of small-scale individual farming, and bring modern benefits to the countryside more rapidly through rural industrialization.

These objectives are attained largely through the economies of scale of communes; that is, it is presumed that things done on a large scale are more efficient and cost-effective than when done on a small scale. Thus, using tractors, harvesters, trucks, and other agricultural machinery makes sense when large tracts of land can be planted with the same crops and plowed at one time. Similarly, small-scale industries may be based on the communal unit of 30,000 to 70,000 people, since, in such a large work unit, some people can take care of agricultural needs for the entire commune, leaving others to work in commune-based industries.

Because of its size, a commune may also support other types of organizations that smaller work units would find impossible to support, both financially and otherwise. A commune, for example, can support a hospital, a high school, an agricultural-research organization, and, if the commune is wealthy enough, even a "sports palace" and a cultural center for movies and entertainment.

During the Great Leap Forward, launched in 1958, peasants were—much against their will—forced into these larger agricultural and administrative units. They were particularly distressed that their remaining private plots were taken away from them. Communal kitchens, run by women, were to prepare food for everyone while workers went about their other productive work. Peasants were told that they had to eat in the communal mess halls rather than in the privacy of their own homes.

When the combination of bad policies and bad weather led to a severe famine, widespread peasant resistance forced the government to retreat from the Great Leap Forward and abandon the communes. But a modified commune system remained intact in much of China until the late 1970s, when the government ordered communes to be dissolved. A commune's collective property was then distributed to the peasants belonging to it, and a system of contract responsibility was launched. Today, with the exception of a few communes that refused to be dissolved, agricultural production is no longer collectivized. Individual households are again, as before 1953, engaged in small-scale agricultural production on private plots of land.

try were ordered into "higher-level agricultural producer co-operatives" of 10 times that size, and the size of the private plots allotted to them was reduced to 5 percent of the cooperatives' total land.

Many peasants felt cheated by these wholesale collectivization policies. When in 1958 the central leadership ordered them to move into communes 10 times larger still than the cooperatives they had just joined, they were infuriated. Mao Zedong's Great Leap Forward policy of 1958 forced all peasants in China to become members of huge communes—economic and administrative units consisting of between 30,000 and 70,000 peasants. With communization, all of the peasants' private plots and private utensils, as well as their household chickens, pigs, and ducks, were to be turned over to the commune. Resisting this mandate, many peasants killed and ate their livestock. And since private enterprise was no longer permitted, home handicraft industries ground to a halt.

CCP chairman Mao Zedong's vision for catching up with the West was to industrialize the vast countryside. Peasants were therefore ordered to build "backyard furnaces" to smelt steel. Lacking iron ore, much less any knowledge of how to make steel, and under the guidance of party cadres who themselves were ignorant of steel making, the peasants tore out metal radiators and pipes, metal fences, pots and pans. Almost none of the final smelted product was usable. Finally, the central economic leadership ordered all peasants to eat in large, communal mess halls. This was reportedly the last straw for a people who

valued family above all else. Being deprived of time alone with their families for meals, the peasants refused to cooperate further in agricultural collectivization.

When the catastrophic results of the Great Leap Forward policy poured in, the CCP retreated, but it was too late. Three subsequent years of bad weather, combined with the devastation wreaked by these policies and the Soviet withdrawal of all assistance, brought economic catastrophe. Demographic data indicate that in the "three bad years" from 1959 to 1962, some 20 million to 30 million Chinese died from starvation and malnutrition-related diseases.

By 1962, central planners had condoned peasants returning to production and accounting units the size of the higher- and lower-level cooperatives. Furthermore, peasants were again allowed to farm a small percentage of the total land as private plots, to raise domestic animals for their own use, and to engage in household handicrafts. Free markets at which the peasantry could trade goods from private production were reopened. The commune structure was retained throughout the countryside, however, and until the party leadership introduced the "contract responsibility system" in 1979, it provided the infrastructure of rural secondary education, hospitals, and agricultural research.

Other centrally determined policies, seemingly oblivious to reality, compounded the P.R.C.'s difficulties in agriculture. These included attempts to plant three crops per year in areas that for climatic reasons could support only two; and to plant

DENG XIAOPING: TAKING A "PRACTICAL" APPROACH TO CHINA'S PROBLEMS

(Hsin-Hua News Agency)

Deng Xiaoping, a controversial figure throughout his political career, was twice purged from power. Deng, pictured here, became the dominant figure in Chinese politics after he returned to power in 1978. Under Deng's leadership, China implemented policies of economic liberalization, including the market system of supply and demand for distributing goods, services, and resources. These policies replaced many of China's socialist centrally planned economic policies. Deng's statement "I don't care whether the cat is black or white as long as it catches mice" illustrates his practical, nonideological approach to modernizing China. In other words, Deng did not care if he used capitalist methods as long as they helped modernize China faster than socialist methods.

Deng's economic liberalization policies frequently were blamed when problems such as inflation and corruption occurred in the 1980s and 1990s. Those opposing his policies used this as their rationale for retreating from economic liberalization twice during the 1980s. Since 1992, however, when Deng reasserted the need to move ahead with economic liberalization, the leadership has fairly steadily implemented Deng's policies.

Deng did not hold any official post in his final years of life; but, from 1992 until he died in February 1997, his policies were not successfully challenged. By 1997, the liberalizing reforms he had introduced had enjoyed such remarkable success that it is unlikely they will be undone any time soon, regardless of who leads China.

twice as much grain as was normal in a field, with the result that all of it grew to less than full size or simply wilted for lack of adequate sunshine and nutrients.

A final example of ill-considered centrally determined agricultural policy was the decision in the early 1970s by the Gang of Four radicals that "the whole country should grow grain." The purpose was to establish China's self-sufficiency in grain. Considering China's immense size and diverse climates, soil types, and topography, a policy ordering everyone to grow the same thing was doomed to fail. Peasants plowed under fields of cotton and cut down rubber plantations and fruit orchards, planting grain in their place.

China's planners, who at this point were largely CCP cadres, not economic experts, ignored overwhelming evidence that grain would not grow well in all areas and that China would have to import everything that it had replaced with grain at far greater costs than it would have paid for importing grain. Peasant protests were futile in the face of local-level Communist Party leaders who hoped to advance their careers by implementing central policy. After the arrest of the Gang of Four in 1976, the self-sufficiency in grain policy was abandoned, and each region was told to specialize in growing the most suitable crops for its conditions.

Economic Reforms: Decentralization and Liberalization

In an effort to increase productivity and speed up modernization, the Deng Xiaoping government began in 1979 to implement a program of economic reform and liberalization. In brief, although the program tried to maintain overall state control of the direction of policy and the distribution and pricing of strategic and energy resources, it introduced decentralized decision making down to the level of local enterprises. The purpose of decentralization was to facilitate more rational decision making—based on local conditions, needs, and efficiency criteria—about the best policy for any particular enterprise or part of the country. While retaining the right to set overall economic priorities, the national government allowed a greater number of goods to be produced and allocated according to local market forces of supply and demand instead of centrally determined quotas and pricing. It also encouraged enterprises to contract with each other instead of with the state, thereby limiting the role of the government as the go-between in commercial transactions.

Today, most collective and individual enterprises, instead of fulfilling centrally determined production quotas, meet contractual obligations that they themselves set under the contract responsibility system. After they have fulfilled their contractual obligations and paid their taxes, profitable enterprises are permitted to use the remaining profits to expand production facilities, improve equipment, and award bonuses. The so-called collective enterprises (set up by individuals or small groups), which compete with state-run enterprises to supply goods and services, may become rich or go bankrupt.

(Xinhua News Agency)

Under the economic liberalization program, shops such as this one in Sichuan were allowed to prosper.

This was not the case for state-run enterprises. Although they were threatened with bankruptcy and being shut down if they operated with losses, or produced goods that no one wanted, fear of the political instability that might result from a high level of unemployment left the government in an unfortunate position: It felt it had to continue to subsidize the heavy losses in the state-controlled sector. This, in turn, consumed a significant portion of the state's budget and contributed to China's growing inflation.

By the mid-1990s, however, the state had reached a crisis point. Continuing to underwrite the losses of state-run enterprises was consuming a higher and higher proportion of the budget. Under a very carefully managed scheme, the government has started to spin off some state-run industries to the collective and private sectors. In most cases, whoever buys these state industries must guarantee some sort of livelihood, even if not full employment, to the former employees of the state-run enterprises; but they have far more freedom

(United Nations photo/A. Holcombe)

With the highly centralized or command economy in place until the 1980s, China's manufacturing energy was focused on production, with little regard to need or markets. These women in Shanghai were producing mechanical toys for no defined market.

to make a profit than did the state-run enterprises. Finally, in the face of competition from collective enterprises and under the threat of bankruptcy, some state-run enterprises have in recent years themselves become far more efficient, to the point where they are no longer generating significant losses.

In agriculture, the collectivized economy has been almost completely replaced by the contract responsibility system. Under this system, individuals or individual households, to whom the formerly collective lands and production tools have been distributed, are responsible for planning and carrying out production on their own land. The "10,000 yuan household" (about $2,000), a measure of extraordinary wealth in China, has now become a realizeable goal for many peasants. After fulfilling their contractual responsibilities to the state, they are free to sell remaining produce in free markets where price is determined by the forces of supply and demand, not by a centralized state bureaucracy.

Although theoretically the collectives still own the land that they have "leased" to the peasants, in practice the land is treated as if it is owned by the peasants. Those who choose to leave their land may contract out their own land to others, so that some peasants have amassed large amounts of land appropriate for large-scale farm machinery. To encourage development of the land, the government has permitted land to be leased for as long as 30 years and for leased rights to be inherited. Furthermore, peasants have built houses on what they consider their own land.

The occasional efforts since the early 1980s to revert to collectivized agriculture have repeatedly come up against a stone wall of resistance from the overwhelming number of peasants who have benefited from the reforms. Today wealthy rural towns are springing up throughout the agriculturally rich and densely populated east coast as well as along China's major transportation lines.

With the growth of free enterprise in the rural towns since 1979, some 60 million to 100 million peasants have left the land to work for far better pay in small-scale rural industry or to search for jobs in China's large cities. Many roam the country searching for work. For some, especially those able to find employment in the construction industry that is booming in many of China's cities, this new system has meant vast personal enrichment. However, tens of millions of unemployed peasants clog city streets, parks, and railroad stations. They have contributed to a significant increase in crime and a sense of social instability.

Problems Created by Economic Reforms

Withholding of Profits and Materials
Inevitably, problems arose from the reformers' new economic policies. For example, decentralization prompted profitable

CHINA'S SPECIAL ECONOMIC ZONES

In 1979, China opened four Special Economic Zones (SEZs) within the territory of the People's Republic of China as part of its program of far-reaching reform of the socialist economy. The SEZs were allowed a great deal of leeway in experimenting with new economic policies. For example, Western management methods, including the right to fire unsatisfactory workers (something unknown under the Soviet-style centrally planned economy), were introduced into SEZ factories. Laws and regulations on foreign investment were greatly eased in the SEZs in order to attract capital from abroad. Export-oriented industries were established with the goal of earning large amounts of foreign exchange in order to help China pay for the imported technology needed to hasten modernization. To many people, the SEZs looked like pockets of capitalism inside the socialist economy of the P.R.C.; indeed, they are often referred to as "mini-Hong Kongs."

The largest of the Special Economic Zones is Shenzhen, which is located just across the border from the Hong Kong New Territories. The transformation of Shenzhen over the last few years from a sleepy little rural town to a large, modern urban center and one of China's major industrial cities has been phenomenal. The city now boasts broad avenues and China's tallest skyscrapers, and the standard of living is the highest in the country.

But with growth and prosperity have come numerous problems. The pace of construction has gotten out of hand, outstripping the ability of the city to provide adequate services to the growing population. Speculation and corruption have been rampant, and crime is a more serious problem in Shenzhen than it is elsewhere in China. Strict controls on immigration have been implemented to stem the flood of people who are attracted to Shenzhen in the hopes of making their fortune.

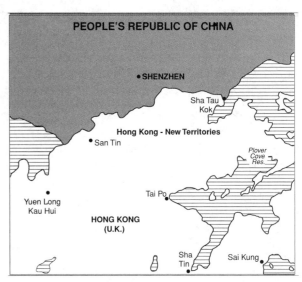

Shenzhen is the largest of China's SEZs. It is located close to the Hong Kong New Territories.

Nevertheless, the success of Shenzhen and other SEZs has led the leadership to expand the concept of SEZs throughout the country. The special privileges, such as lower taxes, that foreign businesses and joint ventures could originally enjoy only in these zones were expanded first along the coast and then to the interior, so that it too could benefit from foreign investment. Eventually, all of these special privileges will be eradicated.

industrial enterprises to refuse to hand over a fair percentage of their profits to the state. In spite of the dramatic increase in the value of industrial output since the 1980s, therefore, the profits turned over to the state actually declined. Moreover, some localities and enterprises withheld materials normally allocated by the state, such as rolled steel, glass, cement, and timber, either to hoard them as a safeguard against future shortages or to resell them at unauthorized higher prices. Not only did these enterprises make illegal profits for themselves; they also deprived the state of access to building materials for its key construction projects. This reflected a basic problem of a mixed economy: With the state controlling the pricing and allocation of some resources and the free market determining the rest, there are many opportunities for corruption and abuse of the system.

The needs of the centralized state economy remain in tension, if not conflict, with the interests of provinces, counties, towns, and individuals, most of which now operate under the dual rules of a part-market, part-command economy. Thus, even as enterprises are determining whether they will expand production facilities based on the demands of a market economy, the state continues to allocate resources based on a national plan. A clothing factory that expands its production, for instance, requires more energy (coal, oil, water) and more cotton. The state, already faced with inadequate energy resources to keep most industries operating at more than 70 percent capacity, continues to allocate the same amount to the now-expanded factory. Profitable enterprises want a greater share of centrally allocated scarce resources but find that they cannot acquire them without the help of "middlemen" and a significant amount of under-the-table dealing. Corruption has, therefore, become rampant at the nexus where the capitalist and socialist economies meet.

Overall, however, the kinds of tensions among the central state, the provinces, the cities, the town, and the enterprises that have been generated by decentralization of economic power have been beneficial to economic growth. Greater economic autonomy at each level has, moreover, led to a concomitant growth in the political autonomy at that level. Thus, provinces, especially those that are producing significant revenues, can now challenge central economic policy—and even refuse to carry it out.[9] The same is true for the cities vis-à-vis the former all-encompassing power of the provinces over them; and so on down to the level of the enterprise. This sort of economic power carries with it, in short, the political power necessary to challenge Beijing's leaders.

Unequal Benefits

Not all Chinese have benefited equally from the contract responsibility system. Peasants living far from cities or transportation lines or tilling less arable land have benefited far less than others from the economic reforms of the Deng Xiaoping period. Further, the commune as the basis of education and medical care in the countryside has disappeared. The peasantry in many areas suffer from even less access to education and medical care than before, whereas wealthy peasants can send their children into larger towns and cities for schooling and their family members can travel to the more comprehensive health clinics and hospitals farther away. In some areas, however, those peasants who have become wealthy have invested in local schools and private hospitals.

In the cities, employees of state-run enterprises, who are on fixed salaries, suffered from the double-digit inflation that resulted from the state's decontrolling of prices in the agricultural sector. Urban dwellers, long accustomed to being the primary beneficiaries of growth, were enraged that the living standards of the peasantry should be rising faster than their own. Some of China's more conservative leaders concluded that soaring inflation, rampant corruption, and the development of a distinctly wealthy class were too high a price to pay for modernization. In the late 1980s, they were temporarily able to halt reforms in their tracks. But this did not resolve China's economic problems, and by the early 1990s, the leadership was moving forward with economic reforms. In 1995 and 1996, the state managed to bring inflation under greater control, and its annual rate dropped to 9 percent. By then, the standard of living in the cities was surging ahead. In contrast, the benefits of reform in the countryside had slowed considerably. As a result, China now faces serious revolts from the peasantry, who are angered by the government's inability to pay them for their grain and to address the needs of China's massive rural population.

Overall, however, China's economy has been experiencing an economic boom for some 15 years. Inflation is under control, and China continues to export more than it imports. As foreign investors consider where to put their money, China is almost always at the top of their list.

Mortgaging the Future

Perhaps one of the most damaging aspects of the capitalist "get-rich" atmosphere prevailing in China is the willingness to sacrifice the future for profits today. The environment is literally being destroyed by uncontrolled pollution; the rampant growth of new towns, cities, and highways; the building of houses on arable land; and the destruction of forests. Some state institutions such as middle schools have turned their basketball courts into parking lots in China's crowded cities, which are unable to provide parking facilities for the huge number of newly owned private cars. And they have used state funds allocated to the schools for education to build shops all along the outside walls of the schools. Teachers and administrators deal themselves the profits, but, in the meantime, classroom materials and facilities are deteriorating.

Economic Crime

Widespread corruption in the economic sector has led the Chinese government to wage a series of campaigns against economic crimes. An increasing number of economc criminals are going to prison, and serious offenders are frequently executed. Until energy and transportation bottlenecks and the scarcity of key resources are dealt with, however, it will be extremely difficult to halt the bribery, smuggling, stealing, and extortion now pervasive in the P.R.C. The relaxation of strong state central controls, the mandate for the Chinese people to "get rich," and a mixed economy have exacerbated what was already a problem under the socialist system. In a system suffering from serious scarcities but controlled by bureaucrats, who gets what—not only goods, but also opportunities, licenses, permits, and approvals—is determined by political power, not by the market.

Although the Chinese may now purchase in the market many essential products previously distributed only through bureaucratically controlled channels, there are still many goods that they can acquire only through the "back door"—that is, through people they know and for whom they have done favors. Scarcity, combined with bureaucratic control, has led to "collective corruption": Individuals engage in corrupt practices, even cheat the state, in order to benefit the enterprise for which they work. Since today's non-state-owned "collectives" survive or perish on the basis of profits and losses, the motivation for corrupt activities is stronger than under the previous system.

Liberalization of the economy is providing a massive number and variety of goods for the marketplace. The Chinese people may buy almost any basic consumer goods in the open markets. But the nexus between continued state control and the free economy still fuels a rampant corruption that threatens the strength of China's economy.

SOCIALIST LEGALITY

China's legal system must be viewed within the particular Chinese cultural context for law and the goals of law in a socialist system. If Western standards of law and justice are used to evaluate the Chinese system, it should be with the understanding that most of these standards have never had a foundation in China. Nevertheless, reforms in China's legal system since 1979 have brought a remarkable transformation in Chinese attitudes toward the law; and China's laws and procedures look increasingly like those used in the West.

This is particularly true in the area of law that relates to the economy, including contract, investment, property, and commercial laws. The Chinese have discovered that the legal system has developed into a strong protector of their rights in economic transactions. Even in the area of intellectual property law, the source of so much controversy between China and the West, the Chinese are finding that it helps defend their own interests against copyright violation and fake products.[10] Criminal law and procedure have also undergone a rapid transformation. In civil law (when it relates to disputes with neighbors and family members), however, the Chinese are still more likely to rely on mediation to settle their disputes.

Ethical Basis of Law
In imperial China, the Confucian system provided the basis for the traditional social and political order: Confucianism posited that ethics were based on maintaining correct personal relationships among people, not on laws. A legal system did exist; but in civil cases, the Chinese resorted to it only in desperation, for the inability to resolve one's problems oneself, or through a mediator, usually resulted in considerable loss of "face," or dignity and pride. (In criminal cases, the state normally became involved in determining guilt and punishment.)

This perspective on law carried over into the period of Communist rule. Until recent years, most Chinese preferred to call in CCP officials, local neighborhood or factory mediation committees, family members, and friends—not lawyers or judicial personnel—to settle disputes. Only when mediation failed did the Chinese resort to the courts. By contrast, the West lacks both this strong support for the institution of mediation and the concept of face. So Westerners have had difficulty understanding why China has never had many lawyers and why the Chinese lack faith in the law.

Like Confucianism, Marxism-Leninism is an ideology that embodies a set of ethical standards for behavior. After 1949, it easily built on China's cultural predisposition toward ruling by ethics instead of by law. Although Marxism-Leninism did not completely replace the Confucian ethical system, it did establish new standards of behavior based on socialist morality. These ethical standards emerge in the works of Karl Marx, in the writings of Mao Zedong, and in the CCP's policies.

Law and Politics
From 1949 until the legal reforms that began in 1979, Chinese universities trained very few lawyers. Legal training consisted

of learning law and politics as an integrated whole; for, according to Marxism, law is meant to reflect the values of the "ruling class" and to serve as an instrument of "class struggle." The Chinese Communist regime viewed law as a branch of the social sciences, not as a professional field of study. For this reason, China's citizens tended to view law as a mere propaganda tool, not as a means for protecting their rights. They have never really experienced a law-based society.

Not only are China's laws and legal education highly politicized, but the party and politics also pervade the judicial system. With few lawyers available, few legally trained judges in the courts, and even fewer laws to refer to for standards of behavior, China's legal system has inevitably been subject to abuse. China has been ruled by people, not by law; by politics, not by legal standards; and by party policy, not by a constitution.

After the Deng Xiaoping leadership gained ascendancy in 1978, the government moved rapidly to write new laws. Fewer than 300 lawyers, most of them trained before 1949 in Western legal institutions, undertook the immense task of writing a civil code, a criminal code, contract law, economic law, law governing foreign investment in the P.R.C., tax law, and environmental and forestry laws. One strong motivation for the Chinese Communist leadership to formalize the legal system was its growing realization, after years of a disappointingly low level of foreign investment, that the international business community was reluctant to invest further in the P.R.C. without substantial legal guarantees.

In fact, even China's own potential entrepreneurs wanted legal protection from the *state* before they would assume the risks of developing new businesses. If, for example, the state should fail to fulfill its part of a contract to supply resources to an enterprise for production, the enterprise wants a legal guarantee that the state can be sued for losses issuing from its nonfulfillment of contractual obligations. Since the objective of economic reform is to encourage investment from individuals and enterprises, the leadership has necessarily had to supplement economic reforms with legal reforms. These efforts to formalize the legal system have fostered a stronger legal basis for modernization. They have, moreover, helped limit abuse of the people's rights by the government and the CCP.

Criminal Law: Presumption of Guilt
Procedures followed in Chinese courts have differed significantly from those in the United States. For example, in China's socialist judicial system, until further legal reform in 1996,[11] it was presumed that people brought to trial in criminal cases were guilty; for before the accused were brought to trial, a branch of the judiciary called the *procuracy,* the investigative branch, had already spent considerable time and effort finding out the facts and establishing whether suspects were indeed guilty. This is important to understand when assessing the fact that, until 1996, some 99 percent of all the

accused who were brought to trial in China were judged guilty. Had the facts not substantiated their guilt, the procuracy would have dismissed their cases before going to court. In short, those adjudged to be innocent were never brought to trial. For this reason, court appearances of the guilty functioned mainly to present the evidence upon which the guilty verdict was based—not to weigh the evidence to see if it indicated guilt—and to remind the public that criminals were punished.

A trial is a "morality play" of sorts: The villain is punished, justice is done, the people's interests are protected. In addition, the trial process continues to emphasize the importance of confessing one's crimes; those who confess and appear repentant in court will usually be dealt more lenient sentences. Even today, criminals are encouraged to turn themselves in, on the promise that their punishment will be less severe than if they are caught.

From the Western perspective, the problem with this system has been that, once the procuracy establishes "the facts," the facts are not open to question by the lawyer or other representative of the accused. (In China, a person may be represented by a family member, friend, or colleague, largely because there are simply not enough lawyers to fulfill the guarantee of a person's "right to a defense.") A lawyer (who is usually handed the case only a day or two before the trial) is not allowed to introduce new evidence, make arguments to dismiss the case based on technicalities or improper procedures (such as wire tapping), or make insanity pleas for the client. Instead, the lawyer's role in a criminal case is simply to represent the person in court and to bargain with the court for a reduced sentence for the repentant client.

The 1996 legal reforms have improved the rights of the accused, however. Now they are pressured to be innocent until proven guilty, and are permitted to have access to a lawyer within several days of being formally arrested. Nevertheless, it has always been assumed that a lawyer will not defend someone who is guilty. The lawyer is, in fact, an employee of the state and is paid by the state. As such, a lawyer's obligation is first and foremost to protect the state's interests, not the individual's interests at the expense of the state. When lawyers have done otherwise, they have risked being condemned as "counterrevolutionaries" or treasonous. Small wonder that, after 1949, the study of law did not attract China's most talented students.

(UN photo by John Isaac)

Settling civil disputes in China today still usually involves neighborhood mediation committees, family members, and friends.

The Need for Lawyers

In the area of civil and commercial law, however, the role of the lawyer has become increasingly important since the opening of China's closed door to the outside world. Now that the leadership views trade with other countries and foreign investment as crucial to China's development, its goal is to train at least one lawyer for every state, collective, or private organization and enterprise. Increasingly, the Chinese recognize that upholding the law is not merely a question of correctly understanding the party "line" and then following it in legal disputes but, rather, of interpreting the meaning of law according to the concrete circumstances of a case. Yet even in economic disputes in the 1980s and 1990s, lawyers who have vigorously defended their clients' interests against the state's interests have occasionally been condemned for being "anti-socialist."

Since China has had so little experience in dealing with civil conflicts and economic disputes in the courts, and since Western investors insist that Chinese courts be prepared to address such issues, the leadership has been forced to train lawyers in Western law and to draft literally thousands of new laws. To protect themselves against what is difficult to understand in the abstract, however, the Chinese often refused to publish their newly written laws. Claiming a shortage of paper or the need to protect "state secrets," they withheld publication of many laws until their actual impact on China's state interests could be determined. The leadership realizes that, once the laws are actually published, it will be much harder to retract them for rewriting. This practice frustrated potential investors, who dared not risk making capital investments in China until they knew exactly what the relevant laws were. However, as relations with foreign investors as well as the entrepreneurial activities of their own citizens have grown increasingly complex, the Chinese government now feels obligated to publish most of its laws as quickly as possible.

THE POLITICAL SYSTEM

The Party and the State

The Chinese Communist Party is the fountainhead of power and policy in China. But not all Chinese people are CCP members. Although the CCP has some 50 million members, this represents less than 5 percent of the population. Joining the CCP is a selective, rigorous process. Some have wanted to join out of a commitment to Communist ideals, others in hopes of climbing the ladder of opportunity, still others to gain access to limited goods and opportunities. By the late 1980s, however, so many students and educated individuals had grown cynical about the CCP that they simply refused to join. Still, those who travel to China today are likely to find that many of the most talented people they meet have been recruited to become members of the CCP.

The CCP is the ultimate institutional authority. It determines the "general line" to which all state policies must conform. Theoretically, the state is distinct from the party. In practice, however, the two have overlapped almost completely since the late 1950s. The state apparatus consists of the State Council, headed by the premier. Under the State Council are the ministries and agencies and "people's congresses" responsible for the formulation of policy. The CCP, however, exercises firm control over these state bodies through interlocking organizations. For example, CCP branches exist within all government organizations, and all key state personnel are also party members. Efforts to separate the CCP from the government have been under way since the reforms that began in 1979, but it is still difficult to uproot party leaders.

China's socialist system is subject to enormous abuses of power. The lines of authority within both the CCP and the state system are poorly defined, as are the rules for succession to the top leadership positions. This has allowed individuals like Mao Zedong and the Gang of Four to usurp power and rule arbitrarily. By the late 1980s, China's bureaucracy appeared to have become more corrupt than at any time since 1949. Anger at the massive scale of official corruption was, in fact, the major factor unifying ordinary citizens and workers with students during the antigovernment protests in the spring of 1989.

Campaigns to control official corruption continue today. Individuals are free to suggest in the country's daily newspapers how corruption might be ferreted out. Some cases are investigated by journalists, thereby focusing public attention on official abuse. Chen Xitong, the head of the CCP in Beijing, was scheduled to go on trial in late 1997. He is one of the highest party officials ever to be tried for corruption.

One approach to cleaning up corruption has been to reform the political system. The Chinese have tried to separate the party from the functions of the state bureaucracy and economic enterprises. For some leadership positions, there are now limits on tenure in office. There are also strict prohibitions on a leader developing a personality cult, such as that which reached fanatical proportions around CCP chairman Mao Zedong during the Cultural Revolution. Reforms have also encouraged, if not demanded, that the Chinese state bureaucracy reward merit more than mere seniority and expertise more than political activism. And, in 1996, the government's practice since 1949 of leading officials staying in one ministry during their careers was replaced by new regulations requiring officials from divisional chiefs up to ministers and provincial governors to be rotated every 5 years. In addition, no high official may work in the same office as his or her spouse or direct blood relative. It is hoped that such regulations will cut down on the building up of power bases that support corruption within ministries.

So far, most efforts to control official corruption have had little effect. Officials continue to use their power to achieve personal gain, trading official favors for others' services (such as receiving better housing, jobs for their children, admission to the right schools, and access to goods in short supply). Getting things done in a system that requires layers of bureaucratic approval still depends heavily upon a complex set of personal connections and relationships, all reinforced through under-the-table gift giving. This is, in part, because of the still heavily centralized aspect of Chinese governance and, in part, because China's bureaucracy remains overstaffed and plagued by red tape. Countless offices must sign off on requests for everything from buying a typewriter to getting a passport. This gives enormous power to individual officials who are willing to take charge of processing an individual's or work unit's request for something, such as a license or a building permit. In today's more market-oriented China, for example, anyone with adequate funds may buy an air conditioner. Then, however, because all electrical service is controlled by the government, the person must pay off an official to allow the electrical service to his or her living unit to be upgraded to actually use the air conditioner. Similarly, brothels can be run in the open, virtually without interference from the police, who are bribed to look the other way.

An example of the difficulty in controlling corruption is this: To cut down on the abuse of official privilege, the government issued a regulation stipulating that governmental officials doing business at a restaurant could order only four dishes and one soup. But, since most Chinese like to eat well, especially at the government's expense, restaurants accommodated them by simply giving them much larger plates on which they put many different foods and wrote them up as one dish. Another example concerns middlemen who are paid for arranging business transactions. They used to be considered corrupt. Now a government regulation says that it is all right for a middleman to keep 5 percent of the total value of a transaction as a "fee," and it is no longer called corruption. The Chinese have also adopted the custom in other countries of permitting tour guides who take tourists to a shop to receive a percentage of the total sales—a practice that earlier was considered corrupt.

ENVIRONMENT FOR DEMOCRACY

When assessing the Chinese political system's level of freedom, democracy, and individual rights, it is important to remember that the Chinese do not share the values and traditions of the West's Greco–Roman political heritage. For millenia, Chinese thought has run along different lines, with far less emphasis on such ideals as individual rights, privacy, and limits on state power. The Chinese political tradition is one of authoritarianism and moral indoctrination. For more than 2,000 years, China's rulers have shown greater concerns for establishing their authority and maintaining unity in the vast territory and population that they have controlled than in Western concepts of democratic liberalism. Apart from China's intellectuals in the twentieth century, the vast majority of the Chinese people have appeared to be more afraid of chaos than rule by an authoritarian despot.

China's limited experience with democracy in the twentieth century has been bitter. Virtually the entire period from the fall of China's imperial monarchy in 1911 to the Communist victory in 1949 (the period of the "Republic of China" on the mainland) was marred by warlordism, chaos, war, and a government masking brutality, greed, and incompetence under the label of "democracy." Although it is not fair to blame this period of societal collapse and externally imposed war on China's efforts to practice "democracy" under the "tutelage of the Kuomintang," the Chinese people's experience of democracy was nevertheless negative.

China's experience of democracy from 1912 until 1949 and China's political culture help to explain the people's reluctance to pursue democracy aggressively. During that period, the existence of both democratic political institutions and a complete legal system (on paper, anyway) proved inadequate to guarantee the protection of individual rights. Under Communist rule after 1949, the period described as "democratic mass rule" (the "10 bad years" or "Cultural Revolution" from 1966 to 1976) was in fact a period of mass tyranny. For the Chinese, the experience of relinquishing power to "the masses" turned into the most horrific period of unleashed terrorism and cruelty they had experienced since the Communist takeover.[12]

When the CCP came to power in 1949, it inherited a country that had been torn by civil war, internal rebellion, and foreign invasions for more than 100 years. The population was overwhelmingly illiterate and desperately poor, the economy in shambles. The most urgent need was for order. Despite some serious setbacks and mistakes, Mao Zedong and his colleagues made great strides in securing China's borders, establishing the institutions of government, and enhancing the material well-being of the Chinese people. But they also severely limited the development of "democracy" as the liberal democratic West would understand it, in the name of order and stability.

Cultural and Historical Authoritarianism
The heavy weight of more than 2,000 years of Chinese history helped shape the development of today's political system. The Chinese inherited a patriarchal culture, in which the hierarchical values of superior–inferior and subordination, loyalty, and obedience prevailed over those of equality; a historical predisposition toward official secrecy; a fear of officials and official power; a traditional repugnance for courts, lawyers, and formal laws that resulted in a legal system inadequately developed to defend democratic rights; and a historical legacy of authoritarianism. These cultural factors provided the context for the introduction of Western democratic values and institutions into China from the nineteenth century onward. As a result,

CENTRAL GOVERNMENT ORGANIZATION OF THE PEOPLE'S REPUBLIC OF CHINA

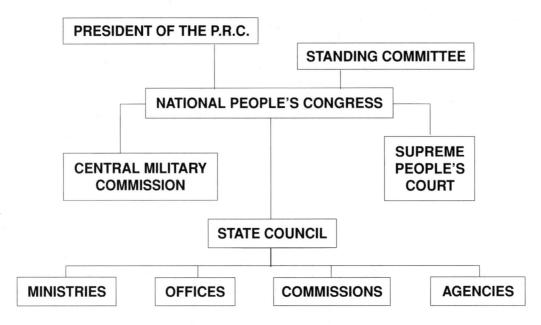

This central government organization chart represents the structure of the government of the People's Republic of China as it appears on paper. However, since all of the actions and overall doctrine of the central government must be reviewed and approved by the Chinese Communist Party, political power ultimately lies with the party. To ensure this control, virtually all top state positions are held by party members.

THE CHINESE COMMUNIST PARTY (CCP)

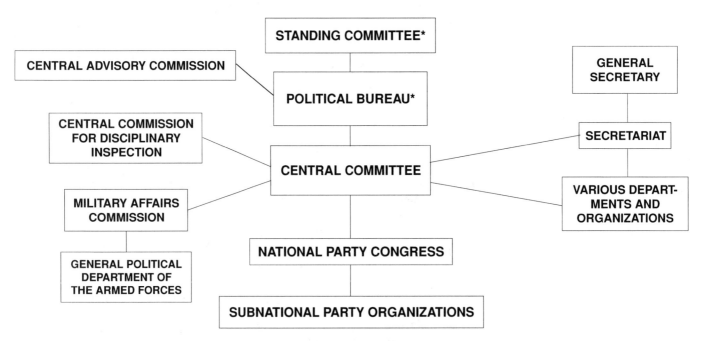

*This Political Bureau and its Standing Committee are the most powerful organizations within the Chinese Communist Party and are therefore the real centers of power in the P.R.C.

Although the Chinese Communist Party (shown here at its 11th National Congress) has hand-picked one candidate for each public office in the past, it is now allowing more than one person to run for the same post.

the Chinese people have not embraced democratic values with fervor.

The Chinese people are accustomed to "eating bitterness," not to standing up to authority. The traditional Confucian emphasis on the group rather than the individual and respect for authority, although now being undercut by the effects of modernization and disenchantment with the CCP leadership, continue to this day.

Today, although an atmosphere of greater freedom is pervasive in China, all will admit that a gnawing fear continues of what *could* happen. As one faculty member in a university remarked that, although he does not think the atrocities of the Cultural Revolution could happen again, he still writes his diary in code. As he put it, when you feel that you have been watched every day of your life for 43 years, it is difficult to rid yourself of deeply ingrained fears when no one any longer is watching. Furthermore, many would admit that although those scholars and students studying abroad who protested the Chinese government's brutal suppression of the 1989 Tiananmen Square demonstrations need not fear being jailed or persecuted if they return to China (unless, of course, like Shen Tong, an actual leader of those demonstrations, they are brazen enough to advocate democratization publicly upon

their return), they might well be punished in other ways—such as the state offering them jobs inappropriate for the level of education they received abroad. Thus, the government continues to decide which rights individuals will receive—and when to withdraw them.

A lack of interest in political participation by the Chinese people is in part because their participation appears "ineffective in getting what they want for themselves. For that purpose, they have found that under-the-table gift giving to, and entertainment of local officials, together with developing a "web of connections," are far more effective. Chinese peasants and workers seem inclined to believe that policies change only when high-level officials mandate it, not in response to popular pressure."[13] This helps to explain the pervasive gift giving and outright bribery in China.

As the impersonal market forces of supply and demand undercut the power of officials to control the distribution of resources and opportunities in the society, these patterns are changing. Participation in the political process at the local level is already reaping significant results. Some officials are eagerly seeking out advice for improving the economic conditions in their localities, and some incompetent officials are unable to gain reelection. Nevertheless, many

Chinese continue to believe that voicing their opinions in some situations is useless and can even be dangerous; and memories of forced participation in the many campaigns and movements in China since 1949 continue to give political participation a negative connotation. The result is that an active political participant is often regarded with deep suspicion.[14]

To the extent that the unwillingness of Chinese to challenge the political institutions and rulers of the CCP regime may be labeled as passive or submissive behavior, not to mention "collusion" with their oppressors, is it in any sense unique to China? One could argue that Central/Eastern Europeans also participated in their own political oppression simply by complying with the demands of the system. The Czech President Vaclav Havel stated, "All of us have become accustomed to the totalitarian system, accepted it as an unalterable fact and therefore kept it running. . . . None of us is merely a victim of it, because all of us helped to create it together."[15] Can it be said that the Chinese, any more than the Czechs, passively *accepted* totalitarianism if they did not go into exile outside of their country or did not refuse to work? Is anyone who does not actively revolt against an oppressive system necessarily in collusion with it? As one person wrote in China in 1989,

> The danger of losing jobs and the threats to survival make many people fearful. Fear also comes from the policy of implication, the personal dossiers. . . . The people, therefore, can only try to cope with the situation by burying anger deep in their hearts.[16]

In short, those who do not challenge the system out of fear of the consequences cannot be said to be supportive of the system, but one cannot assume that the major reason why people are not challenging the Communist system is out of fear of punitive consequences.

Were the CCP to step back from its state policies of punishment for political crimes, then, there is nothing in an abstract Chinese culture that would necessarily cause the Chinese to remain submissive to an authoritarian regime. Rather, it is the political system that has reinforced the authoritarian qualities of Chinese culture. Nor should a lack of rules and institutions be considered an insurmountable object, as "democratic" behavioral skills can be acquired through practice.[17] In short, as the political system becomes more liberal, the political culture is likely to evolve—indeed, it is evolving—in a more liberal direction.

Limited Popular Demands for Greater Democracy

So far, China has experienced only limited popular demand for democracy. When the student-led demonstrations began in April 1989, the demands for democratic reforms were confined largely to the small realm of the elite—that is, students and well-educated individuals as well as some members of the political and economic ruling elite. The workers and farmers of China remained more concerned about bread-and-butter issues: inflation, economic growth, and their own personal enrichment, not democratic ideals. By the mid-1990s, many Chinese had discovered that they could get what they wanted through channels other than mass demonstrations because of the development of numerous alternative groups, institutions, and processes. Many of these groups are fundamentally economic in origin, but the process by which they are pressing for policy changes in the government is highly political.

Lack of an Alternative Leadership

One of the critical problems for democratization in China has been the people's inability to envision an alternative to CCP rule: It has been *unthinkable.* What form would it take? How would it get organized? Wouldn't the organizers be jailed? And if the CCP were overthrown, who would lead a new system? These questions are still far from being answered even today. But one thing is clear: Those dissidents who have left China and remain abroad have lost their political influence with the Chinese people. Apart from everything else, dissidents abroad still have no way to make themselves heard in China, where their articles cannot be published.

For the 40 years of Chinese Communist rule from 1949 to 1989, no dissident leadership capable of offering an alternative to CCP leadership and laying claim to popular support had formed. The result was that, in China, the students' and workers' actions of 1989 were in no sense a "rebellion" under a recognized leader. China's intellectuals were not prepared to offer any sort of comprehensive alternative policies to the CCP's; and in any event, they soon found themselves in prison or in exile abroad.

Furthermore, the democracy movement was led by neither a worker nor a peasant, nor by an intellectual with whom the common people could identify:

> [C]ompared with the intellectuals of Poland and Czechoslovakia, for example, Chinese intellectuals have little contact with workers and peasants and are not sensitive to their country's worsening social crisis; they were caught unawares by the democratic upsurge of 1989, and proved unable to provide the people with either the theoretical or practical guidance they needed.[18]

In fact, during the Tiananmen Square protests in 1989, students were actually *annoyed* with the workers' participation in the demonstrations. They wanted to press their own political demands, not the workers' more concrete, work-related issues. Some Chinese have commented that the students' real interest in demanding respect for their own goals from China's leadership was to enhance their own power vis-à-vis the regime. The students' major demands were for a "dialogue" with the government as "equals" and for free speech—issues of primary interest to them but of secondary interest to the workers of China.

Many Chinese believe that the leaders of the 1989 demonstrations would have differed little from the CCP elite had they suddenly been catapulted to power. The student movement itself admitted to being authoritarian, of kowtowing to its own leaders, and of expecting others to obey rather than to discuss decisions. As one Beijing University student wrote during the 1989 Tiananmen Square protests:

> The autonomous student unions have gradually cut themselves off from many students and become a machine kept constantly on the run in issuing orders. No set of organizational rules widely accepted by the students has emerged, and the democratic mechanism is even more vague.[19]

Apart from students and intellectuals, the major proponents of democratic reform today hail from China's newly emerging business circles. These two groups have not united to achieve reform, however, because they neither like nor trust each other. Intellectuals view venture capitalists "as uncultured, and business people as driven only by crass material interests." For their part, they regard intellectuals and students as "well-meaning but out of touch with reality and always all too willing and eager to serve the state" when it suits their needs.[20]

The Impact of Global Interdependency on Democratization
Since the late 1970s, the cultural context for democracy in China has shifted. Growing awareness of global interdependency, with the expansion of the global capitalist economy to include China, has brought with it a social and economic transformation of China. For the first time in Chinese history, a significant challenge to the "we–they" dichotomy—of China on the one hand, against the rest of the world on the other—is occurring. This, in turn, has led many Chinese to question the heretofore assumed superiority of Chinese civilization to all other civilizations. Such an idea does not come easily for a people long-accustomed to believing in their own superiority. Hence the fuss caused by "River Elegy," a television series first shown on Chinese national television in 1988. In this series, the film producers argued that the Chinese people must embrace the idea of global interdependency—technological, economic, and cultural. To insist at this time in history on the superiority of Chinese civilization, with the isolation of China from the world of ideas that this implied, would only contribute to China's continued stagnation. The film suggested that the Chinese must see themselves as equal, not superior to, others; and as interdependent with, not as victims of, others. Such concepts of equality and opening up China to ideas from outside of China implicitly challenge the CCP's authoritarian rule. These concepts are still resisted by the more conservative reformers remaining in China's top leadership today.

The Press and Mass Media
At the time that the student-led demonstrations for democracy began in the spring of 1989, China's press had witnessed remarkable growth in its diversity and liberalization of its content. With some 1,500 newspapers, 5,000 magazines, and 500 publishing houses, the Chinese were able to express a wider variety of viewpoints and ideas than at any time since the CCP came to power in 1949. The importation and domestic production of millions of television sets, radios, short-wave radios, cassette recorders, CD players, and VCRs also facilitated the growth of the mass media in China. They have been accompanied by a wide array of "un-Chinese" and "non-Communist" audio and video materials. The programs of the British Broadcasting System and the Voice of America, the diversification of domestic television and radio programs (a choice made by the Chinese government and facilitated by international satellite communication), and the importation and translation of foreign books and magazines—all contributed to a more pluralistic press in China. In fact, by 1989, the stream of publications so overwhelmed the CCP Propaganda Department that it was simply no longer able to monitor their content.

During the prodemocracy demonstrations in Tiananmen Square in the spring of 1989, the Chinese press, under pressure from both students and the international press in Beijing (which freely filmed and filed reports on the demonstrations), took a leap into complete press freedom. With cameras and microphones in hand, reporters covered the student hunger strike that began on May 13 in its entirety; but, with the imposition of martial law in Beijing on May 20, press freedom came to a crashing halt.

In the immediate aftermath of the crackdown on Tiananmen Square in June 1989, the CCP imposed a ban on a variety of books, journals, and magazines. Vice Premier Wang Zhen ordered the "cleansing" of media organizations, with offending reporters removed and not permitted to leave Beijing for reporting. All press and magazine articles written during the prodemocracy movement, all television and radio programs shown during this period, were analyzed to see if they conformed to the party line. Those individuals responsible for editing during this period were dismissed. And, as had been the practice in the past, press and magazine articles once again had to be on topics specified by the editors, who were under the control of the CCP. In short, press freedom in China suffered a significant setback because of the prodemocracy demonstrations.

In the new climate of experimentation launched by Deng Xiaoping in 1992, however, the diversity of television and radio programs soared. China's major cities now have multiple television and radio channels carrying a broad range of programs from Hong Kong, Taiwan, Japan, and the West. These programs, whether soap operas about daily life for Chinese people living in Hong Kong and Taiwan or art programs exposing the Chinese to the world of Western religious art

STOCK MARKETS, GAMBLING, AND LOTTERIES

China has had two stock markets since just before the Tiananmen Square demonstrations of 1989. One is in the special economic zone of Shenzhen; the other is in Shanghai. With only seven industries originally registered on them, strict rules about how much daily profit or loss (1.2 percent for the Shanghai exchange until July 1992) a stock could undergo, and deep public suspicion that these original issues of stocks were worthless, these markets got off to a slow start. When these same stocks were worth 5 times their original value one year later, however, the public took notice. Rumors—as important in China as actual news—took over and exaggerated the likelihood of success in picking a winning stock. The idea of investors actually losing money, much less a stock-market crash, did not seem to be an idea whose time had come.

Soon there were so many Chinese dollars chasing so few stocks that the government began a lottery system: Anyone who wanted to buy a stock had first to buy a coupon that was then put into a national lottery. The supply/demand ratio for stocks was so out of proportion that an individual had only a 1 in 100 chance of having a coupon chosen from the lottery. The coupon would, in turn, enable its bearer to buy a mere 5 shares of a stock that might or might not make a profit. Today, thanks to the rapid increase in stocks registered on the two stock exchanges, there is now a 70 in 100 chance of getting the right to buy a stock.

When a set of new issues was scheduled to appear in 1992, literally thousands of people waited in line for as many as 5 days and nights until the lottery coupons went on sale in Shenzhen and Shanghai. The estimated 100,000 people in this "line"—a line so tight that people in it were pressing up against those in front of them so that no one could break into it—carefully calculated their places in line as good enough to ensure their right to purchase lottery coupons for a shot at the stock market. The crowd became an angry mob when, within a short time after opening the lottery, the authorities announced that no more coupons were available for purchase. The crowd's frustration and anger combined with suspicion about official corruption, for how else could most of the shares have been sold so quickly? Violence broke out, with seven people being shot by the police or trampled to death in the resulting melee.

What had happened? Individuals whom the Chinese call the "Mafia" went down the long line and offered people 200 yuan in exchange for their official identification cards—cards that were required in order to buy the lottery coupons. In other words, without incurring the risk of buying a stock that might not increase in value, individuals could receive what was for many of them the equivalent of a month's pay. Working with corrupt officials, the "Mafia" then were allowed to purchase most of the available coupons before the vast majority of those standing in line.

As communications remain poor in China, and as it is still largely a cash economy, making a stock-market transaction does not resemble what happens in a Western country. Instead of simply telephoning a broker and giving an order, with a bank transfer or check to follow shortly, most Chinese must still appear in person, stand in line, and pay cash on the spot. Taiwan has added its own angle to China's stock mania by selling to the Mainlanders small radios that are tuned to only one frequency—stock-market news.

Issuing, buying, and selling stocks has become nearly a national obsession. Not only do ordinary companies selling commercial goods, such as computers and clothing, issue stocks. So do taxi-cab companies and even universities. Thus far, few such stocks are actually listed on the national stock exchanges; but employees of these work units are eager to purchase the stocks. In most cases, the original issues are sold at far higher prices than their face value, as employees (and even nonemployees) eagerly buy up fellow employees' rights to purchase stocks, at grossly inflated prices. Presumably, the right of employees to own stock in their own work units will make them eager to have it do well and thus increase efficiency and profits.

Learning from Western practices and catering to a penchant for gambling (illegal, but indulged in nevertheless, in mahjong and cards), the Chinese have also begun a number of lotteries. Thus far, most of these have been for the purpose of raising money for specific charities or causes. In addition, following Western marketing practices, companies put Chinese characters on the inside of packages or bottle caps to indicate whether or not the purchaser has won a prize. With a little Chinese ingenuity, the world could witness never-before-imagined realms of betting and competitive business practices that appeal to people's desire to get something for nothing.

through a visual art history tour of the Vatican, or in news about protests and problems faced by other nations in the world, are both subtly and blatantly exposing the Chinese to values, ideas, and standards of living previously unknown to them. Today, ownership of televisions is widespread. China even has 40 million cable television subscribers, with 5 million new subscribers being added each year. And virtually all families have radios. Round-the-clock, all-news radio stations broadcast the latest political, economic, and cultural news, and conduct live radio interviews. Radio talk shows take phone calls from anonymous listeners about everything from sex to political corruption. So far, no one seems to be challenging the broadcast of these eye-opening programs.

The printed press has also regained substantial freedom since 1989. "Weekend editions" print just about any story that will sell. Often about the seamier side of Chinese life, all are undercutting the puritanical aspect of CCP rule and expanding the range of topics available for discussion in the public domain. And, because China's official papers are now required to make money instead of being subsidized completely by the state, they now accept advertisements and print stories that cater to the readers' interests. So many publishing houses have sprung up that the CCP no longer has the resources to monitor the content of their publications. And even China's movies, plays, and fine arts have been able to provide commentary on heretofore prohibited topics.[21]

International Pressures to Democratize

For close to 2 decades, China's government has attempted to accelerate economic development by decentralizing the economy, moving out of its isolationist position by trading in the world economy, and bringing foreign investment funds into China. Furthermore, pressures from the West and Japan of a *quid pro quo* sort (greater trade, investment, and more access to technology in exchange for greater liberalization of the economic and political system) have forced the CCP leadership to take certain steps along the road of reform, most notably in the economic and legal systems. For example, to maintain "most-favored-nation" (MFN) trading status with the United States, the Chinese government has agreed to stop using prisoners to make goods for export and to respect intellectual copyright laws.

Finally, Asia's "four little dragons" (Taiwan, Hong Kong, Singapore, and South Korea) have offered to the Chinese leadership an alternative to the Western model of economic development. All four of these systems have maintained a system of tight centralized political control while decentralizing control over the economy. Obviously the CCP leadership prefers the idea of remaining in power while adopting an economic system that provides astounding economic success. With tourists and businesspeople from "the four little dragons" traveling and doing business in China, the Chinese people's understanding of the successes of other Asian societies has increased—as has their desire to emulate them.

Singapore is constructing a complete township from the bottom up, just one hour from Shanghai. All those Chinese who work in Suzhou-Singapore are being trained by Singapore Chinese to think as they do and to adopt similar values. Hong Kong Chinese are developing enterprises throughout China. "Taiwan fever" on the mainland is fed by the Chinese people's access to Taiwan's music, fashions, books, and films. Taiwan is now envied in the P.R.C. for both its economic development and the diversity and richness of its culture. Perhaps most important for the enormous appeal of the Taiwan and Singapore models is that they have been successful within the context of a *Chinese culture*. Thus, the CCP cannot dismiss these models as easily as it does successful models of reform and development within non-Chinese cultures.

The Student and Mass Movement of 1989

Symbolism is very important in Chinese culture; the death of a key leader is a particularly significant moment. In the case of the former head of the CCP, Hu Yaobang, his sudden death in April 1989 became symbolic of the death of liberalizing forces in China. The students used Hu's death as an excuse to place his values and policies in juxtaposition with those of the then-increasingly conservative leadership. The deceased leader's career and its meaning were touted as symbols of liberalization, even though his life was hardly a monument to liberal thought. More conservative leaders in the CCP had removed him from his position as the CCP's general secretary in part because he had offended their cultural sensibilities. Apart from everything else, Hu's suggestions that the Chinese turn in their chopsticks for knives and forks and not eat food out of a common dish because it spread disease were culturally offensive to them.

The students' reassessment of Hu Yaobang's career in a way that rejected the party's evaluation was in itself a challenge to the authority of the CCP's right to rule China. The students' hunger strike during the visit of then–Soviet president Mikhail Gorbachev to China was, even in the eyes of ordinary Chinese people, an insult to the Chinese leadership. Many Chinese later stated that the students went too far, as, by humiliating the leadership, they humiliated *all* Chinese.

Part of the difficulty in reaching an agreement between the students' and China's leaders was that the students' demands changed over time. At first they merely wanted a reassessment of Hu Yaobang's career. But the students quickly added new demands: an end to official corruption, exposure of the financial and business dealings of the central leadership, a free press, dialogue between the government and the students (with the students to be treated as equals with top CCP leaders), retraction of an offensive *People's Daily* editorial, the removal of the top CCP leadership, and still other actions that challenged continued CCP rule.

The students' hunger strike, which lasted for one week in May, was the final straw that brought down the wrath of the central leadership. Martial law was imposed in Beijing; and, when the citizens of Beijing resisted its enforcement and blocked the army's efforts to reach Tiananmen Square to clear out the hunger-strikers, both students and CCP leaders dug in. But both were deeply divided bodies. Indeed, divisions within the student-led movement caused it to lose its direction, and divisions within the central CCP leadership incapacitated it. For two weeks, the central leadership wrangled over who was right and what to do. On June 4, the "hardliners" won out, and they chose to use military power over a negotiated solution with the students.

Did the students make significant or well-thought-out statements about "democracy" or realistic demands on China's leaders? The short and preliminary answer is no; but then, is this really the appropriate question to be asking in the first place? One could argue that what the students *said* was less important than what they *did*: They mobilized the population of China's capital and other major cities to support a profound challenge to the legitimacy of the CCP's leadership. Even if

Students from the University of Law and Politics staged a sit-in during the Tiananmen Square demonstrations in 1989.

workers believed that "You can't eat democracy," and even if they participated in the demonstrations for their *own* reasons (such as gripes about inflation and corruption), they did support the students' demand that the CCP carry out further political reforms. This was because the students successfully promoted the idea that, if China had had a different sort of system, a democratic system rather than authoritarian rule, the leadership would have been more responsive to the workers' bread-and-butter issues and charges of corruption.

Repression Following the Crackdown

By August 1989, the CCP leadership had established quotas of "bad elements" for work units and identified 20 categories of people to be targeted for punishment. But people were more reluctant than in the past to follow orders to expose their friends, colleagues, and family members, not only because such verdicts had often been reversed at a later time but also because few believed the CCP's version of what had hap-

pened in Beijing on June 4. Although many people worried about informers,[22] there seemed to be complicity from top to bottom, whether inside or outside the ranks of the CCP, in refusing to go along with efforts to ferret out demonstrators and sympathizers with the prodemocracy, antiparty movement. Party leaders below the central level appeared to believe that the central-government leadership was doomed and, for this reason, they dared not carry out its orders. Inevitably, there would be a reversal of verdicts, and they did not want to be caught in that reversal.

As party leaders in work units droned on in mandatory political study sessions about Deng Xiaoping's important writings, workers wondered how long it would be before the June 4 military crackdown was condemned as a "counter-revolutionary crime against the people." Individuals in work units had to fill out lengthy questionnaires. One had 24 questions aimed at "identifying the enemy." Among them were such questions as, "What did you think when Hu Yao-bang died?" "When Zhao Ziyang went to Tiananmen Square, what did you think? Where were you?" At one university, each questionnaire had to be verified by two people (other than one's own family); otherwise, the individual involved would not be allowed to teach.[23]

In July 1989 new regulations prohibited all criticism of the Communist Party and the government. Li Peng submitted a new law to the National People's Congress Standing Committee curtailing the right to demonstrate: "Demonstrations can be authorised only after the names and details of every one of the organisers have been submitted to the state security apparatus. In addition, the organisers must provide in advance the planned number of demonstrators and the text of all their placards." Also, "Neither soldiers, nor police, nor public servants may demonstrate. If a factory or work unit manages to obtain a permit to voice their demands, no other factory or work unit may join their rally. People from outside the city are excluded, and foreigners may join a demonstration only with a special permit from the state security organs."[24] Of course, with all names of leaders registered, the government could exert far greater control.

As part of the repression that followed the military crackdown in June 1989, the government carried out announced and unannounced arrests of hundreds of "liberal" intellectuals, students, workers, and others supporting the prodemocracy movement of 1989. Some were summarily executed, although available information indicates that almost all of those executed were workers. During the world's absorption with the Persian Gulf War in 1991, the Chinese government suddenly announced the trials and verdicts on some of China's most famous dissident leaders during the 1989 demonstrations. Only a few dissidents involved with the demonstrations remained in jail by 1993, although the government has occasionally re-arrested these dissidents since that time.

Academicians in the Chinese Academy of Social Sciences, who do state-sponsored research on history, economics, society, anthropology, politics, and international relations, also suffered in the repression following the 1989 crackdown. The government strictly limited which subjects these academicians could research; but, not being interested in these government-approved topics, they remained silent. Because of crowded work conditions, they were not required to appear at their offices anyway, so they were free to do whatever they chose—including nothing.

As with the mass media, most such repressive controls have slowly disappeared. The increasing involvement of Chinese intellectuals in international conferences—the result of China's desire to become a more respected participant in the international community of science, commerce, and economics—has led to far more innovation in scholarship than was formerly tolerated. Moreover, the government now wants its best and brightest to do as much as possible in the way of basic analytical and policy studies to assist it in making the best choices possible for advancing China's modernization.

INTERNATIONAL RELATIONS

From the 1830s onward, foreign imperialists nibbled away at China, subjecting it to one national humiliation after another. As early as the 1920s, both the KMT and the CCP were committed to unifying and strengthening China in order to rid it of foreigners and resist further foreign incursions. When the Communists achieved victory over the KMT in 1949, they vowed that foreigners would never again be permitted to tell China what to do. This historical background is essential to understanding China's foreign policy in the period of Chinese Communist rule.

From Isolation to Openness

The Communists had forced all but a handful of foreigners to leave China by the early 1950s. China charted an independent, and eventually an isolationist, foreign policy. After the end of the "Cultural Revolution" in 1976, and the return to power of more pragmatic "reformers" in 1978, China re-opened its door to the outside world. By the 1980s, it was hosting several million tourists annually, inviting foreign investors and foreign experts to help with China's modernization, and allowing Chinese to study and travel abroad. Nevertheless, inside the P.R.C., contacts between Chinese and foreigners were still affected by the suspicion on the part of ordinary Chinese that ideological and cultural contamination comes from abroad and that association with foreigners might bring trouble.

Today, these attitudes have moderated considerably, to the point where some Chinese are more willing to make friends with foreigners, invite them to their homes, and even date and marry them. But this greater openness to things foreign sits uncomfortably with a sort of neo-nationalism that has crept into the picture. The broad masses of Chinese people remain suspicious, even disdainful, of foreigners. Sensitivity to any suggestion of foreign control and a strong xenophobia (dislike and fear of foreigners) mean that the Chinese are likely to rail at any effort by other countries to tell them what to do.[25] Even after 1978, when China pursued an "open door" policy toward the outside world, the Chinese continued to exhibit this sensitivity on a wide variety of issues; from human rights to China's policy toward Tibet and Taiwan, from intellectual property rights to working conditions in factories. The Chinese people appear, moreover, to be just as nationalistic in their individual responses to foreign criticism of China as is the government.[26]

China's xenophobia continues to show up in its efforts to keep foreigners isolated in certain living compounds; to limit social contacts between foreigners and Chinese; to control the importation of foreign literature, films, and periodicals; and to keep foreign ideas, and diseases, out of China. In some respects, it has been a losing battle, with growing numbers of foreigners in China socializing with Chinese; television swamped with foreign programs; Kentucky Fried Chicken,

McDonald's, and pizza parlors proliferating; "Avon calling" at several million homes; body building and disco becoming part of the culture; and AIDS cases rocketing upward. In 1996, in an effort to protect its own culture, the government ordered television stations to broadcast only Chinese-made programs during prime time.[27] The pride of the Chinese in their culture and country has been enhanced in recent years by their economic success and by China's outstanding performance in the Olympic and Asian Games, music competitions, and film festivals.

China in the 1980s and 1990s has by any measure become a much more open country than at any time since 1949. This is in spite of the concern of the more conservative wing of the CCP with the impact of China's "open door" policy on the political system (the influx of ideas about democracy and individual rights); on economic development (a market economy, corruption, and foreign control and ownership); and on Chinese culture ("pollution" from foreign literature and pornography). Although a large number of foreign businesspeople left in the wake of the crushing of the student-led protests in June 1989, they were soon back. The favorable investment climate created by Deng's 1992 "experiment" (try-anything-that-works) speech accelerated the return of foreign capital. Since then, China has seemed less worried about the invasion of foreign values than it is anxious to attract foreign investments.

The Sino–Soviet Relationship
While forcing most other foreigners to leave China in the 1950s, the Chinese Communist regime invited experts from the Soviet Union to China to give much-needed advice, technical assistance, and aid. This convinced the United States (already certain that Moscow controlled communism wherever it appeared) that the Chinese were Soviet puppets. Indeed, for most of the 1950s, the Chinese Communist regime had to accept Soviet tenets of domestic and foreign policy along with Soviet aid. But China's leaders soon grew concerned about the limits of Soviet aid and the relevance of Soviet policies to China's conditions—especially the costly industrialization favored by the Soviet Union. Ultimately, the Chinese questioned their Soviet "big brother" and turned, in the form of the Great Leap Forward policy, to a Chinese model of development. Soviet leader Nikita Khrushchev warned the Chinese of the dangers to China's economy in undertaking the Great Leap Foward; but Mao Zedong interpreted this as evidence that the Soviet "big brother" wanted to hold back China's development.

The Soviets' refusal to use their military power in support of China's foreign policy objectives further strained the Sino–Soviet relationship. First in the case of China's confrontation with the United States and the forces of the "Republic of China" over the Offshore Islands in the Taiwan Strait in 1958, and then in the Sino–Indian border war of 1962, the Soviet Union backed down from its promise to support China.

The final blow to the by-then fragile relationship came with the Soviet Union's signing of the 1963 Nuclear Test Ban Treaty. The Chinese denounced this as a Soviet plot to exclude China from the "nuclear club" of Great Britain, France, the United States, and the Soviet Union. Subsequently, Beijing publicly broke Communist Party relations with Moscow.

The Sino–Soviet relationship, already in shambles, took on an added dimension of fear during the Vietnam War, when the Chinese grew concerned that the Soviets (and Americans) might use the war as an excuse to attack China. China's distrust of Soviet intentions was heightened when, in 1968, the Soviets invaded Czechoslovakia in the name of the "greater interests of the socialist community," which, they contended, "override the interests of any single country within that community."

Soviet skirmishes with Chinese soldiers on China's northern borders soon followed. Ultimately, it was the Chinese leadership's concern about the Soviet threat to China's national security that, in 1971, caused it to re-assess its relationship with the United States. The Sino–American ties that ensued made the Soviets anxious about their own security. The alleged threat of "Soviet hegemony" to world peace became the main theme of almost every public Chinese foreign policy statement. An estimated 1 million Soviet troops on China's northern borders, the Soviet occupation of Afghanistan on China's western flank, and Soviet support for a territorially aggressive Vietnam on China's southern borders gave the Chinese reason to be concerned about Soviet intentions.

The Sino–Soviet relationship did not really improve until close to the end of the cold war. The Soviets began making peaceful overtures in 1987. They reduced troops on China's borders, and they withdrew support for Vietnam's puppet government in neighboring Cambodia. Moscow's withdrawal from Vietnam provided Beijing with further evidence of Moscow's desire for reconciliation. Beijing responded positively to the glasnost ("open door") policy of the Soviet Communist Party general secretary Mikhail Gorbachev. Ideological conflict between two Communist giants abated; for, with the Chinese themselves abandoning much of Marxist dogma in their economic policies, they could hardly continue to denounce the Soviet Union's "revisionist" policies and make self-righteous claims to ideological orthodoxy. With both the Soviet Union and China abandoning their earlier battle over who should lead the Communist camp, they shifted away from ideological and security issues to economic issues.

The End of the Cold War
With the collapse of Communist party rule, first in Central/Eastern Europe in 1989 and subsequently in the Soviet Union, the dynamics of China's foreign policy changed dramatically. Apart from fear that their own reforms might lead to the collapse of CCP rule in China, the disintegration of the Soviet Union into 15 independent states removed China's ability to

play the two superpowers off against each other: The formidable Soviet Union no longer existed. Yet its fragmented remains had to be treated seriously, for the state of Russia still shares a common border of several thousand miles with China, and Kazakhstan shares a common border of nearly a thousand miles.

The question of what type of war the Chinese military might have to fight has affected its military modernization. China's military leaders have been in conflict for decades over whether or not China would have to fight a high-tech war or a "people's war" in which China's huge army would draw in the enemy on the ground and destroy it. In 1979, the military modernizers won out and jettisoned the idea that a large army, motivated by ideological fervor but armed with hopelessly outdated equipment, could win a war against a highly modernized military, such as that of Japan or even the Soviet Union. The People's Liberation Army began by shedding a few million soldiers and putting its funds into better armaments. A significant catalyst to modernizing the military still further came with the Persian Gulf War of 1991, during which CNN vividly conveyed the power of high-technology weaponry to China's leaders.[28]

Because the military believed it was allocated an inadequate budget for modernization, it struck out on its own along the capitalist road to raise money. Today, the PLA is one of the most powerful actors in the Chinese economy. It has purchased considerable property in the "special economic zones" near Hong Kong, taken over ownership of major tourist hotels and industrial enterprises, and invested in everything from golf courses, brothels, and publishing houses to CD factories and the computer industry as means for funding military modernization.

In recent years, China's military has purchased weaponry and military technology from Russia as Moscow scales back its own military in what sometimes resembles a going-out-of-business sale; but, in doing so, China's military may have simply bought into a higher level of obsolescence, since Russia's weaponry now lags years behind the technology of the West. China possesses nuclear weapons, the second largest submarine fleet in the world and long-distance bombing capability, but its ability to fight a war beyond its own borders is quite limited. Nevertheless, today, China's military power at least counterbalances that of Asia's most feared potential enemy, Japan. Perhaps for this reason, China's neighbors (many of whom are themselves building considerable military power) seem willing to tolerate China's military modernization.[29]

Furthermore, long before the cold war came to an end in the late 1980s, China's leadership was primarily concerned with economic development. Although ever-alert to threats to its national security (including sovereignty over Taiwan), there are no indications that it is preparing for a major war with any country. Instead, China is poising itself to become an integral part of the international economic, commercial, and mone-

tary systems. It has moved quickly to increase trade, not just with the international community but also with its potential enemies across the Russian and Kazakhstani borders. These rapidly increasing commercial links, in which China offers much-sought-after consumer goods, have helped enrich China's border provinces, especially Xinjiang (bordering on Kazakhstan) in the far northwest. This area is rich in natural resources but was, until recently, unable to capitalize on its wealth because of its distance from the east's coastal export area.

The Sino–American Relationship

China's relationship with the United States has historically been an emotionally turbulent one.[30] It has never been characterized by indifference. During World War II, the United States gave significant help to the Chinese, who at that time were fighting under the leadership of the Nationalist Party head, General Chiang Kai-shek. At that time, the Chinese Communists were fighting together with the Nationalists in a "united front" against the Japanese, so American aid was not seen as directed against communism.

After the defeat of Japan at the end of World War II, the Japanese military, which had occupied much of the north and east of China, was demobilized and sent back to Japan. Subsequently, civil war broke out between the Communists and Nationalists. The United States attempted to reconcile the two sides, but to no avail. As the Communists moved toward victory in 1949, the KMT leadership fled to Taiwan. Thereafter, the two rival governments each claimed to be the true rulers of China. The United States, already in the throes of the "cold war" because of the "iron curtain" falling over Central/Eastern Europe, viewed communism in China as a major threat to the world.

Korea, Taiwan, and Vietnam

The outbreak of the Korean War in 1950 helped the United States to rationalize its decision to support the Nationalists, who had already lost power on the mainland and fled to Taiwan. The Korean War began when the Communists in northern Korea attacked the non-Communist south. When United Nations (UN) troops (mostly Americans), led by American general Douglas MacArthur, successfully pushed Communist troops back almost to the Chinese border and showed no signs of stopping their advance, the Chinese—who had been sending the Americans anxious messages about their concern for China's own security—entered the war. China's participation resulted in the pushing back of UN troops to what today is still the demarcation line between North and South Korea. China thereupon became a major target of America's cold war isolation and containment policies.

With the People's Republic of China condemned as an international "aggressor" for its action in Korea, the United States felt free to recognize the KMT government in Taiwan as the legitimate government of all of China. The United States supported the Nationalists' claim that the 600 million people on the Chinese mainland actually wanted the KMT to return to the mainland and defeat the Chinese Communists. As the years passed, however, it became clear that the Chinese Communists controlled the mainland and that the Chinese people were not about to rebel against Communist rule.

Sino–American relations steadily worsened as the United States continued to build up a formidable anti-Communist military bastion in the tiny Offshore Islands, just off China's coast. Tensions were exacerbated when U.S. military involvement in Vietnam steadily escalated in the 1960s and early 1970s. China, fearful that the United States was really using the war in Vietnam as the first step toward attacking China, concentrated on civil-defense measures: Chinese citizens used shovels, even spoons, to dig air-raid shelters in Beijing, with tunnels connecting downtown Beijing to the suburbs. Similar efforts were carried out in other large cities. Some industrial enterprises were moved out of China's major cities in order to make them less vulnerable in the event of a massive attack on concentrated urban areas. The Chinese received a steady barrage of what we would call "propaganda" about the United States "imperialist" as its number-one enemy. But it is important to realize that the Chinese leadership actually *believed* what it told the people, especially in the context of the United States' continuing escalation of the war in Vietnam toward the Chinese border. Apart from everything else, it is unlikely that China's leaders would have otherwise made such an immense expenditure of manpower and resources on civil-defense measures.

Diplomatic Relations

By the late 1960s, China was completely isolated from the world community, including the Communist bloc. In the throes of the "Cultural Revolution," it had withdrawn its diplomatic staff from all but one of its embassies. It saw itself as surrounded on all sides by enemies—the Soviets to the north and west, the United States to the south in Vietnam as well as in South Korea and Japan, and the Nationalists to the east in Taiwan. Internally, China was in such turmoil from the "Cultural Revolution" that it appeared to be on the verge of complete collapse.

In this context, it was the Soviet invasion of Czechoslovakia in 1968 and Soviet military incursions on China's northern borders, combined perhaps with an assessment of which country could offer China the most profitable economic relationship, that led China in 1971 to consider the United States the lesser of two evil giants. In 1972, U.S. president Richard Nixon visited China, the first American public-official contact with China since breaking diplomatic relations in 1950. With the signing of the Shanghai Communique, the inital steps in reversing more than 2 decades of hostile relations were taken. A new era of Sino–American friendship had begun, but it fell short of full diplomatic relations until January 1, 1979.

(UPI/Bettmann Newsphotos)

In 1971, U.S. secretary of state Henry Kissinger made the first overtures toward reversing the hostile Sino–American relationship. In 1972, President Richard Nixon visited China, and a new era of cooperation began. Nixon is pictured above with Vice Premier Li Xiannian on the Great Wall of China during this historic visit.

This long delay in bringing the two states into full diplomatic relations reflected not only each country's domestic political problems but also mutual disillusionment with the nature of the relationship. Although both sides had entered the relationship with an understanding of its strategic importance as a bulwark against the Soviet threat, the Americans had assumed that the 1972 opening of partial diplomatic relations would lead to a huge new economic market for American products; the Chinese assumed that the new ties would quickly bring the United States to end its diplomatic relations with Taiwan. Both were disappointed. Nevertheless, pressures from both sides eventually led to full diplomatic relations between the United States and the People's Republic of China.

The Taiwan Issue

Because the People's Republic of China and the Republic of China both claim to be the legitimate government of the Chinese people, the establishment of diplomatic relations with the former necessarily entailed breaking them with the latter.[31] Neverthe-less, the United States continued to maintain extensive informal economic and cultural ties with Taiwan. It also continued the sale of military equipment to Taiwan. Although these military sales are still a serious issue, American ties with Taiwan have become much less significant, while China's own ties with Taiwan have grown steadily closer since 1988. Taiwan's entre-preneurs (by way of Hong Kong front companies, as certain laws still prohibit their investment in China) have become one of the largest group of investors in China's economy.[32] Although Taiwan used to have one of the cheapest labor forces in the world, its workers now demand wages too high to remain competitive in international trade. Thus, Taiwan's entrepreneurs have dismantled many of its older industries and re-assembled them on the mainland. With China's cheap labor, these same industries are now profitable, and both China and Taiwan's entrepreneurs are the beneficiaries.

Ties between Taiwan and the mainland have also been enhanced by the millions of tourists, most of them with relatives in China, who have traveled to the mainland since the late 1980s. They bring with them both presents and goodwill. Families that have not seen each other for 40 years have re-established contact; the "enemy" now seems less threatening. Furthermore, as China continues to liberalize its economic system and to raise the standard of living, the Chinese leadership hopes that reunification will become more attractive to Taiwan. This very positive context was disturbed only briefly by the military crackdown on the dem-onstrators in Tiananmen Square in 1989, and then in 1995 and 1996 by Taiwan president Lee Teng-hui's visit to the United States and subsequent threats of Taiwan declaring inde-pendence; for neither side wants to do anything to disrupt a peaceful and profitable relationship in which Taiwan contin-ues to act as an independent state—as long as it does not insist that its independence be recognized.

In short, without firing a single shot, Taipei and Beijing are coming steadily closer together. This does not mean that the two will soon be fully reunified in law; but whether or not this happens matters far less as their economies continue to be-come intertwined and mutually benefit from their economic and commercial ties. There remains, however, the black cloud of Beijing possibly using military force against Taiwan, as it threatened to do in 1996, if Taiwan makes efforts to become an independent state. Beijing refuses to make any pledge that it will never use military force to reunify Taiwan with the mainland, on the grounds that what it does with Taiwan is China's internal affair. Hence, no other country has a right to tell China what to do about Taiwan.

Human Rights

The election of Bill Clinton as president of the United States in 1992 caused considerable consternation, both to China's leader-ship and its people. The Chinese people were confused and distraught at the prospect of the punitive economic measures that the new Clinton administration threatened to take in response to China's human rights abuses. They saw their government as having taken economic measures to bring in foreign investment, integrate China into the international economy, and enhance development. Many saw their government's law and order cam-paigns, which sometimes involved jailing dissidents, as neces-sary to China's continued economic growth and political stability. China's phenomenal growth in the 1980s and early 1990s had improved the daily lives of hundreds of millions of ordinary Chinese people. They were far more interested in the prospect of an improved standard of living than in the rights of dissidents. Even China's intellectuals no longer seemed inter-ested in politics. They did not "love the party," but they ac-cepted the status quo. They just wanted a promotion and to make money. As one university professor put it, it is easy to be idealistic in one's heart, but to be idealistic in action is a sign of a true idealist; and there haven't been many of those in China since 1989.

It is not just the number of democratic idealists that is limited; so is the number of idealists committed to commu-nism. Few Chinese want to discuss Marxism or communism. Even government officials rarely mention communism. They prefer to talk about development. In doing so, they are appealing to the strong nationalism in China that has seem-ingly almost replaced communism as the glue holding the country together.

The Chinese perspective is this: They only know what their government tells them. They assume that it lies to them, but they nevertheless know no more than what they are told. Why should they risk their careers to fight for the rights of jailed dissidents when they really know very little about what the dissidents have done? They then argue that the U.S. government has also brutalized its population, pointing to such matters as the Kent State killings during the Vietnam War and the brutality of the Los Angeles police against Rodney King. They also mention the many deaths at the hands of the British in Northern Ireland. They have heard about the abominable behavior of several stu-dent leaders of the Tiananmen Square demonstrations in 1989, both during the movement, and after from some who escaped to the West. They wonder aloud if, upon examina-tion, any of them were more virtuous than their own cor-rupt and brutal government leaders.

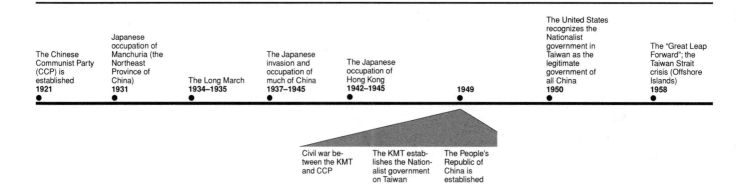

The Chinese Communist Party (CCP) is established
1921

Japanese occupation of Manchuria (the Northeast Province of China)
1931

The Long March
1934–1935

The Japanese invasion and occupation of much of China
1937–1945

The Japanese occupation of Hong Kong
1942–1945

1949

The United States recognizes the Nationalist government in Taiwan as the legitimate government of all China
1950

The "Great Leap Forward"; the Taiwan Strait crisis (Offshore Islands)
1958

Civil war between the KMT and CCP

The KMT establishes the Nationalist government on Taiwan

The People's Republic of China is established

Some Chinese intellectuals argue that the recent difficulties in the United States and in other Western democracies indicate that their citizens frequently elect the wrong leaders, leaders who not only make bad policies but are increasingly being prosecuted in courts for corruption. This, they argue, indicates that democracy does not necessarily work any better than socialism. Furthermore, many support the view that the Chinese people are inadequately prepared for democracy because of their low level of education.

In any event, they do not see the point in punishing hundreds of millions of Chinese for human rights abuses committed not by the people but by their leadership. Not infrequently, moreover, it is the Chinese people themselves who demand ever harsher penalties for common criminals, if not political dissidents. For example, in 1995 and 1996, urban residents in Beijing demanded that the government remove the squatters and shantytowns that had sprung up, on the grounds that they were breeding grounds for criminality in the city. And many ordinary people now seem to believe the government's overall assessment of the events of the spring of 1989, which is that they posed a threat to the stability and order of China. To the Chinese people, no less than to their government, stability and order are critical to continued economic development.

President Clinton quickly abandoned his 1992 campaign platform in favor of breaking the linkage between "most-favored-nation" trade status for China and its human rights record. This was due in part to his conviction—a conviction that President George Bush had had before him—that the United States dare not risk jeopardizing its relations with an increasingly powerful state containing one quarter of the world's population through measures that would probably have given Japan and other countries a better trading position while undercutting the opportunity for Americans to do business with China. But Clinton's China policy was also shaped by a new strategy of "agreeing to disagree" on certain issues such as human rights, while efforts continued to be made to bring the two sides closer together. This strategy of "constructive engagement" came out of a belief that China and the United States had so many common interests that neither side could afford to endanger the relationship on the basis of a single issue.

THE FUTURE

In less than 20 years, China has moved from being a closed and isolated country to one that is fully engaged in the world. China's agenda for the future is daunting: It must avoid war; maintain internal political stability in the context of international pressures to democratize, continue to carry out major economic, legal, and political reforms without endangering CCP control; sustain economic growth while limiting environmental destruction; and limit population growth. Since 1980, the Chinese Communist Party leadership has, with the exception of limiting environmental damage, succeeded in all these efforts. China's name may soon be added to the list of Asia's "dragons"—only it will not be one of the four "little dragons," but a very large one.

There are, however, monumental hurdles on the road. Serious concerns remain since the death of Deng Xiaoping in 1997 that the leadership of President Jiang Zemin will not be strong enough to succeed in addressing China's serious economic and political problems while simultaneously maintaining social stability. There is also concern that the military will interfere in the political sphere more than it has in the past. In general, however, optimism is based on the belief that most of the current leadership core group has been running China for nearly a decade and will continue to handle China's affairs well. Some speculate that, in any event, no effort to topple the leadership will occur until after the return of Hong Kong to China's rule on July 1, 1997.

A continued record of economic success may allow the CCP to feel secure enough to allow still further political liberalization. Although "liberalization" must not be confused with "democratization," it would certainly allow China to continue in the direction of greater pluralization and freedom for its people. In fact, greater political pluralization has already been an important consequence of economic liberalization. As market reforms and privatization continue, literally thousands of interest groups have formed to press the government for measures to protect and enhance their economic positions. Economic growth has also spawned environmental groups concerned about the impact of growth on the environment. It is the same in other sectors: lawyers, health care

Soviet withdrawal of aid to the P.R.C. 1959	The public Sino–Soviet split 1963	The "Great Proletarian Cultural Revolution" 1966–1976	The United Nations votes to seat the P.R.C. in place of the R.O.C. 1971	U.S. president Richard Nixon visits the P.R.C.; the Shanghai Communique 1972	Mao Zedong dies; removal of the Gang of Four 1976	Deng Xiaoping is restored to power 1977	The Democracy Wall movement 1978–1979	The United States recognizes the P.R.C. and withdraws recognition of the R.O.C.; the Sino–Vietnamese War 1979

workers, musicians, althletes—all are now forming their own interest groups to press for legislation and policies that they think are important.

Finally, the integration of China into the global political and economic systems has made China's leaders more sensitive to pressures from the international community on specific issues—human rights, environmental protection, intellectual property rights, prison labor, and legal codes. But it is still likely that China's leadership will insist on moving at its own pace and in a way that takes into account China's culture, history, and institutions.

In the meantime, as is the case in so many other developing countries, China's leadership must worry about the increasing polarization of the population into the rich and the poor, unemployment, uncontrolled economic growth, environmental degradation, corruption that threatens the very foundation of CCP rule, secessionist movements in Xinjiang and Tibet, and the strident resistance by whole regions within China to follow economic monetary policies formulated at the center. These would be formidable tasks for any nation's government. How much more so for a leadership responsible for feeding, educating and controlling the world's largest population.

NOTES

1. Most of these young women are likely to be sold as brides to men who live in remote villages where there are not enough women.

2. For example, they have had paid maternity leave, a child-care support system, the right to divorce, and the right to choose their own marriage partners.

3. Reuters, as reported in *China News Digest* (online), May 19, 1996.

4. That Panchen Lama died in 1989.

5. Report from Xinjiang Television as reported in *Hong Kong Standard,* (June 4, 1996), excerpted in *China News Digest* (June 5, 1996, online.)

6. For excellent detail on Chinese religion practices, see Robert Weller, *Resistance, Chaos, and Control in China: Taiping Rebels, Taiwanese Ghosts, and Tiananmen* (Seattle: University of Washington Press, 1994); and Robert P. Weller and Meir Shanar (eds.), *Unruly Gods: Divinity and Society in China* (Honolulu: University of Hawaii Press), 1996; Alan Hunter and Kim-Kwong Chan, *Protestantism in Contemporary China* (New York: Cambridge University Press, 1993). The latter notes that Chinese judge gods "on performance rather than theological criteria" (p. 144). That is, if the contributors to the temple in which certain gods were honored were doing well financially and their families were healthy, then those gods were judged well. Furthermore, Chinese pray as individuals rather than as congregations. Thus, before the Chinese government closed most temples, they were full of individuals praying randomly, children playing inside, and general noise and confusion. Western missionaries have found this style too casual for their own more structured religions (p. 145).

7. Professor Rudolf G. Wagner, Heidelberg University. Information based on his stay in China in 1990.

8. Steven Mufson, "Maoism, Confucianism Blur into Nationalism," *The Washington Post* (March 19, 1996), p. A12.

9. For example, the wealthier provinces have successfully challenged the central government's right to collect more taxes on provincial revenues.

10. In pursuit of those individuals who are producing products under copyrighted labels, the Chinese have set up an "Anti-Fake Bureau." Fakes have often led to serious problems, including fertilizers that destroy crops, medicines that make people sick, liquor that is marketed under famous labels but is improperly prepared, and compact discs that are of poor quality—and are the patented property of someone else.

11. This is not to suggest that Chinese judicial personnel actually changed their presumptions and procedures as soon as the new law, which assumes innocence until proven guilty, went into effect.

12. Of course, the masses were really manipulated by power-hungry members of China's elite, or ever-shifting nouveau elite, who were in a desperate competition with other pretenders to power.

13. Suzanne Ogden, *China's Unresolved Issues: Politics, Development, and Culture,* 3rd ed. (New York: Prentice-Hall, 1995), p. 143.

14. *Ibid.*

15. Vaclav Havel, as quoted by Timothy Garton Ash, "Eastern Europe: The Year of Truth," *New York Review of Books* (February 15, 1990), p. 18, referenced in Giuseppe De Palma, " After Leninism: Why Democracy Can Work in Eastern Europe," *Journal of Democracy,* Vol. 2, No. 1 (Winter 1991), p. 25, note 3.

16. Anonymous, "Letter to Friends from a County-Level Party Official," June 4, 1992, Document 200, in Suzanne Ogden, Kathleen Hartford, Lawrence R. Sullivan, and David Zweid, eds., *China's Search for Democracy: The Student and Mass Movement of 1989,* p. 439.

17. De Palma, p. 26, *op. cit.,* note 15.

18. Liu Binyan, "China and the Lessons of Eastern Europe," *Journal of Democracy,* Vol. 2, No. 2 (Spring 1991), p. 8.

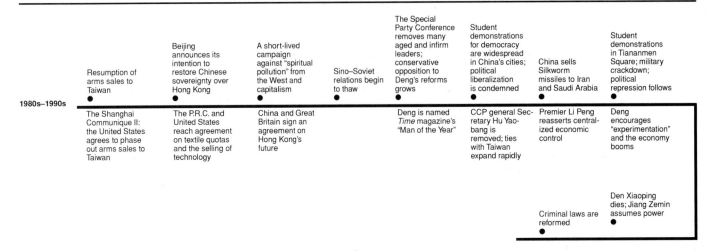

1980s–1990s	Resumption of arms sales to Taiwan	Beijing announces its intention to restore Chinese sovereignty over Hong Kong	A short-lived campaign against "spiritual pollution" from the West and capitalism	Sino–Soviet relations begin to thaw	The Special Party Conference removes many aged and infirm leaders; conservative opposition to Deng's reforms grows	Student demonstrations for democracy are widespread in China's cities; political liberalization is condemned	China sells Silkworm missiles to Iran and Saudi Arabia	Student demonstrations in Tiananmen Square; military crackdown; political repression follows
	The Shanghai Communique II: the United States agrees to phase out arms sales to Taiwan	The P.R.C. and United States reach agreement on textile quotas and the selling of technology	China and Great Britain sign an agreement on Hong Kong's future		Deng is named *Time* magazine's "Man of the Year"	CCP general Secretary Hu Yaobang is removed; ties with Taiwan expand rapidly	Premier Li Peng reasserts centralized economic control	Deng encourages "experimentation" and the economy booms
							Criminal laws are reformed	Den Xiaoping dies; Jiang Zemin assumes power

19. Beijing University student, "My Innermost Thoughts—To the Students of Beijing Universities," May 1989, Document 68, in Ogden, et al., eds., *China's Search for Democracy*, pp. 172–173.

20. Vivienne Shue in a speech to a USIA conference of diplomats and scholars, as quoted and summarized in "Democracy Rating Low in Mainland," *The Free China Journal* (January 24, 1992), p. 7.

21. Because there are relatively few films, however, censorship of them is likely to be greater than for the print media. Furthermore, all films are shot in a small number of film studios, making control easier. Finally, a film is likely to have a much larger audience than most books, so the censors are concerned that it be carefully reviewed before being screened. From Wang Meng, former minister of culture and a leading novelist in China, in a speech at Cambridge University on May 23, 1996. An example of a movie banned in China is the famous movie producer Chen Kaige's latest movie, *Temptress Moon.* This movie, which won the Golden Palm Award at the Cannes Film Festival in 1993, is, however, allowed to be distributed abroad.

22. "Campaign to Crush Dissent Intensifies," *South China Morning Post* (August 9, 1989).

23. Chinese student (anonymous) in the United States, conversation in the summer of 1990.

24. "Clampdown Sparks Rush to Beat Censors," *South China Morning Post* (July 8, 1989).

25. By the mid-1990s, if the United States deigned to lecture the Chinese on their behavior, whether regarding human rights, prison labor, or threats to Taiwan, the Chinese were likely to reciprocate with a lecture of their own. And Asian leaders (notably the leaders of Malaysia and Singapore) have been very supportive of the Chinese leaders' standing up for their right to rule the country as they choose.

26. In addition to seeming to side with the government on its position on Taiwan, Tibet, intellectual property rights, and so on against foreign criticism, the Chinese people exhibited extraordinary anger at losing the Olympics site bid

for the year 2000 because of what they believed to be American engineering of the decision to punish China for its human rights abuses; and at the American broadcasters' suggestion on television during the 1996 Olympics that China's swimmers had only won medals in the 1992 Olympics by using performance-enhancing drugs.

27. Note that the European Parliament earlier in 1996 also passed a bill requiring all major television stations to broadcast at least 51 percent local programs. Using language virtually identical to that used in China concerning the fear of "cultural pollution" and the "destruction of our national culture(s)," the European measure was largely aimed at containing the flood of American programs onto European television screens.

28. It is rumored that China has acquired Patriot missiles, used in the Persian Gulf War with such vaunted success (which has subsequently been seriously questioned), from Israel.

29. Gregor Benton and Alan Hunter, "Chinese Nationalism and the Western Agenda," unpublished paper (spring 1996).

30. For excellent analyses of the Sino–American relationship from the nineteenth century to the present, see Warren Cohen, *America's Response to China: A History of Sino–American Relations,* 3rd ed. (New York: Columbia University Press, 1990); Richard Madsen, *China and the American Dream: A Moral Inquiry* (Berkeley, CA: University of California Press, 1995); Michael Schaller, *The United States and China in the Twentieth Century,* 2nd ed. (New York: Oxford University Press, 1990); David Shambaugh, ed., *American Studies of Contemporary China* (Armonk, NY: M. E. Sharpe, 1993); and David Shambaugh, *Beautiful Imperialist: China Perceives America, 1972–1990* (Princeton, NJ: Princeton University Press, 1991).

31. For more detail on the Taiwan issue, see the Taiwan Country Report, "Taiwan: A Dynamo in East Asia," in this book.

32. By 1996, some 25,000 Taiwanese companies had invested close to $20 billion in China.

Taiwan

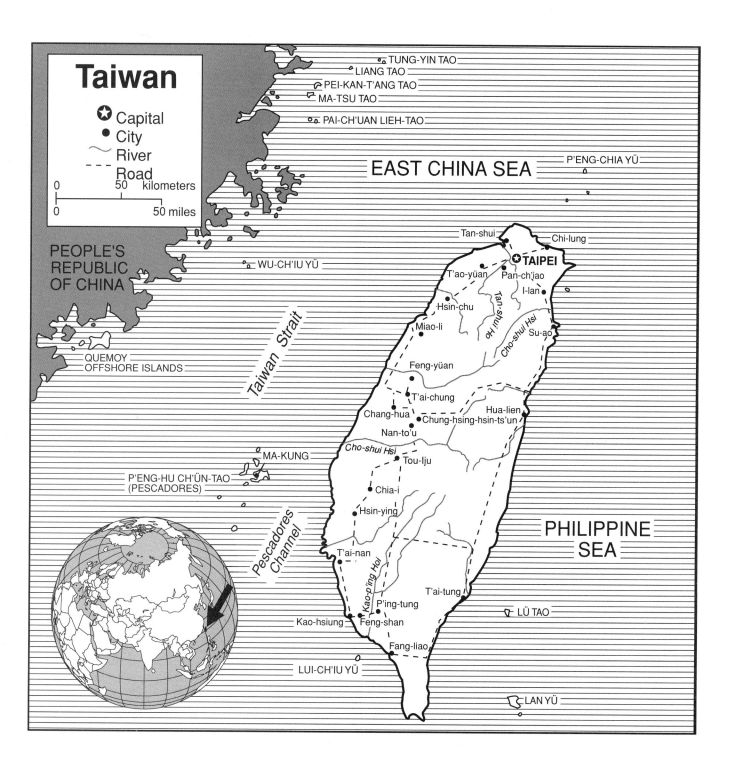

Taiwan has been considered the center of the government of the Republic of China (Nationalist China) since 1949. In the past, the Nationalist government on Taiwan claimed jurisdiction over all the Chinese mainland, while the People's Republic of China continues to claim jurisdiction over Taiwan. Until 1995, the government of Taiwan agreed with the P.R.C. that there was only one China, and that Taiwan was a province of China. The province of Taiwan consists of the main island, 15 islands in the Offshore Islands group, and 64 islands in the Pescadores Archipelago. While the Pescadores are close to Taiwan, the Offshore Islands are only a few miles off the coast of mainland China.

Taiwan (Republic of China)

GEOGRAPHY

Area in Square Kilometers (Miles):
36,002 (22,320) (about the size of West Virginia)
Capital (Population): Taipei (2,720,000)
Climate: subtropical

PEOPLE

Population
Total: 21,500,600
Annual Growth Rate: 0.93%
Rural/Urban Population Ratio: 25/75
Ethnic Makeup: 84% Taiwanese; 14% Mainlander Chinese; 2% aborigine
Major Languages: Mandarin Chinese; Taiwanese and Hakka dialects

Health
Life Expectancy at Birth: 72 years (male); 79 years (female)
Infant Mortality Rate (Ratio): 5.6/1,000
Average Caloric Intake: n/a
Physicians Available (Ratio): 1/804

Religions
93% mixture of Buddhism, Taoism, and folk religions; 4.5% Christian; 2.5% others

Education
Adult Literacy Rate: 92%

COMMUNICATION

Telephones: 7,800,000
Newspapers: 139

TRANSPORTATION

Highways—Kilometers (Miles): 20,041 (12,425)
Railroads—Kilometers (Miles): 4,600 (2,852)
Usable Airfields: 38

TAIWAN: "NONEXISTENT" BUT PROFITABLE

In 1979, the United States recognized the People's Republic of China as the sole legal government of China. Since for diplomatic purposes there could only be one China, recognition of the Nationalist government of the Republic of China on Taiwan was dropped. Officially, this made Taiwan cease to exist as a separate state in the view of the U.S. government. American business interests, however, continued to thrive in Taiwan. U.S. investment in Taiwan is considerable, and American banks have made billions of dollars in loans to Taiwan. Thus, even in the absence of formal diplomatic relations, the economic links between the United States and Taiwan remain extensive.

GOVERNMENT

Type: multiparty democratic regime
Head of State/Government: President Lee Teng-hui; Premier Lee Yuan-tseh
Political Parties: Nationalist Party (Kuomintang); Democratic Progressive Party; China Social Democratic Party; Labor Party
Suffrage: universal over 20

MILITARY

Number of Armed Forces: 425,000 (active); 1,657,000 (reserve)
Military Expenditures (% of Central Government Expenditures): 3.4%
Current Hostilities: none

ECONOMY

Currency ($ U.S. Equivalent): 27.51 New Taiwan dollars = $1
Per Capita Income/GDP: $12,070/$257 billion
Inflation Rate: 5.2%
Natural Resources: coal; gold; copper; sulphur; oil; natural gas
Agriculture: rice; tea; bananas; pineapples; sugarcane; sweet potatoes; wheat; soybeans; peanuts
Industry: steel; pig iron; aluminum; shipbuilding; cement; fertilizer; paper; cotton; fabrics

FOREIGN TRADE

Exports: $93.0 billion
Imports: $85.1 billion

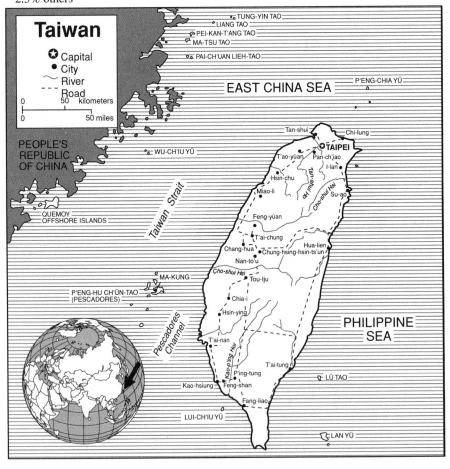

Taiwan

Capital
City
River
Road

0 50 kilometers
0 50 miles

PEOPLE'S REPUBLIC OF CHINA

EAST CHINA SEA

TUNG-YIN TAO
LIANG TAO
PEI-KAN-T'ANG TAO
MA-TSU TAO
PAI-CH'UAN LIEH-TAO
P'ENG-CHIA YÜ

WU-CH'IU YÜ

QUEMOY OFFSHORE ISLANDS

Taiwan Strait

Tan-shui
Chi-lung
TAIPEI
T'ao-yüan Pan-ch'iao
I-lan
Hsin-chu
Miao-li
Feng-yüan
T'ai-chung
Chang-hua Chung-hsing-hsin-ts'un
Nan-to'u
Tou-liu
Chia-i
Hsin-ying
Su-ao
Hua-lien

Cho-shui Hsi

MA-KUNG
P'ENG-HU CH'ÜN-TAO (PESCADORES)

Pescadores Channel

T'ai-nan
Kao-hsiung Feng-shan
P'ing-tung
T'ai-tung
Fang-liao

LUI-CH'IU YÜ

PHILIPPINE SEA

LÜ TAO

LAN YÜ

Taiwan

A Dynamo in East Asia

HISTORY AND PEOPLE

Taiwan,* a powerful economic center in Asia, was once an unknown island off the coast of China, just 90 miles away. It was originally inhabited by aborigines from Southeast Asia. By the seventh century A.D., Chinese settlers had begun to arrive. The island was subsequently discovered by the Portuguese, in 1590, and Dutch as well as Spanish settlers followed. Today, the aborigines' descendants, who have been pushed into the remote mountain areas by the Chinese settlers, number fewer than 400,000, a small fraction of the 21 million people now living in Taiwan. Furthermore, most of the current population are descended from those Chinese who emigrated from the Chinese mainland's southern provinces before 1885, when Taiwan officially became a province of China. Although these people originally came from China, they are known as *Taiwanese,* as distinct from the Chinese who came from the China mainland from 1947 to 1949. The latter are called *Mainlanders* and represent less than 20 percent of the island's population. After 1949, the Mainlanders dominated Taiwan's political elite; but the "Taiwanization" of the political realm that began after Chiang Kai-shek's death in 1975 and the political liberalization of the late 1980s and early 1990s have allowed the native Taiwanese to take up their rightful place within the elite.

The Manchus, "barbarians" who came from the north, overthrew the Chinese rulers on the mainland in 1644. In 1683, they conquered Taiwan; but because Taiwan was an island 90 miles distant from the mainland, the Manchus paid less attention to it and exercised minimal sovereignty over the Taiwanese people. With their defeat in the Sino–Japanese War (1894–1895), the Manchus were forced to cede Taiwan to the Japanese. The Taiwanese people refused to accept Japanese rule, however, and proclaimed Taiwan a republic. As a result, the Japanese had to use military force to gain actual control over Taiwan.

For the next 50 years, Taiwan remained under Japan's colonial administration. Taiwan's economy flourished under Japanese rule. Japan also helped to develop Taiwan's agricultural sector, a modern transportation network, and an economic structure favorable to later industrial development. Furthermore, by creating an advanced educational system, the Japanese developed an educated workforce, which proved critical to Taiwan's economic growth.

With Japan's defeat at the end of World War II in 1945, Taiwan reverted to China's sovereignty. By this point, the Chinese had overthrown the Manchu Dynasty (1911) and established a republican form of government. Beginning in 1912, China was known as the Republic of China (R.O.C.).

*Taiwan has also been known as Formosa, Free China, the Republic of China, and Nationalist China. Today, the government in Taiwan calls the island "Taiwan" and the government the "Republic of China."

Thus it was Chiang Kai-shek who, as head of the R.O.C. government, accepted the return of the island province of Taiwan to R.O.C. rule in 1945. Relations between Taiwanese and Mainlanders were, however, full of tension: The rag-tag, undisciplined military forces of the KMT (Kuomintang, or Nationalist Party,) who arrived in Taiwan were met with hatred and contempt from the local people, who had grown accustomed to the orderliness and professionalism of the Japanese occupation forces. Angered by the incompetence and corruption of KMT officials, demonstrations against rule by Mainlanders occurred in February 1947. Relations were badly scarred when KMT troops brutally killed thousands of Taiwanese opposed to mainland rule. Among those killed were many members of the island's political elite.

Meanwhile, the KMT's focus remained on the mainland, where, under the leadership of General Chiang Kai-shek, it was continuing to fight the Chinese Communists in a civil war that had ended their fragile truce during World War II. Civil war raged from 1945 to 1949 and diverted the KMT's attention away from Taiwan. As a result, Taiwan continued, as it had under Manchu rule, to function fairly independently of Beijing. In 1949, when it became clear that the Chinese Communists would defeat the KMT, General Chiang and some 2 million members of his loyal military, political, and commercial elite fled to Taiwan to establish what they claimed to be the true government (in exile) of the Republic of China. This declaration reflected Chiang's determination to regain control over the mainland and his conviction that the more than 600 million people living on the mainland would welcome the return of the KMT to power.

During the McCarthy period of the "Red scare" in the 1950s—a period during which Americans believed to be Communists or Communist sympathizers were persecuted by the government—the U.S. government supported Chiang Kai-shek. In response to the Chinese Communists' entry into the Korean War in 1950, the United States applied its "cold war" policies of support for any Asian government that was anti-Communist—regardless of how dictatorial and ruthless that government might be—in order to "isolate and contain" the Chinese Communists. It was within this context that the United States committed itself to the military defense of Taiwan and the Offshore Islands in the Taiwan Strait, by ordering the U.S. Seventh Fleet to the strait (in 1950) and by giving large amounts of military and economic aid to Taiwan. General Chiang Kai-shek continued to lead the government of the Republic of China on Taiwan until his death in 1975, at which time his son, Chiang Ching-kuo, succeeded him.

Two Governments, One China

Taiwan's position in the international community and its relationship to the government in Beijing have been determined by perceptions and values as much as by actions. In 1949, when the R.O.C. government fled to Taiwan, the Chinese Communists renamed China the *People's Republic of China* (P.R.C.) and proclaimed the R.O.C. government illegitimate. Mao Zedong, the P.R.C.'s preeminent leader, was later to say that adopting the new name instead of keeping the old name of the *Republic of China* was the biggest mistake he had ever made, for it laid the groundwork for future claims of "two Chinas." Beijing claimed that the P.R.C. was the legitimate government of all of China, including Taiwan. Beijing's attempt to regain de facto control over Taiwan was, however, forestalled by the outbreak of the Korean War and later by the presence of the U.S. Seventh Fleet in the Taiwan Strait. Nevertheless, Beijing has always insisted that Taiwan is an "internal" Chinese affair, that international law is therefore irrelevant, and that other countries have no right to interfere. For its part, until 1995, the government of Taiwan agreed that there was only one China and that Taiwan was a province of China; however, the KMT still claims that this "one China" must be the Republic of China.

Although the Chinese Communists' control over the mainland was long evident to the world, the United States managed to keep the R.O.C. in the China seat at the United Nations by insisting that the issue of China's representation in the United Nations was an "important question." This meant that a two-thirds affirmative vote of the UN General Assembly, rather than a simple majority, was required. With support from its allies, the United States was able to block the P.R.C. from winning this two-thirds vote until 1971.

At this critical moment, when the R.O.C.'s right to represent "China" in the United Nations was withdrawn, the R.O.C. could have put forward the claim that Taiwan had the right to be recognized as an independent state, or at least to be granted observer status. Instead, it steadfastly maintained that there was but one China and that Taiwan was merely a province of China. As a result, today the Republic of China has no representation in any international organization under the name of the R.O.C.; and it has representation only as "Taipei–China" in organizations in which the P.R.C. is a member—if the P.R.C. allows it any representation at all.

International Acceptance of the People's Republic of China
The seating of the P.R.C. in the United Nations in 1971 thus led to the serious erosion of the R.O.C's position in international affairs. Not wanting to anger China, which has a huge and growing economy and significant military power, the state members of international organizations have given in to Beijing's unrelenting pressure to exclude Taiwan. Similarly, Beijing insists that, in bilateral state-to-state relations, any state wishing to maintain diplomatic relations with it must accept China's "principled stand" on Taiwan—notably, that Taiwan is a province of China and that the People's Republic of China is the sole representative of the Chinese people.

New York Public Library

McCARTHYISM: ISOLATING AND CONTAINING COMMUNISM

The McCarthy period in the United States was an era of rabid anticommunism. McCarthyism was based in part on the belief that the United States was responsible for losing China to the Communists in 1949 and that the reason for this loss was the infiltration of the U.S. government by Communists. As a result, Senator Joseph McCarthy (pictured above) spearheaded a "witch-hunt" to ferret out those who allegedly were selling out American interests to the Communists. McCarthyism took advantage of the national mood in the cold war era that had begun in 1947, in which the world was seen as being divided into two opposing camps: Communists and capitalists.

The major strategy of the cold war, as outlined by President Harry Truman in 1947, was the "isolation and containment" of communism. This strategy was based on the belief that if the United States attempted—as it had done with Adolf Hitler's aggression against Czechoslovakia (the first step toward World War II)—to appease communism, it would spread beyond its borders and threaten other free countries.

The purpose of the cold war strategy, then, was to contain the Communists within their national boundaries and to isolate them by hindering their participation in the international economic system and in international organizations. Hence, in the case of China, there was an American-led boycott against all Chinese goods, and the United States refused to recognize the People's Republic of China as the legitimate representative of the Chinese people within international organizations.

CHIANG KAI-SHEK: DETERMINED TO RETAKE THE MAINLAND

Until his dying day, Chiang Kai-shek (1887–1975), pictured here with his wife, maintained that the military, led by the KMT (Kuomintang, or Nationalist Party), would one day invade the mainland and, with the support of the Chinese people living there, defeat the Communist government. Daily during the years of Chiang's presidency, banner headlines proclaimed that the Communist "bandits" would soon be turned out by internal rebellion and that the KMT would return to control on the mainland. In the last years of Chiang Kai-shek's life, when he was generally confined to his residence and incapable of directing the government, his son, Chiang Ching-kuo, always had two copies of the newspaper made that proclaimed such unlikely feats, so that his father would continue to believe these were the primary goals of the KMT government in Taiwan. In fact, a realistic appraisal of the situation had been made long before Chiang's death, and most of the members of the KMT only pretended to believe that an invasion of the mainland was imminent.

Chiang Ching-kuo, although continuing to strengthen Taiwan's defenses, turned his efforts to building Taiwan into an economic showcase in Asia. Taiwan's remarkable growth and a certain degree of political liberalization were the hallmarks of Chiang Ching-kuo's leadership. A man of the people, he shunned many of the elitist practices of his father and the KMT ruling elite, and he helped to bring about the Taiwanization of both the KMT party and the government. The "Chiang dynasty" in Taiwan came to an end with Chiang Ching-kuo's death in 1988. It was, in fact, Chiang Ching-kuo who made certain of this, by barring his own sons from succeeding him and by grooming his own successor, a native Taiwanese.

Commercial ventures, foreign investment in Taiwan, and Taiwan's investment abroad have not, however, suffered as a result of ending diplomatic relations with Taipei. After being forced to close all but a handful of its embassies, as one state after another switched recognition from the R.O.C. to the P.R.C., Taipei simply substituted offices that actually function as if they are embassies. They handle all commercial, cultural, and official business (including the issuance of visas to those traveling to Taiwan).

To adjust to its loss of official international recognition, the KMT has adopted a new approach in the 1990s. Entitled "flexible diplomacy," it essentially allows Taiwan to justify its own decision to join international organizations to which China already belongs by calling itself "Taipei–China." Beijing has, with only a few exceptions (such as the Olympic Games), been adamant about not letting this happen. This has led to increasing frustration and a sense of humiliation in Taiwan.

The frustration came to a head in early 1996. Under increasing pressure to respond to demands from its people that Taiwan get the international recognition that it deserves for its remarkable accomplishments, Taiwan's President Lee Teng-hui engaged in a series of maneuvers to get the international community to confer de facto recognition of its statehood. Not the least of these bold forays was President Lee's offer of $1 billion to the United Nations in return for a seat for Taiwan, an offer rejected by Secretary General Boutros Boutros-Gali.

President Lee's campaigning for reelection in the spring of 1996 proved to be the final straw for Beijing. Lee had as one of his central themes the demand for greater international recognition of Taiwan as an independent state. Beijing responded with a military buildup of some 200,000 troops in Fujian Province and the "testing" of missiles in the waters around Taiwan. Under pressure from the United States not to provoke a war with the mainland and a refusal on the part of the United States to say exactly what it would do if a war occurred, Lee toned down his campaign rhetoric. A military conflict was averted, and Taipei and Beijing agreed to move forward with their temporarily shelved plans to link Taiwan with the mainland, in almost every conceivable way except for governance.

THE OFFSHORE ISLANDS

Since crises of serious dimensions erupted between China and the United States in 1954–1955, 1958, 1960, and 1962 over the blockading of supplies to the Taiwan-controlled Offshore Islands in the Taiwan Strait, the importance of these tiny islands grew out of all proportion to their intrinsic worth. The two major island groups, Quemoy (about 2 miles from the Chinese mainland) and Matsu (about 8 miles from the mainland) are located almost 90 miles from Taiwan. Thus, Taiwan's control of them made them strategically valuable for pursuing the government's professed goal of retaking the mainland and for linking Taiwan psychologically to the mainland.

The civilian population is about 50,000 (mostly farmers) in Quemoy and about 6,000 (mostly fishermen) in Matsu. The lack of industry and manufacturing on the islands has led to a steady emigration of their natives to Southeast Asia for better jobs. The small civilian population in Quemoy is significantly augmented, however, by an estimated 10,000 to 100,000 soldiers. The heavily fortified islands appear to be somewhat deserted, though, since the soldiers live mostly underground: hospitals, kitchens, sleeping quarters—everything is located underground in tunnels blasted out of granite, including two-lane highways that accommodate trucks and tanks. Heavily camouflaged anti-artillery aircraft dot the landscape.

In the first years after their victory on the mainland, the Chinese Communists fairly steadily shelled the Offshore Islands. When there was not a crisis, their shells were filled with pro-Communist propaganda materials, which littered the islands. When the Chinese Communists wanted to test the U.S. commitment to the Nationalists in Taiwan and the Soviet commitment to their own objectives, they shelled the islands heavily and intercepted supplies to the islands. In the end, China always backed down; but in 1958 and 1962, it did so only after going to the brink of war with the United States. After 1979 and Deng Xiaoping's "peace initiatives" toward Taiwan, the confrontation over the Offshore Islands was at the level of an exchange of gifts by balloons and packages floated across the channel. In 1986, it was described as follows:

> The Nationalists load their balloons and seaborne packages with underwear, children's shoes, soap, toys, blankets, transistor radios and tape recorders, as well as cookies emblazoned with Chiang Ching-kuo's picture and audio tapes of Taiwan's top popular singer, Theresa Teng, a mainland favorite.
>
> The Communists send back beef jerky, tea, herbal medicines, mao-tai and cigarettes, as well as their own varieties of soap and toys.
>
> [There is] confirmation from the mainland of the balloons' reaching as far as Tibet. . . . Unpredictable winds make the job harder for the Communists, but enough of the packages reach Quemoy and Taiwan for the authorities to have passed a law requiring people to hand over all pamphlets and gifts.[1]

Although the brutal suppression of the Tiananmen Square demonstrators in Beijing in the spring of 1989 temporarily led to increased tensions in the Taiwan Strait and a military emergency alert, by 1992, the political situation in China had stabilized enough to make an attack unlikely. A sign of the diminished sense of threat came in November 1992, when Taiwan's military administration of Quemoy and Matsu ended. By the mid-1990s, however, a furious debate had broken out over the future of these Offshore Islands. The opposition Democratic Progressive Party (DPP) argues that, given today's military technology, these islands just off the China coast could easily be taken as "hostages" by the Chinese Communists. The DPP is therefore proposing that the Quemoy and Matsu island groups be made into an international monetary zone. As such, they would attract foreign investment while simultaneously making it less likely that China would invade. As an international monetary zone, they could also compete with Hong Kong's role as the financial center in Asia. The ruling KMT considers this proposal treasonous and argues that the islands are still vital to the defense of Taiwan.[2]

CULTURE AND SOCIETY

Taiwan is a bundle of contradictions: "great tradition, small island; conservative state, drastic change; cultural imperialism, committed Nationalism; localist sentiment, cosmopolitan sophistication."[3] Over time, Taiwan's culture has been shaped by various cultural elements—Japanese, Chinese, and American culture, localism, nationalism, cosmopolitanism,

(Photo credit Dean Collinwood)

As Taiwan enjoys an economic boom, residents suffer the complications of having more wealth than they know what to do with. Individuals now have easy access to owning cars, but the sheer number of private automobiles overwhelms the infrastructure's capacity.

materialism, and even Chinese mainland culture (in the form of "mainland mania"). At any one time, several of these forces have coexisted and battled for dominance. Since the mid-1980s, as Taiwan has become tightly integrated into the international economic system, the power of the central government to control cultural development has declined. This has unleashed not just global cultural forces but also local culture, which has flourished at the expense of centrally mandated culture.[4]

The Taiwanese people were originally immigrants from the Chinese mainland; but their culture, which developed in isolation from the mainland's culture, is not the same as the "Chinese" culture of the Mainlanders who arrived from 1947 to 1949. Indeed, although the KMT saw Taiwan largely in terms of security and the bastion from which to fight against and defeat the Chinese Communist regime on the mainland, "it also cultivated Taiwan as the last outpost of traditional Chinese high culture. Taiwanese folk arts, in particular opera and festivals, did thrive, but as low culture."[5] The Taiwanese have continued to speak their own dialect of Chinese, distinct from the standard Chinese spoken by the Mainlanders, and almost all engage in Taiwanese folk-religion practices. However, from education and the officially sanctioned language to the mass media, the Mainlander-controlled central government has dictated a cultural policy that emphasizes Chinese cultural values. As a result, the distinctions institutionalized in a political system that discriminated against the Taiwanese have been culturally reinforced. In recent years, the Taiwanese have grown increasingly resistant to efforts by the KMT Mainlanders to "Sinify" them—to have them speak standard Chinese and adopt the values of the dominant Chinese Mainlander elite. State-controlled television now offers programs in the Taiwanese dialect, and many more radio programs are in Taiwanese; still, Taiwanese must fight to maintain their cultural indentity.

Generally speaking, however, Taiwanese and Mainland Chinese culture need not be viewed as two cultures in conflict, for they share many commonalities. As Taiwanese move into leadership positions in what used to be exclusively Mainlander institutions and intermarriage between the two groups grows more common, an amalgamation of Taiwanese and traditional Chinese practices is becoming evident throughout the society. As is discussed later in this report, the real source of conflict is the desire of the Taiwanese not to have their culture or political system controlled by Chinese from the mainland of China, whether they be KMT Nationalists or Communists.

On the other hand, rampant materialism as well as the importation of foreign ideas and values are eroding both Taiwanese *and* Chinese values. The "Big Mac" culture affects more than waistlines. Although the KMT government has engaged in a massive campaign to reassert Chinese values, the message seems lost in its larger message, which asks all to contribute to making Taiwan an Asian showplace. The government's emphasis on hard work and economic prosperity has seemingly undercut its focus on traditional Chinese values of politeness, the sanctity of the family, and the teach-

ing of culturally based ethics (such as filial piety) throughout the school system. Materialism and an individualism that focuses on personal needs and pleasure seeking are slowly undermining collectively oriented values.[6] The "I can do whatever I want" attitude is, in the view of many, leading to a breakdown in social order.[7]

While playing a part in Taiwan's economic boom of the past decade, the emphasis on materialism has contributed to a variety of problems, not the least of which are the alienation of youth, juvenile crime, the loosening of family ties, and a general decline of community values. The pervasive spread of illicit sexual activities through such phony fronts as dance halls, bars, saunas, "barber shops," movies-on-video, and music-video establishments, as well as at hotels and brothels, grew so scandalous and detrimental to social morals and social order that the government suggested cutting off their electricity.[8] Another major activity that goes virtually uncontrolled is gambling. Part of the problem in clamping down on either illicit sexual activities or gambling (both of which are often combined with drinking in clubs) is that organized crime is involved; and part of the problem is that, in exchange for bribes, the police look the other way.[9]

THE ENVIRONMENT

The pursuit of individual material benefit without a concomitant concern for the public good has led to uncontrolled growth and a rapid deterioration in the quality of life, even as the people in Taiwan have become richer. Although recycling and efforts to prevent environmental degradation throughout the island have begun, individuals continue to do such things as dump and burn refuse in public places; purchase cars at the rate of 300,000 per year, even though the expansion of the island's roads has not kept pace and even though most cars can only be parked illegally, either by double parking, which further clogs traffic, or parking on sidewalks meant for pedestrians; build illegal structures that similarly obstruct sidewalks; and spit bright red betle-nut juice on the pavement.

As Taiwan struggles to catch up with its own success, the infrastructure has faltered. During the hot, humid summers in Taipei, both electricity and water are frequently shut off; roads are clogged from 7:00 A.M. until 10:00 P.M.; and the city's air is so dense with pollution that eyes water, hair falls out, and many people suffer from respiratory illness. Inadequate recreational facilities leave urban residents with few options but to join the long parade of cars out of the city on weekends.

Taiwan's citizens have begun forming public-interest groups to address such problems, and public protests about the government's neglect of quality-of-life issues have grown increasingly frequent. Environmental groups, addressing such issues as building more nuclear plants in Taiwan, wildlife conservation, industrial pollution, and waste disposal, have burgeoned. However, environmental campaigns and legislation have hardly kept pace with the rapid growth of Taiwan's material culture.

RELIGION

A remarkable mixture of religions thrives in Taiwan. The people feel comfortable placing Buddhist, Taoist, and local deities—and even occasionally a Christian saint—in their family altars and local temples. Restaurants, motorcycle-repair shops, businesses small and large—all maintain altars. The major concern in prayers is for the good health and fortune of the family. The focus is on life in this world, not in the afterlife. People pray for prosperity, for luck on the stock-market, and even more specifically for the winning lottery number. If the major deity in one temple fails to answer prayers, people will seek out another temple where other deities have brought better luck. Alternatively, they will demote the head deity of a temple and promote others to his or her place. The gods are thought about and organized much in the same way as the Chinese bureaucracy is; in fact, they are often given official clerical titles to indicate their rank within the deified bureaucracy.

Offerings of food and money are important in making sure that the gods answer one's prayers; it is equally important to appease one's deceased relatives, for, if neglected or offered inadequate food, money, and respect, they will cause endless problems for their living descendants by coming back to haunt them as ghosts. Thus, those having trouble getting their computer programs to work or those with car trouble will take time out to go to the temple to pray to the gods and ancestors.

The Chinese designate the seventh month of the lunar calendar as "Ghost Month." For the entire month, most Chinese do whatever is necessary "to live in harmony with the omnipotent spirits that emerge to roam the world of the living." This includes

preparing doorway altars full of meat, rice, fruit, flowers and beverages as offerings to placate the anxious visitors. Temples [hang] out red lanterns to guide the way for the roving spirits. . . . Ghost money and miniature luxury items made of paper are burned ritualistically for ghosts to utilize along their desperate journey. . . . The influence of Ghost Month is widespread in society, with Chinese heeding a long list of taboos that have a strong impact on business activity during this cautious time.

The real estate industry feels the negative forces more so than any other business sector. Buying or moving into new houses is the last thing citizens would dare do, fearing that homeless ghosts might become permanent guests. . . . [M]any customers do not want their new cars delivered until after Ghost Month.

Traditionally, the number of newlyweds drops drastically. According to folk belief, a man who marries during the period could discover before long that his bride is actually a ghost. . . . Some pregnant women, after realizing they will most likely

undergo childbirth during Ghost Month, [ask] that Caesarean sections be performed prior to the beginning of the month.

Busy lawyers on the island know they can take a breather in Ghost Month. Legal suits traditionally decrease due to the common belief that ghosts do not appreciate those who sue.[10]

Finally, there continues to be a preference for seeking medical cures from local temple priests over either traditional Chinese or modern Western medicine.

What is unusual in the case of Taiwanese religious practices is that as the island has become increasingly "modern" and wealthy, it has not become less religious. Technological modernization has seemingly not brought secularization with it. In fact, aspiring capitalists often build temples in hopes of getting rich. People bring offerings of food; burn incense and bundles of paper money to honor the temple gods; and burn expensive paper reproductions of houses, cars, and whatever other material possessions they think their ancestors might like to have in their ethereal state.

They also pay real money to the owner of their preferred temple to make sure the gods are well taken care of. Since money goes directly to the temple owner, not to a religious organization, the owner of a temple whose constituents prosper will become wealthy. Given the rapid growth in per capita income in Taiwan over the last 20 years, then, temples to local deities have proliferated, as a builder of a temple was almost guaranteed to get rich if his or her constituents' wealth grew steadily.

Although the vast majority of Taiwan's citizens follow folk religions, Christianity is not left out of the melange of religions. About 4.5 percent of the population are Christians. Christianity does not escape local adaptations, however, such as setting off firecrackers inside a church during a wedding ceremony to ward off ghosts or flashing neon lights around representations of the Virgin Mary. The Presbyterian Church, established in 1865 in Taiwan by missionaries, has frequently been harassed by the KMT because of its activist stance on social and human rights issues and because it has generally supported the Taiwan independence viewpoint.[11]

As for Confucianism, it is really more a philosophy than a religion. Confucianism is about self-cultivation, proper relationships among people, ritual, and proper governance. Although Confucianism accepts ancestor worship as legitimate, it has never been concerned directly with gods, ghosts, or the afterlife. In imperial China, if drought brought famine, or if a woman was thought to have given birth to a cow, the problem was ascribed to the lack of morality on the part of the emperor, not the lack of prayer, and required revolt.

In an effort to restore Chinese traditional values, the KMT has tried to reinstitute the formal study of Confucianism within the schools. Students are apathetic, however, and will usually borrow Confucian texts only long enough to study for

(United Nations photo)

This masonry course at Taiwan University is part of a vocational arts program designed to train prospective teachers in the industrial arts.

their examinations for college entrance: Unlike the system of getting ahead in imperial China through knowledge of the Confucian classics, in Taiwan, students need to excel in science and math. Yet, even though the government's plea for the formal study of Confucianism has fallen on deaf ears in Taiwan, Confucian values suffuse the culture. Streets, restaurants, corporations, and stores are named after major Confucian virtues; advertisements to sell everything from toothpaste to computers appeal to Confucian values of loyalty, friendship, and family; children's stories focus on Confucian sages in history; and the vocabulary that the KMT government and party officials use to conceptualize issues is the vocabulary of Confucianism: moral government, proper relationships between officials and the people, loyalty, harmony, obedience.

EDUCATION

The Japanese are credited with establishing a modern school system in Taiwan in the early twentieth century.

Under KMT rule since 1949, Taiwan's educational system has grown steadily. Today, Taiwan offers 9 years of free, compulsory education. Almost all school-age children are enrolled in elementary schools, and most go on to junior high schools. More than 70 percent continue on to senior high school. Illiteracy has been reduced to about 8 percent and is still declining. Night schools that cater to those students anxious to test well and make the cut for the best senior high schools and colleges flourish. Such extra efforts attest to the great desire of the Taiwanese to get ahead through education.

Taiwan has one of the best-educated populations in the world, a major factor in its dramatic economic development. Yet its educational system is coming under growing criticism for its insistence on uniformity through a unified national curriculum, a lecture format that does not allow for participation of students, the high school and university examinations, tracking, rote memorization, heavy homework assignments, and humiliating punishments. Its critics say that these practices inhibit creativity.[12] Reforms in recent years have tried to modify some of these practices.

The island has more than 100 colleges and universities, but the demand for higher education still outstrips the ability of the system to provide spaces for all qualified students. As a result, many students go abroad for study—and many never return. From 1950 to 1978, only 12 percent of the some 50,000 students who studied abroad returned, a reflection of both the lack of opportunity in Taiwan and the oppressive nature of government in that period. This outward flood of human talent, or "brain drain," was stemmed in the 1980s and 1990s as Taiwan grew more prosperous and its political system more open.

WOMEN

The societal position of women in Taiwan reflects an important cultural ingredient of Confucianism. "Women in classical Chinese society were expected to obey their fathers before marriage, their husbands after, and their sons when widowed. Furthermore, women were expected to cultivate the 'Four Virtues': morality, skills in handicrafts, feminine appearance, and appropriate language."[13] In Taiwan, as elsewhere throughout the world, women have received lower wages than men for similar work and have rarely made it into the top ranks of business or government. Moreover, women are treated differently in the workplace from men—this in spite of the fact that it was women who managed the tens of thousands of small businesses and industries out of their own homes that fueled Taiwan's economic boom. "For example, all female civil servants, regardless of rank, are expected to spend half a day each month making pants for soldiers, or to pay a substitute to do this."[14]

Today, there are countervailing values and new trends toward greater opportunities and respect for women. Women are more visible in politics and the media than before. The fact that women may now receive an education the equal of a man's has helped promote their social and economic mobility, as has the advocacy by Taiwan's feminists of equal rights for women. It has also made the typical marriage pattern, in which a man is expected to marry a woman with an education inferior to his own, far more difficult.

THE ECONOMY

The rapid growth of Taiwan's economy and foreign trade has made Taiwan wealthy as well as one of the world's largest holders of hard-currency reserves. A newly industrialized country (NIC), Taiwan has shed its " Third World," underdeveloped image. With a gross domestic product per capita income that has risen from $100 in 1951 to more than $12,000 in 1996, and a highly developed industrial infrastructure and service industry, Taiwan has entered the ranks of some of the most developed economies in the world. As with the leading industrial nations, however, the increasing costs of manufacturing in an economy where labor demands ever higher wages has meant that the percentage of the economy in the industrial sector is steadily declining, and manufacturing jobs are being relocated to other countries with cheaper wages and raw materials.

Taiwan's economic growth rate over the last 3 decades has been phenomenal, averaging more than 8 percent per year. If Taiwan's GDP per capita income continues to grow at the rate of 6 to 8 percent annually, as it has for more than 20 years, it will soon find itself with one of the world's highest per capita incomes. Yet, as with Japan, this high per capita income will not necessarily mean a commensurate lifestyle: The cities are crowded; housing is too expensive for most urbanites to afford more than a small apartment; and the overall infrastructure is inadequate to handle traffic, parking, sewage, electricity, and other social needs.

Most of the critical reforms that helped Taiwan's economy grow were initiated by the KMT government elite's state-regulating policies. These have included land redistribution, currency controls, central banking, and the establishment of government corporations.[15] Taiwan's success may also be attributed, however, to a largely free enterprise economy in which businesspeople developed international markets for their products and promoted an export-led economy, and in which Taiwan's labor force has contributed through its high productivity. In fact, workers have tended to lack class consciousness because they progress so rapidly from being members of the "proletariat" to becoming capitalists and entrepreneurs, because even factory workers are often involved in small businesses—and because the government has repressed any signs of an active labor movement. This task has been made easier because unions have been under the control of the KMT.[16]

A stable political environment has also facilitated Taiwan's rapid growth. So has a protected market, which has brought protests against unfair trade policies from those suffering from an imbalance in their trade with Taiwan. Taiwan has slowly shed most of the regulations that have protected its industries, including agriculture, from international trade competition. In the last decade, it has also invested heavily abroad, including $20 billion in the China mainland. It has also established nonprofit foundations in the United States and helped fund U.S. university-research centers that study Taiwan. Such investments abroad have helped shrink the trade imbalance, but Taiwan still holds billions of U.S. dollars in its central reserve bank.

Agriculture and Natural Resources

After arriving in Taiwan, the KMT government carried out a sweeping land-reform program: The government bought out the landlords and sold the land to their tenant farmers. The result was equalization of land distribution, an important step in promoting income equalization among the farmers of Taiwan. The land-reform program was premised upon one of Sun Yat-sen's famous Three Principles, the "people's liveli-

(Photo credit Dean Collinwood)
Taiwan is almost self-sufficient in agriculture, but the amount of natural resources is quite limited and must be carefully utilized.

hood." One of the corollaries of this principle was that any profits from the increase in land value attributable to factors not related to the real value of farmland (such as urbanization, which makes nearby agricultural land more valuable) would, when the land was sold, be turned over to the government. Thus today, although the price of land has skyrocketed around Taiwan's major cities, and although many farmers feel that they are being squeezed by low prices for their produce, the farmers would get almost nothing for their land if they sold it to developers. As a result, many farmers have felt trapped in agriculture. Evidence of the high productivity of Taiwan's farmers is that Taiwan is almost self-sufficient in agriculture. This is an impressive performance for a small island where only 25 percent of the land is arable.

Natural resources are quite limited in Taiwan. Taiwan's rapid industrialization and urbanization have put a strain on what few resources do exist. Energy sources, such as coal, gas, and oil, are particularly limited. The result is that the government has had to invest in the building of a number of nuclear power plants to provide sufficient en-

ergy to fuel Taiwan's rapidly modernizing society and economy. Popular protest against further nuclear power plants, however, has brought an energy crisis in the 1990s. Investment in developing China's vast natural resources and moving industries to countries where resources, energy, and labor are cheaper are ways in which Taiwan is postponing its energy and resource crisis.

Taiwan as a Model of Economic Development
Taiwan is often cited as a potential model for other developing countries seeking to lift themselves out of poverty. They could learn some useful lessons from certain aspects of Taiwan's experience, such as the encouragement of private investment and labor productivity, an emphasis on basic health care and welfare needs, and policies to limit the gross extremes of inequality. But Taiwan's special advantages during its development have made it hard to emulate: its small size, the benefits of improvements to the island's economic infrastructure and educational system made under the Japanese occupation, massive American

(Photo credit Dean Collinwood)
The considerable economic wealth of Taiwan has been distributed in a judicious fashion. This street is illustrative of Taiwan's consumer economy. The result of this widespread prosperity has been a stable middle class.

financial and technical assistance, and a highly favorable international economic environment during Taiwan's early stages of growth.

What has made Taiwan extraordinary among the rapidly developing economies of the world is the ability—and the commitment—of the government to achieve and maintain income equality. Taiwan has been able to develop without relying on the exploitation of one economic class to support the growth of others. Although there are beggars in Taiwan today, it is difficult to find them. Government programs to help the disabled and a thriving economy that offers employment to almost everyone certainly help, as does a tight-knit family system that supports family members facing difficult times. The KMT's commitment to Sun

Yat-sen's principle of the "people's livelihood," or what in the West might be called a "welfare state," is still an important consideration in policy formation.

One truly major economic division within Taiwan is between farmers and urban workers. In the last few years, however, the growth of Taiwan's stockmarket—a market built on the thin air of gossip and rumor—has created (and destroyed) substantial wealth almost overnight. Yet Taiwan's economic wealth is still fairly evenly distributed, contributing to a strongly cohesive social system and political stability.

Taiwan's economy is not without growing pains. The government has so far seemingly been unable to address many of the problems arising from its breathtakingly fast modernization: massive pollution; an inadequate urban infrastructure for housing, transportation, electricity, and water; and rampant corruption as everyone tries to get ahead in a now relatively open economy. The rapid acquisition of air conditioners and automobiles has made the environment unbearable and transportation a nightmare. In spite of, and in some cases because of, Taiwan's astounding growth, the quality of life has deteriorated greatly. Complaints of oily rain, ignitable tap water, stunted crops due to polluted air and land, and increased cancer rates abound. "Garbage wars" over the "not-in-my-backyard" issue of sanitary landfill placement have led to huge quantities of uncollected garbage.[17] Numerous public-interest groups have emerged to pressure the government to take action. Antinuclear activists have even tried to use the recall vote to remove seven legislators who favored building Taiwan's fourth nuclear power plant.[18]

Inflation, although still under 6 percent per year, has been fueled by labor's demand for higher wages. Higher wages have, in turn, priced Taiwan's labor-intensive products out of the international market. This has caused foreign investors to look elsewhere as Taiwan loses its competitive advantage. Even Taiwan's own entrepreneurs have set up shop outside of Taiwan, notably in Thailand, the Philippines, and China, where labor is far cheaper.

To encourage Taiwan's manufacturers to keep their plants in Taiwan instead of moving overseas for cheaper labor, since 1988 the government has allowed businesses to import an increasing number of laborers from Southeast Asia to do work at wages too low, hours too long, and conditions too dangerous for Taiwan's own citizens. Numbering 143,000 by the mid-1990s, these workers introduce their own invisible "costs" to Taiwan. Lonely and isolated within a society where they are considered socially inferior and where they rarely speak the language, they tend to engage in heavy drinking, gambling, and other socially dysfunctional behaviors.[19]

By positioning itself as a major investor and financier in the international economy, Taiwan has continued to run a trade and international-currency surplus. Internationalization of its economy is also part of Taiwan's strategy to thwart China's efforts to cut off Taiwan's relationships with the rest of the world: With Taiwan an increasingly important actor in the

SUN YAT-SEN: THE FATHER OF THE
CHINESE REVOLUTION

New York Public Library

Sun Yat-sen (1866–1925) was a charismatic Chinese nationalist who, in the declining years of the foreign-ruled Manchu Dynasty, played upon Chinese-nationalist hostility to both foreign colonial powers and to the Manchu rulers themselves.

Sun (pictured at the left) drew his inspiration from a variety of sources, usually Western, and combined them to provide an appealing program for the Chinese. This program was called the Three People's Principles, which translates the American tenet "of the people, by the people, and for the people" into "nationalism," "democracy," and "the people's livelihood."

This last principle, the people's livelihood, is the source of dispute between the Chinese Communists and the Chinese Nationalists, both of whom claim Sun Yat-sen as their own. The Chinese Communists believe that the term means socialism, while the Nationalists in Taiwan prefer to interpret the term to mean the people's welfare in a broader sense.

Sun Yat-sen is, in any event, considered by all Chinese to be the father of the Chinese Revolution of 1911, which overthrew the feeble Manchus. He thereupon declared China to be a republic and named himself president. However, he had to relinquish control immediately to the warlord Yuan Shih-K'ai, who was the only person in China powerful enough to maintain control over all other contending military warlords in China.

When Sun died, in 1925, Chiang Kai-shek assumed the mantle of leadership of the Kuomintang, the Chinese Nationalist Party. After the defeat of the KMT in 1949, Sun's widow chose to remain in the People's Republic of China and held high honorary positions until her death in 1982.

international economy, it is virtually impossible for its trade, commercial, and financial partners to ignore it. And this, in turn, saves Taiwan from the international diplomatic isolation it might otherwise face in light of its current nonstate status. In the meantime, its economy is also becoming increasingly integrated with that of the China mainland, to the mutual benefit of both Taiwan and the P.R.C.

THE POLITICAL SYSTEM

From 1949 to 1988, the KMT justified the unusual nature of Taiwan's political system with three extraordinary propositions. First, the government of the Republic of China, formerly located on the mainland of China, was merely "in exile" on China's island province of Taiwan. Second, the KMT was the legitimate government not just for Taiwan but also for the hundreds of millions of people living on the Chinese mainland under the control of the Chinese Communist Party. Third, the people living under the control of the Communist "bandits" would rush to support the KMT if it invaded the mainland to overthrow the Chinese Communist Party regime. Taiwan's political and legal institutions flowed from these three unrealistic propositions. Underlying all of them was the KMT's acceptance, in common with

the Chinese Communist Party, that there was only one China and that Taiwan was a province of that one China. Indeed, until the early 1990s, it was a *crime* in Taiwan to advocate independence.[20]

The Constitution

In 1946, while the KMT still was the ruling party on the mainland, it promulgated a Constitution for the Republic of China. This Constitution took as its foundation the same political philosophy as the newly founded Republic of China adopted in 1911 when it overthrew China's Manchu rulers on the mainland: Sun Yat-sen's "Three People's Principles" (nationalism, democracy, and the people's livelihood). Democracy was, however, only to be instituted after an initial period of "party tutelage." During this period, the KMT would exercise virtually dictatorial control while preparing China's population for democratic political participation.

The Constitution provided for the election of a National Assembly, with the responsibility of electing a president and vice president; a Legislative Yuan "branch" to pass new laws, decide on budgetary matters, declare war, and conclude treaties; an Executive Yuan to interpret the Constitution and all other laws and to settle lawsuits; a Control Yuan, the highest supervisory organ, to supervise officials through its powers of censure, impeachment, and auditing; and an Examination Yuan (a sort of personnel office) to conduct civil-service examinations. The Examination Yuan and Control Yuan were holdovers from Chinese imperial traditions dating back thousands of years.

Because this Constitution went into effect in 1947, while the KMT, as the governing party of the Republic of China, still held power in the mainland, it was meant to be applicable to all of China, including Taiwan. The KMT government called nationwide elections to select delegates for the National Assembly and then, in 1948, held elections for representatives to the Legislative Yuan and indirect elections for members of the Control Yuan. Later in 1948, as the civil war between the Communists and the Nationalists on the mainland raged on, the KMT government amended the Constitution to allow for the declaration of martial law and a suspension of regular elections. They did this because, by this time, the Communists were taking control of vast geographical areas of China. Soon afterward, the Nationalist government under Chiang Kai-shek fled to Taiwan. With emergency powers in hand, it was able to suspend elections—and all other democratic rights afforded by the Constitution.

By October 1949, the Communists controlled the entire Chinese mainland. As a result, the KMT, living in what it thought was only temporary exile in Taiwan, could not again hold truly "national" elections for the National Assembly or for the Legislative and Control Yuans, as mandated by the 1946 Constitution. But to foster its claim to be the legitimate government of all of China, the KMT retained the 1946 Constitution and governmental structure, as if the KMT alone could indeed represent all of China. With "national" elections suspended, those individuals elected in 1947 from all of China's mainland provinces (534 out of a total 760 elected had fled with General Chiang to Taiwan) continued to hold their seats in the National Assembly, the Legislative Yuan, and the Control Yuan—usually until death—without standing for reelection. Thus began some 40 years of a charade in which the "National" Assembly and Legislative Yuan in Taiwan pretended to represent all of China. In turn, the government of the island of Taiwan was considered as a mere provincial government under the "national" government run by the KMT.

Although the commitment to retaking the China mainland was quietly abandoned by the KMT government even before President Chiang Kai-shek's death in 1975, the 1946 Constitution and governmental structure remained in force. Over these many years, of course, many members of the three elected bodies died, and special elections were held just to fill their vacant seats. But the continuation of this atavistic system raised serious questions about the legitimacy of the no-longer-elected government. The Taiwanese, who comprised more than 80 percent of the population, accused the KMT Mainlanders of keeping a stranglehold on the political system and pressured them for

greater representation. Because the holdovers from the pre-1949 period were of advanced age and often too feeble to attend meetings of the Legislative Yuan (and some of them no longer even lived in Taiwan), it was virtually impossible to muster a quorum. Thus, in 1982, the KMT was forced to "reinterpret" parliamentary rules to allow the Legislative Yuan to get on with its work.

By the time a Taiwanese, Lee Teng-hui, succeeded President Chiang Ching-kuo upon his death in January 1988 as the new KMT party leader and president of the "Republic of China," 70 percent of the KMT were Taiwanese. Pressures therefore built for party and governmental reforms that would undercut the power of the old KMT Mainlanders. In July 1988, behind the scenes at the 13th KMT Party Congress, the leadership requested the "voluntary" resignation of the remaining pre-1949 holdovers: Allegedly as much as $1 million was offered for some of them to resign, but few accepted. Finally, the Council of Grand Justices forced all those Chinese mainland legislators who had gained their seats in the 1946 elections to resign by the end of 1991.

Under the Constitution, the Legislative, Judicial, Control, and Examination Yuans hold certain specific powers. Theoretically, this should result in a separation of powers, preventing any one person or institution from abusing power arbitrarily. In fact, however, until after the first completely democratic legislative elections of December 1992, none of these branches of government exercised much, if any, power independent of the president (himself chosen by the KMT instead of by a democratic election until 1996) or the KMT.

A final consequence of the three propositions upon which political institutions in Taiwan were created is that, since 1949, Taiwan has maintained two levels of government. One is the so-called "national" government of the "Republic of China," which rules Taiwan as just one province of all of China. The other is the actual provincial government of Taiwan, which, as on the Chinese mainland, reports to the "national" government that pretends to control all of China. In this provincial-level government, native Taiwanese have always had considerable control over the actual functioning of Taiwan province in all matters (e.g., the economy and culture) not directly related to the Republic of China's relationship with the Chinese mainland. Taiwan's provincial government thus became the training ground for native Taiwanese to ascend the political ladder once the KMT reformed the political system after 1988.

MARTIAL LAW

The imposition of martial law over Taiwan from 1949 to 1987 is critical to understanding the dynamics of Taiwan's politics. Concerned with the security of Taiwan against subversion or an invasion by the Chinese Communists, the KMT had declared a state of martial law on Taiwan in 1949. Martial law allowed the government to suspend civil liberties and to limit political activity, such as organizing political parties or mass demonstrations. Thus, it was a convenient weapon for controlling potential Taiwanese resistance by the KMT Mainlanders, who were by then occupying the seat of power of Taipei. In particular, the KMT invoked martial law to quash any efforts to organize a "Taiwan independence" movement. Police powers were widely abused, press freedoms were sharply restricted, and dissidents were jailed. As a result, the Taiwan Independence Movement was forced to organize abroad, mostly in Japan and the United States. Taiwan was run as a one-party dictatorship supported by the secret police. Beginning in 1977, non-KMT candidates were, however, permitted to run for office under the informal banner of *tangwai* (literally, "outside the party"); but they had to run as individuals, not as members of new political parties, which were forbidden until 1989.

The combination of international pressures for democratization, the growing confidence of the KMT, a more stable situation on the China mainland, and diminished threats from Beijing led the KMT to officially lift martial law in July 1987. Thus ended the state of "Emergency" under which almost any governmental use of coercion against Taiwan's citizens was justified.

The Mass Media

With the official end of martial law, the police powers of the state were radically curtailed. The media abandoned former taboos and grew more willing to address social and political problems openly, including the "abuse of authority and unwarranted special privilege."[21] A free press, strongly critical of the government and the KMT, now flourishes. Taiwan, with only 21 million people, boasts close to 4,000 magazines, well over 100 newspapers with a total daily circulation of 5 million, 150 news agencies, 3 domestic television channels, and more than 30 radio stations, which now include foreign broadcasts such as CNN, NHK (from Japan), and the BBC. Thus, although television and radio are still controlled by the government, they have become far more independent since 1988; and 1.2 million households receive 20 to 30 channels through satellite dishes.[22] Television stations show programs from all over the world, exposing people to alternative ideas, values, and lifestyles, and contributing to social pluralism.[23]

Political magazines, which are privately financed and therefore not constrained by governmental financial controls, have played an important role in undercutting state censorship of the media and developing alternative perspectives of issues of public concern. But their ability to establish a profitable niche in the press has not been easy, for they have suffered from denial of access to official sources, a less well-trained press corps, and inadequate funds. Even Taiwan's major opposition party, the DPP, has lacked adequate finances to run a daily newspaper that could compete against the two major papers, both of which are state-owned and-operated—as are the three television stations. New technology that defies national boundaries (including satellite broadcasts

from Japan and mainland China), cable television, and VCRs are, nevertheless, diminishing the relevance of the state monopoly of television.[24]

Civil Rights

Until the late 1980s, the rights of citizens in Taiwan did not receive much more protection than they did on the Chinese mainland. The R.O.C. Constitution has a "bill of rights," but most of these civil rights never really existed until martial law was lifted. Civil rights have been suspended when their invocation by the citizenry has challenged KMT power or policies. Because the "Emergency" regulations provided the rationale for the restriction of civil liberties, the KMT used military courts (which do not use normal judicial procedure) to try what were actually civil cases,[25] arrested political dissidents, and used police repression, such as in the brutal suppression of the Kaohsiung Incident.[26] Even in 1988, government police and government intimidation were used to halt the farmers' street protests against imports of American agricultural products, lack of insurance, and other concerns. And there were strict limits on what the opposition parties could say. Today, individuals may be imprisoned for political crimes, but it is far less likely than before.

Political Reform

Taiwan's economic growth and rapidly rising standard of living over several decades gave the KMT regime much of the legitimacy it needed even without democratic participation. Minimally, the government's success in developing the economy meant that economic issues did not provide fuel for political grievances. The KMT could, then, beginning in 1987, undertake political reform with a certain amount of confidence. Its gradual introduction of democratic processes and values eroded much of its former authoritarian style of rule. Reform simultaneously generated considerable tensions, but these tensions have not been destabilizing. By the early 1990s, the KMT realized that it could ride out repeated demonstrations against government policies and win elections even if it did not suppress the opposition. This being the case, the KMT liberalized the political realm still further. Today, it is in most respects functioning as a democracy.

Taiwan possesses a condition important for political liberalization: a large middle class with increasingly diverse and complex social and economic interests of its own that arise from ownership of and concern for private property. Moreover, because of the remarkably egalitarian distribution of economic wealth and the lack of a large underclass, economic discontent is low.[27] Thus, the KMT regime has gradually modified its authoritarian rule and become responsive to demands from an ever more politically aware and active citizenry.

One way in which the KMT has maintained dominance as it reforms is by opening up its membership to a broader segment of the population. Social diversity and political pluralism may now be expressed *within* the KMT. The "Taiwanization" of both the KMT and governmental institutions after Chiang Kai-shek's death actually permitted the KMT not to respond to the demands of the Taiwanese until the late 1980s. By "Taiwanization" and, subsequently, by *co-opting* the most appealing platforms of the Democratic Progressive Party (DPP),[28] Taiwan's political system has been able to institutionalize channels for conflict within a party–government system still under the KMT's control. In short, as Taiwan has become more socially and politically diverse, the KMT has been willing to move away from authoritarian instruments and toward persuasion, conciliation, and open debate as the means to maintain control.[29]

External pressures have played a significant role in the democratization of Taiwan's institutions. Substantial U.S. aid was accompanied by considerable American pressure for liberalizing Taiwan's economy and political institutions. Taiwan's dependence on foreign trade has made it anxious to become accepted into membership in the World Trade Organization (to replace the General Agreement on Tariffs and Trade), even though this will hurt its agricultural sector and domestic industries such as car manufacturing. To gain acceptance, Taiwan must open up its domestic market to foreign imports, through such measures as cutting tariffs, lifting trade barriers, and reducing government subsidies on agricultural products.[30] Taiwanese businesspeople have added their own pressures to these.

The KMT government's efforts to bolster integration of Taiwan into the international economy has allowed Taiwan to reap the benefits of internationalization. Furthermore, since 1987, the KMT has responded positively to demands from its citizens for greater contact with China and for reform of the party and government. As a result, the KMT can continue to claim responsibility for Taiwan's prosperity and political liberalization.

With the KMT moving quickly to assume key elements of most opposition party policies, the opposition has had to struggle to lay claim to providing an alternative to the KMT. In the December 1992 elections, the Democratic Progressive Party did so. Without making a point of pushing Taiwan's independence, an issue that could inflame Beijing's aggressive sentiments as much as those of the KMT elite (and an issue that had alienated the public in the 1991 elections), the DPP took on the KMT, demanding more rapid political reforms and criticizing corrupt practices of the KMT. During those elections, moreover, the DPP was permitted to campaign against the KMT's claims to be the legitimate government of mainland China.

By the time of the first democratic elections for the president of R.O.C. in March 1996[31] (which the KMT candidate President Lee Teng-hui won handily, with 54 percent of the vote), however, much had changed in the platforms of both the KMT and the DPP. The KMT, which

THE U.S. SEVENTH FLEET HALTS INVASION

In 1950, in response to China's involvement in the Korean War, the United States sent its Seventh Fleet to the Taiwan Straight to protect Taiwan and the Offshore Islands of Quemoy and Matsu from an invasion by China. The aircraft carrier Enterprise, a part of the Seventh Fleet, is shown above. Because of improved Sino–American relations in the 1970s, the enhanced Chinese Nationalist defense capabilities to defend Taiwan and the Offshore Islands, and problems in the Middle East, the Seventh Fleet was eventually moved out of the area. In 1996, however, part of the Seventh Fleet briefly returned to the Taiwan Strait when China threatened to use military force against Taiwan if its leaders sought independent statehood.

had by this time developed a powerful internal faction demanding greater international recognition of Taiwan as an independent state, adopted what amounted to an "independent Taiwan" position, at least in the eyes of Beijing. Although President Lee denied this as a misinterpretation on Beijing's part—stating that Taiwan just wanted more international "breathing space"—his offer of $1 billion to the United Nations if it would give Taiwan a seat was hardly open to interpretation.

Political Parties
Not until 1989 did the KMT pass new laws legalizing opposition political parties. This decision was made in the context of

growing resistance to KMT rule, because of the continued restriction of democratic rights, and in the favorable environment created by widespread prosperity and economic growth. The DPP, a largely Taiwanese-based opposition party, was officially recognized as a legal party. Even after 1989, however, the KMT continued to regulate political parties strictly, in the name of maintaining political and social stability, which might be jeopardized by a truly competitive political system.[32]

The first real elections, for 101 of the total seats in the Legislative Yuan (Parliament), occurred in December 1989. Vote buying and general dishonesty were serious issues during this first competitive election, but the results indicated the DPP's appeal as an opposition party. However, in both these and the 1991 elections, internal differences marred the ability of the DPP to project a unified electoral strategy. Since then, DPP leaders have proven more willing to compromise with one another in order to present a united front against the KMT. Yet, whether out of general frustration as the minority party or because of inexperience with democratic parliamentary procedures, DPP representatives continue to engage in physical brawls on the floor of the Legislature, ripping out microphones and throwing furniture.

For its part, the KMT has grown increasingly factionalized between progressive reformers and those who are reluctant to move ahead with further liberalization of the economic and political systems. Factionalism has become even more serious over the issue of whether Taiwan should press for greater international recognition as a state. One wing of the KMT, angry that the KMT was not moving more actively to bring about reunification with the mainland of China and in general holding more conservative views than the liberalizing KMT, broke off to form the New Party. It took 7 percent of the vote in the 1994 elections, making it an up-and-coming third party.

Because the KMT and the DPP have moved toward each other's positions on the issue of Taiwan independence and because they are in basic agreement on most social and economic issues, there is not a major ideological rift between the two parties. Both are committed to democracy, both vehemently oppose communism and advocate capitalism, both believe that it is important to maintain good relations with the P.R.C., and both support an equitable distribution of wealth, even though this requires governmental intervention. As a result, the growing power of the DPP and other opposition parties does not significantly threaten the policies that the KMT so carefully laid out during its many decades in power.

Interest Groups

As Taiwan has become more socially, economically, and politically complex, alternative sources of power have developed that are independent of the KMT. Economic-interest groups comprised largely of Taiwanese, whose power arises from private property and wealth, are the most important. However, there are also public-interest groups that challenge the KMT's policies in such areas as civil rights, the environment, women's rights, consumer protection, agricultural pol-

icy, aborigine rights, and nuclear power. Even before the actual lifting of martial law in 1988, these and other groups were organizing hundreds of demonstrations each year to protest government policy.

By the mid-1990s, every adult in Taiwan belonged on average to at least one of the thousands of interest groups. They have been spawned by political liberalization and economic growth and have, in turn, added to the social pluralism in Taiwan. They have also increased the pressures for a still greater institutionalization of democratic procedures. Still, the KMT strictly regulates the personnel, budgets, and representation of interest groups in the Legislature; and, if the KMT believes that any group is voicing support for interests inimicable to the KMT's own or that opposition forces might coalesce around those interests, it does not hesitate to restrict or eliminate the group.[33] Nevertheless, the KMT government is finding it increasingly difficult to control all the interest groups, and they have become important instruments for democratic change.

The Future of Political Reform in Taiwan

The KMT, then, has been able to harness popular pressure, in part by allowing dissent to have an outlet through interest groups and opposition parties. At this point, should the KMT feel its power threatened, it would be difficult to remove the many democratic rights it has bestowed on the Taiwanese people in the last decade. Undoing them would be easier, of course, if Taiwan's security were threatened—either because of internal political turmoil (resulting, say, from an economic downturn) or an external political threat from China. Were internal pressures to threaten KMT control, it might try to revert to authoritarian measures—and it is even plausible that the majority of the population would accept this as necessary. Since the late 1980s, however, the KMT has benefited from the legitimation of its rule by the gradual introduction of a more democratic system.

Finally, the ability of the KMT to keep the lid on the expression of political discontent is aided by the politically conservative value system of the majority of people in Taiwan, who fear the consequences for stability of too many different ideas. Much like the Chinese living on the mainland, people in Taiwan fear instability more than they treasure freedom.

THE TAIWAN–P.R.C.–U.S. TRIANGLE

From 1949 until the 1960s, Taiwan received significant economic, political, and military support from the United States. Even after it became abundantly clear that the Communists effectively controlled the China mainland and had the support of the people, the United States never wavered in its support of President Chiang Kai-shek's position that the R.O.C. was the legitimate government of *all* of China. U.S. Secretary of State Henry Kissinger's secret trip to China in 1971, followed

(United Nations photo/Chen)

The Chinese Communists have said that Taiwan may maintain its free market economy after reunification with the mainland, but many Taiwanese fear that the island's textile and other industries would falter under Communist control.

by President Richard M. Nixon's historic visit in 1972, led to an abrupt change in the American position and to the gradual erosion of the R.O.C.'s diplomatic status.

Allies of the United States, most of whom had loyally supported its diplomatic stance on China, soon severed diplomatic ties with Taipei, a necessary step before they could in turn establish diplomatic relations with Beijing. Only one government could claim to represent the Chinese people; and, since the KMT was in complete agreement with the Chinese Communist regime that there was no such thing as "two Chinas" or "one Taiwan and one China," the diplomatic community had to make a choice between the two contending governments. Given the reality of the Chinese Communist Party's control over a billion Chinese people and the vast territory of mainland China, and, more cynically, given the desire of the business community throughout the world to do business in China, Taipei found itself increasingly isolated diplomatically.

The United States found it painful to desert its long-time Asian ally. After all, the R.O.C. had always been a loyal ally in Asia and a bastion against communism, if not a democratic oasis. The United States had, moreover, invested heavily in Taiwan's economy. But on January 1, 1979, President Jimmy Carter announced the severing of diplomatic relations with Taipei and the establishment of full diplomatic relations with Beijing. Although the disappointment and anger of the KMT government at the time cannot be overstated, the relationship flourished between the United States and what became known as simply the "Taiwan government." American interests in Taiwan are overseen by a huge, quasi-official "American Institute in Taiwan," while Taiwan is represented in the United States by multiple branches of the "Taipei Economic and Cultural Office." In fact, the personnel in these offices continue to be treated in most respects as if they are diplomatic personnel. Except for the handful of countries that

(Photo credit Fred J. Maroon)

The signing of the Shanghai Joint Communique during President Richard Nixon's visit to China was the first of several steps by which the United States diplomatically deserted its long-time ally, Taiwan. The power of the economic relationship between the United States and Taiwan, however, eventually overcame the lack of diplomatic recognition, and Taiwan continued to do business with the West.

officially recognize the R.O.C., and who therefore are not even permitted by China to have diplomatic relations with Beijing, Taiwan's commercial, cultural, and political interests are represented abroad by these unofficial offices.

Once the United States agreed to the Chinese Communists' "principled stand" that Taiwan is a province of China and that the People's Republic of China is the sole legal government of all of China, it could hardly continue to maintain a military alliance with one of China's provinces. Recognition of Beijing, therefore, required the United States to give the mandated 1-year termination notice to its mutual-defense treaty with the R.O.C. In the Taiwan Relations Act of 1979, however, the United States stated its concern for the island's future security, its hope for a peaceful resolution of the conflict between the KMT government and Beijing, and its decision to put a moratorium on the sale of new weapons to Taiwan.

Renewal of Arms Sales

In spite of this agreement, by 1981, the newly ensconced Reagan administration had announced its intention to resume arms sales to Taiwan. It argued that Taiwan needed its weapons upgraded in order to defend itself. Irate, Beijing demanded that, in accordance with American agreements and

implicit promises to China, the United States phase out the sale of military arms over a specified period. The issue of U.S. arms sales to Taiwan has plagued relations with Taiwan and the P.R.C. ever since. Agreements were concluded in 1992 to deliver 150 F-16 fighters to Taiwan in 1996. Given Beijing's punitive measures against countries such as the Netherlands and France when they wanted to sell military equipment to Taiwan, Taiwan has further developed its own defense industry. As a result, by 1994, it had produced its own squadron of 20 jet fighters, armed with Taiwan-made air-to-air missiles.[34]

China's conflicts with the United States over its own sales of military equipment, such as medium-range missiles to the Saudi Arabians, Silkworm missiles to the Iranians (used against American ships), nuclear technology to Pakistan, and massive sales of semiautomatic assault weapons to the United States (one of which was used to attack the White House in 1994) have put it in a weak position for protesting American military sales to Taiwan. In the end, Beijing seemed to put a good trade relationship with the United States ahead of its insistence that the United States cancel the sale of fighter jets, and its protests faded into mutterings.[35]

One of the critical stumbling blocks to controlling the growing arms race between Taipei and Beijing is the insistence by the United States that Beijing agree to the "peaceful resolution of the Taiwan issue." But "on principle," China refuses to make any such a commitment, insisting that Taiwan is an "internal" affair, not an international matter over which other states might have some authority. From China's perspective, then, it has the right as a sovereign state to choose to use force to settle the Taiwan issue; and in 1996, apart from a mild statement from Japan, no Asian country even questioned China's right to use force when it appeared that President Lee was challenging Beijing's claim of sovereignty over Taiwan.

CHINA'S "PEACE OFFENSIVE"

Since the early 1980s, the People's Republic of China has pursued a "peace offensive" in an effort to get the KMT leaders to negotiate a future reunification of Taiwan with the mainland. Beijing has invited the people of Taiwan to visit their friends and relatives on the mainland and to witness the progress made under Communist rule. In the first year (1987–1988) since 1949 that Taiwan's government agreed to allow visits to the mainland, more than 170,000 people seized the opportunity. Since then, more than 8 million Taiwan residents (over one third of the population) have traveled to the mainland. In turn, fewer than 2 million Chinese mainlanders have been permitted by the KMT government to visit Taiwan (although more may have entered through a third area such as Hong Kong or the United States.).[36] The KMT goverment has, however, arranged for mainland Chinese students studying abroad to come for "study tours" of Taiwan. They have treated them as if they were visiting dignitaries, and the students have usually returned to their universities full of praise for Taiwan.

China's "peace offensive" has included a nine-point proposal originally made in 1981. The major points include Beijing's willingness to negotiate a mutually agreeable reintegration of Taiwan under the mainland's government; encouragement of trade, cultural exchanges, travel, and communications between Taiwan and the mainland; the offer to give Taiwan "a high degree of autonomy as a special administrative region" of China after reunification (the same status it has offered to Hong Kong when it comes under Beijing's rule in 1997); and promises that Taiwan could keep its own armed forces, continue its socioeconomic systems, and maintain political control over local affairs—far more, incidentally than China has offered to Hong Kong. Beijing has also offered to allow Taiwan's leaders to participate in the national leadership of a unified China.

Until 1988, the KMT's official response to Beijing's "peace offensive" was negative. The KMT's bitter history of war with the Chinese Communists, and what the KMT sees as a pattern of Communist duplicity—making and breaking promises—explain much of the government's hesitation. Since late 1992, however, Taiwan has been engaged in "unofficial" discussions on topics of mutual interest. These include such issues as the protection of Taiwan's investments in the mainland, tourism, cross–Taiwan Strait communication and transportation links, and the dumping of Taiwan's nuclear waste on the mainland. Taipei remains sensitive, however, to the Taiwanese people's concern about the unification of Taiwan with the mainland implicit in Beijing's "peace offensive." The Taiwanese have said that they will never accede to rule by yet another mainland Chinese government, especially a Communist one. And they have insisted that no deals be struck between the KMT Mainlander leadership and the Chinese Communist regime. Their concern has been that the KMT Mainlander elite could join in an agreement with the Beijing leadership at the expense of the Taiwanese. However, the 1996 democratic presidential elections, in which Lee Teng-hui, a Taiwanese, was elected by a popular majority of 54 percent, did much to diminish their concerns.

At the same time, any serious negotiations for reunification could strengthen those who are pressing for Taiwan's independence. Those supporting outright independence, as opposed to a gradual accretion of greater international recognition for Taiwan's de facto statehood, realize the risks involved in doing so. Indeed, the military threats that Beijing hurled at Taiwan in 1996 in response to President Lee's campaign rhetoric about greater international recognition for Taiwan indicated that Beijing meant business. In the weeks leading up to Taiwan's first truly democratic elections for president in March 1996, China began missile "tests" in the waters close to Taiwan. Fortunately, none of the missiles accidentally hit Taiwan. President Lee's reassurances that the missiles did not have warheads and were meant only to intimidate the Taiwanese people did not alleviate anxieties completely. Many stockpiled rice, and some swapped their savings in local currency for hard currency, to the point that some of the banks ran out of U.S. dollars.[37] Since the March 1996 elections, both sides have made serious efforts to end the tensions and to return to mutually cooperative endeavors.[38]

With only a handful of countries recognizing the R.O.C. instead of the P.R.C., and with Beijing blocking membership for the R.O.C. in most international organizations, the KMT has to be able to show some positive results in its evolving relationship with Beijing. Thus, it has been eager to promote links between Taiwan and the mainland. "Indirect" trade between China and Taiwan by way of Hong Kong has continued to soar. (It had already surpassed $10 billion by 1994, making China Taiwan's third-largest trading partner, after the United States and Japan.) Meanwhile, "illegal" trade between mainland fishermen and Taiwanese continues at a brisk pace (as much as an estimated $2 billion a year by the mid-1990s), with fishermen trading much-coveted traditional Chinese medicines for made-in-Taiwan VCRs, televisions, and videotapes. Originally, the KMT permitted such aspects of its relationship with China to develop in part to let some of the steam out of the Taiwan Independence Movement. Now, it is more concerned with countering the DPP's arguments that, under KMT policies, Taiwan has essentially been excluded (at the official level) from international diplomatic circles.

To keep up at least the pretense of moving toward unification with the mainland, Taiwan's government-controlled television presents travelogues about China as if it were just another place that any ordinary citizen in Taiwan could visit (no longer a land occupied by Communist "bandits"). News about China, including weather forecasts, is included under the topic of "national news" on Taiwan's radio and television programs, symbolizing the fact that Taiwan is indeed a part of China. Since 1988, individuals from China who have ailing relatives on Taiwan, or whose funerals they wish to attend, could for the first time go to Taiwan and stay for up to 3 months. The KMT's policy on mainland spouses is particularly stringent, with few Taiwanese residents who marry individuals from the mainland being permitted to bring them to live in Taiwan. This is in startling contrast to Beijing's policy, which welcomes Taiwanese spouses. The KMT government's argument is that the mainland spouses could be spies. Since 1992, while the KMT government permitted several hundred mainlanders to come to reside with their spouses in Taiwan, thousands are still prohibited from doing so.

Although temporarily interrupted by the military confrontation in early 1996, China's policy of preparing for the eventual reintegration of Taiwan with the mainland has been resumed. China continues to deepen and widen harbors to receive ships from Taiwan; wines and dines influential Taiwanese; gives preferential treatment to Taiwan's entrepreneurs in trade and investment on the mainland; opens direct telephone lines from Taiwan to the mainland; allows luggage at Taipei's airport to be checked directly to China (even though, thus far, flights do not go directly there); rebuilds some of the most important temples to local deities in Fujian Province, favorite places for Taiwanese to visit; establishes special tourist organizations to care solely for people from Taiwan; and refurbishes the birthplace of Chiang Kai-shek, the greatest enemy of the Chinese Communists in their history.

Various segments of the Taiwan population view the relationship differently. Businesspeople and scholars want direct trade and personal contacts. They feel that there is little to fear and that political concerns should be separated from economic interests and international scientific exchanges. Those in the economic sector are particularly worried that, unless they are allowed to penetrate the China market, others will establish control over it, at their expense. They have insisted that trade will remain limited and that the government need not fear Taiwan becoming dependent on trade with China.

For those faced with Taiwan's ever-higher labor costs, which price their goods out of the international market, and

the need for cheap raw materials unavailable in Taiwan, investing in China offers definite advantages: They can move Taiwan's outdated labor-intensive factories and machinery to the mainland. There, significantly cheaper labor allows these same factories to continue to make a profit. Since the factories are not profitable if left in Taiwan, not much can be lost by relocating them on the mainland.

Many are concerned, however, that Taiwan, which already has put 15 percent of its total foreign investment in the mainland, could become "hostage" to Beijing. That is, if China were to refuse to release Taiwan's assets or repay investors for their assets on the mainland in case of a political conflict between Taipei and Beijing, Taiwan's enterprises would form a pressure point that would give the advantage to Beijing. Furthermore, without diplomatic recognition in China, Taiwan's businesses on the mainland are at risk in case of a conflict with local businesses or the government. Yet, so far, affairs have turned out quite the opposite: China has actually *favored* Taiwan's businesses over all others. As for Taiwan's investors, they have in general managed to make such a quick profit and to put in so many safeguards that they have little to lose from any possible seizure of assets.

PROSPECTS FOR REUNIFICATION

Many of those opposed to reunification would nevertheless agree that the KMT government's policy toward China should be progressive, assertive, and forward-looking; and that lacking a long-term plan and simply reacting to Beijing's initiatives puts the real power to determine the future relationship in the Chinese Communist Party's hands. Reform-minded individuals in the KMT have insisted that the government abandon its head-in-the-sand behavior and actively structure how that relationship evolves. In 1990, therefore, the KMT set up a "National Unification Council" for the purpose of accelerating the process of "unification of all China as a free, democratic nation."[39] Taiwan's former premier proposed a "one country, two regions" model "as a means for handling legal and other disputes arising from unofficial contact."[40]

This model would not necessarily be used, however, if reunification were to occur. Nor would Taiwan's leaders necessarily agree that Taiwan would follow Beijing's model for Hong Kong once it reverted to China's control in 1997. Indeed, after winning Taiwan's presidential elections in 1996, Lee Teng-hui asserted that the "one country, two systems" model that China has said that it would carry out in Hong Kong clearly would not work—for either Hong Kong or Taiwan. President Lee stated, in a remarkably unambiguous way: "Our 'One China' is the Republic of China which will for the first time become the true 'One China' after reunification [with mainland China]." He added that Beijing's perspective of a "One China" ruled by Beijing, with Taiwan as a province, would be unacceptable to Taipei; and he repeated his hope that Taiwan would be admitted to the United Nations.[41] This view does not, however, necessarily challenge the agreement Taipei and Beijing reached in 1992: ". . . each would maintain its own interpretation of the one-China concept. [Beijing] equates China with the present People's Republic of China government and ignores the existence of the R.O.C. Taipei holds that Taiwan and the mainland are separate and politically equivalent parts of one China. . . ."[42] In short, President Lee is not necessarily rejecting the concept of "One China"—if Taipei is in charge. He is rejecting the idea that it would be called the People's Republic of China or that Beijing would be in charge of the new unified government. He did not indicate why he imagined that the government of the "Republic of China" would, even if free and democratic elections for all of the mainland and Taiwan were to be held, come out the winner.

In spite of rhetoric such as this, changes in Taipei's policies toward the P.R.C. have been critical to an improvement to cross–Taiwan Strait ties. For example, the KMT ended its 40-year-old policy of stamping "Communist bandit" on all printed materials from China and prohibiting ordinary people from reading them. Taiwan's government officials and others formerly prohibited from visiting relatives in China are now also permitted to go. Scholars from Taiwan may now attend some international conferences in the P.R.C., and Taipei now permits a few P.R.C. scholars to attend conferences in Taiwan. Furthermore, retired KMT veterans, who fought against the Communists and retreated to Taiwan in 1949, are actually encouraged to return to the mainland to live out their lives, because their limited KMT government pensions would buy them a better life there! Certainly, some members of Taiwan's upper class are acting as if the relationship will eventually be a harmonious one when they purchase large mansions in the former international sector of Shanghai.

Other circumstances also encourage Taiwan to expand its ties, if not yet reunify with the mainland. For example, both Taiwan and China would prefer the establishment of a Chinese trading zone to a Japan-dominated East Asian trading zone. A "Chinese common market" would incorporate China, Taiwan, Hong Kong, Macao, and perhaps other places with large ethnic Chinese communities, such as Singapore and Malaysia. Economically integrating these Chinese areas would strengthen them against the Japanese powerhouse. Adopting common policies on taxes, trade, and currencies would be an important step toward eventual reunification of Taiwan with the mainland.[43]

Growing ties between Taiwan and the mainland do not, however, add up to a desire on Taipei's part for reunification. And, with an ever smaller number of first-generation Mainlanders in top positions in the KMT and Taiwan's government, few are keen to push for reunification. Indeed, the majority of people in Taiwan still oppose reunification. They are particularly concerned about the gap in living standards,

and they are fully aware of the high price West Germany has paid to reunify with East Germany. Obviously, the price tag to close the gap with mammoth China would be prohibitive for tiny Taiwan. Furthermore, whether Mainlander or Taiwanese, KMT or DPP, the Chinese Communist Party's crackdown on Tainanmen Square demonstrators in June 1989, the subsequent repression throughout society, and the reversal of economic reforms—in spite of the fact that all these events occurred back in the late 1980s—have continued to dampen enthusiasm for formal reunification. Combined with a fear of loss of certain political freedoms and control over their own institutions, such as they perceive as certain to happen in Hong Kong, the population generally wonders what further benefits would accrue to them from reunification. While some would find it deeply satisfying, many more would mourn the loss of Taiwan's separate identity.

Thus, the KMT has been caught in a dilemma. Its efforts to move more quickly toward reunification were not fast enough to avoid alienating both the military and the conservatives within the KMT, who in 1993 broke off to form the New Party; and they were *too* fast to avoid giving more appeal to the DPPs platform encouraging greater independence. Over the years, many have pushed the KMT to propose a new model for reunification. Germany's reunification and the possibility of reunification between North and South Korea increases the pressure on Taiwan to reunify with the mainland.

More contacts and exchanges between the two sides may in themselves help lay the basis for mutual trust and understanding. Greater contacts have led to a greater appreciation on the mainland of an alternative to communism in a Chinese society. The Chinese Communist regime has been closely watching to see if political and economic liberalization in Taiwan will lead to the sort of chaos that followed on the heels of political and economic liberalization in Eastern Europe and the former Soviet Union. So far, in spite of both the growing economic polarization of society into rich and poor and the increasing number of protests and demonstrations challenging government policies, the KMT government has had few problems in controlling the effects of liberalization and rapid growth. Beijing cannot help but be impressed.

At many levels, ties between the P.R.C. and Taiwan are expanding exponentially. Taiwan's premier even said that the government would create a "Special Economic Zone" for direct trade with the China mainland.[44] Furthermore, China's government has displayed remarkable stability. And the likelihood of Beijing using military force against Taiwan—unless Taiwan again pushes for recognition as an independent state—seems less and less likely as it continues to benefit from Taiwan's trade and investment as well as remittances and tourism from Taiwan. China's leadership, committed to rapid economic development, would also have to consider the risks involved in draining its limited resources into a war that it might not win. Beijing would not know in advance, moreover, whether an attack on Taiwan would cause the United

States to intervene on its behalf; but Beijing could well worry that it might. The American policy of "strategic ambiguity" has, in fact, left both Taipei and Beijing in the dark as to what the United States would do in case of a conflict.

For its part, Taiwan's high labor costs and lack of natural resources and China's abundance of both natural resources and cheap labor mean that closer ties with China offer Taiwan a chance to continue its rapid growth into the twenty-first century. Combined with Taiwan's heavy dependence on trade, Taipei must at least talk as if it is interested in unification, even if it simultaneously pursues "a policy which, if effective would create the basis for both *de facto* and *de jure* independence." It is, in short, a strategy aimed at using "the unification *process* to set up conditions advantageous for the emergence of some form of *de jure* independent Taiwan with no commitment to unification with China."[45]

Of course, no guarantee exists that reunification will ever take place. China's low level of economic development and lack of a pluralistic culture are unacceptable even to Taiwan's Mainlanders. Furthermore, the KMT would never be interested in reunification unless it would be in control of the mainland government. A situation of "coalition government," especially one in which it would be a minority voice, would at this point be unacceptable to the KMT. Since there is no evidence that most people in China would welcome the return to power of the KMT government—a government unable to address China's problems successfully before 1949—the question of the future role of Taiwan's leadership in any unified government remains an intractable issue.

Thus, it seems to be in Taiwan's best interests for the relationship with China to develop in a careful and controlled manner—and to avoid public statements on the issue of reunification versus an independent Taiwan, even as that issue haunts every hour of the day in Taiwan. It is also in Taiwan's interest to wait and see how China integrates Hong Kong under its formula of "one country, two systems." In the meantime, Taiwan's international strategy—acting like an independent state, while insisting it is not attempting to become independent, and conducting business and diplomacy with other states as usual—has proved remarkably successful. It has allowed Taiwan to get on with its own economic development without too many concerns for military security.

As Taiwan's relationship with China deepens and broadens, it is possible that more arrangements could be made for the representation of both Taiwan and China in international organizations without Beijing putting up countless roadblocks. Meanwhile, although both Beijing and Taiwan have set the year 2000 as a target for the reintegration of Taiwan, China's hands are already full with the reversion of Hong Kong (1997) and Macao (1999) to its sovereignty.

Beijing's leadership knows Taiwan acts as a de facto independent state, but it is willing to turn a blind eye as long as Taipei does not push too openly for recognition. The reality does not matter to Beijing as long as the symbolism of Taiwan being a province of China is recognized. Beijing's leadership is far more interested in putting its resources into China's economic development than fighting a war with no known outcome. But, because China's sovereignty over Taiwan has been an emotional patriotic, even nationalistic, issue for the Chinese people ever since 1949, Beijing will not make a "rational" cost-benefit analysis of the costs of using force against a rebellious Taiwan.

In any event, the concrete results of Taiwan declaring independence would be virtually nil. Already Beijing refuses to have diplomatic relations with any country that officially recognizes the Republic of China as the legitimate government of China. Those countries that do recognize the R.O.C. cannot trade with the P.R.C.; and, given the size of the China market, this is an unacceptable price for most countries to pay. Beijing would no doubt use this trump card to punish those who would dare to recognize an independent state of Taiwan, just as it does now.

NOTES

1. John F. Burns, "Quemoy (Remember?) Bristles with Readiness," *New York Times* (April 5, 1986), p. 2.

2. Susan Yu, "Lien Vows Defense Outposts to Stay," *The Free China Journal* (November 4, 1994), p. 1.

3. Edwin A. Winckler, "Cultural Policy on Postwar Taiwan," in Stevan Harrell and Huang Chun-chieh, eds., *Cultural Change in Postwar Taiwan* (Boulder, CO: Westview Press, 1994), p. 22.

4. *Ibid.,* p. 29.

5. Thomas B. Gold, "Civil Society and Taiwan's Quest for Identity," in Harrell and Chun-chieh, eds., *Cultural Change in Postwar Taiwan* (Boulder, CO: Westview, 1994), p. 60.

6. Thomas A. Shaw, "Are the Taiwanese Becoming More Individualistic as They Become More Modern?" Taiwan Studies Workshop, *Fairbank Center Working Papers*, No. 7 (August 1994), pp. 1–25.

7. David Chen, "From Presidential Hopeful, Frank Words on Democracy," *The Free China Journal* (September 9, 1994), p. 6.

8. "Premier Hau Bristling about Crime in Taiwan," *The Free China Journal* (September 13, 1990), p. 1.

9. Winckler, p. 41.

10. Lee Fan-fang, "Ghosts' Arrival Bad for Business," *The Free China Journal* (August 7, 1992), p. 4.

11. Marc J. Cohen, *Taiwan at the Crossroads* (Washington, D.C.: Asian Resource Center, 1988), pp. 186–190. For further detail, see his chapter on "Religion and Religious Freedom," pp. 185–215. Also, Gold, p. 53.

12. See *The Free China Review*, Vol. 44, No. 9 (September 1994), which has a series of articles on educational reform, pp. 1–37.

13. Cohen, p. 107.

14. *Ibid,* p. 108. For more on women, see his entire chapter on "Women and Indigenous People," pp. 106–126.

15. James A. Robinson, "The Value of Taiwan's Experience," *The Free China Journal* (November 6, 1992), p. 7.

16. Gold, pp. 50, 53. Under martial law, strikes were prohibited.

17. Robert P. Weller, "Environmental Protest in Taiwan: A Preliminary Sketch," Taiwan Studies Workshop, *Fairbank Center Working Papers*, No. 2 (1993), pp. 1, 4.

18. Susan Yu, "Legislature Acts to Protect Lawmakers from Recall Movements," *The Free China Journal* (October 14, 1994), p. 2.

19. Dianna Lin, "Alien Workers Face Problems in New Life," *The Free China Journal* (September 9, 1994), pp. 7–8.

20. The maps of China in Taiwan's schools still include not just Taiwan and all of China proper but also Tibet, Inner Mongolia, and even Outer Mongolia.

21. Lee Changkuei, "High-Speed Social Dynamics," *The Free China Review* (Taipei), Vol. 39, No. 10 (October 1989), p. 6.

22. Yu-ming Shaw, "Problems and Prospects of the Democratization of the Republic of China on Taiwan," Taiwan Studies Workshop, *Fairbank Center Working Papers*, Harvard University, No. 2 (October 1993), pp. 1–2.

23. For more detail on television programming, see Minh-ha Nguyen, "Telecommunications: Business Is Beaming," *The Free China Review* (September 1994), pp. 54–59.

24. Chin-chuan Lee, "Sparking a Fire: The Press and the Ferment of Democratic Change in Taiwan," in Chin-Chuan Lee, ed., *China's Media, Media China* (Boulder, CO: Westview Press, 1994), pp. 188–192.

25. From 1950 to 1986, military courts tried more than 10,000 cases involving civilians. These were in violation of the Constitution's provision (Article 9) that prohibited civilians from being tried in a military court. Hung-mao Tien, *The Great Transition: Political and Social Change in the Republic of China* (Palo Alto, CA: Hoover Institution, Stanford University, 1989), p. 111.

26. The Kaohsiung rally, which was followed by street confrontations between the demonstrators and police, is an instance of KMT repression of *dangwai* activities, which were seen as a challenge to the KMT's absolute power. The KMT interpreted the Kaohsiung Incident "as an illegal challenge to public security." For this reason, those arrested were given only semi-open hearings in a *military,* not civil, tribunal; and torture may have been used to extract confessions from the defendants. *Ibid.,* p. 97.

27. In recent years, however, Taiwan has had to cope with the effect of a growing disparity in income distribution. By 1994, the wealthiest 20 percent of the population possessed 54 percent of the total wealth of Taiwan. See Philip Liu, "Discontent with a Growing Wealth Gap," *The Free China Review* (June 1994), pp. 36–41.

28. E.g., the DPP's demand for more flexible treatment of relations with the P.R.C.; ecology and environmental issues; including DPP in discussions; and permitting greater freedom of the press. By the time of the 1996 elections, the dominant wing of the KMT had even co-opted the DPP's platform for a more independent Taiwan.

29. Tien, p. 72.

30. Philip Liu, "Revving Up for the GATT Shock," *The Free China Review* (September 1994), pp. 47–53.

31. Prior to this, the head of the KMT, chosen by the KMT itself, was the president of R.O.C.

32. Jiang Ping-lun, "Competition Mixed with Consensus," *The Free China Review* (October 1989), p. 36.

33. Tien, pp. 43, 45 ff.

34. Peter Chen, "Taiwan-made Fighters Go into Active Service," *The Free China Journal"* (December 30, 1994), pp. 1, 2.

35. Perhaps Beijing was wise not to clamor too much; for, just before the end of his term in office, President George Bush authorized the first shipments of military equipment to China since the 1989 Tiananmen military crackdown on the dissidents. This equipment, including radars, torpedos, and aviation electronics, had been kept in storage for $3\frac{1}{2}$ years after it was sold to China. The release of it at the end of 1992 was justified on the grounds that it had become outdated and was of limited use to China. "Arms Shipments to China Cleared," *The Boston Globe* (December 23, 1992), p. 7.

36. As excerpted in *China News Digest,* on the Internet (May 5, 1996).

37. *South China Morning Post* (March 7, 1996), as excerpted in *China News Digest* on the Internet (March 8, 1996).

38. Concerned about the growing tensions with China, the three major political parties in Taiwan agreed to set up a committee to repair the damage to relations. Reuters report, by *China News Digest* on the Internet (February 9, 1996).

39. "NUC's Charter Approval May Hasten Unification," *The Free China Journal* (September 17, 1990), p. 1.

40. "One China, Two Regions," *The Free China Journal* (September 6, 1990), p. 1.

41. Japan Economic Newswire, as excerpted on Internet by *China News Digest* (June 21, 1996).

42. Virginia Sheng, "Lee Restates Offer to Visit Mainland for Talks," *The Free China Journal* (July 12, 1996), p. 1.

43. Willy Wo-lap Lam, "Beijing 'Reconsidering' 'Chinese Common Market,'" *Foreign Broadcasts Information* (FBIS-China-89-043) (March 7, 1989), pp. 58–59.

44. "Lien Chan Proposed Plan to Sign 'Peace Accord' with the Mainland," *China News Digest* (May 6, 1996), as excerpted.

45. Alastair I. Johnston, "Independence through Unification: On the Correct Handling of Contradictions Across the Taiwan Straits," *Contemporary Issues,* No. 2, Fairbank Center for East Asian Research, Harvard University (September 1993), pp. 5–6.

Hong Kong

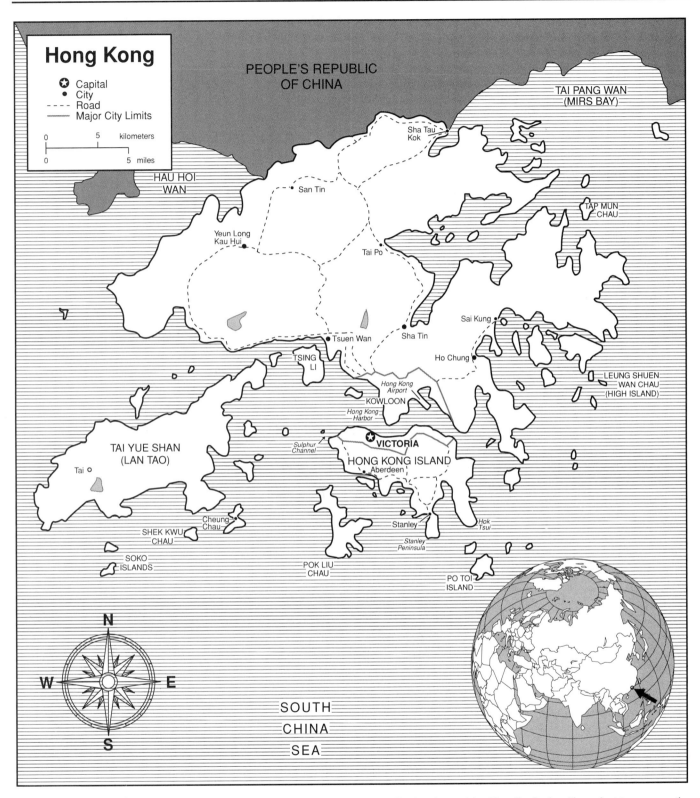

Hong Kong
- ✪ Capital
- • City
- --- Road
- — Major City Limits

0 ——— 5 kilometers
0 ——— 5 miles

PEOPLE'S REPUBLIC
OF CHINA

TAI PANG WAN
(MIRS BAY)

HAU HOI
WAN

Sha Tau
Kok

San Tin

TAP MUN
CHAU

Yeun Long
Kau Hui

Tai Po

Sai Kung

Tsuen Wan

Sha Tin

Ho Chung

TSING
LI

Hong Kong
Airport

LEUNG SHUEN
WAN CHAU
(HIGH ISLAND)

KOWLOON

Hong Kong
Harbor

TAI YUE SHAN
(LAN TAO)

Sulphur
Channel

✪ VICTORIA

HONG KONG ISLAND

Tai

Aberdeen

Cheung
Chau

Stanley

Hok
Tsui

SHEK KWU
CHAU

Stanley
Peninsula

SOKO
ISLANDS

POK LIU
CHAU

PO TOI
ISLAND

N W E S

SOUTH
CHINA
SEA

Hong Kong consists of the island of Hong Kong, adjacent islets, the Kowloon Peninsula, and the New Territories (these last two are on the mainland of China). More than 230 islands make up Hong Kong. Since land is constantly being reclaimed from the sea, the total land area of Hong Kong is continually increasing by small amounts.

Hong Kong

GEOGRAPHY

Area in Square Kilometers (Miles):
1,062 (658) (about twice the size of
New York City)
Capital: Victoria
Climate: subtropical

PEOPLE

Population

Total: 6,300,900
Annual Growth Rate: 0.12%
Rural/Urban Population Ratio: 9/91
Ethnic Makeup: 98% Chinese (mostly
Cantonese); 2% European and
Vietnamese
Major Languages: Cantonese; other
Chinese dialects; English

Health

Life Expectancy at Birth: 77 years
(male); 84 years (female)
Infant Mortality Rate (Ratio): 5.8/1,000
Average Caloric Intake: n/a
Physicians Available (Ratio): 1/1,000

Religions

90% a combination of Buddhism and
Taoism; 10% Christian

Education

Adult Literacy Rate: 77%

HONG KONG'S UNCERTAIN FATE

As July 1, 1997, the date when Great Britain must relinquish its colony of Hong
Kong to the People's Republic of China nears, there are vastly differing
opinions as to what will happen. While the Chinese and the British have signed
an agreement stating that Hong Kong's way of life will remain basically
unchanged after the reestablishment of Chinese sovereignty, some people
doubt whether an enclave of capitalism can continue to thrive under the control
of the People's Republic of China.

Others feel, however, that China will do little to threaten the stability and
prosperity that have marked Hong Kong under British rule, since the P.R.C.
has so much to gain, both politically and economically, from a smooth transfer
of power. Whatever the outcome, Hong Kong is clearly in the midst of a major
period of transition.

COMMUNICATION

Telephones: 3,000,000
Newspapers: 69

TRANSPORTATION

Highways—Kilometers (Miles): 1,100
(683)
Railroads—Kilometers (Miles): 35 (22)
Usable Airfields: 3

GOVERNMENT

Type: colonial (British Crown colony)
Independence Date: Chinese sovereignty

to be reestablished on July 1, 1997
Head of State/Government: Queen
Elizabeth II; Governor Christopher
Patten (appointed by Great Britain), to
be replaced by Tung Chee-hwa
Political Parties: United Democrats of
Hong Kong; Liberal Democratic
Federation; Hong Kong Democratic
Federation; Association for Democracy
and People's Livelihood; Progressive
Hong Kong Society
Suffrage: residents over age 21 who have
lived in Hong Kong for at least 7 years

MILITARY

Number of Armed Forces: Until July 1,
1997, foreign relations and defense the
responsibility of British Armed Forces,
12,000 of whom are stationed in Hong
Kong. After July 1, China will assume
responsibility for Hong Kong's foreign
policy and defense.
*Military Expenditures (% of Central
Government Expenditures):* 0.2%
Current Hostilities: none

ECONOMY

Currency ($ U.S. Equivalent): 7.74
Hong Kong dollars = $1
Per Capita Income/GDP:
$24,530/$136.1 billion
Inflation Rate: 8.5%
Natural Resources: none
Agriculture: vegetables; livestock
(cattle, pigs, poultry); fish
Industry: light—textiles and clothing;
electronics; clocks and watches; toys;
plastic products; metalware; footwear;
heavy—shipbuilding and ship
repairing; aircraft engineering

FOREIGN TRADE

Exports: $168.7 billion
Imports: $160 billion

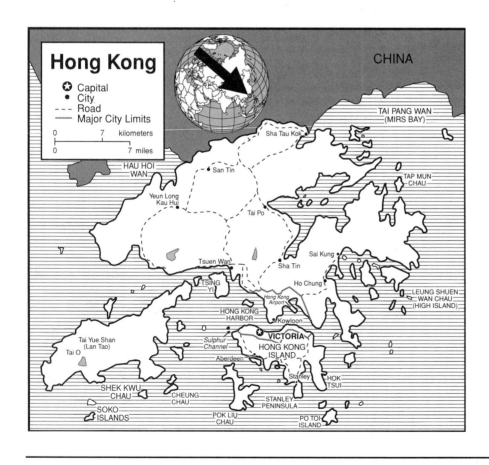

Hong Kong

From British Colony to China's Special Administrative Region

Hong Kong, the "fragrant harbor" situated on the southeastern edge of China, has been characterized as a "capitalist paradise," the "pearl of the Orient," a "borrowed place living on borrowed time," and a "den of iniquity." Under a British colonial administration committed to a laissez faire economy, but in the context of a highly structured and tightly controlled political system, Hong Kong's dynamic and vibrant people have shaped the colony into one of the world's great success stories. The history of Hong Kong's formation and development, its achievements, and the complex problems that it must address today as it makes the transition to becoming integrated under the government of the People's Republic of China in 1997 affect how Beijing, London, and the Hong Kong people themselves view its future. Hong Kong's "borrowed time" is at an end.

HISTORY

In the 1830s, the British sale of opium to China was creating a nation of drug addicts. Alarmed by this development, the Chinese imperial government banned opium; but private British "country traders," sailing armed clipper ships, continued to sell opium to the Chinese by smuggling it (with the help of Chinese pirates) up the coast and rivers. In an effort to enforce the ban, the Chinese imperial commissioner, Lin Zexu, detained the British in their warehouses in Canton and forced them to surrender their opium. Eventually Imperial Commissioner Lin took the more than 21,000 chests of opium that he had seized and destroyed them in public. [1]

The British, desperate to establish outposts for trade with an unwilling China, used this siege of British warehouses as an excuse to declare war on the Chinese. Later called the Opium War (1839–1842), the conflict ended with China's defeat and the Treaty of Nanking.

All would no doubt agree that, had Great Britain waged a war in order to sell a drug banned by the Chinese government, an additive and debilitating drug that destroyed people's lives, it would be disgraceful. But the attack on the British selling of opium only provided the excuse the British government needed to get what it really wanted: to gain free trade with a

THE SECOND ANGLO/CHINESE CONVENTION CEDES THE KOWLOON PENINSULA TO THE BRITISH

The second Anglo/Chinese Convention, signed in 1860, was the result of a string of incidents and hostilities among the Chinese, the British, and the French. Although the French were involved in the outbreak of war, they were not included in the treaty that resulted from conflict.

The catalyst for the war was that, during a truce, the Chinese seized the chief British negotiator and executed 20 of his men. In reprisal, the English destroyed nearly 200 buildings of the emperor's summer palace and forced the new treaty on the Chinese. This called for increased payments ("indemnities") by the Chinese to the English for war-inflicted damages as well as the cession of Kowloon Peninsula to the British.

New York Public Library

government that restricted foreign trade to one port—Canton (Guangzhou)—and to assert Great Britain's diplomatic and judicial equality with a country that considered itself the "Central Kingdom," superior to all other countries. At the political level, the Chinese imperial government's demand that all "barbarians," including the British, kowtow to the Chinese emperor, incensed the British and gave them further cause to set the record straight.

More pragmatically, the British treasury was being drained of its gold and silver species, for the British purchased large quantities of Chinese porcelain, silk, tea, and spices, while the Chinese, smug in their belief that their cultural and moral superiority was sufficient to withstand any military challenge from a "barbarian" country, refused to purchase goods being manufactured during the Industrial Revolution going on in Great Britain. An amusing example of the thought process involved in "Sinocentrism" (the Chinese belief that China was the center of the world, hence superior to all other countries) was Imperial Commissioner Lin's letter to Queen Victoria. Here he noted "Britain's dependence on Chinese rhubarb, without which the English would die of constipation."[2]

China's Sinocentric world view blinded its government to the growing power of the West and resulted in China's losing the opportunity to benefit from the Industrial Revolution at an early stage. The Opium War turned out to be only the first step in a century of humiliation for China—but the step that led to a British foothold on the edge of China.

As for the British public, it did not generally understand that the Chinese might have a problem with addiction, and it largely ignored moral considerations. Opium was available for self-medication in Great Britain, "was even administered by working mothers as a tranquilliser for their infants," and was not considered toxic by the British medical community at that time.[3]

The Treaty of Nanking gave the British the right to trade with the Chinese from five Chinese ports; and Hong Kong, a tiny island off the southern coast of China, was ceded to them "in perpetuity." The island's total population of Chinese villagers and people living on boats numbered fewer than 6,000. From that point onward, Hong Kong became the primary magnet for Chinese immigrants fleeing the chaotic conditions of the mainland in favor of the relatively peaceful environment of Hong Kong under British rule.

In 1860, again as a result of a British victory in battle, the Chinese ceded to the British "in perpetuity" Cutter Island and a small (3½ square miles) but significant piece of land facing the island of Hong Kong: Kowloon Peninsula. Just a few minutes by ferry (and, since the 1970s, by tunnel) from Hong Kong Island, it became an important part of the residential, commercial, and business sector of Hong Kong. The New Territories, the third and largest part (89 percent of the total area) of what is now known as "Hong Kong," were not granted "in perpetuity" but were merely leased to the British

for 99 years, under the second Anglo–Chinese Convention of Peking in 1898. The New Territories, which are an extension of the Chinese mainland, comprise the major agricultural area supporting Hong Kong.

The distinction between those areas that became a British colony (Hong Kong Island and Kowloon) and the area merely "leased" for 99 years (the New Territories) is crucial to understanding why by the 1980s the British had to negotiate with the Chinese about the future of "Hong Kong"; for although colonies are theoretically colonies "in perpetuity," the New Territories were merely leased and would automatically revert to Chinese sovereignty in 1997. Without this large agricultural area, the rest of Hong Kong could not survive. The leased territories have, moreover, been tightly integrated into the life and business of Hong Kong Island and Kowloon.

With the exception of the Japanese occupation (1942–1945) during World War II, Hong Kong was, then, administered as a British Crown colony since the nineteenth century. After the defeat of Japan in 1945, however, Great Britain almost did not regain control over Hong Kong because of the United States, which insisted that it had not fought World War II in order to return colonies to its allies.

At the end of the civil war that raged in China from 1945 to 1949, the Communists' Red Army stopped its advance just short of Hong Kong. Beijing never offered an official explanation. Perhaps it did not want to get into a war with Great Britain (even though the Red Army probably would have won it); or perhaps the Communists thought that Hong Kong would be of more value to it if left in British hands. Indeed, at no time did the Chinese Communists attempt to force Great Britain out of Hong Kong, even when Sino-British relations were greatly strained, as during China's Cultural Revolution.[4]

This did not mean that Beijing accepted the legitimacy of British rule. It did not. After coming to power on the mainland in 1949, the Chinese Communist Party held that Hong Kong was a part of China stolen by British imperialists and that it was merely "occupied" by Great Britain. The People's Republic of China insisted that Hong Kong *not* be treated like other colonies; for the process of decolonization has in practice meant sovereignty and freedom for a former colony's people.[5]

China was not about to allow Hong Kong to become independent. After the P.R.C. gained the China seat in the United Nations in 1971, it protested Hong Kong and Macao (a Portuguese colony) being listed as colonies by the General Assembly's Special Committee on Colonialism. In a letter to the Committee, Beijing insisted they were merely

part of Chinese territory occupied by the British and Portuguese authorities. The settlement of the questions of Hong Kong and Macao is entirely within China's sovereign right and does not at all fall under the ordinary category of colonial territories. Consequently they should not be included in the list

Hong Kong's economy is supported by a hard-working and dynamic population. The people at this outdoor market typify the intense entrepreneurial tendency of Hong Kong's citizens.

of colonial territories covered by the declaration on the granting of independence to colonial countries and peoples. . . . The United Nations has no right to discuss these questions.[6]

The Chinese Communists found it ideologically uncomfortable to proclaim China's sovereign rights and spout Communist principles while at the same time tolerating the continued existence of a capitalist and British-controlled Hong Kong on its very borders. China could have acquired control within 24 hours simply by shutting off Hong Kong's water supply from the mainland. But China profited from the British presence there and, except for occasional flareups, did little to challenge it.

Declaring independence was not, in any event, the option for Hong Kong's colonial subjects that it was for other colonies, for it was clear to them that overthrowing British colonial rule would have led directly to the reimposition of China's control. And, although there is for the Hong Kong Chinese a certain amount of cultural identity as Chinese, after 1949 few wanted to fall under the rule of China's Communist Party government. Furthermore, Beijing and London as a rule did not interfere in Hong Kong's affairs, leaving these in the capable hands of the colonial government. Although the colonial government reported to the British Parliament, in practice it was left to handle its own affairs. In 1958, London gave it even greater power by ceding financial authority in Hong

Kong to its colonial government. On the other hand, the colonial government did not in turn cede any significant political power to its colonial subjects.[7]

In the meantime, the Hong Kong and foreign business communities grew increasingly concerned over the expiration of the British lease on the New Territories in 1997. The problem was that all land in the New Territories was *leased* to businesses or individuals. However, since the New Territories were themselves originally leased from the Chinese for only 99 years, the British colonial government could not grant any land lease that expired after the lease on the New Territories expired. Thus, all land leases—regardless of which year they were granted—would expire 3 days in advance of the expiration of the main lease on the New Territories on July 1, 1997. Thus, as 1997 grew closer and closer, the British colonial government had to grant shorter and shorter leases. Investors found buying leases increasingly unattractive; therefore, by 1980, the British colonial government felt that it had to do something to calm investors.[8]

Thus it was the British, not the Chinese, who took the initiative to press for an agreement on the future status of the colony as well as the rights of its people. Everyone recognized the inability of Hong Kong Island and Kowloon to survive on their own because of their dependence upon the leased New Territories for food, as well as because of the integrated nature of the economies of the colonial and leased parts of Hong Kong. Everyone (everyone, that is, except for British Prime Minister Margaret Thatcher) also knew that Hong Kong was militarily indefensible by the British, and that the Chinese were unlikely to permit the continuation of British administrative rule over Hong Kong after it was returned to Chinese sovereignty.[9] So a series of formal Sino–British negotiations over the future of Hong Kong began. By 1984, the two sides had reached an agreement to restore all three parts of Hong Kong to China on July 1, 1997.

The Negotiations over the Status of Hong Kong

Negotiations between the People's Republic of China and Great Britain over the future status of Hong Kong got off to a rocky start. Prime Minister Thatcher set a contentious tone for the talks when she claimed, after meeting with Chinese leaders in Beijing, that the three nineteenth-century treaties that gave Great Britain control of Hong Kong were valid according to international law and that China, like other nations, had an obligation to honor its treaty commitments. Thatcher's remarks infuriated China's leaders, since they considered the treaties to be the result of an imperialist aggression that had no legitimacy in the contemporary world.

While both sides realized that Chinese sovereignty over Hong Kong would be reestablished in 1997 when the New Territories lease expired, they disagreed profoundly on what such sovereignty would mean in practice. The British claimed that they had a "moral commitment" to the people of Hong Kong to maintain the stability and prosperity of the colony.

Both the British and the Hong Kong population hoped that Chinese sovereignty over Hong Kong might be more symbolic than substantive and that some arrangement could be worked out that would allow for continuing British participation in the administration of the area. The Chinese vehemently rejected what they termed "alien rule in Chinese territory" after 1997. In the end, the Chinese insisted on sovereignty and ignored the possibly greater economic value of a Hong Kong *not* under its administrative power.[10]

After several months of stalemate, both sides compromised enough to allow progress to be made in the talks. Great Britain agreed to end its administration of Hong Kong in 1997, while China agreed to work out a detailed and binding arrangement for how Hong Kong would be governed under Chinese sovereignty. Negotiations speeded up after China declared that, if no agreement was reached by mid-1984, it would cease negotiations and unilaterally announce its plans for Hong Kong's future. It was a threat, to be sure, but one that the British could not ignore, as a breakdown of the talks would seriously harm their relations with China and jeopardize the stability of Hong Kong.

The people of Hong Kong did not formally participate in the negotiations over the colony's fate. Both the British and the Chinese consulted various interested parties in the colony about their views on 1997 and beyond, but they simply ignored many of their viewpoints. China was particularly adamant that the people of Hong Kong were Chinese and that the government in Beijing represented *all Chinese* in talks with the British.

In September 1984, Great Britain and the People's Republic of China initialed the Joint Declaration on the Question of Hong Kong. The Joint Declaration stated that, as of July 1, 1997, Hong Kong would become a Special Administrative Region (SAR) of the People's Republic of China. The Sino–British Joint Liaison Group was created to oversee the transition to Chinese rule. Any changes in Hong Kong's laws made during the transition period, if they were expected to continue after 1997, had to receive final approval from the Joint Liaison Group. If there were disagreement within the Joint Liaison Group between the British and Chinese, they had to talk until they reach agreement. This procedure gave China veto power over any proposed changes in Hong Kong's governance and laws proposed before 1997,[11] and China eventually used it to veto changes in the laws of which it did not approve.

The Basic Law

The Basic Law is the crucial document that translates the *spirit* of the Sino–British Joint Declaration into a legal code. It will function as a "mini-constitution" for the governance of Hong Kong to be as an SAR as of July 1, 1997. The British had no role in formulating it, as the Chinese considered it an internal, sovereign matter. China established a Basic Law Drafting Committee in 1985 under the direction of the National People's Congress (NPC). This Committee had 59

The refugees who came to Hong Kong and settled in squatter communities such as the one shown above voluntarily subjected themselves to foreign (British) rule.

members, 36 from the mainland, 23 from Hong Kong. Of the latter, almost all were "prominent figures belonging to high and high-middle strata," with Hong Kong's economic elites at its core. In addition, China established a Consultative Committee in Hong Kong of 180 members. The purpose of the Consultative Committee was to function as a nonofficial representative organ of the people of Hong Kong from all walks of life—an organ that would channel their viewpoints to the Basic Law Drafting Committee. By so including Hong Kong's elite and a Hong Kong–wide civic representative organ in consultations about the Basic Law, China hoped to provide political legitimacy to the Basic Law.[12] Once the Basic Law was approved in April 1990 by China's NPC, the final draft was promulgated.

The Basic Law gives the Hong Kong SAR a high degree of autonomy after 1997, except in matters of foreign policy and defense, which will be under the direct control of Beijing. The SAR government will be made up of local inhabitants and a chief executive "elected by a broadly representative Election Committee in accordance with [the Basic] Law and appointed

by the Central People's Government" (that is, the Standing Committee of the National People's Congress).[13] The 800 members of the Election Committee will be drawn from the industrial, commercial, and financial sectors (200); the professions (200); labor, social-services, religious, and other sectors (200); and members of the Legislative Council and other representative organs (200).[14] The chief executive will appoint key officials of the SAR (although they likewise must be approved by Beijing).

In the end, provisions were made to allow some British and other foreign nationals to serve in the administration of the SAR, if the local government chose to do so. An elected legislature would be responsible for making the laws of the SAR.[15] The maintenance of law and order would be the responsibility of the local authorities, but China retained the right to station military forces in the SAR. The judicial and legal system in Hong Kong was to remain basically unchanged, but China's NPC reserved the right to approve of all new laws written between 1990 and 1997.[16]

The Basic Law is critical to understanding China's anger in 1992 when Governor Christopher Patten proceeded to push for democratic reforms in Hong Kong without Beijing's agreement—particularly since his predecessor, Governor David Wilson, always did consult Beijing and never pushed too hard. After making numerous threats to tear up the Basic Law, Beijing simply stated in 1994 that it would nullify any efforts by the British to promote political liberalization that would go beyond the provisions in the Basic Law. Many observers feel, however, that it is Hong Kong's commercial value, not the Basic Law, that will protect it from a heavy-handed approach by the Chinese government.

In essence, the Joint Declaration and Basic Law bring Hong Kong under China's rule but allow it some measure of independence, such as continuing to control its own finances, budgeting, and revenue. In doing so, they commit China to preserving Hong Kong's "capitalist system and lifestyle" for 50 years. In other words, China has promised not to impose the Communist political, legal, social, or economic system on Hong Kong and to allow Hong Kong to remain a free port, with its own internationally convertible currency, over which China will not exercise authority. The free flow of capital will still be allowed. In addition, Hong Kong will be able to enter into economic and cultural agreements with other nations, participate in relevant international organizations, and issue its own travel documents to citizens and visitors. The Basic Law states that all Hong Kong residents shall have freedom of speech, press, publication, association, assembly, procession, and demonstration, as well as the right to form and join trade unions and to strike. Freedom of religion, marriage, choice of occupation, and the right to social welfare are also protected by law.[17]

However, some residents of Hong Kong fear the Basic Law may not actually protect the autonomy of Hong Kong as an SAR within China. When China promulgated the Basic Law in the spring of 1990, Hong Kong residents by the thousands took to the streets in protest, burning their copies of the Basic Law. As one quip went, "Basic Law for the poor; immigration law for the rich!" Hong Kong's population tends to see the British side as having repeatedly capitulated to China's opposition to plans for political reform in Hong Kong before 1997 and believe that the British have traded off Hong Kong's interests in favor of their own interests in further trade and investment in China.

THE SOCIETY AND ITS PEOPLE

Immigrant Population

In 1842 Hong Kong had a mere 6,000 inhabitants. Today it has reached about 5.6 million people. What makes this population distinctive is its predominantly immigrant composition. Waves of immigrants have flooded Hong Kong since 1842. Even today, barely half of Hong Kong's population were actually born in Hong Kong. This has been a critical factor in the political development of this colony, for instead of a foreign government imposing its rule on submissive

(United Nations photo/A. Jongen)
Chinese cultural values are still very strong in modern-day Hong Kong. Here, women in traditional Chinese dress take a work break.

natives, the situation has been just the reverse. Chinese people have voluntarily emigrated to Hong Kong, even risking their lives to do so, to subject themselves to alien British colonial rule.

In recent history, the largest influxes of immigrants came as a result of the civil war in China (1945–1949), when 750,000 fled to Hong Kong; as a result of the "3 bad years" (1959–1962) following the economic disaster of China's Great Leap Forward policy; and from 1966 to 1976, when more than 500,000 came to escape the societal turmoil generated by the Great Proletarian Cultural Revolution. After the Vietnam War ended in 1975, Hong Kong also received thousands of refugees from Vietnam as that country undertook a policy of expelling many of its ethnic-Chinese citizens. Many Chinese from Vietnam have risked their lives on small boats at sea to attain refugee status in Hong Kong. China's improving economic and political conditions beginning in the 1980s have, however, greatly stemmed the flow of immigrants from the mainland. Nevertheless, the absorption of refugees into Hong Kong's economy and society remains one of the colony's biggest problems, in spite of the British tightening of both legal and illegal immigration. The injection of another distinct group (the Chinese from Vietnam) has also generated tension and conflict among the Hong Kong population.

Because of a severe housing shortage and strains on the provision of social services, the British colonial government first announced that it would confine all new refugees in camps and prohibit them from outside employment. It then adopted a policy of sending back almost all refugees who

(United Nations photo/M. Hayward)

The refugees who have flocked to Hong Kong during the last few years have often ended up living in squatter settlements and on boats such as these in Aberdeen Harbor.

were caught before they reached Hong Kong Island and were unable to prove that they had relatives in Hong Kong to care for them. By 1988, the British had reached an agreement with Vietnam's government to return some of those Chinese immigrants from Vietnam who were believed to be economic rather than political refugees. The first few attempts at this reportedly "voluntary" repatriation raised such an international furor that the British were unable to systematize a policy meant to discourage further illegal immigration. By the mid-1990s, however, the improvement of economic and political conditions in Vietnam made it easier for the British colonial government once again to repatriate Vietnamese refugees.[18] In the meantime, the economy of southern China was expanding so rapidly that the pressure of immigrants from China dropped to a trickle.

Language
Ninety-eight percent of Hong Kong's people are Chinese, with the bulk of the other 2 percent being European and Vietnamese. Although a profusion of Chinese dialects is spoken, the two official languages—English and the Can-

tonese dialect of Chinese—are still dominant. Since the Chinese written language is in ideographs and is written fairly much the same regardless of how it is pronounced in a dialect, all literate Hong Kong Chinese are able to read Chinese newspapers.

There is concern in Hong Kong, however, that, after July 1, 1997, the Beijing government will require Mandarin to be the language of instruction in the schools and the Mandarin dialect to be the official dialect—as it is in the rest of China. Whether the "one country, two systems" that Beijing guaranteed to Hong Kong for the next 50 years will include allowing its civil servants to speak their own dialects is still unresolved. In the period before the changeover, both the workforce and the students were intensively studying Mandarin.

Living Conditions
Hong Kong has a large and growing middle class, but its people suffer from extremes of wealth and poverty. The contrast in housing that dots the landscape of the colony dramatically illustrates its great inequalities of wealth. The rich live in luxurious air-conditioned apartments and houses

on some of the world's most expensive real estate. They are taken care of by cooks, maids, gardeners, and chauffeurs. They enjoy a social life that mixes such Chinese pleasures as mahjong, banqueting, and participation in traditional Chinese and religious rituals and festivals with British practices of cricket, horseracing, rugby, social clubs, and athletic clubs for swimming and croquet. By contrast, the vast majority of Hong Kong's people live in crowded high-rise apartment buildings, with several poor families sometimes occupying one apartment consisting of a few small rooms and having inadequate sanitation facilities. Since the mid-1950s, the government has built extensive low-rent public housing, which accommodates about half of the population.[19] These government-subsidized housing projects easily become run-down and are often plagued by crime. But without them, a not-insignificant percentage of the new immigrant population might have continued to live in squalor in squatter villages, with no running water, sanitation, or electricity.

The tensions that might be expected to result from the enormous gap between rich and poor have been substantially diminished by the government's commitment to social-welfare programs, including public housing, social services, and education. Hong Kong's rapid post–World War II economic growth, which has improved the lives of almost all Hong Kong residents, as well as the resulting opportunities for economic and social mobility, have also allayed tensions.

A poor, unskilled peasant who fled across China's border to Hong Kong, to an urban life of grinding poverty—but opportunity—could usually be rewarded before he died by a government-subsidized apartment, and his grandchildren would likely graduate from high school and move on to white-collar jobs. The reasons why most Hong Kong Chinese wanted to maintain the status quo as a British Crown colony, and refugees sought to go to Hong Kong in the first place, were the same: freedom of choice, the chance to live better, freedom of speech, and freedom to make money.[20]

Some of these opportunities may be threatened by an uncertain political future and a change from an economy of hundreds of thousands of entrepreneurs to one dominated by large corporations in a number of sectors. Furthermore, a class of "the super rich addicted to conspicuous consumption and crass materialism" has led to a growing class consciousness.[21]

A good example of this is that some Hong Kong business tycoons, who have seemingly run out of other ways to spend their money, ask for restaurants to decorate their food with gold leaf; others spend several hundred thousand U.S. dollars just to buy a lucky number on their car license plate. Another is a successful Hong Kong businessman who, confident of the future, has built a multimillion-dollar mansion in Beijing that features 1,000 brass dragons on the ceilings, decorated with 3 pounds of gold leaf (at more than $400 per gram).[22]

Chinese cultural values of diligence, willingness to sacrifice for the future, commitment to family, and respect for

education have contributed to the success of Hong Kong's inhabitants. What is more, the colonial government has provided 9 years of compulsory and free education for children through age 15, helping to reinforce these cultural values. Hong Kong's people continue to view education as the key to material success. But their children are educated in schools modeled on a now

out-of-date British grammar school, complete with uniforms, lists of rules, and a packed academic timetable. Many of the most prestigious schools are Christian foundations; their medium of instruction is English and the pupils are still given English Christian names by their teachers . . . .[23]

Since access to higher levels of education is strictly limited, students work hard to gain access to an upper middle school and then to the even fewer places available in Hong Kong's universities. An alternative that many of Hong Kong's brightest students take is to go abroad for college education. Universities in the West have benefited from the presence of these highly motivated and achievement-oriented students.

Until recent years, then, the allure of Hong Kong was its combination of economic success with enlightened social-welfare policies. These were possible not just because of the British colonial government's commitment to them but also because the flourishing Hong Kong economy provided the resources for them. Hong Kong has had a larger percentage of the gross domestic product (GDP) available for social welfare than most places, for two reasons. First, it has had a low defense budget to support its approximately 12,000 British troops (including some of the famous Gurkha Rifles) stationed in the colony for external defense (only 0.4 percent of the GDP, or 4.2 percent of the total budget available). Second, the government was also able to take in substantial revenues (18.3 percent of GDP) through the sale of land leases.[24]

The real question is whether Beijing, when it starts exercising oversight over the preparation of Hong Kong's budget,[25] will continue to allocate as high an amount in per capita terms to the support of a social-welfare system in Hong Kong as the colonial government has done. Beijing may choose either to scale down the budgetary allocation of funds to Hong Kong's welfare sector after 1997, or to let what will become the Hong Kong Special Administrative Region continue to have the same budgetary resources in the 50 years of the "one country, two systems" plan. Beijing is concerned that, in the countdown to the handover of Hong Kong, the colonial administration dramatically increased welfare spending—65 percent in a mere 5 years. Governor Christopher Patten denounced Beijing for challenging how much is spent on social-welfare programs and stated that such questions are the prerogative of Hong Kong's citizens to decide after 1997.[26] From Beijing's perspective, however, such dramatically increased spending suggests that the British were trying to pump all of Hong

Kong's assets into its people and economy so that there would be nothing left for Beijing to take out and use elsewhere in China; and that, in doing so, they were setting a pattern and standard that Hong Kong as an SAR will be able to use to justify continuing expenditures in the next 50 years of protected autonomy in the same way.

In the educational sector, there is a similar sort of concern about the fate of Hong Kong's first-rate public universities. Professors have been paid very high salaries even by Western standards, but all professors are considered government "civil servants." As such, Beijing has proposed that their salaries be scaled back gradually until they are no higher than those in China's own universities. Again, the question is whether this violates the principle of China's 50-year guarantee of "one country, two systems."

Finally, as for "law and order," Hong Kong will continue to have its own public security forces. The British colonial military forces of about 12,000 will be replaced by a smaller Chinese People's Liberation Army (PLA) force of about 9,000. Most of these will probably be stationed just outside the Hong Kong border for the purpose of preventing illegal entry into Hong Kong, but some will also be stationed in the colony, to serve as a deterrent to social unrest and mass demonstrations against the Chinese government.

China has done much to ensure that the PLA troops do not become a source of tension. Quite the contrary, China wants them to be a positive force, a vanguard in developing a positive view of what Chinese control of Hong Kong will mean. As part of their "charm offensive," the soldiers must be tall (at least 5 feet 10 inches); have "regular features" (i.e., be attractive); be well read (with all officers having college training and all ordinary soldiers having a high school education); know the Basic Law; and speak both the local dialect of Cantonese and simple English.[27]

In short, the PLA, which does not have these requirements for its regular soldiers and officers, is sending an elite corps of soldiers to Hong Kong. No doubt the hope is that a well-educated military will be less likely to provoke problems with Hong Kong residents through misunderstandings. In fact, PLA troops will even be permitted to date and marry local Hong Kong women! Fears remain in Hong Kong that this public relations effort will count for little if or when PLA soldiers, whose monthly wages are the equivalent of lunch money for many people in Hong Kong, resort to shady business activities to redress the disparity in income. Nevertheless, the PLA is going to take charge of Hong Kong and will have the military installations of the British forces at its disposal.[28] In the meantime, British naval ships in Hong Kong are up for sale.

Social Problems

Hong Kong does suffer from significant problems, including serious environmental pollution, ignored in the pursuit of profits, and an appallingly high crime rate. Violent crime continues to rise, as does white-collar crime, which is spreading into the highest levels of government. For more than a decade, ordinary criminality has been steadily augmented by crime under the control of competing Chinese criminal societies called *triads*. Organized crime has moved beyond extortion from massage parlors, bars, restaurants, and clubs, illegal gambling, smuggling, the sale of handguns, prostitution, and drugs, to take advantage of a fluctuating real estate market. Opium, largely controlled by the triads, continues to be used widely by the Chinese. As a commentator once put it,

> Opium trails still lead to Hong Kong . . . and all our narcotic squads and all the Queen's men only serve to make the drug more costly and the profits more worthwhile. It comes in aeroplanes and fishing junks, in hollow pipes and bamboo poles and false decks and refrigerators and pickle jars and tooth paste tubes, in shoes and ships and sealing wax. And even cabbages.[29]

Today, unfortunately, Hong Kong is still one of the world's greatest entrepôts for drugs. This is in no small part because social and economic liberalization on the mainland has diminished the ability of the P.R.C.'s police to control the purchase and sale of drugs. As a result, the number of drug addicts in China is skyrocketing. Although the Hong Kong drug squad and the P.R.C.'s drug squad cooperate, China is now cooperating less than before. The reason is the lack of mutuality: When Hong Kong drug investigators have asked the Chinese to find and turn over certain individuals dealing in drugs, the Chinese have expended significant resources to find the criminals and then turned them over to the Hong Kong authorities. But when the Chinese have asked the Hong Kong drug authorities to do the same, they have gone so far as to arrest the suspects but have refused to turn them over to the P.R.C. public-security office. The reason? There is a fairly strong chance that a person convicted on charges of selling drugs in China will be executed, but capital punishment is illegal in Hong Kong, and is considered a derogation of human rights. It is still unclear what will happen to the prohibition of capital punishment in Hong Kong after 1997. Certainly, however, the drug enforcement agencies in Hong Kong and the mainland will work together more closely.[30]

Triad influence has always been vast in the areas of real estate, drugs, prostitution, and gambling, and triad gangs are often hired by corporations to deal with debtors and others. Now triad influence is expanding into unexpected areas. As an example, in 1992, when the then–new British governor, Christopher Patten, upset Beijing by his proposals for further democratization of Hong Kong before 1997, the Chinese Communist regime (by way of its estimated 60,000 supporters working in Hong Kong) recruited triad members to begin harassing those within the Hong Kong government who were supporting Patten's proposals. (And, when Patten's dog disappeared one day in November 1992 during the crisis stage of Sino–British relations, one rumor had it that the Chinese Communists had kidnapped the dog and were going to ransom it in exchange for halting political reform in Hong Kong; the other rumor was that Patten's pet had been flown into China to be served up for breakfast to Deng Xiaoping. Of course, neither rumor was true.)

POLITICS AND POLITICAL STRUCTURE

From a developmental perspective, Hong Kong's record of combining economic growth with political stability has been remarkable. This was not due to any effort on the part of the British to transplant a form of Western-style democracy to Hong Kong. Instead, the colonial Hong Kong government "deliberately created hundreds of consultative committees at various levels of the bureaucracy, through which the views and feelings [of the population] fed back into the administrative decision-making processes." Similarly, the Legislative and Executive Councils have functioned to get Hong Kong's socioeconomic elites to participate in the administration. The administration has also absorbed more than 300 advisory groups and numerous partly elected bodies. These include the Urban Council (for Hong Kong Island and Kowloon), the Rural Committees (for the New Territories), and district boards, all of which have considerable say in managing the affairs under their jurisdiction. By institutionalizing consultation among Chinese administrators and the colonial government, Hong Kong "developed a unique brand of political system which can be characterized as one variant of elitist politics." Political dissent outside the government was, therefore, almost unnecessary.[31]

Under colonial rule, most people in Hong Kong were basically satisfied with the government, which may help explain why only a small portion of the mere 6 percent who were registered as voters actually voted. Hong Kong people seem to have taken little interest in politics, focusing their time and energy on economic pursuits. It is also likely that the limited scope of democracy in Hong Kong was a disincentive for local people to get involved in politics.

The problem for Hong Kong's residents was not that their demands were ignored by the colonial government but, rather, a perception that Hong Kong lacked competent and trustworthy leaders to take charge as the colonial government closed down. In a 1988 survey, 69.9 percent of those queried replied that there were no trustworthy political leaders among the Hong Kong Chinese. Among those who did believe that Hong Kong could produce acceptable leaders, the largest number named David Wilson, at that time the British governor of Hong Kong, as the single most trustworthy leader! Similarly, the Hong Kong Chinese placed extraordinary trust in their British-controlled political institutions: 75 percent endorsed the statement that Hong Kong's political system, while not perfect, was "already the best under existing cir-

cumstances."[32] And this survey, it should be noted, was taken before Governor Patten began introducing political reforms to promote greater democratization in Hong Kong.

The concerns of the people of Hong Kong about the commitment to its welfare by those who hold foreign passports or rights of residence abroad will largely become moot after July 1, 1997. By then, Beijing will have a far greater say. Although Beijing has withdrawn its demand that all governmental civil servants must swear an oath of allegiance to the government of the P.R.C. and that they cannot be holders of British passports, the P.R.C. will no doubt pressure Hong Kong's civil servants to move along these lines.

Hong Kong's government has remained stable in large part because it has functioned well and has been perceived to be trustworthy and capable of addressing the needs of Hong Kong's people. A solid majority of Hong Kong's citizens believe that a strong political authority is indispensable to prosperity and stability and that the formation of multiple political parties could disrupt that strong authority. Thus, what in the West is seen as a critical aspect of democracy is viewed by the people in Hong Kong as suspect: "Political parties conjure up pictures of conflict, sectional interests, political repression and corrupt government."[33] This is, incidentally, a view they share in common with their neighbors in China.

Hong Kong's colonial government was well institutionalized. The British monarch, acting on the advice of the prime minister, would appoint a governor, who presided over the Hong Kong government's colonial administration. Colonial rule in Hong Kong may be characterized as benevolent, consultative, and paternalistic, but it was nonetheless still colonial. Although local people were heavily involved in running the colony and the colonial government interfered very little in the business activities and daily lives of Hong Kong Chinese, the British still controlled the major levers of power and filled the top ranks in the government. As was common in British colonial administration elsewhere, the lower levels of government were filled with the local people.

The concern of many Hong Kong Chinese that democratic political reforms be institutionalized before the Chinese Communists took over in 1997 generated greater political demands. In turn, the ability of the departing colonial government to deal with these increased pressures declined, because it was a "lame duck" government whose ability to make laws or policies that would apply after 1997 was seriously constricted. The people of Hong Kong awoke to the fact that their interests and those of the colonial government, which since the signing of the Joint Declaration in 1982 had become a mere appendage of British policy toward China, were no longer compatible.[34] Indeed, the Joint Declaration and the 1990 Basic Law "basically [froze] the status quo and hence circumscribed the policy-making sphere of the government."[35] Thus, although the people of Hong Kong after 1982 steadily increased pressure on the colonial government to address their own interests, rather than Great Britain's, they did so largely by trying to get the support of the two governments that were really in charge—Beijing and London. The Hong Kong colonial government was perceived to have lost its independence to these more powerful governments.[36]

Executive and Legislative Branches

The Constitution of Hong Kong provided for a separation of powers among the executive, legislative, and judicial branches of government as a check on the arbitrary use of power by any single individual or institution of the government. The separation of powers in Hong Kong's government, however, never did exist within the framework of a representative democracy.

The structure of government after 1997, which is outlined in great detail in Hong Kong's post-1997 Constitution (the Basic Law), will remain similar in some respects to what it was under colonial rule. However, China will also make changes in it to bring it into greater correspondence with its own structure of government, even if in some cases this is merely a matter of changing names. As the government stood in 1997, an Executive Council, composed of several top civil servants and "unofficial" (that is, non-civil servant) members appointed by the governor, functioned as a cabinet of sorts, although sole decision-making authority was vested in the governor. The British governor Chris Patten, whose position ends with the handover, is being replaced by a "chief executive," Tung Chee-hwa, who is by law a resident of Hong Kong. He was chosen by Beijing's hand-picked Preparatory Committee, which was led by China's foreign minister, Qian Qichen.[37]

Furthermore, China has refused to accept any legislation to move Hong Kong toward direct elections of the Executive and Legislative Councils.[38] It has also rejected Governor Patten's expansion of the franchise, first, by lowering the voting age to 18, and second, by extending it to all of Hong Kong's adult population (the electorate would be 3.7 million people) in time for the 1995 legislative elections. This expanded the franchise beyond 1 percent of the population to all adults ages 18 and over.

In March 1996, China's Preparatory Committee of 149 members voted to abolish[39] the Hong Kong Legislature elected under the laws introduced since 1992 by Governor Patten (which were, in the Committee's view, in violation of principles agreed to in the Sino-British Joint Declaration). The members of China's Preparatory Committee are Hong Kong residents (many of them well-known personalities in their field as well as business leaders) chosen by Beijing, 14 elected representatives from the pre–1997 Hong Kong Legislature, and senior Chinese officials. Unfortunately, the people of Hong Kong have not trusted the Preparatory Committee to take their interests into account, in large part because it has conducted much of its business in secrecy. After voting to abolish the Hong Kong Legislature, the Preparatory Commit-

tee selected a 400-member Provisional Legislature to replace it on July 1, 1997, which, in turn, the British say, was not agreed to in the handover treaties.

According to Beijing, the purpose of the Provisional Legislature is to provide a "legal" legislature until new elections take place after Chinese rule begins so that there will be a smooth transition from British to Chinese rule. As under the British, the Provisional Legislature will advise Hong Kong's chief executive on laws. Even before Chinese rule began on July 1, 1997, it had already voted to abolish a number of laws promoting democratic rights that the "illegally" elected 1995 Hong Kong Legislature had promulgated, causing a furor within some segments of the Hong Kong community.[40]

Beijing's position is understandable—during more than 100 years of British colonial rule, the people of Hong Kong had virtually no rights to participate in the electoral process. Then, at the eleventh hour, Great Britain pushed to give them those rights. Were Beijing to allow this increased democratization, it would create a situation in which China would be unable to exercise the same level of control over Hong Kong's people and political system as it does on the mainland. It would therefore mean that one part of the population—those living in Hong Kong—would enjoy rights that the rest of China's population did not have. This situation could easily lead to pressure on Beijing to extend those rights to all Chinese; if Beijing is going to give greater political rights to its people, it would rather do so on its own timetable.

From Beijing's perspective, the colonial government's efforts to develop a representative government in Hong Kong were part of a conspiracy to use democracy to undercut China's rule in Hong Kong after 1997. This concern led Beijing to resist further efforts by the colonial government's efforts since 1992 to carry out political reform in Hong Kong. China's leaders argued that the last-minute political reforms could, in fact, jeopardize Hong Kong's prosperity and stability by permitting special interests and political protest to flourish. They also said that Hong Kong's social problems—narcotics, violence, gangs, prostitution, an underground economy—required that Hong Kong be controlled, not given autonomy. In fact, China has adopted a very status quo approach to Hong Kong. After all, Hong Kong's political system under British colonial control was imposed from the outside. This system worked well and kept Hong Kong stable and prosperous. All Beijing wants to do is to replace the colonial ruler with a leader selected by the Chinese Communist Party ruler.[41]

Until Governor Patten came along in 1992, London seemed implicitly to accept this idea—pushing Beijing to allow further political reforms only to the point where Beijing said no. Those pressing for greater democratization, led by Martin Lee (who heads Hong Kong's most popular party, the Democratic Party),[42] had denounced the British approach as giving precedence to Sino–British relations at the expense of Hong Kong's political liberalization.

Hong Kong's supporters of greater democratization have vowed to press Beijing for more political reforms after July 1, 1997. Thus far, however, signs are not favorable that Beijing will be responsive to such requests. For example, on July 1, 1996, a delegation of Hong Kong democracy advocates flew to Beijing to present a petition with signatures of 60,000 Hong Kong residents to the Chinese National People's Congress to protest its decision to abolish Hong Kong's elected legislature on July 1, 1997; but they were detained at the airport and were forced to return to Hong Kong without being permitted to present their petition. Beijing considers many of these political activists to be subversive elements, determined to undermine Beijing's control over Hong Kong.[43]

Judiciary

Hong Kong's judiciary is independent, and it should remain so after 1997. Judges are appointed until they are no longer able to function for mental or physical reasons. English common law, adapted to accommodate Chinese custom, has been at the heart of the legal system. Much of the international and local communities' confidence in Hong Kong as a good place to live and do business in has been based on the reputation of its independent judiciary for integrity and competence, the stability of the legal and constitutional system, and Hong Kong's adherence to the rule of law.

China has promised to continue to allow Hong Kong's legal system to rely on such legal concepts as habeas corpus, legal precedent, and the tradition of common law, which do not exist in China. Beijing has said that it will not subject Hong Kong's legal system to the Politburo's guidelines for the rest of China. But on political matters such as legislation, human rights, civil liberties, and freedom of the press, there remains considerable concern that the Basic Law offers inadequate protection. For example, the Basic Law provides for China's Standing Committee of the NPC, not the Hong Kong SAR courts, to interpret the Basic Law and to determine whether future laws passed by the Hong Kong SAR legislature conflict with the Basic Law. Nor will the Hong Kong courts be able to question whether China's political and administrative decisions are compatible with Hong Kong's Basic Law.

Furthermore, although Beijing had promised Hong Kong that executive authorities would be accountable to the Legislature, the Basic Law states that the chief executive—to be appointed by China's NPC until at least the year 2012—will have the power to dissolve the Hong Kong Legislature and veto bills. Of even greater concern, Beijing has yet to state the relationship of Hong Kong's Basic Law to China's own Constitution and whether, after 1997, Hong Kong will be required to recognize the leading role and authority of the Communist Party, as required in China's Constitution. The fundamental incompatibility between the British tradition (in which the state's actions must not be in conflict with the laws) on the one hand, and China's practice of the state using law as a tool as well as conferring and withdrawing rights at will on the other hand, is at the heart of the concern about future Chinese rule over Hong Kong.[44]

Press, Civil Rights, and Religious Freedom

China's forceful crackdown on protesters in Beijing's Tiananmen Square on June 4, 1989, and subsequent repression traumatized the Hong Kong population. China's leadership warned the Hong Kong authorities that foreign agents might use such organizations as the Hong Kong Alliance in Support of the Patriotic Democratic Movement in China (a coalition of some 200 groups) to advance their intelligence activities on the mainland.[45] China even accused that group of "playing a subversive role by supporting the pro-democracy movement."[46]

Such statements have aroused fears that the Beijing regime might use force in Hong Kong after 1997 against politically motivated demonstrations. Beijing has, in fact, used subtle—and not so subtle—intimidation to discourage Hong Kong from supporting prodemocracy activities, suggesting that to do so would be "treasonous." The implication is that, once China controls Hong Kong, these people might be accused of a political crime and punished for it, just as they might happen in the rest of China. Were this to occur, few in Hong Kong believe the Joint Declaration or the Basic Law would protect their rights. In addition, China has already announced that it will not permit mass rallies or demonstrations against the central government of China after July 1, 1997.

One freedom that British subjects in Hong Kong have cherished and are concerned about losing is freedom of the press, including television, although it has actually been restricted to some extent by the colonial government. Hong Kong has had a dynamic press, one that represents all sides of the political spectrum. Indeed, it has been free to the point of tolerating the Chinese Communists' having in Hong Kong their own pro-Communist, pro-Beijing newspaper as well as a news bureau (the New China News Agency), which has also functioned as the unofficial foreign office of the P.R.C. in Hong Kong.

In the years between the agreement on the handover treaties and the actual handover, press freedom across the Hong Kong border in China made significant progress. While it is not yet clear how Beijing will respond to a Hong Kong press that openly challenges the Chinese Communist Party's right to rule, in China itself, political analyses no longer merely reflect the Communist Party's line. And, beyond politics, just about any type of journalistic article is now tolerated.

In short, it does not seem likely that China will roll back press freedom in Hong Kong in any significant way. Nor it is likely that information coming into Hong Kong will be cut off, for to do so would jeopardize continuation of the very economic success for Hong Kong that China wants to ensure after 1997. A more likely scenario is that Hong Kong will

SHANGHAI: THE HONG KONG THAT MIGHT HAVE BEEN

Situated on China's eastern coast, Shanghai (pictured above) was China's major port before 1949. Various groups of foreigners lived there in areas called concessions, and, together with the Chinese, they built Shanghai into a bustling world port in the nineteenth and twentieth centuries. It was also a city of crime and vice, and large numbers of its citizens lived in terrible poverty.

After 1949, both because China's former major trading partners joined the American embargo against trade with the People's Republic of China and because China itself at times pursued isolationist policies, Shanghai's role in international trade was eclipsed. The situation was aggravated by socialist policies that took trade out of the hands of independent trading corporations and placed it in the hands of a single state-run trading corporation. The state determined what was bought and sold, thus eliminating competition among Chinese companies. Some observers fear that Chinese control of Hong Kong after 1997 may rob it of its economic dynamism.

The reforms in China in the 1980s and the opening of China to world trade did much to revive Shanghai's economy. Earlier in their rule, the Chinese Communists took steps to rid the city of notorious problems, like prostitution and drug dealing, and to establish a basic standard of welfare for most of its residents. Unfortunately, the return of the capitalist style to Shanghai in recent years has brought with it many of the problems that before 1949 had made it a "city of sin."

become a center for disseminating information to the rest of China.

As for religious freedom, Beijing has guaranteed that, as long as a religious practice does not contravene the Basic Law, it will be permitted. Given the fact that China's tolerance of religious freedom within the mainland has expanded dramatically since 1983, this does not seem to be a likely area of tension for the post-1997 Hong Kong Special Administrative Region.

THE ECONOMY

From the beginning, the British designated Hong Kong as a free port. This has meant that Hong Kong never applied tariffs or other major trade restrictions on imports. Such appealing trade conditions, combined with Hong Kong's free market economy, deep-water harbor, and location at the hub of all commercial activities in Asia, have made it an attractive place for doing business. Indeed, from the 1840s until the crippling Japanese occupation during World War II, Hong Kong served as a major center of China's trade with both Asia and the Western world.

The outbreak of the Korean War in 1950 and the subsequent United Nations embargo on exports of strategic goods to China, as well as a U.S.–led general embargo on the import of Chinese goods, forced Hong Kong to reorient its economy. To combat its diminished role as the middleman in trade with the mainland of China, Hong Kong turned to manufacturing.

At first, it manufactured mainly textiles. Later, it diversified into other areas of light consumer products and developed into a financial and tourist center. Today, it continues to serve as a critical trade center, with thousands of companies (especially Taiwanese ones) still located in Hong Kong for the purpose of doing business with the P.R.C.

Hong Kong's many assets, including its hard-working, dynamic people, have made it into the world's second-largest container port, third-largest gold-dealing center, and perhaps its largest banking and financial center. Yet because of Hong Kong's lack of natural resources, it has remained vulnerable to international political and economic currents, such as trade restrictions and international monetary fluctuations. For example, in the early 1980s, Hong Kong's economy, which relies heavily on exporting, suffered considerably from the protectionist measures taken by its major trading partners, including the United States. Similarly, the repeatedly threatened withdrawal of most-favored-nation (MFN) status for China put Hong Kong in as much of a state of panic as Beijing, for, as the largest single investor in China's export sector, Hong Kong would have been badly hurt by the elimination of MFN treatment for China. The favorable resolution of these negotiations brought a collective sigh of relief from Hong Kong.

Since 1979, when China initiated major internal economic reforms that opened it up to foreign investment, Hong Kong's economy has become deeply integrated with China's contiguous province of Guangdong. Hong Kong entrepreneurs have taken advantage of China's cheap labor (Hong Kong industries operating on Chinese soil employ some 3 million Chinese workers) and turned Guangdong into "a huge processing zone for Hong Kong based manufacturers."[47] Hong Kong's investment accounts for 66 percent of China's total foreign investment and a full 80 percent of Guangdong's total. Hong Kong owns 16,000 factories in Guangdong, factories that export goods worth some $11 billion annually.[48] More than 35 percent of China's trade is through Hong Kong.

As part of its economic reform program and "open door" policy, China has created Special Economic Zones (SEZs) in areas bordering or close to Hong Kong, in order to attract foreign investment. These SEZs, under far more liberal regulations than the rest of China, have blossomed in the last decade. Various parts of China's government have themselves invested heavily in the SEZs in hopes of making a profit. Even China's military has developed an industrial area catering to foreign investors and joint ventures in Shenzhen—and SEZ bordering on Hong Kong—as part of its effort to compensate for insufficient funding for the military since 1981. It calls its policy "one army, two systems"—that is, an army involved with both military and economic development.[49] Brushing aside its earlier concern for a puritanical society, China's military is as likely to invest in nightclubs, Western-style hotels, brothels, and health spas as it is in industry.

The bulk of foreign investment in the SEZs and in the rest of China actually comes, however, from Hong Kong Chinese, either with their own money or acting as middlemen for investors from Taiwan, South Korea, the United States, and other countries. Two thirds of direct foreign investment in China, in fact, comes *through* Hong Kong. Thus, this integrated area, encompassing Hong Kong, the SEZs, and Guangdong Province, has the potential to become a powerful new regional economy on a par with other newly industrialized countries (NICs). Indeed, it is increasingly evident that, rather than China taking over Hong Kong in 1997, Guangdong will already have become part of Hong Kong's empire.

Hong Kong's growth has been challenged by the rapidly expanding economies of the other "little dragons" of East Asia—Singapore, Taiwan, and South Korea. These robust economies compete with Hong Kong in the manufacture and export of light industrial and consumer goods. South Korea, which previously had had to use Hong Kong as an entrepôt for trade and business with China, established full diplomatic relations with China in 1992, thereby allowing it to deal directly with China. Still, Taiwan's indirect trade through Hong Kong in 1992 was estimated at $7 billion.[50] And China remains Hong Kong's largest trading partner.

Sensitivity of the Economy to External Political Events
Hong Kong's economic strength rests on the population's belief in Hong Kong's future, which has fluctuated with its vacillating confidence in the future. Concern over Great Britain's unwillingness to negotiate more democratic rights for Hong Kong before 1997 periodically threatened Hong Kong's economic stability, diminished confidence, and generated an outward flow of professionals from Hong Kong.

So did China's economic retrenchment policies and partial closing of the "open door" to international trade and investment, as well as Beijing's verbal intimidation in the period following the Tiananmen crackdown in 1989, and again when Governor Patten began whipping up Hong Kong fervor for greater democratic reforms in 1992. China's statement in December 1992 that contracts that the enterprises or the government in Hong Kong signed with foreign companies would be invalid after 1997 sent shock waves throughout the colony. The Hang Sang stock exchange took a nose dive, for such a policy would mean that, after 1997, China would in fact control Hong Kong's economy completely—a wholesale abrogation of the Basic Law.

Such volatility has demonstrated just how vulnerable Hong Kong is to Beijing's policies and actions. China is well aware of this, and it is deeply concerned that Hong Kong not be destabilized either by Beijing's own policies or by potentially destabilizing changes in policies and laws in Hong Kong, such as it fears greater democratization in Hong Kong could bring. Beijing has stated that it would allow Hong Kong to become a separate member of the World Trade Organization

(United Nations, 74037)

The Hong Kong government has constructed new apartments in an effort to address the severe overcrowding in tenements and squatter communities.

(WTO). This means that Hong Kong need not worry about whether China is meeting WTO standards, as it will not affect its own membership.

Although Hong Kong's economy has recovered since 1989, in no small part aided by the remarkable growth of the P.R.C.'s own economy since 1992, Hong Kong's resulting labor and capital shortage has fueled inflation in the 1990s. The uncertainty of economic conditions after 1997 has made it more difficult to attract the capital investment necessary for continued strong growth. Indeed, although much of the potential imbalance is redressed by international capital flowing in, capital continues to flow out of Hong Kong—and into China.[51] Since the value of these investments depends on a stable political and economic environment in China, Hong Kong's wealthy entrepreneurs are far less interested in supporting a quest for democratic rights in China if these would come at the expense of political stability. Hong Kong's business people and its new chief executive Tung Chee-hwa are, in fact, among the strongest supporters of China's "law and order" approach to governing Hong Kong.

Emigration from Hong Kong (at the rate of about 60,000 per year since 1990) largely comes from among its better-educated, wealthier class.[52] Thus, both talent and investment dollars leave. Once emigrants gain a second passport (a guarantee of residency abroad in case conditions warrant flight), however, they often return to Hong Kong, where there is still money to be made and opportunities available for professional success (e.g., for architects, engineers, dentists, doctors, and businesspeople). This outflow of talent is largely counterbalanced by an inflow of immigrants as well as by the education of new professionals in Hong Kong's excellent schools.[53]

And many are in Hong Kong to stay. Certainly most foreign corporations already located in Hong Kong have no intention of leaving. Indeed, because they are already well positioned in Hong Kong, many foreign corporations will never have to go through the unpredictable, lengthy, and expensive bureaucratic hassle of trying to break into the China market: As of July 1, 1997, they are already in it! Even Taiwan's enterprises in Hong Kong are standing firm, for without direct trade and transport links between China and Taiwan, Hong Kong is still the major entrepôt for trade between the two places. Predictions are that the Hong Kong Special Administrative Region's GDP will grow by at least 10 percent annually from 1997 through 2002, with trade and investment flowing between Hong Kong and the mainland driving blossoming for both sides.[54]

THE FUTURE

Of course, no one can predict Hong Kong's future with certainty. China's leaders have stated that the relationship between China and the Hong Kong SAR will be "one country, two systems" for 50 years after 1997. By this they mean that Hong Kong may maintain its current social, political, economic, and legal system alongside China's system. Yet China is changing so quickly—indeed, it is day by day becoming more like Hong Kong in its commercial and economic features as it phases out its state-run economy in favor of a market economy—that the imposition of a socialist economy on Hong Kong is unthinkable. With China's commercial banks acting much the same as banks in any capitalist economy, a budding stock market, and a currency whose value is no longer regulated by the state, China's economy is looking ever more like Hong Kong's than like a centrally planned socialist economy. China's leaders have repeatedly stated the importance of foreign investment, greater openness, and experimentation.

The extraordinary economic boom since 1991 in southern China has made the Hong Kong population more optimistic than at any time since 1982. They see a new "dragon" emerging, one that combines Hong Kong's technology and skills with China's labor and resources. For many, the major worry is not that there will be political repression and centralized controls imposed on Hong Kong's economy after 1997, but, rather, that China's bureaucracy and corruption may simply smother the economic vitality of Hong Kong.

Even in the political realm, China is changing so profoundly that the two systems that, just 20 years ago, seemed so far apart, are now much closer. China has itself been undertaking significant political liberalization, especially in respect to increasing electoral rights at the local level, permitting greater latitude in individual lifestyles, and according greater freedom to the mass media. And, because of the rapid growth of private property and business interests, China is undergoing major social changes, including the blossoming of numerous interest groups.

Nevertheless, the legal safeguards of civil rights in Hong Kong are unmatched thus far on the mainland. The Chinese Communist Party had denounced calls for more democracy in Hong Kong, especially multiparty democracy, as "bourgeois liberalization," and it has reaffirmed the party's unchallengeable authority. It has repeatedly stated hostility to Western notions of democracy and insisted that any political reforms in Hong Kong must be in line with China's own vision of political reform.

Because China has an important stake in having a successful takeover of Hong Kong, one that does not disrupt the economic sphere, it is concerned that Hong Kong's residents and the international business community believe in its future prosperity. China's rulers know that, in the 1980s, policies and events that were threatening to that confidence led to the loss of many of its most talented people, technological know-how, and investment. They do not want to risk losing even more. China also wants to maintain Hong Kong as a major free port and the regional center for trade, financing, shipping, and information—although it is also doing everything possible to turn Shanghai into another major center that competes with Hong Kong.

Finally, regardless of official denials by the government in Taiwan, Beijing's successful management of "one country, two systems" in Hong Kong will profoundly affect how Taiwan feels about its own peaceful integration with the mainland. As Beijing wants to regain control of Taiwan by peaceful means, it is critical that it handle Hong Kong well.

NOTES

1. R. G. Tiedemann, "Chasing the Dragon," *China Now,* No. 132 (February 1990), p. 21.

2. Jan S. Prybyla, "The Hong Kong Agreement and Its Impact on the World Economy," in Jurgen Domes and Yu-ming Shaw (eds.), *Hong Kong: A Chinese and International Concern* (Boulder, CO: Westview Special Studies on East Asia, 1988), p. 177.

3. Tiedemann, p. 22.

4. Robin McClaren, former British ambassador to China, seminar at Cambridge University, Centre for International Relations, February 28, 1996.

5. Ambrose Y. C. King, "The Hong Kong Talks and Hong Kong Politics," in Domes and Shaw, p. 49.

6. Hungdah Chiu, Y. C. Jao, and Yual-li Wu, *The Future of Hong Kong: Toward 1997 and Beyond* (New York: Quorum Books, 1987), pp. 5–6.

7. Siu-kai Lau, "Hong Kong's 'Ungovernability' in the Twilight of Colonial Rule," in Lin Zhiling and Thomas W. Robinson, *The Chinese and Their Future: Beijing, Taipei, and Hong Kong* (Washington, D.C.: The American Enterprise Institute Press, 1994), pp. 288–290.

8. McLaren, February 28, 1996.

9. *Ibid.* McLaren noted that it was not easy to convince Prime Minister Margaret Thatcher, in her "post-Falklands mood" (referring to Great Britain's successful defense of the Falkland Islands, 9,000 miles away, from being returned to Argentinian rule), that Hong Kong could not stay under British administrative rule even after 1997.

10. T. L. Tsim, "Introduction," in T. L. Tsim and Bernard H. K. Luk, *The Other Hong Kong Report* (Hong Kong: The Chinese University Press, 1989), p. xxv.

11. Norman J. Miners, "Constitution and Administration," in Tsim and Luk, p. 2.

12. King, pp. 54–55.

13. Annex I, Nos. 1 and 4 of *The Basic Law of the Hong Kong Special Administrative Region of the People's Republic of China* (hereafter cited as *The Basic Law*). Printed in *Beijing Review*, Vol. 33, No. 18 (April 30–May 6, 1990), supplement. This document was adopted by the 7th National People's Congress on April 4, 1990. Tung Chee-hwa, an extraordinarily wealthy shipping tycoon, was chosen as chief executive by these procedures in 1996.

14. Annex I, No. 2, *The Basic Law* (1990).

15. For specifics, see Annex II of *The Basic Law (1990)*.

16. Article 14, *The Basic Law* (1990).

17. Articles 27, 32, 33, and 36 of *The Basic Law* (1990).

18. When riots again flared in Hong Kong's refugee camps for Vietnamese, Beijing expressed annoyance at the British for not just getting on with sending them back to Vietnam and emptying the camps. All Vietnamese in these camps will have been repatriated or given refuge in other countries by July 1, 1997.

19. Tsim, in Tsim and Luk, p. xx.

20. See "Hong Kong," *Asia 1983 Yearbook* (Hong Kong: Far Eastern Economic Review, 1983), p. 146.

21. Lau, p. 300.

22. Keith B. Richburg, "Uptight Hong Kong Countdown," *The Washington Post* (July 2, 1996), pp. A1, A12.

23. Chairman Suttill, "Chinese Culture in Hong Kong," *China Now,* No. 132 (February 1990), p. 14.

24. Tsim, p. xxi.

25. Even in the last years leading up to the handover, any significant change "in revenue or spending strategies" required Beijing's approval; and China's preference by 1996 was for keeping the status quo. "Currently, Hong Kong has no income tax, no sales taxes, no capital gains tax, no taxes on dividends, a profit tax of 16.5 percent for corporations and a flat 15 percent salary tax starting at thresholds that leave tens of thousands of workers unscathed." Ironically, calls to change the taxation system in Hong Kong have come not from Beijing but from Singapore, Hong Kong's major competitor to Hong Kong's position as the financial center of Asia. Kevin Murphy, "Hong Kong: Taxing Question," *International Herald Tribune* (March 6, 1996).

26. Keith B. Richburg, "Chinese Muscle-Flexing Puts Hong Kong Under Pessimistic Pall," *The Washington Post* (December 26, 1996), p. A31.

27. Kevin Murphy, "Troops for Hong Kong: China Puts Best Face on It," *International Herald Tribune* (January 30, 1996), p. 4.

28. Edward A. Gargan, "Chinese General's Visit Shakes Up Hong Kong," *International Herald Tribune* (July 24, 1996), p. 2.

29. John Gordon Davies, "Introduction," *Hong Kong Through the Looking Glass* (Hong Kong: Kelly & Walsh, 1969).

30. The transition to China's sovereignty is also raising a host of questions over what will happen to Hong Kong's other criminals already in jail or awaiting trial. Considerable debate surrounds the question of whether it is fair to those awaiting trial to be tried under the laws of a country (China) in which the crime was not committed. Other countries are refusing to extradite criminals to Hong Kong, on the grounds that, as of July 1, 1997, China may deal more harshly with them than they would have been treated in Hong Kong; and on the grounds that the trial procedures still being used in China are not as protective of the rights of the accused as they are in Hong Kong.

31. Ambrose Y. C. King, in Domes and Shaw, op. cit., pp. 45–46.

32. *Ibid.,* pp. 196–197; and Lau, p. 302.

33. *Ibid.,* p. 205.

34. Lau, pp. 293, 304–305

35. *Ibid.,* p. 294.

36. *Ibid.,* p. 294.

37. Tung Chee-hwa, who was a vice chairman of China's Preparatory Committee, had also been chosen by Governor Chris Patten to be on the Hong Kong Executive Council but resigned in mid-1996 because of the conflict of interests in simultaneously holding both positions.

38. By the end of 1992, Hong Kong public opinion had already begun to turn against Governor Patten because of concern that his democratization proposals might, by provoking retaliatory measures from China, destabilize the situation in Hong Kong. Many in Hong Kong (especially the businesspeople who have so much invested both in Hong Kong and China) wonder whether more democracy is worth the risks. Vincent Lo, who chaired the Hong Kong Business and Professionals Federation, publicly stated the Federation's opposition to the governor's political reform package. "The Federation, whose 159 members include some of Hong Kong's biggest companies, politely asked Mr. Patten to withdraw his proposals." "Sheriff Patten Comes to Town," *The Economist* (November 14, 1992), p. 35.

39. Beijing censured the one dissenter among the 149 committee members and said he would not be permitted to serve on any committees planning the handover or any governing role after July 1, 1997.

40. Reuters, "Hong Kong Is Pessimistic On Transfer, 2 Polls Find," *International Herald Tribune* (June 25, 1996), p. 5.

41. Ambrose Y. C. King, in Domes and Shaw, *op. cit.,* pp. 51, 56, 57.

42. The Democratic Party has 19 members (out of a total of 60) in the Hong Kong Legislature, all of whom will be unseated after July 1, 1997.

43. Kevin Murphy, "Banned Hong Kong Party to Fight On," *International Herald Tribune* (March 26, 1996).

44. James L. Tyson, "Promises, Promises . . . ," *The Christian Science Monitor* (April 20, 1989), p. 2.

45. Miu-wah Ma, "China Warns Against Political Ties Abroad," *The Hong Kong Standard* (September 1, 1989), p. 4.

46. Viola Lee, "China 'trying to discourage HK people,' " *South China Morning Post* (August 21, 1989). The article, which originally appeared in a *People's Daily* article in July, was elaborated upon in the August edition of *Outlook Weekly,* a mouthpiece of the CCP.

47. T. L. Tsim, p. xix.

48. Jan S. Prybyla, "China's Economic Dynamos," *Current History* (September 1992), p. 263.

49. Tammy Tam, "Shenzhen Industrial Estate Developed to Boost Military Funds," *The Hongkong Standard* (September 5, 1989), p. 1.

50. Jan Prybyla, "China's Economic Dynamos," *Current History* (September 1992), p. 263.

51. Yun-wing Sung, "The Hong Kong Economy—To the 1997 Barrier and Beyond," in Zhiling Lin and Thomas W. Robinson, *The Chinese and Their Future: Beijing, Taipei, and Hong Kong* (Washington, D.C.: The American Enterprise Institute Press, 1994), pp. 319–323.

52. London's refusal to allow Hong Kong citizens to emigrate to the United Kingdom contributed to a sense of panic among the middle and upper classes in Hong Kong, those most worried about their economic and political future under Communist rule. Other countries have, however, been more than willing to accept these well-educated, wealthy immigrants who come ready to make large deposits in their new host country's banks.

53. Yun-wing Sung, *op. cit.,* pp. 316–319.

54. "Investors to Gain after Hong Kong Handover," *China News Digest* (June 22, 1996), as excerpted on the Internet.

Annotated Table of Contents for Articles

People's Republic of China Articles

Taiwan Articles

Hong Kong Articles

Topic Guide to Articles

TOPIC AREA	TREATED IN	TOPIC AREA	TREATED IN
Industrial Development	8. China Is No Threat 11. Who Will Feed China? 12. Developing China's Hinterland 17. The Long River's Journey Ends	**Private Enterprise**	1. China since Tiananmen Square 7. Economic Liberalization vs Political Authoritarianism 9. Boom-at-a-Glance
Media	6. The Short March	**Regime**	1. China since Tiananmen Square 2. Engaging China
Military	8. China Is No Threat	**Regional Cooperation**	3. The Giant Wakes 5. China's New Nationalism 8. China Is No Threat 12. Developing China's Hinterland 25. How China Lost Taiwan 28. Hard and Soft Policies 29. Learning to Survive with 'Gulliver'
Music and Art	22. The First Asians 23. Script Reform in China		
Nationalism	4. Back to the Future 5. China's New Nationalism		
National Reunification	1. China since Tiananmen Square 26. Vibrant, Popular Pantheon	**Religion**	24. Red Envelopes 26. Vibrant, Popular Pantheon 27. Every Number an Omen
Natives	14. A Floating Population 26. Vibrant, Popular Pantheon	**Rule of Law**	2. Engaging China 6. The Short March 12. Developing China's Hinterland
Natural Resources	11. Who Will Feed China? 17. The Long River's Journey Ends	**Rural Life**	6. The Short March 10. How Poor Is China?
Patriotism	1. China since Tiananmen Square 5. China's New Nationalism	**Taiwan Independence**	25. How China Lost Taiwan 29. Learning to Survive with 'Gulliver'
Peasants	6. The Short March 10. How Poor Is China? 12. Developing China's Hinterland 13. China's Human Avalanche 26. Vibrant, Popular Pantheon	**Territorial Problems**	3. The Giant Wakes 25. How China Lost Taiwan 28. Hard and Soft Policies 29. Learning to Survive with 'Gulliver' 30. China's Golden Goose
Philosophy	4. Back to the Future 5. China's New Nationalism 26. Vibrant, Popular Pantheon	**Trade**	1. China since Tiananmen Square 2. Engaging China 6. The Short March
Political Reform	4. Back to the Future 5. China's New Nationalism 7. Economic Liberalization vs Political Authoritarianism 12. Developing China's Hinterland	**Urbanization**	10. How Poor Is China? 12. Developing China's Hinterland 13. China's Human Avalanche 14. A Floating Population
Politics	4. Back to the Future 5. China's New Nationalism 7. Economic Liberalization vs Political Authoritarianism	**Women**	9. Boom-at-a-Glance
		World Role	1. China since Tiananmen Square
Poverty	10. How Poor Is China?	**Youth**	1. China since Tiananmen Square 20. As a Pampered Generation Grows Up

Articles from the World Press

People's Republic of China

Article 1

The World & I, April 1996

China since Tiananmen Square

China: The Good, the Bad, and the Dangerous

*Most young Chinese now agree that economic development,
not greater democracy, is the most pressing national need.*

Stanley Rosen

Stanley Rosen is professor of political science at the University of Southern California, Los Angeles.

When Americans think of the People's Republic of China, certain indelible images inevitably spring to mind. Who can forget the spring of 1989, marked by student demonstrations for democracy, the hunger strike in Tiananmen Square, and the tragic denouement of the military crackdown on June 4? Since those dark days, as the Sino-American relationship has struggled to recover its pre-1989 momentum, the American press continues to document the enduring tensions between the two countries.

On global issues, there is the strong suspicion that in a variety of areas, including intellectual-property rights, trade policy, and nuclear proliferation, China is unwilling to play according to long-established international rules. On what China considers domestic issues as well, the regime has been repeatedly condemned for violating the human rights of its citizens, from prominent dissidents to disabled orphans to unborn fetuses.

While editorials and op-ed contributors debate whether MFN (most-favored nation) renewal should be tied to improvements in China's international and domestic behavior, there is remarkably little discussion beyond the broadest generalities of the changes in China since 1989 and the views of China's own citizens. Such information is crucial, at a minimum, if the United States is to avoid obvious missteps in its relationship with China; it is available through published survey research, public opinion polling, press reports, and discussions with a wide range of individuals in China. What these sources reveal is a China that has changed significantly from the late 1980s.

China Before and After 1989

Following the 13th Party Congress in October 1987 and prior to June 1989, China was a very lively place for intellectual discussion and contention. There was, by today's standards, a surprising amount of official tolerance toward those questioning China's past, present, and future. One of the clearest examples of this was a six-hour documentary shown on Chinese television in 1988 titled *River Elegy,* which attacked some of the major icons of Chinese civilization, including the Great Wall, the image of the dragon, and the Yellow River.

The message of the documentary was that a hopelessly backward Chinese civilization could only advance by following a Western model of development, and that only China's intellectuals were capable of serving as a bridge to link China with the West. The leader of the Communist Party at that time, Zhao Ziyang, was so taken with this documentary that he ensured that it was rebroadcast, thereby guaranteeing it a larger audience.

Conservative political leaders in China—and many Chinese abroad—were appalled by this frontal assault on Chinese civilization, but the policy at that time was to discourage the Communist Party from interfering in academic and cultural debates, so it could not be suppressed.

There were also debates in the press and before large audiences on university campuses over the best way for China to become democratic, whether a "neoauthoritarian" model à la South Korea, Singapore, and Taiwan or a more direct, Western-derived model best fit China's conditions. This openness, along with the self-imposed circumscribed role of the Communist Party, ended after June 1989.

Following Tiananmen, a decision was made to control political life and strictly limit academic debates that might have political implications. The overriding empha-

Democracy no longer a priority: In 1989 young Chinese fought for their democratic rights in Tiananmen Square.

sis was placed on maintaining stability. Many intellectuals who had been tarnished in the eyes of the regime because of their "antigovernment" activities had their professional lives either sharply curtailed or ended completely. At the same time the regime knew that it had to restore its legitimacy and polish its own severely tarnished image.

The new policy had several components. One priority was to focus on raising the standard of living of the urban population, particularly those in the coastal cities who were best situated to take advantage of the state's new economic initiatives. Indeed, for the "tarnished" intellectuals, their only recourse was to engage in business, which many did with surprising success.

In addition to offering them more bread, circuses were provided in the form of a far more varied cultural life, albeit of a nonthreatening nature. Thus, China witnessed an explosion of tabloid newspapers and sensationalistic magazines, which was further fueled by the elimination of state subsidies and the necessity for all cultural organizations to adjust to the new requirements of the market.

Evening entertainment was enhanced with increased numbers of discos and karaoke bars and the importation of 10 "blockbuster" movies per year, such as *Forrest Gump, True Lies,* and *The Fugitive.* A virtual revolution in consumer goods was spearheaded by the increasing penetration of cosmetics, toiletries, and other such wares of Western multinational corporations.

The government's strategy can easily be seen in the field of popular music. In place of the pounding rock music of rebellion that had been so important a part of the 1989 student movement, sentimental love songs from Hong Kong and Taiwan were encouraged and became dominant.

The Stress on Patriotism over Politics

Finally, indirectly acknowledging that heavy doses of obviously outdated political dogma had become counterproductive, the leadership has taken steps to promote patriotism while deemphasizing politics. Thus, beginning in fall 1994, for the first time since university entrance examinations were restored in the late 1970s, students applying to study science did not have to take an examination in politics. Many educators expect the exemption to be extended to humanities and social science students in due course.

At the same time, however, there has been a sharp increase in "patriotic education," to teach students to be proud of being Chinese and to emphasize the achievements of Chinese culture, the Chinese people, and the role of the Communist Party in honoring and furthering these achievements. This is an astute move, because so few young people now believe in Marxism–Leninism–Mao Zedong's thought anyway.

The State Education Commission appears to have concluded that forcing students to memorize and regurgitate

A Different China

• China has changed significantly since the late 1980s.

• The regime has raised the standard of living of the urban population and encouraged a more varied cultural life.

• Patriotism has been promoted and politics deemphasized.

• The United States and democracy no longer have a favorable image among the Chinese public, especially young Chinese.

what they consider to be outmoded theories had created constant tension between the students and authorities. in its view, the periodic student protests of the mid and late 1980s were in part a reaction against the hypocrisy the students felt these political education examinations and courses represented.

This new strategy thus far appears to have paid dividends. In addition to the absence of the type of demonstrations that marked the 1980s, surveys have suggested that the regime's message is getting through. Citing a recent survey conducted by private researchers based in Beijing, the *Far Eastern Economic Review* noted that 54 percent of urbanites agreed with the official line that economic development, not greater democracy, is the most pressing national need.

Moreover, many surveys have documented a resurgence in patriotism among Chinese youth. One of the most interesting is a survey of 698 youths in Shanghai and surrounding areas that compared the results to earlier surveys of a similar nature conducted in 1984 and 1990. Respondents were given a list of 18 values and asked to rank their top four and bottom four. Perhaps most striking was the fact that patriotism—which had ranked fifth in 1984—ranked second in 1994. Indeed, among workers, peasants, and science students, it was ranked first. Only a relatively low ranking by liberal arts students prevented patriotism from replacing "self-respect" as the most valued concept.

More detailed analysis, however, reveals that present-day patriotism is far different from its Maoist variant, that in significant ways it actually presents a strong current of individualism and a rejection of authority. To be more specific, surveys of groups as diverse as peasant youth and graduate students at the elite Beijing University all show strong support for patriotism in the abstract. When asked to evaluate a statement such as

"defending the nation is every young person's sacred duty," around 85 percent of respondents would concur. But when asked to make sacrifices for the benefit of the country, the response is far different.

For peasant youth, politics is very practical and is associated with changes in their own village or the behavior of local officials. Most of them were only concerned about politics if it directly impinged on their own lives or the livelihood of their families. Only 10 percent in a recent survey agreed with the famous motto of Lei Feng, a model youth of the Maoist period, that one should serve the nation in whatever capacity one is needed, as a "rust-free screw" in the great machine of the state.

There were similar results in a survey on the meaning of patriotism under a market economy conducted among graduate students at Beijing University. Despite overwhelming support for patriotism as a cherished value, only 6.6 percent said they were willing to take a job assignment after graduation wherever the country needed them. Those who said they would "serve the people and make a contribution to society" were also a very small percentage.

Over 50 percent said that the old model of making selfless contributions was out of date, no longer credible, not sensible, unnecessary, and not worth the effort. Fewer than 7 percent said they still wanted to emulate this model, but even they felt they would be ridiculed and isolated and would not have the understanding and support of society. It is therefore not surprising that in the Shanghai survey cited above, the value ranked consistently lowest over the last decade—last at number 18 in 1984 and again in 1994—was "obedience to authority."

Chinese Youth and the Outside World

Some of the most riveting and moving moments for Americans who watched the coverage of the students in Tiananmen Square during the "democratic spring" of 1989 were the frequent references to American political history and political values. Six and a half years later, the United States and democracy more generally no longer have such a favorable image.

One public opinion poll published in early 1995 in the *Beijing Youth Daily*, which has arguably become China's liveliest and most widely read newspaper, attracted particular attention. Titled "Foreign Countries in the Eyes of Urban Young People in China," the poll was part of an annual survey of Chinese youth. What was unusual was the addition for the first time of four questions on foreign countries. Respondents were asked to choose (1) the country you like best; (2) the country you like least; (3) the country you believe is most friendly to China; (4) the country you believe is most unfriendly to China.

On all four of these questions, the United States ranked among the first three choices. in fact, 74 percent of Chinese youth said that the United States is the foreign country with the greatest influence on China. Still, the surveyors expressed their surprise at some of the results. While the United States was third (12.1 percent) among the countries most liked, following only China itself (46.1 percent) and Singapore (14.1 percent), it was a clear first among the countries most disliked (39.8 percent), well ahead of Japan, Vietnam, and Russia, which were the next three choices.

Again, the United States was third among the countries considered most friendly to China (3.9 percent), but far and away No. 1 among those considered most unfriendly (71.9 percent).

To provide some context, it should be noted that North Korea was considered most friendly by a whopping 67.7 percent, followed by Japan at 8.4 percent. Following the United States as most unfriendly were Japan, Vietnam, and Great Britain. Even some youths who listed the United States as their favorite country felt it was the most unfriendly toward China.

To be sure, public opinion in China tends to be quite volatile and survey techniques are commonly less than state-of-the-art. Nevertheless, many Chinese youth have told me that they do not find these results particularly surprising. Indeed, as Liu Xiaobo, one of the country's leading dissidents and among the last four hunger strikers to leave Tiananmen, wrote recently in a Hong Kong publication: "History moves in such rapid cycles. Many an advocate of Westernization who clamored for 'democracy' and 'freedom' on or before June 4 have in an instant become nationalists rejecting Western hegemony."

It is important for those outside China to understand some of the reasons for the change in sentiment. One source of disillusionment is the lack of success the former Soviet Union and eastern European countries have had in transforming and consolidating their new political and economic systems.

When I was in Beijing in August 1991 during and after the abortive coup attempt in the Soviet Union, many young Chinese intellectuals told me excitedly that the final demise of communism in its homeland would have an immense, albeit not immediate, impact in China. Such palpable enthusiasm no longer exists. In fact, some openly suggest that, given the situation in 1989, China was fortunate to avoid the fate of the Soviet Union. This perceived failure of postcommunist systems has given credibility to the government's continual stress on stability as the overriding value.

At the same time, the leadership appears to have been extremely successful in its presentation of the United States as the ringleader of those who seek to deny China its rightful place in the hierarchy of nations. The Chinese press consistently argues that American policy is premised on "containing" China, citing as evidence not only American policy during the Cold War years but recent articles in such premier publications as *Time*, the *Economist*, the *New York Times*, and the *Washington Post*.

The regime has been inadvertently aided and abetted by certain policy decisions emanating from the White House and Congress. A prime example is related to China's failed bid to host the Olympics in the year 2000. After Beijing barely lost out to Sydney as the host site, the Chinese press—on its best behavior on this subject until the decision was reached—unleashed a torrent of abuse against foreigners who were said to have bullied China before the communist victory, then sought to encircle, contain, and isolate the growing strength of the socialist nation. China's defeat on the Olympics issue was seamlessly tied to a consistent pattern of Western efforts to humiliate and perpetuate a weak China, neatly turning the setback into a lesson in patriotism.

Public opinion polls on college campuses revealed that the large majority of students were particularly incensed by the congressional resolution urging the international Olympic Committee not to award China the games because of human rights violations. Regardless of their views of the government or human rights issues, most students fervently supported China's Olympic bid and saw this resolution as blatant interference by a "superpower bully."

The authorities have used the media to portray a China on schedule to become a world power in the next century but being resisted by a resentful West.

As if to reinforce such an interpretation in their minds, around the same period in 1993 the U.S. Navy shadowed and eventually searched a Chinese ship suspected of carrying chemicals to Iran that could be used to manufacture weapons. When no such chemicals were found, the government-controlled press once again took the lead in excoriating the United States for groundlessly violating Chinese sovereignty and attempting to police the world.

Conclusion

China has changed significantly since June 1989. The regime appears to have willingly sacrificed many of its former socialist goals and offered its citizens an opportunity to make money and enjoy life in return for their political acceptance of the status quo. It has had many takers. Public opinion polls show one of the most popular slogans among youth today is "Money isn't everything, but without money you can't do anything."

At the same time, the authorities have used the media to portray a China on schedule to become a world power in the next century but being resisted by a resentful West, spearheaded by the United States, reluctant to share its hegemonic control. Considering the government's isolation back in 1989 and its estrangement from society, the current strategy to this point must be considered a singular success.

Whereas Chinese youth in the 1980s became obsessed with Western philosophical and political thought, embracing Sartre, Freud, Nietzsche, and many others one after another, there is much more interest now in the success of the East Asian economic miracle and China's prospects for replicating it. Singapore—authoritarian, rich, without corruption, and willing to cane Americans—has become the most popular foreign country. indeed, Singapore was rated first by Chinese youth among countries they most wanted to visit (26.8 percent), even outpolling the United States (21.8 percent).

The United States, of course, remains the foreign country of greatest importance to China's future. But the influence we exert is strictly limited and, when exercised unwisely has led to counterproductive results. In future, we would do well to consider how our policy decisions will be interpreted by the Chinese people, particularly the younger generation, which combines a growing individualism marked by a pattern of conspicuous consumption with a desire to see a strong and respected China.

Article 2   *Current History*, September 1996

Engaging China: Exploiting the Fissures in the Facade

"China is not a monolith; there are fissures in the facade . . . and the outside world would do well to exploit them were possible . . . [The international community] should not deviate from the long-term goal of peaceful economic engagement but react with a large measure of flexibility and pragmatism to China's response to what it sees as threats to its regime economic security."

James Shinn

James Shinn is the senior fellow for Asia at the Council on Foreign Relations. He is the director of the council's multiyear Asia Project and the editor of Weaving the Net: Conditional Engagement with China (New York: Council on Foreign Relations Press, 1996). The views presented here are those of the author.

Officials of the People's Republic of China equate the political security of the governing regime in Beijing with the national security of all of China. This accounts in part for the rigidity and neuralgic sensitivity China's foreign security policy often exhibits. Does the conduct of China's foreign economic policy exhibit a similar equivalence? Is the economic security of the governing regime in Beijing synonymous with the economic security of China as a nation? How does economic interdependence impinge on regime economic security in China, and what does this suggest for a strategy of economic engagement with China?

Defining Economic Security

The classic definition of economic security, which conflates traditional military strength with economic prowess, is embodied in the slogan "rich country, strong military," or *fu guo qiang bing* in Chinese. Like the Meiji

Japanese, China's Qing dynasty patriots yearned for an economy strong enough to build warships to keep the Western (and later Japanese) imperialists at bay.

Viewing GNP as a proxy for national power is an economic security definition of more recent vintage. This view is a form of raw neomercantilism, a zero-sum game in which economic security is measured by a sustained balance of payments surplus and by foreign currency reserves piling up in the Bank of China. This narrow view of economic interdependence is being erased as more economists rise within the Chinese nomenklatura, but it is still a common mindset of ruling Communist Party elders.

China's economic security has also been defined as freedom from dependence on external resources, such as energy and food. China is shifting from being a net exporter of petroleum to a net importer, and will require imports of almost 1.2 million barrels of oil per day by the year 2000. But there is no obvious way to purchase resource security with military forces. For example, the People's Liberation Army (PLA) could seize the islands of the South China Sea, but then China would be unable to tap their petroleum resources without the capital and technology of the oil majors.

Another definition of economic security is the degree to which the domestic economy is insulated from external macroeconomic forces. All national economic authorities wish they had the latitude to pursue their own macro targets in isolation from international arbitrageurs and footloose international investors. But the Beijing government is acutely aware of China's dependence on exports and inflows of foreign capital to sustain the current growth rates of 10 percent per year, and absorb China's huge labor force.

For China, all four definitions of economic security have been overtaken by interdependence. The benefits of China's integration with the world trading and financial systems have effectively offset the appeal of pursuing any of these more traditional definitions of economic security. Yet some aspects of interdependence do pose a stubborn threat to the security of the governing regime in Beijing, which is acutely aware of what could be termed its own regime economic security.

What do I mean by "regime"? For the purposes of this argument, it is equivalent to the "selectorate." Coined by political scientist Susan Shirk, the selectorate is based on "a term adopted from British parliamentary politics to define the group within a political party that has effective power to choose leaders."[1] The selectorate in the People's Republic of China is composed of three major elements: the roughly 300 members of the Central Com-

mittee, several dozen Communist Party elders, and the top officers of the PLA.

As with most governments, the prime goal of the regime in Beijing is to hold on to the reins of power. The regime's central problem is how to run a closed political system in concert with an open economy while ensuring that there is no spillover effect from the open economy in the direction of political pluralism, which would challenge the regime's monopoly of political power.

The regime's apprehension of economic security is the mirror image of a constructive engagement strategy for dealing with China. Constructive engagement is predicated on the assumption that spillover effects from economic interdependence will moderate and then modify the Beijing regime. The authorities in Beijing are justifiably haunted by such a devolution of power, since it would almost certainly invoke a challenge to their position, such as another Tiananmen, or resistance to the state that includes demonstrations by students, workers, the urban middle class, or—the most threatening case—splinter groups of the PLA or other state security organs.

How do we distinguish economic threats to the security of the regime from purely political threats to it? The former include events that diminish the economic well-being of key regime constituencies such as state-owned enterprises or business interests of the PLA. Political threats include the creation of alternative centers of political power, such as the challenge posed by the National People's Congress (NPC), the application of the rule of law to the party in the courts, or separatist agitation in Tibet or Xinjiang province.

Threats to Regime Security

What aspects of economic interdependence threaten regime security in China? In *Weaving the Net: Conditional Engagement with China*, I examine four moderating factors arising from China's dramatically expanding economic interdependence. These moderating factors include the tyranny of markets, corrosive capitalism, decentralization, and changing elite stakes.

The tyranny of markets stems from the Chinese economy's growing dependence on world markets for essential inputs for sustained growth, including energy, food grains, capital, and technology, all of which impose a price for belligerent behavior by the Chinese government. Corrosive capitalism follows from the spread within China of international liberal practices such as the rule of law standardized public financial disclosure, and managerial accountability. Decentralization encompasses fiscal reform and privatization of the media that result in a loss of control by the central government. Changing elite stakes include the expanding personal and professional investment of key regime constituencies in eco-

1. Susan Shirk, *The Political Logic of Economic Reform in China* (Berkeley: University of California Press, 1993), p. 71.

nomic integration, including the PLA's expanding business empire.

How will these four moderating factors undermine regime economic security in China, and how will the regime resist this process?

The World Bank has shown far more concern for [China's] environment than for political pluralism or the rule of law.

The tyranny of markets poses little risk to regime security in China. The international commodity markets are quite comfortable dealing with authoritarian regimes, and although financial markets take a longer term and more probing interest in the internal politics of debtor states, creditworthiness is far more important than internal political behavior. For example, China's premium on long-term sovereign debt (measured in terms of its pricing over United States Treasury debt of comparable maturity) while higher than that of a small democratic state such as Malaysia, is still less than 100 basis points, or 1 percent. There is some evidence that this risk premium widens in response to external tensions between China and its trading partners, but not necessarily in response to internal political tensions or repression—at least not unless that internal repression is particularly bloody and is featured on CNN.

Ironically, quasi-public financial institutions such as the World Bank and the Asian Development Bank (ADB) are also relatively unconcerned with China's internal political behavior. Aside from a brief hiatus after Tiananmen, the World Bank has rapidly expanded its lending activities to China, and the country is currently the bank's largest single borrower ($13.5 billion as of May 1996).

Beijing has been increasingly assertive in negotiating the terms and conditions of these concessional loans. For example, in its lending practices to China the World Bank has shown far more concern for the environment than for political pluralism or the rule of law. The ADB is equally accommodating. Its five long-term strategic development objectives are "promoting economic growth, reducing poverty, supporting human development (including population planning), improving the status of women, and protecting the environment"—but nothing about political pluralism. With $5.3 billion in loans as of December 1995, the People's Republic is the

ADB's largest current borrower and third-largest cumulative borrower.

Regime economic security suggests that the Chinese Ministry of Finance will continue to exercise close control over concessional loans, and will strive to keep such loans free of conditions on domestic political change or economic reform when it threatens regime security interests.

Capitalism's Corrosive Effects

An equally important source of capital and technology for China is foreign direct investment. But from a regime security standpoint, FDI is a transmission belt of both the tyranny of markets and more insidiously, the second moderating factor, corrosive capitalism. Once established inside China, foreign-invested firms can pose a competitive threat to state-owned enterprises; they can also spread unwelcome liberal practices such as organized labor unions and the rule of law.

For example, the state-owned enterprises problem reflects a collision between regime economic security and the imperatives of economic reform. The collapse of state-owned firms would pose a huge risk to the Beijing government. Millions of cashiered workers would spill into the streets of Beijing and other key urban areas. Collapse would also shock the already weak state banking sector because of its huge lending exposure to the state firms. And it would devastate the industrial supply base of the PLA. Yet state-owned enterprise losses already account for about 5 percent of GDP, which represents a staggering drain on China's economy.

Regime economic security suggests that government authorities will resist economic interdependence when it undermines state-owned enterprises. A good example is China's embryonic industrial structure policy, allegedly formulated to promote pillar industries such as autos, electronics, and pharmaceuticals. This policy tightly restricts FDI in pillar industries; it also includes coerced technology transfer from foreign firms (as a condition for FDI and trade licenses), and a host of restrictive nontariff barriers. These protectionist tactics violate World Trade Organization (WTO) rules, as well as Organization for Economic Cooperation and Development investment principles.

Regime economic security also predicts that the government will stiffen resistance to other liberal practices by foreign investors. For example, organizing independent labor unions outside the state-controlled All-China Federation of Trade Unions will remain anathema to the state authorities.

And If the Center Cannot Hold?

The third moderating factor, decentralization, which includes tax reform, privatization, and the free flow of information, would also undermine regime economic security.

Despite periodic so-called tax reforms—earnestly supported by the ADB—China's reformed tax system is no more objectively codified than the old tax system. The reforms have not brought more codification, transparency, recourse, or rule of law. Enormous latitude is still granted to government authorities to assess and collect a complex web of different taxes on the basis of negotiation, with a heavy input of *guanxi*, entertainment, back-scratching, and garden-variety corruption. This latitude increases with the level of authority, thus providing the government (and the Communist Party) with an intricate level of power on a national scale.

The free flow of information presents a sharp dilemma to the Chinese government. It is hard to sustain a modern industrial economy without the open exchange of information; yet a truly free media could allow a local political spark to ignite a national conflagration. The government has dealt with this problem by fighting a rear guard censorship campaign.

This campaign consists of self-censorship in the print media—enforced by the periodic prosecution of reporters for crossing the line—and direct censorship of the broadcast media, which are easier to monitor. Strong-arming StarTV to drop the British Broadcasting Corporation from its satellite transmissions into China is one example; Asia-Pacific Telecommunity Satellite (owned by several Chinese ministries) will go one step further by actually controlling the satellite transmission.

The computer-networking medium of the Internet and online services provides yet a third decentralization problem for the authorities, one that is less dangerous (at least today) because of a narrow audience, but somewhat more difficult either to monitor or censor. Regime economic security predicts Chinese experiments with network firewalls or other monitoring technologies for the Internet, and more heavy-handed interventions, such as the recent attempt by the Xinhua News Agency to monopolize inbound financial data services.

Oddly enough, regime economic security should encourage Beijing to strictly enforce intellectual property rights (IPR) agreements such as the WTO Trade-Related Aspects of Intellectual Property and the IPR agreement with the United States. These agreements would restrict the free circulation of many foreign materials and would improve the state's surveillance of publishing and media houses. Unfortunately IPR enforcement collides at the local level with graft, local party interests, and the cash flow of some PLA units, thus rendering the IPR issue extremely painful for the regime in Beijing.

Regime security also creates an incentive for the Chinese government to regularize its tariff and customs procedures as required by the WTO. Such regularized procedures, combined with more sophisticated scanning technologies and data-processing systems, would assist the Chinese government in intercepting shipments of subversive materials. Widespread smuggling of everything from automobiles to narcotics suggests that China has lost control over parts of its borders. Regime economic security predicts that this is likely to change; China will establish stricter incoming customs and immigration controls even if it slows down international commerce.

Protecting Who Gets What

The fourth moderating factor, changing elite stakes, presents the Chinese government with the most ambiguous trade-off between sustained economic growth and regime security. For example, the growing number of party members with technocratic backgrounds in the Central Committee and other party organs is changing the composition of the governing regime. But this technocratic metamorphosis is not necessarily making the regime any more accountable to outside parties beyond the selectorate or to the Chinese people.

Another example: the "princelings," or taizi, the offspring of Beijing leaders who are intimately involved with China's international trade, are more closely identified with continuing the regime's monopoly of power than with economic progress. Many taizi have little enthusiasm for expanding liberal trading practices, a transition to political pluralism, or public accountability.

Moreover, the influence peddling of the *taizi* and millions of other party members is the wellspring of pervasive official corruption in the People's Republic. Corruption is a glue that binds the interests of the members of the regime, but it is also a major threat to the legitimacy of the regime and thus to regime security. But regime economic security predicts no real progress in stamping out corruption in China, simply because the three elements that would solve the problem—the rule of law, political accountability, and a free press—directly challenge the security of the regime. As a result, the party's periodic anticorruption campaigns will remain a tool of factional infighting.

The growing business interests of the PLA, another important element in the changing stakes of the elite, pose a similar tough choice for the regime. The party's control of the military is partly based on controlling the military budget. Independent income from PLA businesses tends to undermine this party check as well as corrode the operational efficiency and integrity of the officer corps. However, the PLA is playing a key role in the power transition from Deng Xiaoping (a military man) to President Jiang Zemin (a party man), and Jiang cannot afford to displease the generals. Moreover, in the future the party will have to call on the PLA, as well as the People's Armed Police, to suppress popular dissent.

Regime economic security dictates that the commercial interests of PLA-affiliated businesses will take priority over economic efficiency and normal commercial interests. For example, WTO principles of public procurement and transparency conflict with the business practices of PLA-affiliated enterprises in civil engineering, transportation, and telecommunications; these principles will likely get short shrift by the regime when economic integration looms.

In sum, regime economic security predicts that the central government will broadly resist the domestic impact of interdependence. The cumulative effect of this resistance may explain the general slowdown in the speed of China's integration with the world trading and financial systems—what Margaret Pearson describes as a "plateau." She suggests that "China views the process of integration through a model [under the terms of which] it is practical and optimal for China to control carefully the process and depth of the country's integration. Full integration is only one outcome, and for a country with the degree of leverage China has [particularly with its large domestic market], it may only be possible to integrate in ways that suit the beliefs of the dominant leadership."

Given this plateau in the rate of integration, what sort of policies does China's regime economic security suggest for Japan, South Korea, and the Association of Southeast Asian Nations (ASEAN), as well as Europe and the United States, in their long-term strategy toward China?

The first element of any policy is a clear realization of the consequences of the failure of economic engagement of China, and for realistic expectations about the rate of change that may result from economic engagement. The goal of economic engagement is not necessarily Western- or Asian-style democracy, but rather political moderation and a modicum of pluralism.

For example, if the central government were to collapse and not be replaced by another effective civil authority, then any security threat posed by China would be replaced by terrible costs in human suffering: floods of refugees, famine, disease, crime, drug trafficking, environmental disaster, and international terrorism. The peaceful devolution of power is a tricky process, and the mechanisms by which economic integration is supposed to bring about political moderation are not well understood: some of the consequences of economic integration can actually undermine stability and the positive consequences of economic engagement appear to take a long time.

Despite this note of caution, it is very much in the interest of the pluralist countries of Asia, North America,

and Europe to persistently counter Beijing's resistance to the threats posed by interdependence to regime economic security. If China is permitted to merely pick and choose which aspects of integration it finds palatable, and to resist those that push in the direction of moderation and pluralism, then the time scale required by economic engagement will stretch toward infinity.

Both bilateral and multilateral negotiations with China should be used to selectively advance the very practices that threaten the regime, including the rule of law, transparency, the free flow of information, a regularized taxation system, independent labor unions, a reasonable degree of rectitude on the part of public officials, and a level playing field for all enterprises, including state-owned and PLA-affiliated firms. This also includes a key role for the World Bank and the ADB in advancing liberal practices and political pluralism as a condition for sustained lending activity to China.

In general, the North Americans and the Europeans appear more willing to advance liberal practices in China than the Asian states. American officials are increasingly suspicious of the depth of the Chinese government's commitment to the free trade principles of the WTO, and are taking a tougher line on the conditions of China's entry into the WTO—a line that is being supported by the European Union as well. Asian authorities—including Japan, South Korea, and ASEAN—have been publicly circumspect about China and the WTO. This reluctance to help "bell the Chinese cat" is due, among other things, to Asian success at industrial structure policy, widespread mercantilist practices in the region, unpleasant experiences at the hands of the United States trade representative, and a general distaste for Western hectoring of the Chinese.

But China is not a monolith; there are fissures in the facade of regime economic security and the outside world would do well to exploit them where possible. The desire to stifle the free flow of information may collide with the investment of PLA-affiliated enterprises in telecommunications. Rich provinces, which have influential members on the Central Committee, may support the rule of law if it can keep their assets from being expropriated by a revenue-hungry Ministry of Finance in Beijing. *Taizi* equity interests in importing firms may help resist arbitrary taxation or tariffs. A state-owned enterprise may embrace the WTO if a joint-venture partner or foreign export market is its only path to survival. All this suggests that outside actors should not deviate from the long-term goal of peaceful economic engagement but react with a large measure of flexibility and pragmatism to China's response to what it sees as threats to its regime economic security.

Article 3   *Harvard International Review*, Spring 1996

The Giant Wakes

The Chinese Challenge to East Asia

Gerald Segal

Gerald Segal is a Senior Fellow at the International Institute for Strategic Studies, Director of Britain's Pacific Asia Program, and Co-Chairman of the European Council for Security Co-operation in Asia Pacific.

The rise of China undeniably poses a problem for East Asian security. Those who suggest that there is not a problem are either strategically myopic or have prematurely capitulated to the notion of a Sinified East Asia. The real question is how to define the nature and extent of the Chinese challenge. Although China is often compared to the Soviet Union, a more appropriate comparison might be to Japan or Germany in the 1930s. China is undergoing far-reaching and destabilizing social and economic reform, while its authoritarian leadership is losing its ability to control China's rapidly changing social, economic and political system. Meanwhile, China is spending increasing amounts (in absolute terms) on its armed forces. Most importantly, China, like 1930s Germany or Japan, is a non-status quo, increasingly nationalistic power that seeks to change its frontiers and to reorder the international system. These trends do not necessarily prove that China is a threat. But it is instructive that these are precisely the characteristics of great powers in the past century that have posed the biggest challenge to their neighbors and to international order.

If these fundamental features of China are not cause enough for concern, consider China's past and present weight. For centuries China was the world's greatest civilization. It is still the world's longest lasting empire. Until 1850 it was the world's largest economy. In short, there is nothing extraordinary about the current rise of China, for in fact it is the re-rise of China. As a result, there is nothing especially odd about the people who live close to China deciding that when China is strong, they must accommodate rather than confront their giant neighbor.

During the past 150 years East Asians had grown used to a weaker and divided China. While China was tearing itself apart, other East Asian nations achieved remarkable economic success. Now that China too is on the rise, East Asians have to decide if they wish to allow China to regain its suzerain status in the region, or whether they wish to constrain Chinese behavior. If China is to be constrained, then it will have to be while it is still vulnerable to being tied into the international system.

Before the notion of "constrainment" is misread as "containment," it should be noted that China, as has already been suggested, is not very much like the Soviet Union during the Cold War. China's military is not poised to thrust through the Asian equivalent of the German plains. China is far more interdependent in the global market economy than the USSR ever was, and it is becoming even more so. China has abandoned its support for revolutionary Communist movements in East Asia, and its ruling Communist Party has abandoned Marxism-Leninism in all but name. But accepting that China is not to be contained like the Soviet Union should not mean abandoning all notion of constraining China's international behavior. It is important to avoid over learning the lessons of the Cold War and forgetting the lessons of earlier struggles against unstable and unsatisfied great powers.

Territorial Ambitions

China has territorial disputes with most of its neighbors and has refused to forswear the use of force to regain lost land. While its disputes with India are not a problem at the moment, this is only because India has essentially recognized the current lines of control, and China claims no Indian land beyond what it now holds. China and Russia have made some progress in delineating frontiers, and China has apparently abandoned its wider claims for territory seized by Czarist forces. Interestingly, Russia is the only resident power in East Asia with military power superior to that of China. China also claims islands currently held by South Korea and Japan but has put these issues aside while it seeks the economic benefits of good relations with these two countries.

The current focus of Chinese territorial ambition i[s] further south. In 1984, China obtained the agreement of the United Kingdom to return Hong Kong and its six million people to Chinese control in 1997. China clearly could have taken Hong Kong whenever it wanted to, but it saw the benefit of receiving a Hong Kong in decent economic shape, and this required a modicum of cooperation with Britain. That deal is now done, and as 1997 approaches China has shown ever more clearly that [it] feels unconstrained in molding Hong Kong to suit its interests. China promised to safeguard Hong Kong under the slogan of "one country-two systems," but it is already apparent that there will be one system for all.

The fate of Hong Kong is being watched by the 21 million people of Taiwan. The Taiwanese government once claimed to be the rightful government of all China, but it has now abandoned such a pretense. The rulers in Beijing have done no such thing. They view the signs of increasing support for self-determination in Taiwan as a fundamental threat to Chinese sovereignty and see no reason why they should eschew the use of force to prevent such a trend. In 1995 and again in 1996, China closed air and sea lanes in East Asia in order to "test-fire" missiles as a sign that it was still prepared to use force to crush even a democratically-elected government in Taiwan committed to self-determination.

Few doubt the sincerity of Beijing's threats, and therefore no East Asian government is prepared to suggest that it might be sympathetic to the Taiwanese people's calls for assistance in exercising their democratic right of self-determination. Only the more distant Western powers, especially the United States, remain less equivocal. They tell China that it should not use force to settle this dispute, but stop short of giving Taiwan a blank check to declare independence and trigger just the kind of crisis that everyone hopes will somehow go away. Many hope that Taiwan and China can reach some sort of pragmatic accommodation, perhaps in a loose federal structure, but even if such an accord could be reached, it would be a long time in the future.

Just as East Asians do not doubt China's determination to regain Taiwan, so they do not doubt China's desire and eventual ability to take the disputed islands, shoals, and rocks of the South China Sea. In the 1970s, China claimed and eventually took the more northerly Paracel islands. In the 1990s, it is working its way through the Spratly islands, taking all it can, albeit in a relatively cautious manner. In 1995, China took on a member state of the Association of Southeast Asian Nations (ASEAN) for the first time, seizing territory claimed by the Philippines. China has agreed to be bound by the United Nations Law of the Sea Convention, but only on the basis of Chinese sovereignty over the disputed territory. Thus China promised to allow freedom of navigation, but was determined to take and to hold the territory and the resources that might lie in its vicinity. East Asians know that everything China takes, it keeps. They also know that China is a threat in the sense that it is taking what they once thought was theirs. But they feel China cannot be stopped and, in any case, China has no desire to take their main territory.

A Chinese Order

Even if China satisfies its territorial ambitions in Hong Kong, Taiwan, and the South China Sea, and persuades Japan and South Korea to surrender their islands, it will not necessarily become a satisfied power. What China, like the Soviet Union during the Cold War, seems to want is a predominant voice in managing regional international relations.

Consider Chinese policy toward the most important regional security issue where China is not a direct protagonist: the Korean conflict. China is a neighbor of North Korea—indeed, it is North Korea's only ally. While China was flexible enough to open economic relations with South Korea, much to the chagrin of its ally in Pyongyang, it only normalized diplomatic ties when it was the last major power without decent relations with South Korea. In short, China's natural inclination was to take what economic benefit it could get from the relationship with the South, while not budging on political issues until it was too embarrassed to be so isolated.

As for security issues, China's behavior throughout the tension surrounding North Korea's nuclear program in 1993–1994 was at best passive and at worst obstructive of international efforts to force North Korea to comply with the International Atomic Energy Association (IAEA). China did not want a nuclear-armed North Korea, but it also did not want North Korea to be bullied into submission by the United States and its Western allies. So China equivocated. It declined to press North Korea to make concessions and most often claimed to be without influence in Pyongyang. Western negotiators remain uncertain about whether China did anything through private channels, but they certainly decline to say China was being helpful.

The 1994 agreement with North Korea accorded almost perfectly with Chinese desires, as North Korea was both shored up with Western assistance and not forced to capitulate. Pyongyang was allowed to remain ambiguous about whether it had diverted enough nuclear material into a weapons program. Japan and South Korea were persuaded that China would not cut off food and fuel supplies to North Korea so there was no point in seeking sanctions, with all the attendant risks of conflict. Thus the outcome of the Korea negotiations demonstrated that China was the major power in Northeast Asia—quite a change from earlier in the century when Russians and Japanese could pillage Chinese territory in Northeast Asia at will.

The lessons of the Korean nuclear crisis suggest that, while China is prepared to talk about regional security, it will seek to, and often can, win the result most favorable to its own national interests rather than to the interests of general security. Much the same lesson can be drawn from China's approach to regional security in East Asia as a whole. East Asians are only at the earliest stage of building what might someday be worthy of the name "regional security." East Asia made abortive attempts to establish regional security structures during the Cold War, but by the time the Soviet Union collapsed and its regional allies deflated, there was little left of regional security thinking, let alone any formal structures. The only formal multilateral arrangement in East Asia was a leftover of the British empire, the Five Power Defense Arrangements.

When East Asians began to think seriously about formal multilateralism, they began with the only half-way serious regional institution, ASEAN. ASEAN itself is more of a mutual confidence-building club, and it is certainly not an intrusive organization designed to constrain national security policy. Thus, when ASEAN formed the ASEAN Regional Forum (ARF), it did so with the dual recognition of its limited ability to constrain national security policy, even well into the future, and the need to accommodate the main post-Cold War feature of regional security—the rise of China. The combination of these two notions gave China a de facto veto over the development of regional security.

If China were committed to interdependence of security, openness, transparency, and confidence building measures, it could have seized the initiative by setting the ARF on a dynamic course of building regional security. China's actual behavior was quite the opposite and quite understandable from the Chinese point of view. China, and probably most of its neighbors, felt that it was natural for China to dominate regional security and saw no reason why Beijing should encourage the strengthening of international forces that would merely constrain China's ability to act as it sees fit.

So far, the result of this attitude has been predictable. The ARF is little more than a gentleman's dining club. The non-governmental partner of the ARF, the Council on Security and Cooperation in Asia Pacific (CSCAP) has not moved much further, largely because China is blocking any attempt to have Taiwanese representation in CSCAP. Neither the ARF nor CSCAP will discuss the Taiwan question. The South China Sea issue was raised in the ARF, but China made no change to its position regarding sovereignty. China has agreed to consider publishing a report on its military, but China's record on publishing accurate military information is abysmal. In sum, there is no regional security in East Asia that is not Chinese security.

Shaping Regional Order

One might well ask whether there [is] anything necessarily wrong with China taking the territory that it wants and ordering the international relations of East Asia in its own image, so long as China leaves us alone to live in peace. However, while China may become a satisfied and cooperative power when it has what it wants and its neighbors know their place, the logic of an increasingly interdependent East Asia suggests that such a future is not likely.

For example, China has already made it clear that it will tell its neighbors what policies they should have toward Taiwan. ASEAN states provoke Chinese wrath when Taiwanese officials visit for vacations, and Beijing even tells Japan which Taiwanese officials can visit without causing a diplomatic row. China also tells East Asians and others how they should handle visiting Chinese dissidents or the Dalai Lama. Even journalists and academics are told that they should stop writing critical things about China, or else they will be denied visas. When the writers remain uncowed, China then goes after the investors and even charities that support such freedom of expression by threatening to close access to the Chinese market.

> *China's policies and the ASEAN response suggest that China is not willing to accept the constraints of economic interdependence. As China grows strong and incorporates Hong Kong, its economic clout will be such that it can drive most of its neighbors into submission.*

Indeed, Chinese behavior on trade issues also suggests that it sees nothing wrong with hegemonic behavior in economic affairs. When Japan's trade surplus with China began to grow very large, Chinese officials instructed the Japanese government to restore a better balance, and China's brow beating succeeded where US threats of trade retaliation had failed. It is quite possible that China may soon demand the transfer of technology from the developed states of East Asia, even technology banned by the United States and the European Union (EU).

Not surprisingly, China is resistant to being constrained by the rules of the World Trade Organization (WTO), and Chinese negotiators still reject the idea that it should be subject to the WTO dispute settlement mechanism. Most ASEAN states have already accepted the Chinese argument, but Japan remains quietly supportive of US and EU demands that China be bound by the rules. China's policies and the ASEAN response suggest that China is not willing to accept the constraints of economic interdependence. As China grows strong and incorporates Hong Kong, its economic clout will be such that it can drive most of its neighbors into submission. China is unlikely to accept the kind of constraints that the United States accepted in joining the North American Free Trade Agreement.

The notion of China engaging in free trade in East Asia is so far in the future that there is little point in prolonging the discussion. But before moving on to considering responses to the Chinese challenge, consider a few other problems China might pose in the future. For instance, there is the possibility that if Russia collapses even further, China will seek to solve its dependence on foreign energy by taking the Russian Far Eastern territories. After all, China once claimed these territories as its own. China might also take a more active role in defense of beleaguered ethnic Chinese in Southeast Asia. Should Indonesia or Malaysia suffer internal struggles where ethnic Chinese are the targets of discrimination or worse, China would not sit idly by. Even if China does not use force to intervene, the ASEAN states would still find that their domestic affairs are ordered in part by the fear of what China might do.

Constraining China

Whether there is a will in East Asia to constrain China is unclear. The current conventional wisdom is that China should be "engaged." Of course it should. Few could argue with the noble goals of the ARF and of expanding economic relations. The problem is that engagement is a necessary but not sufficient condition of successful policy. All too often those who suggest that something more than engagement is necessary are dismissed as supporters of "containment" who oppose engagement. But engagement alone does not constrain China, especially an increasingly nationalistic China that sees talk of interdependence as a challenge to Chinese sovereignty.

If East Asians want [to] formulate a policy of "constrainment," they must start with a determination of interests. Most East Asians do not want China to take Taiwan or the South China Sea, but they feel there is little they can do to stop it. This legacy of Sinification is a major psychological affliction, as it tends to become a self-fulfilling prophecy. The assumption that nothing can be done means that those in the United States, Australia, Japan, Indonesia, Malaysia, the Philippines, and Thailand who might wish to build a de facto deterrence of China are not given the support to try. Hence US troops find it hard to establish bases. We are left with talk of "virtual alliances" and a "virtual American presence" in East Asia. That is a virtual policy.

If China is to be constrained, it will have to be told what others do not want it to do. It will have to be deterred from doing so. And if it persists, it will have to be compelled to cease. To some extent such a firm policy has only recently been adopted by the United States regarding Chinese threats to Taiwan. The United States can be firm if it wants to.

Constraining the Soviet Union was a tall order during the Cold War, and the current international conditions are far from propitious for constraining China. What is far more likely is a pre-Cold War type of international relations, in which timid powers shy of confrontation appease rising nationalists. Should this scenario come to pass, China will dominate East Asia and take what it wants. But if East Asians want to prevent Chinese domination and defend the freedom of action that they still have, they will have to recognize that the challenge posed by China's growing power is real and demands a firm response.

Article 4   *Far Eastern Economic Review,* August 29, 1996

Back to the Future

Nationalism replaces the drive to reform while leaders jostle for power

By Matt Forney in Beijing

An American academic recently went "way out on a limb" to predict that at some point, probably in this century, Deng Xiaoping will die. With China's communist patriarch reaching the age of 92 on August 22, the "daring" seems justified—and in broader terms than merely physical demise. But China's current leaders aren't waiting.

Nor are their possible successors: Proxies for the next generation of leaders are already debating the meaning of "Dengism" in the pages of state newspapers. Even Deng's family members have broken a centrally imposed taboo against commenting on his legacy.

The hullabaloo comes at a time of grave uncertainty in the leadership. Two high-level conclaves next year—the springtime National People's Congress and the Communist Party's seminal 15th Congress in the autumn—should settle a raft of personnel changes. In the meantime, China's top leaders will spend the next year jostling for position, forming and reforming alliances as each searches for more security in post-Deng China.

For whoever leads China after the patriarch dies, now is no time for bold initiatives to solve the longer-term issues that most threaten China's economic health. Instead, they'll stay the course: protecting state enterprises, easing inflation and hoping the non-state sector will grow away their worries.

They might succeed, assuming their plans aren't scuppered by a paradox of their own creation: strident nationalism serves the leadership's domestic agenda, but might frighten away the $100 million a day in foreign investment that keeps China's economy humming.

China has apparently been successful in putting the brakes on the headlong rush of economic expansion that Deng called for in 1992. This should remove the threat of an immediate crisis that would precipitate a political end-game. The latest round of economic indicators looks positive.

Retail inflation, which two years ago soared to more than 21%, shrank to only 7.4% in the first five months of this year

compared with the same period a year ago. Beijing's municipal government felt confident enough that the days of spiraling increases are past to boost rice prices in state stores by 10%—a bold move in a city where people spend the bulk of their incomes on food.

Foreign reserves stand at a record $85 billion, giving Beijing a comfortable cushion whenever it restarts rapid reforms. Economic growth, once racing ahead, shrank in the first six months to the single digits the government is aiming for. And actual foreign investment, irreplacable in making the economy more efficient, soared 20% in the first six months to $20 billion.

But there are still skunks in China's economic garden party—the state enterprises. Even as Beijing declares state enterprises to be "pillar industries," the numbers begin to stink. Far from turning towards prosperity, they're haemorrhaging even more money than last year. For every dollar China's industrial enterprises made in profit for the first six months, only one cent came from state enterprises.

"It's a worrisome trend," understates an economist from a multilateral lending institution in Beijing. And it's one likely to continue—pre-tax profits at state enterprises plunged nearly 9% in the first half compared to that period last year.

Beijing's response to the state-enterprise mess has been protectionist. Last month, China announced it will limit competition for 10 Chinese beer makers, including the struggling Tsingtao Brewery, to curb foreign domination in the market. Separately, Guangdong province recently limited imports of cars, computers and air-conditioners, among other household goods, for the same reasons.

China's current political winds help puff away opposition to such protectionism. A glance through the media reveals particularly virulent strains of nationalism, often with strong economic components.

Consider these recent headlines: "American-style French fries on the offensive, Chinese producers take what countermeasures?" *(Economic Research News);* "National tea defense battle waged in Hagzhou" *(Wenhui News);* and

a marketing report on powdered milk by the Chinese consultancy Taxon Marketing & Management concluded that "our countrymen were finally given a beating by foreign powdered milks . . . it was a soundless slaughter."

Such thinking permeates mainstream discourse. China's ascendant political doctrine—neoconservatism—states that markets alone can't enrich China's impoverished hinterland. Instead, it says, a reinvigorated central government should take a stronger hand in redistributing wealth to inland areas.

This sounds benign, and in theory in is. But the emphasis on strengthening the Party and the central government weds nicely with authoritarian leadership, xenophobia and crackdowns on dissent. A prominent writer at *Strategy and Management* magazine—China's lightning rod for neoconservative thought—recently thumped the table as he blazed with anger at foreign businesses for "disrupting China's state enterprises." Foreigners, he said, "are snatching them up for nothing and selling off the assets. Managers are glad for kickbacks and don't care if foreigners control our pillar industries."

It's hard to believe that's the main problem with state enterprises these days. And indeed, such knee-jerk nationalism worries many Chinese intellectuals, who see a need for flexibility. A daring article recently published in a small liberal monthly, *Reading,* argued that "probably no country resembles China in elevating [patriotism] to the highest moral standard."

The author, the former head of American studies at the prestigious Chinese Academy of Social Sciences, Zi Zhongjun, safely embedded her critique in a review of Qing-dynasty foreign policy. Zi notes that Chinese who propose working with foreigners have always been liable to accusations of being unpatriotic, whereas anti-foreign forces have not. This, she says, is folly: "Only when China can treat stronger and weaker countries with modesty . . . will the spirit of our country be genuinely healthy and mature."

Party chief Jiang Zemin is struggling to build a platform broader than mere patriotism. His signature "spiritual civilization" programme, announced last year, remains little more than a slogan. A Central Committee meeting in September should define the term, but only its energetic implementation would signal a boost to Jiang's power.

Meantime, the leadership tries to map Deng's legacy. Recent articles in the military's *Liberation Daily* have mentioned Deng's 1992 tour of southern China, when he issued his plea for fast growth that is largely ignored today. Deng's wheelchair-bound son, Pufang, last month violated a gag order by warning that many in government deviate from his father's legacy, and ascribing the

1989 Tiananmen Square demonstrations to both "leftists" and "rightists."

In the longer run, next year will bring major reshuffles. Jiang is lobbying for support to revive Mao Zedong's former post of Party Chairman, which was abolished in 1982 during an early brush of political reforms. As chairman, Jiang would acquire the leadership's most powerful title. That might not be enough; as head of the military, party and state, Jiang already holds the country's three most powerful positions. It's unclear that a new post would protect him, though the mere act of promoting himself would signal his authority.

One unanswered question: Where to shunt Premier Li Peng, the current leader most tainted by the June 4, 1989,

Tiananmen Massacre? "Li is the only top figure who shakes hands with foreign leaders and leaves a bad taste in their mouths," says a Western diplomat in the capital. But Li's strong following in the industrial ministries makes him a difficult man to sideline.

Most options point to demotion, to a position such as a vice-chairmanship of the party. That would leave smaller fry to take the premiership, with Vice-Premier Li Lanqing and politburo Standing Committee member Li Ruihuan the names most bandied about. But if the economy sours or if Jiang pins blame for the Tiananmen Square killings on Deng, then even the darkest horses—such as deposed party secretary Zhao Ziyang—could reappear.

Article 5   *The Washington Post National Weekly Edition,* April 1–7, 1996

China's New Nationalism

A mixture of the ancient and the modern, it keeps outsiders at a distance

Steven Mufson

Washington Post Foreign Service

BEIJING

As 150,000 troops, lashed by cold rains, massed in late February on China's southern coast to prepare for an exercise in missile diplomacy, people across the rest of the nation celebrated the Chinese New Year with family, food, drink and the most popular holiday pastime: tuning in to the annual Spring Festival TV variety show.

This year, the show featured a rendition of the hit song "Big China." Dressed in a tailored, off-white, two-piece suit that combined the simplicity of the uniform made popular by the late Communist Party chairman Mao Zedong with the collar worn by Confucian scholars in imperial times, singer Gao Feng crooned:

We all have a family whose name is China . . .

Look at that 10,000-mile Great Wall shuttle through the clouds . . .

Our big China, what a big family

This is what Chinese nationalism has become in the 1990s: a ladle of militarism, a pinch of Maoism, a spoonful of Confucianism; one part modern, one part traditional, one part belligerent—and one part lounge act.

And yet Chinese nationalism, however muddled, is emerging as a potent force in a country that is striving to shake off its image as the sick man of Asia and regain ancient glory in a modern era. Driven by recent economic achievements and dreams of ancient splendor, Chinese nationalists also harbor a sense of wounded national pride left over from the 19th century, a love-hate relationship with Western culture and an uncomfortable feeling that China's 5,000 years of history are as much a burden as they are a foundation for the future.

The nationalist ferment has been greeted with mixed emotions in Asia and the rest of the world. Americans have waited eagerly for China to open its doors to the outside world, but from behind those doors some strong anti-foreign sentiments have emerged. And Asians who see a stable, healthy China as the key to their regional prosperity now worry that resurgent Chinese nationalism will lead to a modern form of the Qing Dynasty tribute system of centuries ago, with China's neighbors providing investment, technology, cheap credit and diplomatic compliance in place of the 18th-century ritual prostrations and gifts.

The political disappearance of the 91-year-old Chinese leader, Deng Xiaoping, has added to regional concerns. Deng, a revolutionary war veteran, did not need to prove his nationalist credentials. He smoothed out foreign policy problems and kept his focus on the economy. Today's weaker Chinese leaders, including President and Communist Party leader Jiang Zemin and Premier Li Peng, must prove their strength through tough talk and military exercises and perhaps bend more toward nationalist hard-liners.

The definition of Chinese nationalism remains fuzzy. The country has at least 55 ethnic groups, dialects that cannot be understood from one part of the country to another, at least five major religions and a history subject to divergent interpretations. Small wonder that Sun Yat Sen, who founded the Chinese republic in 1911, once called China "a dish of loose sand."

The current crisis over Taiwan encapsulates the region's fears about Chinese nationalism, even though China claims it is purely an internal matter. Regardless of the merits of the dispute, China's nationalist rhetoric and missile diplo-macy are seen as endangering Asia's prosperity. Singapore Senior Minister Lee Kwan Yew, an ethnic Chinese, has tried to calm the diplomatic waters by urging both China and Taiwan to put aside their differences. "After suffering so patiently for two centuries, the Chinese people and their leaders can surely afford to be patient a little longer," Lee says. "East Asia's high economic growth depends on continuing peace and stability."

But the new Chinese nationalists have other priorities. "You can't deny the Chinese nation," says a prominent Communist Party official with close ties to top military leaders. "This isn't a question of what the party says. This is what the Chinese people say. There's not much to say about theory and international relations. That's just the way it is."

China's nationalist rhetoric is largely driven by China's own internal dynamics. Many Communist Party leaders and theorists are looking to nationalism to serve as a crutch now that the pillars of Marxist ideology and class struggle have crumbled. Mao also appealed to Chinese nationalism; on the founding of the People's Republic on Oct. 1, 1949, he declared from the top of Beijing's Tiananmen gate that "the Chinese people have stood up." But contemporary Communist leaders have gone to new lengths to wrap themselves in the flag and identify the party with the nation—and thus make criticism of the party line an unpatriotic act.

The Communist rulers have reshuffled icons in Tiananmen Square, itself symbolic of the mandate of heaven in imperial times. National day celebrations no longer include large portraits of Communist philosophers Marx and Engels; instead, a giant portrait of the non-Communist Chinese nationalist Sun Yat Sen stands alone in the square.

In 1994, one of China's most powerful leaders, Li Ruihuan, broke a long-standing Communist taboo against ancestor worship by laying flowers and planting a pine tree by the mausoleum of China's Yellow Emperor, the legendary ancestor of the Chinese people. That legend was spun by nobles in 450 B.C. who transformed a local agrarian god into a common ancestor to legitimize their claim to power. Today, the mausoleum draws tourists from China, Japan and the Chinese diaspora.

"The previous ideology has gone into decline," says Xiao Gongqin, a professor at the Shanghai Normal University. "A large country such as China needs something to keep the country together. So nationalism is taking the place of the previous ideology as the coalescing force."

One obstacle to that strategy is that the definition of Chinese nationalism remains fuzzy. The country has at least 55 ethnic groups, dialects that cannot be understood from one part of the country to another, at least five major religions and a history subject to divergent interpretations. Small wonder that Sun Yat Sen, who founded the Chinese republic in 1911, once called China "a dish of loose sand."

As a result, the answers to the Communist Party's nationalist rallying cries often seem unfocused. When the party called for "patriotic education" in September 1994, enterprising business people from Hainan and Beijing responded by announcing that they were planning a patriotic theme park in the capital. The Chinese military has initiated weekly patriotic sing-alongs. Qinghua University students do 10-day stints of military training, with uniforms and gas masks.

"What is Chinese nationalism?" asks Beijing writer Wang Xiaobo as he sips a cup of tea at a Kentucky Fried Chicken outlet here. "People always talk about traditional culture. I as a Chinese don't know what they're talking about."

He points to a small paper windmill the franchise is giving away, the sort of gimmick that fast-food franchises use around the world. "Is this nationalism?" he asks. "The government says we have missiles, an army, a seat at the United Nations, and ordinary people have been brainwashed to feel proud on hearing these things. But the Belgians have national pride and they have no missiles, they don't have a big army, and they can't threaten other people."

American political scientist Lucian W. Pye has written that Chinese nationalism lacks substance or common vision. Instead, it is fueled by a set of common enemies—imperialism, hegemonism and corrupting foreign influences. And that is what many people in Asia find unsettling.

"China's nationalism is: 'We won't allow anyone to come and tear us apart.' This is the deepest part of the Chinese soul," declares a ranking government official who says he belongs to the Communist Party only because it's the best vehicle for his nationalist sentiments.

The anti-foreign dimension is a product of Chinese history. For a century, starting in 1842, when British troops defeated the Qing emperor to defend the British-dominated opium trade, China struggled to rid itself of foreign imperial powers. In 1860, British troops marched into Beijing and burned down the emperor's summer palace. In 1900, anti-Westernism fueled the Boxer Rebellion and the slaughter of foreign missionaries and their converts. In the 1930s, Japanese forces invaded, occupied much of the country and massacred millions.

"Chinese nationalism is almost exclusively based on an anti-foreign mentality and is a rather recent product," says Huang Yasheng, a professor at the University of Michigan. "It evolved in the last 150 years or so mainly in reaction to the forcible opening by the West, and for that reason it can be virulent and almost always anti-Western."

Even though it is reestablished as an important power, China still acts like a country with something to prove, and it collects what it sees as new slights to its pride. In 1993, the Olympic Committee's decision to hold the 2000 Olympics in Sydney was interpreted as being orchestrated by foreign bullies. An influential middle-ranking party official complained that Hillary Rodham Clinton snubbed a Chinese delegation that greeted her at the airport during the U.N. women's conference last year. President and party chief Jiang Zemin refused to go to Washington to meet President Clinton for a "working visit" because he wanted the 21-gun salute that goes with a state visit.

Asian countries are not immune to China's anti-foreign sentiments. Last year, on the 50th anniversary of the end of World War II, Chinese state-run media heaped abuse on Japan for its savage occupation and its insufficient remorse. In popular television series and movies, the Japanese are almost universally demonized. When Chinese champion swimmers flunked drug tests at the Asian Games in Hiroshima in October 1994, that too was portrayed as a Japanese plot by a popular Beijing newspaper.

The tensions between China and the United States are particularly important to Asian nations. In an unusually frank assessment, Singapore leader Lee said recently that Asia needs the American security umbrella for protection against China and to guarantee the stability in which economies thrive.

Yet China's attitude makes American policymaking tricky. The United States wants to tame China's aggressiveness and prevent it from trying to dominate other countries in Asia. But American pressure risks awakening China's sense that it is being pushed around. Despite repeated denials by Clinton administration officials, it has become widely accepted within Chinese government circles that Washington wants to contain Beijing's economic and geopolitical expansion.

China's increasing integration with the rest of the world through its economic growth has also helped awaken nationalism. Just as the Great Wall failed to keep foreign invaders out of China, the rhetorical great wall of the ruling party's anti-Western ideology is being scaled by the forces of cultural imperialism. McDonald's golden arches tower over the Avenue of Eternal Peace. Coca-Cola, which sold its first soda here in 1979, sold 2.4 billion cans in 1993. Last year, the Internet opened new gateways to the West for tens of thousands of Chinese citizens, and the sound of the BBC and Voice of America can be picked up on portable short-wave radios.

Intellectuals bemoan the loss of China's "Chineseness," though few people can pinpoint what that means.

"We should have our language purified," commentator Duan Gang has written, suggesting that foreign words such as MTV, CD and karaoke be outlawed. Language, he says, is the key to national development and independent thinking and links Chinese people all over the world. "It is a language with a long history and strong life," he says.

"Whoever uses foreign phrases in our own language should be regarded as knowing next to nothing."

A recent Beijing Daily article cited a student survey of 20 consumers who all chose a shirt with a foreign brand name over one with a Chinese brand name. The paper quoted a student as saying: "What kind of social mentality is this? It's very hard to imagine that a generation of young people who hanker after American food, are infatuated with Japanese electronics and wallow in French fashion can have national pride and dignity." A group of delegates to the national legislature called on the government to restrict foreign names with "colonial and feudal colors."

What do all these conflicting sentiments mean? Is China's amorphous nationalism something that needs to be contained? Will China reach out to claim territory or tribute from other parts of Asia?

Xiao, the Shanghai professor, says no. China, he says, lacks the messianic or utopian tradition of Europe that fueled Nazism, for example. He says China's Confucian tradition and relatively agnostic attitude would prevent its nationalism from becoming expansionist. "There's no Vladimir Zhirinovsky in China," says one neo-nationalist promoter in Beijing government circles, referring to the Russian ultra-nationalist politician.

But others note that Japan in the 1930s was expansionist without the fire of religious fervor. And China itself has often extended its influence far from Beijing. Some scholars note that China already occupies most of the territory that was once the object of its imperialist ambitions, including the regions of Xinjiang and Tibet, making further expansion unnecessary or even risky. In both Tibet and Xinjiang, the Chinese government has settled more people from the Han ethnic group in an effort to make the Uighurs of Xinjiang and the Tibetans into minorities in their own home areas. Still outside China's borders but within its orbit lie Vietnam, Korea and Mongolia, all of which paid tribute in earlier times.

Over the past five years, official documents have used the term "living space" when discussing Chinese claims on the disputed Spratly Islands. And Chinese navy ships have tangled with Vietnamese and Philippine forces near the islands.

The average Chinese citizen seems somewhat removed from nationalist geopolitics. The Chinese are deeply patriotic. They crowd around the flag-raising and -lowering ceremonies in Tiananmen Square. They root mightily for Chinese world champion runners and swimmers. They are angered that they were kept out of the World Trade Organization at its founding. But their private interests, such as making money, dominate the minds of most Chinese, and the average person seems reluctant to fight for Taiwan.

Chinese interviewed here said this year's Spring Festival variety show was not as popular as last year's because of the heavy emphasis on patriotic themes. They said they preferred last year's program, which featured skits poking fun at corrupt government and party officials.

There are occasional hints of more virulent or mystic strains of Chinese nationalism outside the stilted official Communist Party literature. Recently the government said it had discovered a group of students with Nazi books and memorabilia. Dissident lawyer and labor organizer Yuan Hongbing, who is now in detention, has written that the Chinese race needs a national hero and savior.

"This race that dwells on the continent of East Asia once shone with a brilliance bestowed by the sun. Now it has its back to the icy wall of history, driven there by the forces of Fate," he wrote. "We must prove whether we are an inferior race or not."

How that wall of history is viewed holds the key to the future of Chinese nationalism. It could become a source of inner strength during rapid social and economic transformation and an inspiration for a cultural renaissance. Or it could become a tool used by the party-run state to crush dissent and diversity at home and intimidate China's neighbors.

"Today, China's leaders talk about the greatness of China's civilization, but they only emphasize the most authoritarian aspects of Confucianism, such as hierarchy, ideological unity and rule by an elite," says Merle Goldman, a professor of intellectual history at Boston University. "They don't explain that the elite had higher principles than just staying in power, such as loyalty to Confucian principles that dictates that leaders not abuse their power, be honest and listen to the voice of the people."

And while he doesn't share Goldman's view of Chinese history, a neo-nationalist party official with connections to top government leaders agrees that, "If you want to understand China, there's only one class you have to take, and that's history."

Article 6   *The National Interest*, Fall 1996

The Short March

China's Road to Democracy

Henry S. Rowen

Henry S. Rowen is professor emeritus of public management at the Graduate School of Business, and senior fellow of the Hoover Institution, Stanford University. The author is grateful for the comments and suggestions of several colleagues, especially to Minxin Pei of Princeton University.

When will China become a democracy? The answer is around the year 2015. Some might think such a prediction foolhardy but it is based on developments on several fronts, ones inadequately reported in the American media. There are, indeed, unmistakable signs of important positive changes in China. These changes are undoubtedly related to China's steady and impressive economic growth, which in turn fits the pattern of the way in which freedom has grown in Asia and elsewhere in the world.

Bad But Getting Better

According to the latest survey of political rights and civil liberties by Freedom House, China's freedom rating is, in effect, zero.[1] At first glance it is easy to see why. The country remains a one-party state under the rule of the Communist Party; the Justice Ministry admits to having 2,700 "counter-revolutionaries" in prison (many of them actually political dissidents and labor and human rights activists); officials admit to over 2,000 summary executions in 1994; people are often detained for long periods without trial; and many people, especially peasants, are ill-treated by local authorities.

On the other hand, things have improved. China has come far since the disastrous Great Leap Forward of the 1950s, and the lunatic Cultural Revolution in the 1960s and early 1970s. Higher incomes have given people more personal space, agents of the state have less control over citizens' lives, and the typical Chinese is freer to move about the country. The coercive one-child policy is being flouted in the countryside, causing authorities to adopt economic incentives in an effort to gain compliance.

The progress that has been made, and the prospect for more of the same, can be considered under three headings: the growth of grassroots democracy; the struggle toward a rule of law; and the liberalizing of the mass media.

Grassroots Democracy

Reforms in village elections came out of the disasters of collectivized agriculture. Faced with starvation in the late 1970s, peasants in Anhui province disbanded local communes and returned to family plots. Thus began a process of de-collectivization and transition to a market economy, which is now far advanced.[2]

The dissolution of the commune system left in place no institution capable of addressing infrastructure needs, schooling, or any of the other functions of local government. In Guangxi province, villagers responded by organizing committees to maintain social order, mediate disputes, and manage public utilities and welfare. The political vacuum created by de-collectivization led to the amendment of the Chinese constitution in 1982 to provide for village government. A crucial decision concerned the role of the Communist Party in the new arrangement. Was the Party to appoint village officials? Were provincial and town officials to appoint them? Instead of adopting either of these arrangements, in 1987 the central government decided that they would be chosen by elections, and these began in 1988. The political crackdown after the Tiananmen massacre immediately raised questions about the future of this institution, but it has survived.

Village government now consists of a Village Committee functioning as the executive, and a Representative Assembly as a form of legislature. By the early 1990s, 90 percent of village committees had been elected, but the process has been ragged. Elections were unfamiliar phenomena and procedures were understandably irregular. Many people did not take them seriously, as past elections had been only a formality. At first most presumed that upper levels of the government and party would rig the outcomes, and in fact local Party cadres have continued to resist relinquishing their privileges, and non-Party members have often been subjected to various forms of discrimination. Some representative assemblies dominated by members of the old establishment still hold that Party membership is the main qualification for candidacy. Foreign observers have witnessed instances of probable ballot fraud, and it is safe to assume that in elections without such observers the incidence of fraud is higher. Although the law provides for a secret ballot, provisions for privacy in voting are inadequate.

Despite all these drawbacks, substantial progress has been made. Fujian province is perhaps the most advanced in this process, with four rounds of elections behind it. (It has the advantage of being on the coast and benefits from contact with the Taiwanese.) In 1993, the Fujian People's Congress passed an election law, the first provincial legislature to do so. Among other things it changed the basis of voting from one vote per household to one vote per person. In the 1991 elections, 49 percent of the winners were non-Party members; however, in 1995, the *Washington Post* reported that although 40 percent of the candidates who won were not members of the Communist Party, half of them joined later.

Observers of the 1994 elections in Fujian reported, not surprisingly, that Party members were worried about their diminishing control of the various village economies, and expressed these concerns through active lobbying efforts. But these were not always successful in preventing competition. It is up to local officials to decide if an election will be competitive, as distinct from voters facing a "choice" of only one candidate. When there is no competition the only recourse for those who object is abstention. If a significant number do abstain the election is perceived as a failure, and this constitutes a form of pressure for future competition.

In Nanping City in Fujian province, more than thirty peasants from Tiantou village wrote an open letter to election organizers claiming that, "In the past few years, the work style and morality of the village officials have become intolerable and the situation is really serious." They proposed the election of one Chen Jinman and four other lesser local luminaries to the village committee. When the five nominees posted a three-year work plan at the gate of the village committee office, some officials complained that this was going too fast toward democracy. Nonetheless, the nominees' management plan was advertised, a competitive election was held, and the five were elected.

For all the defects of the electoral process, the principle of selecting village leaders by competitive election rather than appointment from above is established, as is the principle of fixed terms of office. Local government is becoming more transparent, and information on village affairs, including finances and officials' salaries, is being posted in public. More elections are being contested. "Class struggle" is no longer employed in dealing with political and social conflicts, nor are those who stand against Party members automatically denounced as "enemies of the people."

It is likely that this process will continue, with election procedures steadily becoming more comprehensive, standardized, and transparent. Growing numbers of peasants are learning about legal procedures, and may be expected to use the law to protect their rights. The Communist Party will face more competition from businessmen, clan organizations, and others expressing a variety of interests. What was begun at the grassroots has already started to influence behavior higher up in the system, too. Recently, several provincial deputy governors who were not on the official slate have been appointed, and they have been accepted by Beijing; and some prominent members of the Party, scheduled for election to the National People's Congress, have lost.

A Rule of Law

The rule of law was never established in modern China, and under Communist rule law has been until recently a political and administrative instrument of the Party dictatorship.[3]

As late as 1980 there were only three thousand lawyers in a country of over one billion people. Since then there has been more than a twentyfold increase in the number of legal professionals, and Chinese courts now hear over three million cases a year. But this is still seen to be inadequate: In June 1992 President Jiang Zemin said that China needs 300,000 lawyers, and the current goal is to have 150,000 by the year 2000. That about equals the combined number of lawyers in Germany, France, Benelux, and Denmark—though China has nine times as many people.

This expansion comes in response to a growing demand for the rule of law. Specifically, the Chinese people are demanding that the government observe its own stated rules. Values consistent with Western ideals of equality, justice, and legality—as well as with ancient Chinese ideals—are being expressed at all levels of society, and are finding their way into legislation.

Chinese officials are explicit in acknowledging that China needs a more developed legal system, because a market economy must be governed by law. Foreign firms in particular require consistency and transparency in the laws to which they must adhere, and these are often lacking. In Shanghai, a principal center of foreign business activity,

> There is no distinction between official policy and officials' references. . . . Lawyers report that when they contact the tax bureau to ask about changes in the law . . . they are advised to consult the bureau's consulting company (for a substantial fee). . . . In the absence of laws, there are rules and then clarifications. And because these often appear contradictory to confused foreign businessmen, it seems that there are no rules at all, just the arbitrary interpretation or whim of the official asked.[4]

There is good reason to question China's ability to sustain rapid growth in the absence of stable and fairly enforced rules that foreign investors find acceptable. (This applies less, however, to overseas Chinese, who have a comparative advantage in a game without formal rules, because of their contacts and skill in personal dealings.)

The growing weakness of the state also elicits demands for law and order. This is evident in the general frustration with massive corruption at all levels: illegal businesses run by government agencies, the theft of government assets, and evasion of price controls and taxes. At the same time, the weakening power of the state makes it more difficult to achieve an effective judicial system.

Among the many shortcomings of the legal system, Anthony Dicks asserts that the most fundamental is the fact that "the Communist Party is outside the jurisdiction of the ordinary courts", despite a 1982 constitution that says that "the political parties . . . must abide by the Constitution and the law", and that "no organization or individual is privileged to be beyond the Constitution or the law."

There are several other serious problems, including slack enforcement of decisions in civil proceedings. In practice, enterprises run by the military are not penalized and large and medium sized state owned enterprises are often protected by local officials, which amounts to being outside the law. Nor are courts themselves exempt from the endemic corruption; lawyers bribe judges, who often make it known to those appearing before them that they are interested in stepping down soon from the bench to enter private practice.

The criminal process is the least reformed of all, and it still serves functions established by a totalitarian regime. Pre-trial detention often exceeds the statutory three months, and arbitrary arrest, detention, and torture continue. Police can impose low-level punishments for minor offenses and may also sentence offenders to "labor re-education" of up to three years for offenses that are defined loosely and in moralistic language.

However, in Beijing, the National People's Congress is rewriting the criminal laws to state that defendants shall not be presumed guilty, that they shall have lawyers, and that the police shall no longer be able to hold them without charge. Doubtless, for some time to come these new laws will often be observed in the breach, but their passage is an indicator of the growing demand for democratic procedures.

The level of competency and professionalism of lawyers in China is low. According to Alford and Lubman, few lawyers (and even fewer members of the judiciary) have university law degrees, and many of those who do studied law for a centrally planned economy, much of which has been superseded. They are better suited to be state legal workers than autonomous lawyers. There is not yet a widely shared understanding of the distinction between public and private interests, or of how these are to be reconciled. Tripling the number of lawyers by the year 2000 will not by itself solve these problems.

For all these many shortcomings, notes Alford, Chinese lawyers in some instances "are now able to represent in an unprecedentedly vigorous manner clients whose interests may not be wholly synonymous with the state's." Arguably, the Supreme People's Court has begun to make law through its interpretations and decisions, a role that is contrary to communist dogma, which allows no place for an independent institution. This process seems likely to continue.

Among academics, and increasingly in the public security bureaucracy, there are calls for change—at least for rationalization, if not for liberalization. According to Lubman, "as institutions of the Party-state erode, legal rules and institutions, however incomplete and tentative by Western standards, may grow more able to exercise the functions of Western private law in the emerging sectors of the economy outside the economic plan."

Another indication of a shift from an ad hoc to a rule-based system is a recent change in China's tax system. In 1994, separate national and local taxes and tax services were established. Such a separation, it is important to note, is an essential feature of a federal system of government—fiscal federalism—as distinct from one that is merely administratively decentralized.[5] While the latter can be easily reversed, fiscal federalism is more likely to endure, becoming de facto constitutional. Within the American constitutional structure, fiscal federalism has been the source of enormous economic and political benefits. It is, of course, far too early to predict similar benefits for China from an initiative that is still in its infancy, but it is another bit of evidence for the emergence of a system based on rules.

The demands of a market economy require such rules, as well as transparency and fairness—all attributes directly at odds with a Leninist ruling party. A choice must be made and it is evident that, slowly and irregularly, the market path is being chosen.

Media Self-Liberalization

As described by Minxin Pei, the liberalization of the Chinese economy after 1979 had the unintended, and to the regime unwelcome, effect of leading to the self-liberalization of the mass media.[6] This came about through the combined effects of market forces, foreign influences, and changes in technology. Together with a more active and critical Chinese intelligentsia, these factors have produced a remarkable increase in freedom of information. The process was led by book publishing and was followed by journals and newspapers. The electronic media lagged, evincing little liberalization in the 1980s, but it too is following the general trend in the 1990s. The net effect of all this has been significant. For example, a history of the Cultural Revolution was published despite government efforts to ban it; a book attacking the Chinese character (*The Ugly Chinese*) became a bestseller; stories about official corruption began appearing; and works opposing the Three Gorges Dam and favoring deeper respect for the rule of law were published.

The shift to the market was the major cause of this Chinese glasnost. The market increased the channels of production and distribution of materials because there was money to be made by entrepreneurs; at the same time, the government was losing money in its many state-owned publications and outlets. As it cut back on state subsidies for publication, many journals and newspapers were forced into the market. In 1984 the government permitted collective private publishing houses (in effect partnerships) to function. This soon led entrepreneurs to adopt many of the functions of the former state publishing houses: finding authors, translators, paper, and printers. In Xinhua's bookstores in 1979, the huge state media empire held 95 percent of the market; by 1988, its share had shrunk to one-third. In Beijing in 1992 there were about two thousand kiosks, and for many of them, profits came largely from the sale of illicit publications.

The newspaper business has evinced a similar trend: non-Party papers have gained market share at the expense of Party publications. According to Pei, 1,008 newspapers were founded between 1980 and 1985, only 103 of which were Party controlled.[7] As Party papers lost, market share they reduced their propaganda content in order to compete. Nonetheless, hampered as they still were by censorship, circulation and advertising decreased.

Initially, the government was better able to manage the electronic and film media. This was partly because the costs of entry were much higher than for print media. But the market eventually made its power known. The government's censored materials were unpopular and falling demand led to mounting losses. Unprofitable government operations were spun off to private operators. Government stations such as Dongfang TV in Shanghai introduced live coverage of breaking stories, talk shows, call-in programs, 24-hour broadcasting, and celebrity interviews of liberal intellectuals whom the hardliners had silenced after 1989. Callers complained about the quality of government services, putting pressure on them to improve. Taken together, these developments have made censorship increasingly impractical. Hence something very basic has changed: The state is losing control of information.

The film business went through a similar evolution. Dreary and unpopular state productions resulted in revenue losses. Already in the 1980s, the government allowed foreign films and TV programs to enter China and in 1992 it ended the state monopoly on film distribution. The result: more private activity, leading to greater competition, which in turn has led to greater variety and higher quality.

The Chinese government's decision to seek foreign investment in order to acquire advanced technology and expertise reinforced these domestic changes. This meant admitting many more foreign businessmen, sponsoring more technological and business exchanges, and creating more electronic links to the rest of the world. Western newspapers found their way to major tourist hotels (and beyond) and access to CNN was approved in the mid-1980s.

Both were cut off after the Tiananmen massacre and restrictions on foreign investment in media were imposed—all to little effect on the flow of information. Working against the regime's efforts to maintain control were growing incomes combined with advances in technology. Televisions, radios, cassette players, and VCRs proliferated widely. In 1985, the government allowed local TV stations and educational and research institutions to set up their own satellite ground stations; by 1990 more than sixteen thousand had been established, creating a system too large for the authorities to monitor effectively. In the 1990s Chinese manufacturers began to make home satellite dishes. The national authorities decreed prohibition but failed to enforce it; by the early 1990s an estimated 4.5 million were operational. Broadcasts from Hong Kong greatly increased their penetration of the market in south China, to the discomfiture of the censors in Beijing. Also, by 1991 more than eighty thousand firms, institutions, and government units were equipped with fax machines, with a projected market increase of ten thousand a year through the decade.

The Chinese government has not pursued a consistent policy line on freedom of information. Between 1978 and 1993 there were waves of liberalization with intervening periods of repression. These oscillations have resulted from shifts among factions in Beijing, developments in the market, and in response to some unpleasant events. Even the crackdown after the Tiananmen massacre did not prevent further liberalization in late 1992, after Deng's visit to south China. The message is clear: Once a totalitarian regime ventures down the path of market reforms, it loses control of its information organs. In China this process was hastened by the gradual loss of control over many other aspects of political life.

Clearly, there is a widening zone of tolerance within which journalists and editors operate. Because those in the media have a financial stake in not being shut down, they stay clear of the (ill-defined) far edge of the zone; in short, there is a good deal of self-censorship and government monitoring. Unsurprisingly, too, a great deal of what is published freely is commercial in character—instructions on how to get rich, for example—and politically unthreatening. What Ramon Myers of the Hoover Institution calls the "ideological marketplace" of politics is still outside the zone of tolerance. Dissidents who oppose the government do not have access to the media because they are considered by editors to be too hot to handle, and they must resort to distributing leaflets and to hunger strikes. But with the exception of some journalists accused of selling state secrets to Hong Kong, there have been no criminal proceedings against journalists for several years.

There will continue to be waves of progress and regression, no doubt, but the underlying tide is raising the overall level of freedom of information. This, taken together with the strengthened rule of law and democracy at the grassroots, shows clearly that the long march away from the totalitarian character of the Communist Party is well underway.[8]

China Is No Different

These changes at the grassroots in China are similar to those that took place in Taiwan at a comparable stage of development. China's per capita GDP is now about $2,500. When Taiwan reached that level in the early 1970s, the Kuomintang Party (KMT) was firmly in charge but changing its ways, much as the Chinese Communist Party is today. Local elections had been held every three years after 1950; over time local bosses had become more responsive to the popular mood, and non-KMT individuals had become active in local politics. In 1973, Taiwan's Freedom House democracy score was 25 (on a scale of 0 to 100). Then its political liberalization began to increase significantly (as is happening to China today)—although at first no organized opposition was allowed (again, as in China). The first open, free election for parliament occurred in 1992, and in March of this year Taiwan held its first presidential election—also deemed free and fair.

The path of political liberalization in South Korea was different but the end point was similar. After the coup that brought Park Chung Hee to power in 1961, elections were held but results were determined by the ruling party. The country's 1974 freedom rating was 33. Political change came rapidly during the mid-1980s and by 1995 its rating had jumped to 84. South Korea was becoming increasingly wealthy as these changes were taking place.

The political evolution of Taiwan and South Korea are but two examples of a wider phenomenon. The worldwide norm, first clearly established by Seymour Martin Lipset, is "the richer the country the freer" (the exception being those enriched through oil, such as Saudi Arabia and Brunei).[9] The curve marked Worldwide Freedom-Income Regression in the figure below shows the relationship between per capita income and Freedom House's 1995 ratings for all countries, indicating an average. The correlation is not perfect in East Asia or anywhere else; Singapore, for example, has a low freedom rating for its income level and the Philippines a high one. But the overall fit is good and it shows that the wealth-democracy connection is not a European artifact. This bears on the assertion by various Asian authorities and intellectuals, mostly in Singapore and Malaysia, that Asian democracy is different from its Western cousin. Perhaps it is in some ways, but the reality is that, although the East Asian income-freedom pattern shown in the figure is a bit lower than the worldwide average, this region is like others in that the wealthier a country, the more (Western-style) freedoms its people enjoy.

The prospects for Chinese liberalization thus rest, above all, on continued rapid economic progress. Since 1979, China has grown annually at over 5 percent per capita (at international prices).[10] If it continues on this trajectory—by no means a certainty—China's per capita GDP will be between $7,000 and $8,000 (in 1995 dollars) by the year 2015. This figure is very significant. Several scholars have suggested that the transition to stable democracy correlates with mean incomes between $5,000 and $6,000, and becomes impregnable at the $7,000 level.[11] There is a compelling logic behind the statistical relationship. Growing wealth is accompanied by increased education, the building of business and government institutions with some autonomy, and the formation of attitudes that enable democratic governments to survive when they have a chance at power. Spain, Portugal, Chile, and Argentina, in addition to Taiwan and South Korea, all made the transition to democracy while they were within this income range.

No one can know precisely how democracy in China will evolve, but its record over the past fifteen years and the experience of other countries in East Asia suggest more competition in local and provincial politics, ultimately reaching the National Congress—although organized political opposition on the national level might be banned for a long time. Freedom of information will expand further and the rule of law will become ever stronger. This process is unlikely to be smooth and there may well be setbacks, as in the regime's reaction to the 1989 Tiananmen demonstrations. To the extent that China's current leaders anticipate a political evolution, as they must if they are realistic, they probably prefer the Singapore model, although Taiwan's seems more in keeping with the Chinese character—and the political history of Taiwan is well known to elites across the strait.

What could go wrong? Although there is a consensus on Deng Xiaoping's dictum, "To get rich is glorious", sustained rapid growth is not assured. Lagging growth in the poor interior provinces might impede political evolution of the country, and an ongoing conflict with

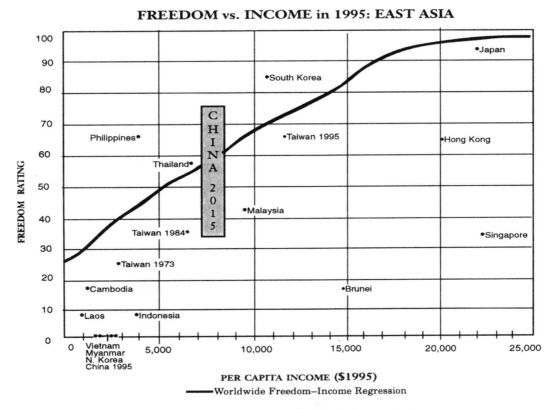

FREEDOM vs. INCOME in 1995: EAST ASIA

PER CAPITA INCOME ($1995)
— Worldwide Freedom-Income Regression

Sources: Freedom House, World Bank, and the author's estimates.

Taiwan could become an obstacle. Or, after all, China might just be different—but in light of the evidence reported above, that is not the way to bet.

This Is the Deal

The key inference for everyone is patience: Only twenty-odd years separate us from 2015, and the advent of Chinese democracy promises abatement of several current problems. For the people of Taiwan, to be a province of a prospering China—or perhaps a member of a Chinese confederation—in which governments on both sides of the Taiwan Strait are popularly elected and the rights of their citizens are protected by law, should be a far more attractive prospect than joining today's China. But the period between now and 2015 (or whatever the precise year) will be volatile, because Beijing will not give up on the goal of unification. And it will become militarily more powerful as time passes. Taiwan needs to keep its powder dry and behave prudently.

For the United States there are two main implications. The first is that it is a good thing that the Chinese become rich, for it will benefit the American economy in the process. The second, and more important, reason is that a richer China will become more democratic. This will not necessarily make it easier to deal with, but experience has shown that democracies are less dangerous interlocu-

tors for other democracies than are dictatorships. Washington should therefore stop holding trade relations hostage to an array of current political disputes. The United States should instead make most-favored nation status for China permanent, and impose no extra obstacles to its admission to the World Trade Organization. Our economic interests need to be pressed on the many trade issues in contention, but it is much better to address them in the WTO forum than in the current, highly politicized bilateral tit-for-tat manner in which we have been engaged in recent years.

If trade sanctions are ruled out-of-bounds in dealing with non-trade matters, how are we to dissuade China from exporting weapons and delivery systems capable of mass destruction? This is a question the Clinton administration has failed adequately to address, and it is a failure that is likely to encourage similar transfers in the future. One answer lies in our taking actions in the security domain rather than in economics. There is much in the way of arms for defense that we have not provided to Taiwan or to other countries in the region that worry about China that we might supply.

The second main policy implication for us is to defend strongly Taiwan's de facto independence. We have an interest in a peaceful East Asia, and we share more values with a democratic Taiwan today than we did with the authoritarian one of days gone by. If Beijing resumes military pressures against the island, we should not only supply more advanced arms to Taiwan but make it clear to China that it will confront American military power if it crosses our red line. We need also to make it clear to Taipei that a condition of our support is that it abjure de jure independence, for that would escalate the confrontation with Beijing, something that we and the Taiwanese should both want to avoid. This merely restates long-standing American policy that there is only one China but that we resist any attempt to unify by force. The difference now is that political evolution in China can be expected to ease the problem.

It follows from this analysis that we should not assume that China will inevitably become a threat to U.S. interests. We have a common interest with China in seeing its people prosper, in peace, in dealing with environmental problems, and in coping with the dangers associated with the spread of weapons capable of mass destruction. This common agenda would be better advanced if China were a member of the various organizations that make the rules on such matters. Nonetheless, American criticism of China's human rights violations should and will continue, but it should not be linked to trade issues. Our criticisms will have increasing resonance inside a China with a better educated and informed population that has access to greatly improved telecommunications, one that is growing freer year by year.

Put another way, the deal—better left tacit than made explicit—is this: Beijing bets on the many benefits of getting rich, including military power and peaceful reconciliation with Taipei. Taipei bets that a democratic China will emerge and holds off declaring itself independent. Washington bets that a rich China will become democratic and that the Taiwan issue will be peacefully settled in the context of a moderated Chinese foreign policy.

Americans sustained the Cold War with the Soviet Union for forty-five years until victory came. The prospect of a twenty-year (more or less) effort to help the Chinese people to become free—while helping Taiwan to retain its freedoms—is a much less daunting prospect. There may be trouble with China during its passage to democracy—or even after—but the odds should go down as it becomes more prosperous. We should do nothing to interfere with that process.

Notes

1. *Freedom in the World: The Annual Survey of Political Rights and Civil Liberties, 1995–6* (New York: Freedom House, 1996).
2. Material in this section draws on the "Study on the Election of Villagers' Committees in Rural China" (December 1, 1993) and the "Report on Villagers' Representative Assemblies in China" (December 1994), both by the China Rural Villagers Self-Government Research Group, China

Research Society of Basic Level Government; on the "Election Observation Report of the People's Republic of China" by the International Republican Institute (a private U.S. nonprofit organization dedicated to promoting democratic institutions), May 1995; and on *Far East Economic Review,* June 23, 1994.
3. This section is based on "China's Legal Reforms", in a special issue of *The China Quarterly* (March 1995). In particular, the contributions of Stanley Lubman, "Introduction: The Future of Chinese Law"; William Alford, "Tasseled Loafers for Barefoot Lawyers: Transformation and Tension in the World of Chinese Legal Workers"; Pittman B. Potter, "Foreign Investment Law in the People's Republic of China: Dilemmas of State Control"; Donald Clarke and James Feinerman, "Antagonistic Contradictions: Criminal Law and Human Rights in China"; Donald Clarke, "The Execution of Civil Judgments in China"; and Anthony R. Dicks, "Compartmentalized Law and Judicial Restraint: An Inductive View of Some Jurisdictional Barriers to Reform."
4. Far East Economic Review, June 23, 1994, p. 55; quoted by Potter.
5. Yingyi Qian and Barry Weingast, "China's Transition to Markets: Market-Preserving Federalism, Chinese Style", Hoover Institution, 1995.
6. Minxin Pei, *From Reform to Revolution: The Demise of Communism in China and the Soviet Union* (Cambridge: Harvard University Press, 1994).
7. Pei, p. 161.
8. A Lexis/Nexis search of coverage on these topics—and of human rights abuses—in five major U.S. publications (the *New York Times, Wall Street Journal, Washington Post, Time,* and *Newsweek*) for the period January 1991 through June 1996 shows, on the one hand, 356 stories on abuses of various kinds, and, on the other, three on local elections, sixteen on efforts to introduce a rule of law, and ten on the liberalizing of the mass media; in short, an overall ratio of twelve to one. How can one explain such scant coverage of such important developments? Aside from the propensity of the press to print bad news, one explanation is that the Tiananmen Square massacre imprinted on the minds of American editors that Beijing is unrelentingly repressive.
9. Seymour Martin Lipset, *Political Man: The Social Bases of Politics* (Baltimore: Johns Hopkins University Press, 1981).
10. In using international prices, all goods and services produced in a country are valued in the same currency, usually dollars, and not in local currencies.
11. Samuel P. Huntington, *The Third Wave: Democratization in the Late Twentieth Century* (Norman, OK: University of Oklahoma Press, 1991), and Adam Przeworski, Michael Alvarez, Jose Antonio Cheibub, and Fernando Limongi, "What Makes Democracies Endure?" *Journal of Democracy* (January 1996).

Article 7   *The World & I, April 1996*

China: The Good, the Bad, and the Dangerous

Economic Liberalization vs. Political Authoritarianism

China is trying to build capitalism within a Leninist political power structure.

Jan S. Prybyla

Jan S. Prybyla is professor of economics emeritus at Pennsylvania State University. He is the author of Reform in China and Other Socialist Economies *(Washington, D.C.: American Enterprise Institute Press, 1990) and coauthor/coeditor of* Russia and China on the Eve of a New Millennium: Differential Responses to Totalitarianism *(1997).*

In 1979, China embarked on three pragmatically driven structural transformations of its socialist economy, a liberalization of sorts that has been successful but not without problems for China and its neighbors near and far. The three transformations have been marketization of a socialist administrative command economy; diversification of property forms away from almost total state ownership; and a partial "opening-up" to the world market, more convincing on the export side and in its receptivity to foreign direct investment than on the side of imports and foreigners' access to China's domestic market.

By the mid-1990s, the bulk of consumer goods, including much farm produce and 80 percent of industrial producer goods, was sold at market-determined prices, and only a few categories (less than 20) of producer goods were physically allocated by the central plan (700 in 1979). However, an austerity program, initiated in 1993, restored price controls over several key commodities (especially food) and services, as a matter of anti-inflationary policy rather than Marxist dogma. So, for the moment at least, price liberalization is in a comatose state.

All agricultural output and 60 percent of industrial production now come from the nonstate sector of the economy, compared to about 95 percent in the mid-1970s, a transformation brought about by the comparatively rapid growth of the nonstate sphere rather than through outright privatization of state-owned firms. Moreover, according to Nicholas Lardy (*China in the World Economy*), China's investment regime is relatively open, far more liberal than those of South Korea and Taiwan.

Although the economic liberalization trend in China has been cumulative, it has also been erratic and often capricious. Because of several factors—the still-important government ownership of industry, transportation, and communications (100,000 mostly large industrial firms employ 110 million people); the blurred lines separating private from public spheres; the fluid state and arbitrary interpretation of laws governing property rights; and endemic corruption of monoparty officials-turned-entrepreneurs—China's economic system today is at what might be called a "red robber baron" phase of capitalist evolution, or at the stage of "elementary insider capitalism."

In its 1996 *Index of Economic Freedom*, the Heritage Foundation classifies China's economy, perhaps a little too harshly, as "mostly not free," assigning it an overall index of 3.8 (where 1 = free, 5 = repressed, and 3–3.99 = mostly not free). The index rates it as 121st among 140 national economies, with Hong Kong first (1.25) and Cuba, Laos, and North Korea last (5).

Achievements

Whatever its precise place on the scale of freedom, the reformist post–1978 Chinese economy has been very successful in raising material welfare. Under several major performance indicators, China has done remarkably well. These criteria include growth rates of domestic product (overall and per capita), industrial and agricultural output and retail sales, savings and investment ratios, acquisition of technology and financial and marketing know-how, growth of external trade, foreign direct investment (FDI), foreign exchange reserves, and avoidance of excessive foreign indebtedness.

The average annual growth rate of real gross domestic product (GDP) during the reform period has been close to 10 percent—among the fastest in the world. Other things remaining the same, the rate is expected to be about 9 percent per annum over 1996–2000.

Prosperity and Politics

• Beijing has seemingly secured widespread public acceptance of its balance of economic liberalization and political authoritarianism.

• There are, however, reports of independent thinking and action on behalf of a more humane society.

• At some point the Chinese people, like other Asians, will probably make the connection between prosperity and democracy.

In 1995, per capita GDP in terms of purchasing power parity (PPP), which takes into account price differences among countries, was put by *Asiaweek* (15 Dec. 1995) at U.S. $2,660 (not the meaningless nominal $435 used by the World Bank). This is still quite modest, the same as the Philippines, and compares with South Korea's $10,534, Taiwan's $13,235, and Singapore's $21,493 ($25,900 for the United States). But it is more than double India's and rising at a brisk annual clip of around 8 percent per head. Exports have surged from under $10 billion in 1978 to $135 billion in 1995, with a current account surplus in the neighborhood of $8 billion. Actually materialized FDI in 1995 was about $38 billion ($33 billion in 1994), the largest in the developing world, and foreign exchange reserves were pushing $70 billion, the third largest in Asia after Japan and Taiwan.

Euphoria and Panic Alert

China's unquestioned economic achievements since 1979, traceable to liberalizing changes in the economy's coordination mechanism, property structure, and foreign trade and investment relations, have caused some China watchers to make euphoric predictions, marginally tempered by apprehension, about that country's prospects in the twenty-first century. I have warned against these overreactions in the past in "China Euphoria Alert: The Case of the Peripatetic Capital." Here, I note three additional points.

The first has to do with the inherent predictive incapacities of the social sciences, economics included. Contrary to conventional wisdom, the past is not necessarily a reliable guide to the future, particularly where interacting, complex, dynamic societies made up of intractable individuals are concerned. Think of the economic achievements of and predicted bright future for Argentina in the 1930s and '40s and the exemplary performance of Brazil from the mid-1960s through the mid-1970s (an 11 percent growth rate per year).

Recall also the World Bank's naming of Burma (Myanmar) in 1960 as one of Asia's success stories and the widespread predictions made in the late 1950s about the dim future of South Korea. In 1995 Burma's per capita gross domestic product (in PPP terms) was $676, the lowest in the region.

The second point, made by Paul Krugman in "The Myth of Asia's Miracle," is more controversial because of disagreement and uncertainty surrounding the measurement of economic efficiency Krugman argues that East Asian growth (China included) has been based on the mobilization of formerly unused or underutilized resources, especially labor and capital, rather than on increases in efficiency—that is, improvements in total factor productivity—somewhat like Soviet growth in the 1950s and early '60s.

Switching to efficiency-based (intensive) growth, once the sources of extensive (additional resource-based) growth encounter diminishing returns or are exhausted, is not only difficult but likely to result in a slowdown in the near future of the rate of product growth, to perhaps 7 percent a year in China's case. Although the overall size of China's economy compared to that of the United

The World & I

Entrepreneur: A recurring problem is how to deal with inflation in the absence of a market that is not subservient to political authority.

States would, in those circumstances, be narrowed from 40 percent now to 80 percent in 2010, China's economy would not be the largest in the world by the latter date, as is often predicted. More important, its product would have to be divided among some 2.2 billion people.

Like inflation, the state enterprise problem is structural and politically explosive.

The third point deals with current concerns: the inescapable problems and dislocations accompanying China's transition to a full-fledged market system. To achieve this unstated objective in the long run the economy will have to solve several difficult but not insuperable structural short-and medium-term problems.

Economic Problems

A troublesome and recurring problem is inflation and how to deal with it in the absence of market instruments of monetary control that are not subservient to political authority (in other words, without a truly autonomous central bank and a commercial banking system not beholden to local party bosses). This is as much as to say that China's inflation problem is structural. Official data almost certainly understate the degree of inflation. They indicate a peak retail price inflation of 27 percent in 1994 compared with the previous year. This was reduced to around 15 percent in 1995 by an administratively ordered tightening of credit, particularly for large construction projects.

Actual inflation is believed to be at least twice the official rate for many key commodities and services. The growth of money supply (M2, or currency + bank demand deposits) has been too high (34.4 percent in 1995 over 1994), but slowed in recent months to a yearly rate of about 30 percent—still excessive. Actual inflation is accompanied by fears that the austerity measures currently in force will depress the growth rate without curbing inflation enough to avoid stagflation: stagnant growth with inflation. Consequently, strong pressures have been building up on the monetary authorities to ease credit restrictions, and illegal ways of obtaining investment funds have proliferated.

The tight credit policy has aggravated the precarious condition of most large state enterprises, almost half of which are operating in the red, their losses having risen by 20 percent in 1995 to just under 800 billion yuan (about $100 billion). Half the state enterprise debts are "triangular," that is, nonperforming debts among firms unable to pay for the goods and services they supply one another. The average debt-to-assets ratio of state enterprises has risen from under 19 percent in 1981 to more than 80 percent in 1995.

Like inflation, the state enterprise problem is structural and politically explosive. State firms still operate under the *danwei* ("iron rice bowl") system, paying their workers wages unrelated to performance, assuring them quasi-permanent employment and retirement pay, and acting as providers of all kinds of social and welfare services, including health, education, and housing, albeit at modest levels of comfort. The monthly wage (paid mostly out of loans nowadays) in many of these firms comes to about 80 yuan, or $10. For doctrinal reasons, privatization of these enterprises is not contemplated.

More important, liquidation through bankruptcy would add at least 20 million presently underemployed workers to the unemployment rolls, on top of an ex-

S. Kanino/The World & I

pected influx over the next several years of perhaps as many as 150 million (out of 450 million) peasants who will seek to leave farming for better work and higher pay in the cities, a movement already in full swing. Currently, 7–8 million peasants leave farming each year.

The "floating population" in search of urban employment is already in the neighborhood of 100 million, worsening the housing shortage, putting enormous strain on urban infrastructures, and pushing up the crime rate. The problem is particularly acute in China's northeastern rust-belt Liaoning Province but is also present in remote parts of China's southwestern Sichuan Province and other inland places, which under the Maoist policy of the "Third Line" were the recipients of huge state investments in heavy defense-oriented industries.

Much of the impetus for the staggering and even bigger future migrations of people is due to the geographically uneven pace of development.

Some of the surplus rural labor has been absorbed in labor-intensive, relatively low-tech township industries operating under market discipline, located mostly along the coast, in some 50,000 old and new, small and medium-sized towns, another 20,000 of which are expected to come into being before the year 2010. These private, joint-venture (with Hong Kong and Taiwan businessmen), and cooperative factories and workshops are heavily involved in the export trade and the production, assembly, and processing of consumer goods, consumer electronics included. They account for more than one-third of rural employment, up from 15 percent in 1985.

The sectoral and geographical transfer of labor, now in progress—a normal phenomenon of industrialization but for its magnitude—calls for the creation of new social institutions to replace the *danwei* system and provide unemployment insurance, old age and disability pensions, and health care, a good deal of it out of taxes, on a countrywide basis.

Much of the impetus for the staggering and even bigger future migrations of people is due to the geographically uneven pace of development—with the dynamic

coastal provinces geared to exports leading the way—and the highly skewed intersectoral distribution of income and wealth, with agriculture (especially in the inland regions) lagging behind since the mid-1980s. The income differential between coastal and poorest inland provinces is 1:15 or greater. More than 90 percent of foreign investment to date (most of it from overseas Chinese) has found its way into a handful of coastal provinces near Hong Kong and Taiwan.

There are also wide and widening interpersonal disparities of wealth and income, particularly between individuals with access to the newly emerging markets and those on fixed pay, including teachers and workers in the larger state industrial enterprises. The relatively backward financial and technical condition of agriculture, the sector that pioneered the marketization and property reforms, has given rise to discontent and social unrest in the countryside.

The near-crisis is due to a combination of causes, most of them having to do with distorted financial incentives and unfinished institutional business:

- niggardly state investments in rural infrastructures (e.g., irrigation and drainage);
- suboptimal size of family farms, uncertainty surrounding property rights;
- low state purchasing prices for grain compared with market prices and the prices farmers have to pay for inputs;
- inadequate transportation, marketing, and storage facilities;
- outdated technology;
- insufficient and not very knowledgeable technical assistance;
- poor maintenance of public goods;
- low level of social services; and
- high-handedness on the part of rural officials (including the enforcers of the one child per family rule), who are often assaulted by the peasants in return.

Even a partial solution to these and other problems could lead to improvements in agricultural productivity and help feed—and feed better—a population that every year adds about 15 million people to its multitudes. But such productivity improvements would necessitate an even larger than hitherto outflow of rural labor: perhaps 200 million people over the next decade.

For reasons of space, other structural problems of equal importance and heroic proportions can only be noted in passing. They include:

- The need to reconstruct the banking system so as to free it from extortion by local political authorities and relieve it of the burden of subsidizing debt-ridden state enterprises, a socialist policy relic that makes the recipients persist in their wasteful ways;

• An equally urgent need to reform the fiscal system, which in its present condition encourages widespread tax avoidance and leaves the central government strapped for cash. Government revenue as a proportion of GDP has fallen below 10 percent. The budgetary deficit, when properly counted, represents about 6 percent of GDP, forcing the government to resort to heavy borrowing from its subservient banking system, renege on tax rebates promised to exporters, and trim tax incentives and other allurements offered foreign investors;

• Official corruption has assumed epidemic dimensions and, worse, the status of a behavioral principle fundamentally incompatible with the emergence and survival of a modern market system. Corruption on this scale and of this depth has a great deal to do with lack of transparency and political accountability.

Political Authoritarianism

A totalitarian political system does what its name suggests: The autocratic one-party state through its bureaucracy purports to control directly every segment of social and all facets of private life, even though theoretically perfect control never occurs. Once a significant degree of marketization (that is, liberalization) of economic life occurs, deliberately or by happenstance, central control is no longer total and the political system becomes authoritarian.

T. S. Lam/The World and I

Life in the interior: People in the coastal provinces earn 15 times more than those in the poorest inland provinces.

The ideology of authoritarianism can run, in a circle, from extreme left (communism) to extreme right (fascism), with various, usually nationalist, admixtures in between. But one thing remains constant: the determination of the autocratic regime to rule alone forever. This determination may be hard (as in contemporary China) or soft (as in Gorbachev's Russia). China today, despite rhetorical protestations to the contrary, is trying to build capitalism within an untypically market-friendly Leninist political power structure. Will it succeed?

With respect to accommodation and coexistence with alien institutional elements, social systems have different degrees of tolerance at different stages of their maturation process. The market system is in this respect very tolerant, adjusting to all kinds of ill-fitting institutions and social pathologies borrowed from other economic and political systems. This flexibility is particularly pronounced during the early stages of capitalist development and can be quite prolonged (e.g., the two centuries of mercantilist transition to capitalism in western Europe). It concerns primarily the combination of diffused market decision making and concentrated state political power that readily lends itself to corruption.

Over the long run and at a technologically and financially higher level of development, capitalism requires for its efficient operation an open, democratic, and competitive political system, if only to guarantee and protect from deceit the free flow of ideas, people, and capital that is the indispensable ingredient of innovation and economic modernization.

Although, to my knowledge, no historical laws exist that would inevitably make this optimal combination of market and democracy come about, there is considerable presumption in favor of its happening in the contemporary context of an increasingly interpenetrating, interrelating, and competitive world economy. This is so because of what Minxin Pei (*From Reform to Revolution: The Demise of Communism in China and the Soviet Union*, 1994) describes as "state-to-society resource transfers and institutional decay within the state" under marketizing economic reforms.

The authoritarian state, unlike its totalitarian counterpart, is no longer the sole possessor of the country's resources. Some of the resources generated outside the state sector by nonstate entities can and have been used in China and elsewhere to support social movements demanding political pluralization.

Every autocrat worth his salt will insist that political democracy is a luxury that an economically developing country cannot afford, and, moreover, that there is nothing wrong with an "enlightened" autocracy that raises the people's living standard and protects the citizenry from crass commercialism and other moral afflictions that capitalist-induced prosperity allegedly brings in its train.

The authoritarians' naked will to power is almost invariably clothed in the language of social stability. It is a procedure Chinese leaders have used and perfected since the bloody incident at Tiananmen Square. To all appearances, the regime has succeeded in securing the grudging acceptance of those (and they are many, especially along the coast) who have benefited from the reforms. But the acceptance is qualified and conditioned on the solution of the structural economic problems noted earlier: inflation; unemployment; yawning and widening income and wealth gaps between individuals, economic sectors, and geographical regions; atrocious housing conditions for most people; and runaway corruption of merchant-officials.

Reports from China by astute foreign correspondents (who, unlike many of their predecessors in Maoist times, have not succumbed to the myth of China's "exceptionalism"), private conversations with knowledgeable Chinese, and the best Sinological minds in the West (among them, Merle Goldman), reveal signs of an expanding sphere of independent thinking and action in behalf of a more modern, humane, and civil society.

It may only be a question of time (but there is no historical inevitability about it) before the Chinese people, like their Taiwanese and South Korean neighbors before them, make the connection between prosperity and democracy and refuse to be bought off in their quest for justice. Until then, China's rapid economic growth and its desire to play its rightful role among the world's nations will rest on unstable domestic foundations.

Additional Reading

Merle Goldman, *Sowing the Seeds of Democracy in China: Political Reform in the Deng Xiaoping Era,* Harvard Univ. Press, Cambridge, 1994.
Paul Krugman, "The Myth of Asia's Miracle," Foreign Affairs, November 1994.
Jan Prybyla, *China and Pacific Rim Letter,* Washington, D.C., vol. 6, no. 3.
———, "Chinese Puzzle," *Journal of East Asian Affairs,* Research Institute for International Affairs, Seoul, vol. 8, no. 2.

Article 8   *The Bulletin of the Atomic Scientists,* July/August 1996

China Is No Threat

China's defense spending is modest; China is seeking economic, not military, power.

Wang Hao

Wang Hao is chief sub-editor of China Daily *in Beijing. He was a* Bulletin *visiting fellow in the fall of 1995.*

A few Western analysts have expressed great concern about "the China threat," especially last spring when tensions over the Taiwan issue peaked. These analysts argue that as China grows more powerful, economically and militarily, it will adopt a policy of expansion, menacing its neighbors. A few others believe that it is inevitable that China will move to fill the power vacuum in the Asia-Pacific region created by the retreat of the superpowers.

It is true that China is growing stronger. Its economy is soaring—growing at an average annual rate of 9 percent since reforms were instituted in 1978. That alone would put it in the spotlight. Add to that the fact that China has a population of 1.2 billion and is the world's third largest nation in land area, it seems natural that China will be influential in the region and on the world stage.

On the other hand, despite these analysts' claims, China is not spending inordinate amounts on its military, nor is it inclined to threaten its neighbors.

Military Spending

China's military spending is comparatively low. Even if China's military expenditures were double its reported figures—as some Western security specialists claim—its defense budget would still be far lower than those of most developed countries or of Japan, Saudi Arabia, or South Korea, according to *The Military Balance,* published by the International Institute for Strategic Studies in London. China spends less than $12 per capita on defense. India

AP/Wide World

May 1, 1996: China's May Day celebrations begin with a morning flag-raising ceremony in Tiananmen Square.

spends $11.7; Japan, $336; the United States, $1,081. And China's spending per soldier is less than that of India, Thailand, or South Korea—China's defense spending per soldier is less than one-thirtieth that of the United States.

China's military spending is equally low as a percentage of gross domestic product. Again, even if it were doubled to meet some Western estimates, at 1.26 percent it would still be lower than the percent of GDP spent on defense by Korea, Thailand, or Malaysia. It is well below the average of 3.4 percent.

China's defense spending remains low, both proportionately and in absolute terms. And although China regards upgrading national defense as one of the goals of modernization, it is unlikely to make a greater investment in its military. According to an official Chinese government "white paper" on defense, issued in November 1995, China "has placed defense spending in a position subordinate to and in the service of overall national economic construction."

That government report indicated that defense spending increased at an annual rate of 6.22 percent from 1979 through 1994. But the general retail price index grew at an annual rate of 7.7 percent over the same term.

Army officers received an across-the-board increase in monthly wages in 1994; senior officers received an increase of more than 50 percent. One might argue that most of the increase in defense spending in 1994 was designed to restore living standards for armed services personnel by compensating for price hikes.

Western critics also complain that Chinese reports of military expenditures are incomplete because they do not include the costs of military research and development, modernization of defense industry plants and equipment, or the revenues that the army derives from commercial enterprises or weapons sales. However, according to the Stockholm International Peace Research Institute (SIPRI), which compiles and publishes military spending information, most nations' defense spending reports show a similar pattern: there is a "dearth of desegregated military spending data for most countries." SIPRI itself follows NATO guidelines; it does not regard government investments in military enterprises as defense expenditures.

This is particularly appropriate in the case of China where, as part of industrial reform, most defense industries no longer "belong" to the military and many are slated for conversion. On July 28, 1995, Hu Ping, a senior researcher from China's Institute for International Strategic Studies, explained in *People's Daily:*

"In recent years, orders for military materials have dropped, and quite a number of military enterprises have been running under capacity. The government has to give them financial aid and help them convert to the production of civilian goods. This money should be categorized as expenditures to reform state enterprises, not as national defense funds."

Like other state enterprises, China's military industrial enterprises practiced a "contract responsibility system," which required them to pay the government both taxes and a portion of their profits. Remaining profits from the production of civilian goods were used mostly to expand production and increase wages. Hu said that Chinese armies were now withdrawing from most of their civilian businesses, with the exception of traditional farming and some sideline production.

Counting receipts from weapon sales abroad would not change the picture much, either. Alfred Wilhelm, executive vice president of the Atlantic Council, testified before the U.S. Senate Subcommittee on East Asian and Pacific Affairs on October 11, 1995, saying: "Arms sales by defense-related corporations are commonly viewed outside China as a major source of income. However, most major weapons manufactures are not owned or operated by the Peoples Liberation Army (PLA), but by one of the civilian ministries. The proceeds from most foreign arms sales go to the originating ministry and not the PLA.

"Furthermore, a review of arms sales from 1985–92 shows that China's arms sales averaged little more than $1.5 billion a year. Even if the entire amount were profit and all went to the PLA, the addition to the military coffers would be minimal. According to the Chinese government, at least one-third of state-owned enterprises are operating at a loss and only one-third are breaking even. Arms industries are all state-owned and like the rest many are unprofitable, and all are attempting to convert their excess capacity to civilian production. Of those making a profit, at least half of the profits are being reinvested in defense conversion or modernization as part of the state's massive effort to create new jobs."

Meeting Needs

China has realistic defense needs. China's borders, which it shares with 15 countries, extend for more than 22,000 kilometers. As security expert Harry Harding, quoted by Gerald Segal in *Defending China*, points out: "Few other major powers have felt as threatened, for such a long period of time, and by such powerful adversaries, as China has." For the past 46 years, especially during the Cold War era, the country faced direct threats to its security from almost all directions.

China has built up its military forces over the past four decades. Despite the size of its forces, China's limited economy and relative isolation have meant that the quality of its armaments is relatively low. China's military research and development is generally believed to be at least 15 years behind the West. Although China has tried to import better equipment, it takes considerable time to digest advanced weaponry. Western policies that restrict technology transfer have also made it difficult for China to modernize its military. Although China's military strength is now—and will remain in future—on a level that meets defensive needs, China is not in a position to adopt an expansionist policy or pose a threat to Asia-Pacific stability.

China's strategic perceptions can be best understood by reviewing the military thinking of Deng Xiaoping, the designer of China's reform and opening. For a long period of time following its founding, the People's Republic was subject to isolation, blockade, and subversion. As a result, the nation was often on alert, preparing for an "early, massive, and even nuclear world war." But in the mid-1980s, Deng concluded that war was not inevitable and that it was possible to realize a long-standing peace.

In November 1984, Deng told a meeting of the Central Military Commission: "We should make a real soberminded judgment . . . [which] will keep our mind on economic construction. . . . We do not have to spend more money on military spending, so we can spare more money for economic construction. We should make up our mind now."

Within the year the Central Military Commission issued new guidelines, moving from preparing against the threat of invasion to peacetime construction. Simultaneously, the commission reduced the military by one million men. A move of this scale—made even before the Cold War was over—is a rare example of contemporary arms control and disarmament. Since 1986 the army has been reduced from 4.25 million to 3.2 million men, a decrease of more than 24 percent, and the defense industry has been gradually transformed from a monolithic producer of military products to a diversified producer of both military and civilian products.

China's decision in the 1990s to establish diplomatic ties with South Korea and Israel, moves that would have been unthinkable in the past, are also reflections of changing perceptions. The country has played an important role in alleviating tension on the Korean peninsula.

In the past 15 years, China has integrated itself into the international trade and financial communities. It is a member of the World Bank and the Asian Development Bank, and it is applying for membership in the World Trade Organization. According to World Bank statistics, China's imports and exports accounted for about 30 percent of gross national product in the 1990s, up from about 10 percent in 1978. China is now a full participant in the global and regional political, economic, and security arenas.

China's modernization requires a peaceful international environment, and China opposes the threat or use of force to settle international disputes.

Last October, Russia and China reportedly settled their long-running border dispute by demarcating the last 54 contested kilometers along their 4,380-kilometer border. China and India have also reached a peaceful agreement, and border problems with Vietnam are nearly resolved. At a meeting in Shanghai in late April, China and four of its neighbors—Russia, Kazakhstan, Kyrgyzstan, and Tajikistan—signed a confidence-building agreement specifying notification and sharply limiting the scale, scope, and number of border-area military exercises.

Apart from questions on the ultimate disposition of Taiwan and the governance of Hong Kong, which China regards as internal concerns, the only outstanding dispute between China and other Southeast Asian countries concerns the ownership of the Nansha (Spratlys) Islands. There are four other claimants: Vietnam, Malaysia, the Philippines, and Brunei. But all sides have behaved with restraint. In August 1995, China and the Philippines held talks in Manila that concluded with a code of conduct. Both sides vowed to refrain from force or the threat of force to resolve the dispute.

China's relations with its neighbors are the best they have been since the People's Republic was founded. As China's senior military scholar Xu Xiaojun said at a 1994 symposium in Beijing, "China enjoys the [best] security environment since 1949. It is not facing any real military threats. There is no obvious danger of a major attack . . . [and] there is not a single country in its neighboring or surrounding area that China defines as an antagonist."

The Future

It is only 16 years since China opened itself to the outside world and began its drive for reform. When a new but rising power enters the international arena, it is crucial to build an environment of trust and to correct misperceptions.

In terms of both its capabilities and its intentions, China is not a threat to its neighbors in the Asia-Pacific region. There is no doubt that China intends to achieve influence through economic rather than military power. China regards the fall of the Soviet Union as a powerful object lesson—no matter how powerful a country's military, it will not last long without a strong economy.

Any country of the size and population of China will cause concern among its neighbors. Compared to the forces of powers like the United States, Russia, Britain, and France, China's military is weak. But it is a giant in Asia.

China still remains something of a mystery to other countries, and Western analysts believe that China should increase its transparency on strategic doctrine, intentions, and military spending. Last fall's publication of a major white paper on defense was a significant move in that regard.

In Asia, economic prosperity has paved the way for regional economic cooperation. Continued economic growth will require greater cooperation, including agreements in the security area. This may not necessarily lead to the establishment of a European Union–style organization, but there is a move toward a multilateral mechanism for dialogue. Chinese Foreign Minister Zian Zichen took part in the July 1993 inaugural meeting of the ASEAN Regional Forum in Singapore.

The best way to make a friend is to treat someone like a friend. This is also true in international relations. China and its Asia-Pacific neighbors have every reason to remain mutually trusted and understood. It is vital for them to view each other as partners, not enemies. Confrontation serves no one's interest.

Article 9

The New York Times Magazine, February 18, 1996

Jerry-Built . . . Or Built to Last?

Boom-at-a-Glance

Over the next 25 years, China's economy should expand to almost $6 trillion, about 10 times its size in 1994, and the birth rate will be low. But household income today is only $685, pollution is staggering and people are living longer.

Jane H. Lii

Jane H. Lii is a reporter on the Metropolitan staff of the Times.

All the World's a Market

Since China began its economic reform, its gross domestic product (G.D.P.), measured in yuan, has grown nearly tenfold, from **447 billion** yuan in 1980 to **4.4 trillion** yuan in 1994. In U.S. dollars, the G.D.P. rose from **$298 billion** in 1980 to **$508 billion** in 1994. It is an economy that has far outstripped the competition. Here, a few significant G.D.P. growth rates (in percentages):

In 1994, China's trade surplus was $5.2 billion. One of its best customers is the United States, whose trade deficit with China is fast becoming a rival of its better-known deficit with Japan. (See chart at right.)

In 1994, foreign investors poured **$81.4 billion** into China, up from **$2.9 billion** in 1984; American investors spent **$6 billion**, up from **$165 million.** The United States was the second-largest foreign investor in 1994, behind Hong Kong/Macao **($48.7 billion)** and ahead of Taiwan **($5.4 billion)** and Ja-

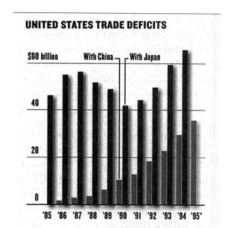

UNITED STATES TRADE DEFICITS

*1995 deficit with China is an estimate based on January-September data; no estimate is available for Japan.

pan **($4.4 billion).** Below, the five American companies whose joint ventures yielded the highest gross sales (in millions of dollars, and with rank among all joint ventures):

- Chrysler $497 (4th)
- Motorola $310 (6th)
- Procter & Gamble $234 (14th)
- United Technologies $184 (33d)
- Coca-Cola $119 (59th)

In 1993, only **0.1 percent** of Chinese owned automobiles, a total of **1.2 million;** about **70 percent** were imports. (Bicycles, meanwhile, number upward of **450 million.**) "China is such a potentially huge market that if 1 percent of Chinese people could afford cars, that would be **12 million,**" says Michael G. Meyerand, a spokesman for General Motors. "That's roughly our market size of Europe."

Big Economy, Tiny Budgets

The national average household income was **$685** in 1994. Per-capita income has

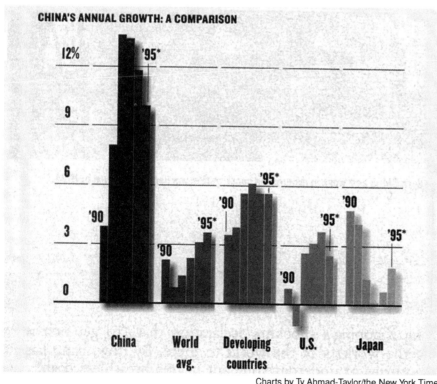

CHINA'S ANNUAL GROWTH: A COMPARISON

Charts by Ty Ahmad-Taylor/the New York Times

risen about **20 percent** over the past two years, and average income should reach **$4,000** by 2020, compared with **$35,000** in the United States (both measured in 1995 dollars).

- The average income of a business-person is **$581** a year.
- A factory worker: **$420.**
- An agricultural worker: **$213.**

A worker for a company that is partly foreign-owned earns at least **200 percent** the salary of a comparable worker at a Government-run company, but Government jobs also provide insurance and subsidized housing.

Before 1979, **100 percent** of agricultural workers had medical insurance; now only **20 percent** do.

How does a Chinese household spend its money?

AVERAGE MONTHLY EXPENSES FOR A CHINESE FAMILY

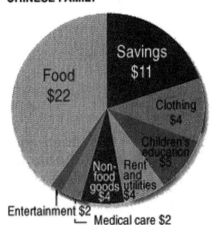

Below, the percentage of families who own certain consumer goods, from a survey of 3,500 households.

• Color television	40%
• Refrigerator	25%
• VCR	12%
• Telephone	9%
• Computer	2%

(A 29-inch foreign-made color television costs about **$1,200.** The paucity of telephone lines, not the cost of the phone itself, accounts for the scarcity of ownership.)

Some of the top items on Chinese wish lists (in percentages):

• Washing machine	22%
• Refrigerator	21%
• Electric fan	15%
• Telephone	11%
• Automobile	4%
• Computer	4%

Population Control (Sort of)

The current Chinese population of **1.2 billion,** but with China's one-child policy, the birth rate has slowed to **1.1 percent.** Still, because of increased life expectancy, the population will continue to grow steadily, reaching **1.5 billion** in 2030.

There are now **40 million** more males than females in China, and that surplus is not expected to diminish substantially. Male babies continue to be more desired, and an estimated **12 percent** of females never enter the population because of sex-selective abortion and infanticide.

A child born in Shanghai, where the infant mortality rate is **9.9 per 1,000,** has a better chance of surviving than one born in Manhattan, where the rate is **10.8 per 1,000.**

The Dirty Downside of an Upsurge

In 1991, about **25 billion tons** of industrial pollutants were dumped in waterways, creating more toxic water pollution in China than in the entire Western world.

In 1992, China produced **728 million tons** of carbon emissions, second only to the United States, which produced **1.3 billion tons.** By 2030, China's emissions should reach **2 billion tons.**

The Government may soon declare serious environmental pollution an offense punishable by death, joining illegal stock speculation, the spreading of superstition, hooliganism and pimping. Violent crime is still relatively rare; of the **1,865 death sentences** handed out in the first six months of 1995, nearly half were for nonviolent crimes, from drug trafficking to corruption to theft.

Not all the smoke in China comes from smokestacks. Some **300 million** Chinese smoke cigarettes, a full **30 percent** of the world's smokers. About **60 percent** of men smoke, and **7 percent** of women. The most popular brand is Red Pagoda, and the tobacco tax is the Government's largest single source of revenue, totaling **$6.6 billion** in 1994.

East Is East ... or Is It?

In 1993, the Chinese Government banned the sale of satellite dishes for private use. But local authorities who share in sales profits are unwilling to enforce the ban, and many Chinese use dishes to pick up "The Simpsons" or "Baywatch."

Some **five billion** movie tickets were sold in China last year, at about **$1.20**

each. Imported films are easily the most popular, even though the Government limits them, allowing only **10** first-run American films last year. "Rumble in the Bronx," starring the Hong Kong martial artist Jackie Chan, was last year's No. 1 film. Rounding out the top five: "True Lies," "The Fugitive," "Speed" and "Forrest Gump."

He Yon, 27, has been called the Kurt Cobain of China. His hit song "A Giant Garbage Dump" says: "The world we live in is like a giant garbage dump/people are like maggots/we fight tooth and nail in this heap ... some go on diets/some starve to death...."

In 1994, the United States lost **$866 million** in pirated copyrighted works to China. (Japan and Germany were even greater culprits, pilfering **$1.3 billion** and **$1.2 billion,** respectively.) On the streets of Beijing, a Madonna CD costs **$4;** Lotus 1-2-3 on CD-ROM costs **$5;** a copy of "Forrest Gump" costs **$8.**

In 1994, Pepsico introduced two flavors of cheeseless Chee-tos—American Cream and Japanese Steak—and sold more than **100 million** bags in a year. Next: seafood flavor.

The economic explosion has boosted prostitution and sexually transmitted diseases. According to the World Health Organization, the number of reported cases of S.T.D.'s in China increased from **2** in 1979 to **200,000** in 1993.

Influenced by Western culture and life style, the divorce rate in China, especially among the educated urban class, is on a sharp rise.

The leading American fast-food restaurant is KFC, with **75** restaurants in **28** cities. McDonald's has **63** restaurants so far. The one in Beijing is the only McDonald's in the world famous for having its own Communist Party secretary. For now, Chinese see fast food primarily as a novelty; noodles and rice remain the centerpieces of their diets.

Last March, the oldest citizen in China, Gong Laifa, died at age **147,** according to the China National Committee on Aging. An illiterate farmer, Gong worked until age **133,** when he broke his leg. A lifelong bachelor, he didn't smoke, but he did drink rice wine every day.

Sources

World G.D.P. growth 1990–1995, China State Statistics Bureau as published in China Today; United States trade deficits with Japan and China, U.S. Department of Commerce, Census Bureau; foreign invest- ment figures, United States-China Business Council; top five American joint ventures, China Trade Report; household-income projection, Lawrence Lau, Stanford University; average monthly expenses, consumer goods, wish list, the Gallup Organization; sex-selective abortion and female infanticide, the East-West Center; carbon emissions, Oak Ridge National Laboratory, Harvard University China Project study; smoking, World Health Organization; piracy data, International Intellectual Property Alliance.

Article 10   *The Economist*, October 12, 1996

How Poor Is China?

New research suggests that poverty in China is more widespread, and the economy much smaller, than previously thought.

In recent years it has become accepted wisdom that China is an economic superpower in the making. Reputable economists have predicted that the Chinese economy could be the largest in the world by 2001. Businessmen have panted at the potential of a market of 1.2 billion consumers. The World Bank has lauded China's achievements in reducing the proportion of its population living in poverty to less than a tenth.

There is only one snag. Many of the numbers on which these claims were based appear to have been wrong. A recent World Bank report, "poverty in China; what do the numbers say?", has substantially revised the statistics put out in other Bank publications. The new figures reduce estimates of the size of the Chinese economy by over 25%. And the Bank has also decided that the proportion of the Chinese population living in poverty is closer to a third, rather than the 7% or so that was commonly cited until recently.

These revisions do not mean that the Chinese economic miracle is a mirage. Chinese growth rates remain among the highest in the world. The country's trade and official reserves continue to swell impressively. But the new figures do suggest that China is further behind the developed countries than had been widely assumed.

The world of statistics can often seem faintly unreal. But the estimates put out by the World Bank and others matter because they affect the real world. China's international rehabilitation after the Tiananmen massacre of 1989 was significantly influenced by awe at the Chinese boom. Disgust at the killings was balanced by respect for the government's increasingly well publicised achievement of lifting hundreds of millions of people out of poverty. Respect of a different sort was created by the idea that China might be the dominant economic power of the next century. And the lure of Chinese markets has created a business lobby keen to get on with China.

If some of the gloss is now taken off the Chinese miracle, will that damage China internationally? Not necessarily. Indeed in some ways it might now suit China to be "poor" rather than "rich". One of the biggest international issues facing today's China is the question of the terms on which it will join the World Trade Organisation. The richer it is seen to be, the faster America and other members will expect it to liberalise its trade rules. So a reminder that much of China remains very poor is actually quite helpful to the Chinese authorities.

Lies and Damned Lies

In its recent poverty report, the World Bank has made two important changes. First, it has raised the income level below which a Chinese is deemed to be poor from $0.60 cents a day to $1.00 a day. This has had the effect of increasing the number of Chinese deemed to be poor from fewer than 100m to well over 300m. Second, the report has lowered estimates for Chinese income per person, measured on a purchasing-power-party (PPP) basis, which adjusts for the local

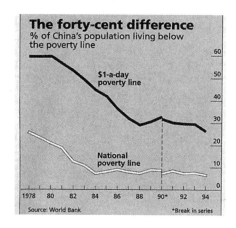

The forty-cent difference
% of China's population living below the poverty line

$1-a-day poverty line

National poverty line

1978 80 82 84 86 88 90* 92 94

Source: World Bank   *Break in series

cost-of-living. The Bank's 1996 *World Development Report* puts Chinese GDP per person, measured on a PPP basis, at around $2,500 in 1994. The new report puts the figure at $1,800.

This change shrinks the estimated size of the Chinese economy dramatically. For example, writing in 1992, Lawrence Summers, who was then chief economist at the World Bank, argued that the size of the Chinese economy was already "greater than that of Germany or Japan". At that time he put Chinese GDP per person at $2,500 on a PPP basis. Extrapolating America's and China's current economic growth rates into the future, Mr Summers went on: "If this growth differential continues, Chinese total output will exceed American total output in 11 years." Unsurprisingly, such a bold prediction from such an eminent source excited much comment.

"The Rise of China", a bullish bestseller by William Overholt, a banker, picked up on Mr Summer's prediction, as did *The Economist*.

The new figures, however, put the date when China becomes the world's largest economy further into the future. At current growth levels, it would now take about 20 more years. In any event, using PPP for extrapolations of this sort, as Mr Summers and others have done, may be misleading. Adjusting incomes for purchasing power is crucial for gauging relative poverty, because it shows how a nominal income of a few hundred dollars—which would mean destitution in America—can translate into an acceptable standard of living in China.

But when it comes to buying western goods, or indeed companies, it is Chinese wealth measured at the real exchange rate, not at PPP, which is of concern to businessmen. Similarly, to extrapolate PPP-based estimates of GDP is probably misleading because rapid economic growth in China, combined with flourishing exports, will almost certainly lead to an appreciation of the Chinese currency, which will narrow the gap between GDP measured on a PPP and on a nominal basis.

It may be for this reason that some Bank officials now seem to be eschewing PPP as a basis for the politically loaded business of measuring the relative sizes of the Chinese and American economies. Pieter Bottelier, the head of the World Bank office in Beijing, makes a back-of-an-envelope calculation using current exchange rates. This suggests that China's economy is now roughly 10% of America's and may catch up in about 40 years' time.

The poverty report is fairly mysterious about the basis on which it has revised the PPP figures, simply citing "better data". When it comes to measuring the numbers of poor Chinese, however, it argues that both the new and the old figures are "right" in different ways. The 60-cents poverty line is a Chinese standard, the $1-a-day line is better for international comparisons.

Maybe so. But in the past, the Bank was not always shy about using the Chinese figure as the basis for international comparisons. For example, in a report on poverty in Vietnam issued in 1995, the Bank observed, "Poverty is considerably higher in Vietnam (51%) than in China (9%), Indonesia (15%), the Philippines (21%) or Thailand (16%)." To some people these figures always seemed implausible. They entailed believing, for example, that, although GDP per person in Thailand (measured on a nominal basis) was five times that in China, the proportion of people liv-

In recent years, China's economy was predicted to become the preeminent world's leader. More recent estimates, based on more balanced assessments of Gross Domestic Product per person, find that China realistically has much further to go to effectively become part of the world economy. Poverty in China is spread much wider than at first thought, and manual labor is still the driving force behind a vast part of their economy.

ing in poverty in Thailand was double that in China. Anybody who had looked around in the two countries would have found that hard to swallow.

Back in the real world, that a third of the population of China is still living in poverty poses more than a humanitarian problem for the Chinese government. Whichever yardstick you use for measuring poverty, the statistics seem to show that the biggest inroads were made in the early 1980s, just after private farming was allowed. For the past decade, the reduction of poverty has slowed. Meanwhile, as a manufacturing-led boom has taken hold on the coasts, the gap between the booming eastern cities and the poorer inland areas has widened. That gap may prove to be the biggest economic and political challenge now facing the Chinese government.

Article 11

The Futurist, January–February 1996

Who Will Feed China?

Industrialization means improved living standards for the Chinese people, but also an accelerating need to import food from elsewhere. The effects on the world's economy could be devastating.

Lester R. Brown

In two years, China shifted from being a net grain exporter of 8 million tons to being a net importer of 16 million tons—a 24-million-ton swing that puts it second only to Japan as a grain importer. Despite these massive imports and the release of government grain stocks, supply failed to keep up with the soaring demand, and grain prices in China climbed nearly 60% in 1994.

The result has been rising prices in world grain markets—and the promise of higher food prices everywhere. If China's rapid industrialization continues—with its attendant rising affluence, land loss, and water shortages—its import demand will soon overwhelm the export capacity of the United States and all other grain-exporting countries. China's rising grain prices are now becoming the world's rising grain prices, China's land scarcity will become everyone's land scarcity, and China's water scarcity will become the world's water scarcity.

Clearly, we are entering a new era. An age of relative food abundance is being replaced by one of scarcity. As the one-fifth of humanity who live in China seek to join the affluent one-fifth already living high on the food chain, the transition into the new era will be accelerated.

Although the 13 million people currently added to China's population each year are expanding the demand for food, most of the growth comes from the extraordinary rise in incomes. Since the economic reforms were launched in 1978, China's economy has expanded fourfold. In economic terms, there are now four Chinas where there was only one 17 years ago.

Can China Feed Itself?

China's leaders publicly argue that they will not become dependent on imported grain, that China will always feed itself. But this is highly unlikely. They argue that they will protect their cropland from conversion to nonfarm uses. It is difficult to imagine any country making a greater effort to do this than Japan, yet that nation has lost half of its grainland since 1950. Some argue that China will increase the productivity of its land so much that it will not have to import grain. But China's yields are already quite high by international standards—with rice yields close to those of Japan and wheat yields well above those of the United States. The bottom line is that, if China continues its rapid industrialization, it will inevitably be forced to import heavily to satisfy future food demand.

Although our projections show China's grain import needs soaring over the next few decades, imports of grain on this scale are never likely to materialize. The small handful of countries with an exportable surplus will simply be overwhelmed by climbing import needs in other countries. As China's grain imports rise, they are likely to drive prices upward, making it increasingly costly to import on the scale projected. The price rise associated with the growing imbalance could lead to economic disruption everywhere and, in low-income countries, to political instability that would dwarf the effects of the oil price hikes in the 1970s. There are, after all, substitutes for oil. But there are no substitutes for food.

Constraints on Food Production

It is an accident of history that China is turning to world markets just when the growing world demand for food is colliding with the sustainable yield of oceanic fisheries, the sustainable yield of aquifers in key food-producing regions, and the limits of available crop varieties to respond to additional applications of fertilizer. The net effect of these constraints is slower growth in world food production.

In the past, rising prices have typically spurred greater growth in output. If seafood prices rose, then fishers would simply invest in more trawlers and expand the catch. That approach today would only hasten the collapse of oceanic fisheries. Similarly, when grain prices went up, farmers would invest in more irrigation wells. Unfortunately, in much of the world today, that response will just accelerate the depletion of aquifers. In the past, rising grain prices stimulated farmers to apply larger amounts of fertilizer. Today, using more fertilizer in many countries has little effect on production.

Neither fishers nor farmers have been able to keep up with the growth in population in recent years. The shift from an era in which both were expanding output much faster than population to one in which both are trailing population growth was well under way before China's prospective emergence as a large importer. But as China turns to the outside world for more grain, it will accelerate the transition from an era of surpluses to one of scarcity.

A Tale of Two Eras

A convenient way of comparing the era of surplus and the new era of scarcity is simply to compare the data from 1950–1990 with projections for 1990–2030. The fish catch, for example, grew from 22 million tons in 1950 to 100 million tons in 1990. During the next 40 years, it is not expected to increase at all. (See Table 1.)

Grain output soared from 631 million tons in 1950 to 1.78 billion tons in 1990. During most of this period, the growth in grain production outstripped that of population, boosting per capita grain output by some 40% between 1950 and 1984. Since then, growth in grain production has slowed.

In contrast to the last four decades, when farmers boosted output by some 28 million tons a year, our projections show grain production growing only 369 million tons in the next four decades, or 9 million tons a year. This projection takes into account the diminishing response of crop yields to additional fertilizer use, the growing scarcity of fresh water, the shrinking backlog of unused agricultural technology, the social disintegration occurring in some countries (mostly in Africa), and the heavy loss of cropland occurring in Asia.

The projection assumes slower growth in production almost everywhere, and in some countries—notably in China—actual declines. China now accounts for one-fifth of the world grain harvest, so if grain production there is declining by roughly 1% a year, as projected, it will take a substantial gain elsewhere just to offset this loss.

Concern for the Future

Four harvests into the new era, there is ample reason to take these projections seriously. Since 1990, there has been no growth in the world grain harvest. Indeed, the 1994 grain harvest is actually smaller than that of 1990. The world fish catch has not increased at all. While four years does not determine a trend for the next four decades, this lack of expansion is a matter of concern.

The new era we are moving into will be so different that many of our traditional reference points will be lost. (See Table 2.) The rise in grain output per person and seafood catch per person that has been under way since mid-century will be replaced by declines of both. Instead of dropping in real terms, food prices will be rising, as we already see with seafood.

> *"The new era will be characterized by a collision between economic trends and the earth's many natural limits."*

Rice scarcity is likely to be next: Rice production is constrained by the availability of both land and fresh water. China's rice harvest in 1994 was 8% less than in 1990 not because of failed technology, but because of the heavy loss of rice land in its southern provinces. Price rises for rice will probably be followed by those for wheat and then other grains.

The era of scarcity that lies ahead is currently most evident with seafood, where human demand is pressing against the sustainable yield of oceanic fisheries. In recent years, seafood prices have been rising by 4% a year in real terms.

Thirty years ago in the United States, poor people who could not afford meat ate fish. Today, seafood costs more than most types of meat. What is happening to seafood prices is instructive, as it provides a glimpse of how future scarcity can affect prices of other foodstuffs. With seafood prices, we are seeing the economic manifestations of our failure to stabilize population before reaching the limits of the ocean's carrying capacity. Unfortunately, we may see price rises for other foodstuffs as similar imbalances between supply and demand begin to develop.

In effect, the era from 1950 to 1990 was shaped by the pursuit of economic growth, including—significantly—record growth in world food production. During most of this period, there were no serious natural constraints on the growth in the seafood catch or in grain production, only economic ones.

The new era, however, will be characterized by a collision between economic trends and the earth's many natural limits, such as the sustainable catch of oceanic fisheries or the sustainable yield of aquifers. Increasingly, economic trends and, indeed, the evolution of the global economy will be shaped by environmental issues, such as the need to use water more efficiently or the need to stabilize climate.

Impacts of China's Demands

China is losing massive amounts of cropland because of its record rate of industrialization. At the same time, incomes are soaring, along with the demands for commensurate quantities and quality of foods. The scale of China's growing demand for food imports is unprecedented. Fully meeting that demand may not be possible:

- To go from consumption of 100 eggs per person in 1990 to the official goal of 200 eggs by the year 2000, it will take more grain than Australia produces.

- For China to consume seafood at the level of Japan, it would need 100 million tons a year—the current world catch.

- In four years, beer consumption is projected to double. To raise consumption for each adult by just three bottles a year would take the equivalent of Norway's annual grain harvest.

Source: Worldwatch Institute

Economic Demands, Environmental Constraints

One consequence of the increasingly frequent collisions between growing human demands and limits on the earth's natural systems is likely to be a further slowdown in world economic growth. (See Table 3.) Although the food-producing sector is a small share of the global economy, it is so basic that any difficulties in adequately expanding output are likely to cause economic disruption and political instability.

A review of global economic growth since mid-century shows growth peaking during the 1960s at an annual rate of 5.2%, then dropping in each of the next two decades. During the first four years of this decade, it has averaged only 1.4%, slightly less than population growth. This means that thus far during this decade income per person has actually declined slightly.

> *"China's leaders stoutly maintain that they will never become dependent on imported grain."*

At issue is how the world economy will be affected if the growth in food production continues to lose momentum. With the continuing loss of cropland not only in China but throughout Asia, a densely populated region that contains at least half the world's people, it will become progressively more difficult to achieve rapid growth in world food output.

The leveling off of the world fish catch and the loss of momentum in grain production overall could further undermine economic expansion. If it does, the world could end this decade with an actual decline in income per person, following the path forged by Africa during the 1980s.

Securing Our Food Future

Future food security for China and the rest of the world may be accomplished with appropriate changes in a variety of strategies and policies, including:

- Reducing consumption of fat-rich livestock products among the affluent. A 10% reduction in the grain used for feed would cover world population growth for 26 months.
- Converting to food production the land now used for nonfood products, such as tobacco and cotton, as well as grains used to produce fuel.
- Implementing topsoil-saving agricultural techniques to reduce loss of agricultural land to erosion.

TABLE 1
World Seafood and Grain Production
(in million tons)

Commodity	1950	1990	2030	Change 1950-1990	Projected Change 1990-2030
Seafood catch	22	100	100	+78	0
Grain output	631	1,780	2,149	+1,149	+369

Source: Food and Agriculture Organization (U.N.)

TABLE 2
Food and Economic Indicators

Indicator	Era of Surplus (1950-1990)	Era of Scarcity (1990-2030)
Seafood catch per person	rising	falling
Grain production per person	rising	falling
Food prices	falling	rising
Grain market	buyer's market	seller's market
Politics of food	dominated by surpluses	dominated by scarcity
Income per person	rising	may decline for much of the world

Source: Worldwatch Institute, based on Food and Agriculture Organization, U.S. Census Bureau, and U.S. Department of Agriculture data

---

TABLE 3
World Economic Growth

Decade	Total Annual Growth	Per Person Annual Growth
1950-1960	4.9%	3.1%
1960-1970	5.2	3.2
1970-1980	3.4	1.6
1980-1990	2.9	1.1
1990-1994 (prel.)	1.4	-0.3

Source: Worldwatch estimates, based on World Bank, Census Bureau, and International Monetary Fund data

Averting a Chinese Dust Bowl

Sand and dust storms resulting from unsustainable agricultural and environmental practices are a growing concern in China's northwestern farmlands, according to a paper published in the *Bulletin of the Chinese Academy of Sciences*.

Overgrazing, over-reclamation of grasslands, overuse of water, and the collection of fuelwood are among the factors blamed for a major dust storm in May 1993, according to Xia Xunchen and Yang Gensheng of the Institute of Desert Research in Lanzhou. That storm in northwestern China killed 85 people, blew away topsoil, and buried large tracts of farmland under sand dunes; direct economic losses totaled 560 million yuan ($67.5 million). "It can be seen from this that sand-dust storm is a major threat to social and economic development in northwest China," the authors argue.

Because dust storms occur naturally in desert and semidesert regions, there may be little that humans can do to prevent them. "On the other hand," note Xia and Yang, "China's practices and experiences have proved that life and property losses caused by sand-dust storms can be reduced through taking some measures, including establishing forecast, early warning, and communication systems; strengthening environmental protection and rehabilitation; and preventing sand-dust storm damage to oases, industrial and mining bases, and roads in desert regions."

The authors recommend five basic principles for saving China's farmlands from dust storms:

1. Stressing prevention by, for example, establishing farmland shelterbelts.

2. Implementing resource development programs that emphasize environmental protection.

3. Using water resources rationally to prevent environmental degradation.

4. Increasing efforts to establish vegetation in oases, industrial and mining bases, and along railway lines and highways.

5. Practicing sustainable farming techniques to reduce loss of topsoil, such as stubble mulch tillage and rotational cropping.

Source: "Problems Concerning Sand-Dust Storms in Northwest China" by Xia Xuncheng and Yang Gensheng, *Bulletin of the Chinese Academy of Sciences* (1995, Vol. 9, No. 2), P.O. Box 8712, Beijing 100080, China. Telephone (86) 10 2542631; fax (86) 10 2542619; e-mail bulletin@bear.ipm.ac.cn.

level at which population will peak before it begins to decline.

Beijing can also alter its industrial policies in a way that will save cropland. At present, it is simply adopting the Western industrial model, emphasizing, for instance, the development of an automobile-centered transportation system that will inevitably consume vast amounts of cropland. Alternatively, China could concentrate on developing a modern national rail transport system for both freight and passengers that would be state-of-the-art and would need only a fraction of the land. For passengers, the bike-to-train commute system that is most highly developed in Japan and the Netherlands provides an appropriate model.

Facing the Future

China's leaders stoutly maintain that they will never become dependent on imported grain. To answer the question, "Who will feed China?" they reply, "The Chinese people will feed themselves." One official has stated unequivocally that "China does not want to rely on others to feed its people and that it relies on itself to solve its own problems."

All the leaders of China today are survivors of the massive famine that occurred in 1959–1961 in the aftermath of the Great Leap Forward—a famine that claimed a staggering 30 million lives. For the Chinese who barely survived that famine, it must be unbelievably difficult to accept the insecurity that is associated with becoming heavily dependent on the outside world for food.

Yet, not to face the issue squarely could have devastating consequences not only for China, but for the rest of the world. Whether China's political leaders are now ready to discuss publicly the dimensions of their likely future dependence on the outside world for food remains to be seen.

About the Author

Lester R. Brown is president of the Worldwatch Institute, 1776 Massachusetts Avenue, N.W., Washington, D.C. 20036. Telephone 202/452-1999; fax 202/296-7365.

This article is based on his new book, *Who Will Feed China? Wake-Up Call for a Small Planet* (W. W. Norton, 1995).

• Introducing water-marketing schemes, such as eliminating subsidies. This will reduce waste and encourage investment in water-efficient technologies.

China in particular can reduce its growing dependence on imported foods in a number of ways. One is to stabilize population before it reaches the peak of 1.66 billion projected for 2045. If, for example, the one-child policy were now extended to minority groups, which make up a substantial share of China's 1.2 billion people, and if incentives to adhere to this goal overall were strengthened, this could help lower the

Article 12

Challenge, March–April 1996

Developing China's Hinterland: From Autarky to Anarchy?

From the vantage point of Western eyes, we tend to see China's remarkable economic development as uniform across the vast country. But as Bernard Weinstein points out, much of China's hinterlands have been left behind. This economist thinks that distributing the benefits of rapid growth throughout China will prove difficult and will sorely try the current political structure.

Bernard L. Weinstein

Bernard L. Weinstein, Ph.D., is Director of the Center for Economic Development and Research and Professor of Applied Economics, University of North Texas, Denton.

For more than a decade, the Chinese economy has been in the throes of a dramatic transformation. From 1949 to the late 1970s, virtually all policies relating to the allocation of resources and the distribution of income were dictated by the central planners of the State Council in Beijing. Committed to a program of economic self-sufficiency, China traded only with countries that shared its puritanical Marxist ardor—such as Cuba, North Korea, North Vietnam, and Albania. Then, under the tutelage of Premier Deng Xiaoping, the Communist party began a process of economic liberalization in 1978, which subsequently led to the ending of agricultural communes, the creation of "special economic zones," and an initial run at privatizing state-owned industries.

On the surface, China's transformation from a centrally directed to a "socialist market" economy appears to be a roaring success. According to the World Bank, China now boasts the third-largest economy on the globe. Since 1978, gross domestic product has increased ten-fold, and real growth rates above 10 percent annually have been common in recent years. China has opened its economy to foreign trade and investment and currently exports more to the United States than any country other than Hong Kong. Indeed, since Deng's liberalization began, China's external trade has ballooned from $10 billion to nearly $300 billion, while foreign investment has jumped from virtually nothing to more than $30 billion in 1994.

But the Chinese "economic miracle" also has its dark side. Rapid growth has been accompanied by rapid inflation, with consumer prices rising 17 percent in 1993 and 27 percent in 1994. Nearly one-half of the state-owned enterprises (SOEs) are losing money, and plans to restructure and privatize these entities have stirred strong resistance from both the Communist party (whose

> *Virtually all of the economic action has taken place in the special economic zones of Zhuhai, Shenzhen, Shantou, and Xiamen or in other east coast cities such as Shanghai, Beijing, and Tianjin, while the hinterlands have experienced little of the new-found prosperity.*

cadres dominate the management of the SOEs) and workers (who fear the loss of secure employment plus the cheap housing and medical care provided by the state). Though the SOEs employ only 76 million workers out of China's labor force of 500 million, they consume 70 percent of state investment funds and contribute less than half the country's economic output.

While technically bankrupt, SOEs remain afloat on government subsidies. China's budget deficit continues to escalate, doubling between 1993 and 1994 to $15 billion—or nearly 25 percent of total government receipts. Seemingly unable (or unwilling) to reform the country's outdated monetary and fiscal systems, the central government sits on the sidelines while the inflationary fires continue to burn and increasingly autonomous provincial and municipal governments invest scarce capital in speculative real estate or foreign ventures.

Though real GDP per capita has increased, income distribution has worsened in recent years because of the bifurcated nature of Chinese development. Virtually all of the economic action has taken place in the special economic zones of Zhuhai, Shenzhen, Shantou, and Xiamen or in other east coast cities such as Shanghai, Beijing, and Tianjin, while the hinterlands have experienced little of the new-found prosperity. With urban workers earning three times the income of their rural cousins, peasants by the hundreds of thousands have been flocking to Beijing and the coastal cities in search of a better life. This, in turn, has overloaded the urban infrastructure and caused a tremendous amount of social unrest in China's eastern cities. The mass migration to the cities, which the authorities seem unable to control, has also had a devastating impact on the farm sector. Since 1993, grain production has been falling and China has become a net food importer.

Graft and corruption are rampant at all levels of government, from influence-peddling by Politburo members to bribe-taking and extortion by municipal employees. The absence of an impartial legal system and a tradition of property rights poses additional dangers for entrepreneurs and foreign investors. Early in 1995, the Communist party began an anticorruption campaign that has resulted in the purging of some 100 party officials and "state entrepreneurs." But the crackdown on graft may have more to do with post-Deng political posturing than a commitment to improve China's perceived business climate.

In stark contrast to the United States and Russia, China's military budget continues to grow, nearly doubling between 1991 and 1995. But there is some leeway in this. The People's Liberation Army (PLA) isn't actually increasing the size of China's armed forces or spending additional billions on military hardware. Instead, the PLA has evolved into a huge business conglomerate that owns hotels, shipping companies, pharmaceutical firms, karaoke bars, brothels, and many other enterprises. In fact, the PLA currently owns or controls more than 20,000 companies across China and earned profits of about $5 billion in 1994.

China's Regional Disparities

Because of growing economic disparities between the coastal provinces and other regions of China, policies to achieve faster growth rates in China's hinterlands have been the topic of much debate in recent years. In the process, a number of Western experts (including this writer) have been asked to render their opinions and recommendations as to the most appropriate strategies to help China realize its regional development goals. But the experience of other countries, especially in the West, may have limited application to the challenges of regional economic development in China.

According to experts and pundits, a new paradigm called the "city-state" will dominate the global economy in the twenty-first century, especially around the Pacific Rim.

These limitations stem partly from the fact that China and the West have different social, cultural, and political traditions and that China is growing at breakneck speed. What's more, China is going through an "industrial" and "post-industrial" revolution at the same time, which is to say that manufacturing and service industries are expanding in tandem. But the key difference between China and other nations, regardless of their stage of development, is that only China has 1.2 billion people. In short, the sheer size of China and the need to control population growth and population mobility limits the transferability of the Western experience to the Chinese setting.

A corollary to this important demographic fact is that at present there is no truly integrated political unit that can be called a "Chinese economy." China, like most large countries, is an agglomeration of regional economies, all growing at different rates with different problems and challenges. Thus, the national statistics for

China are simply weighted averages of China's regional economies. The same is true for more advanced countries, such as the United States, where growth rates, incomes, and unemployment levels vary widely during good times and bad.

Two important policy implications can be drawn from the fragmented nature of the Chinese economic system. First, central or national macroeconomic policies will have differential effects on each region, province, and municipality. Second, central economic policy is de facto regional development policy.

The Urban-Rural Dichotomy

As discussed above, though millions of farmers and peasants have flocked to China's large cities, especially those along the coastal plain, the vast majority of Chinese still live in rural areas. One of the key issues facing economic planners and policy makers in China is whether to bring jobs to people or people to jobs.

Historically, economic development and industrialization have been essentially urban phenomena, with rapid growth first occurring in large metropolitan areas and then fanning out to suburban and, eventually, exurban areas. This has certainly been the case in North America, Europe, and Japan. According to experts and pundits, a new paradigm called the "city-state" will dominate the global economy in the twenty-first century, especially around the Pacific Rim. Singapore, Hong Kong, Tokyo, and Los Angeles are but a few examples of extended urbanized areas that are, and will continue to be, major manufacturing, trade, information, and financial centers.

Against this backdrop, the impulse to direct and reallocate China's internal resources and foreign investment toward lagging hinterland regions may prove ineffective. The experiences of the Western market economies as well as the former Soviet Union suggest that efforts to disperse industry in some sort of "geographically equitable" manner have usually failed. In any event, they've been quite expensive and have resulted in the serious misallocation of scarce human, technical, and capital resources.

Still, because of the huge numbers of people living in China's hinterlands, totally uncontrolled migration could result in perpetual economic and political turmoil. Beijing, Tianjin, Shanghai, Guangzhou, Hong Kong, and other large cities are physically incapable of accommodating another 500 million to 1 billion souls. Thus, China must pursue a strategy of encouraging industrial development in the hinterlands, even if some resource misallocation occurs. To minimize these costs, however, policy makers should strive to define economic areas based on transactional relationships and not political boundaries. A good example would be the Beijing-Tianjin corridor, a

region of nearly 20 million people with complementary industries and infrastructure.

In a similar vein, policy makers must decide whether industrial policy and regional policy are the same or different. In the context of China, they are probably one and the same, since regional development should ideally be based on industrial advantages or opportunities.

Identifying Developmental Goals

Obviously, regional development programs should be framed with specific objectives or goals in mind. But frequently there is confusion or disagreement as to which are the preferred outcomes. Some of the following goals may be complementary, but others may be contradictory:

- job creation
- rising real per capita income
- income redistribution
- poverty reduction
- enhanced quality of life
- broadening the local economic base
- development of export-oriented industries

For example, an emphasis on poverty reduction as an economic development objective may fly in the face of policies designed to enhance efficiency, which should be the overarching goal of regional development programs. Regional development may reduce poverty and improve the distribution of income over time, but then again it may not. The American experience is instructive in this regard.

Though the United States has never embraced explicit regional development policies, with the possible exception of the Appalachian Regional Commission, over the past 60 years a significant degree of regional income convergence has occurred. In 1930, for example, southern incomes were 50 percent below the national norm, while northern incomes were 30 percent above. By 1990, the South was only 10 percent below the national per capita average while the Northeast was only 10 percent above. But over this same period the United States has had limited success in reducing the overall incidence of poverty. Indeed, at present America's official poverty rate—about 15 percent—is more than double that of China. What's more, though interregional income differentials have narrowed, in some parts of the United States intraregional income disparities have actually widened.

Policy Options to Encourage Regional Economic Development

Describing the national and regional economic problems and challenges facing China today is a relatively easy task. But identifying and prioritizing possible solutions—or public policies—is more difficult. This would also be true for any other nation struggling with regional development, but the sheer size of China and its component economic regions, not to mention the dissipation of political power from Beijing to the provinces and the PLA, makes the task even more daunting.

Nonetheless, nine broad policy options can be enumerated that have significant impact on regional economic performance:

1. Conventional Macroeconomic Policy

Macropolicy comprises monetary, fiscal, and regulatory interventions in the marketplace. Though China cannot tailor separate macropolicies for different regions, changes in the money supply, interest rates, the level of taxes and spending, and the regulation of prices will invariably have different regional impacts. Thus, macrolevel policy makers should be sensitive to the regional consequences of their decisions.

2. Intergovernmental Transfers, Grants, and Subsidies

To improve industrial efficiency and international competitiveness, as well as comply with the rules of the General Agreement on Tariffs and Trade (GATT), China must continue the process of reducing subsidies. The socialist market economy must be driven by pricing signals, and subsidies severely distort these signals. In terms of grants and other intergovernmental transfers, the experience of the West has not been positive because the grant-making process has become as politicized as the direct spending process. What's more, intergovernmental grants designed to equalize for differences in per capita incomes, fiscal capacity, or some other measure of "need" have been dismal failures in North America and Europe. So China should proceed with caution in implementing its new revenue-sharing program between the central government and provincial/municipal governments.

3. Industrial Targeting and Development Incentives

Industrial targeting is a reasonable strategy for identifying the best prospects for a particular region or location. The analysis of optimal industries, however, must be based on a candid and realistic assessment of a given location's strengths and weaknesses. To the extent possible, the process should be kept out of the political domain. As regards development incentives—such as low-interest loans, tax abatement, and the like—they should be used judiciously and should be of limited duration. Here again, the experience of North America and Europe with local development incentives has been disappointing. Many noneconomic ventures have been leveraged with government incentives, and a large proportion have failed, leaving taxpayers to foot the bill.

4. Labor and Migration Policies

Resource mobility is the hallmark of an open economy, including the free movement of labor. But given the enormous population pressures in China, labor mobility must be directed and contained except when there is clear evidence of skill shortages in particular regions.

5. Private Ownership and Property Rights

China has already made substantial progress in privatizing industry. The next step must be to establish a system of property rights under law. Though this is clearly the correct approach for ensuring more rapid economic growth in the future, privatization by itself will neither stimulate lagging regions nor narrow income differentials in the short term. What's more, to the extent SOEs simply become private monopolies or oligopolies, industrial inefficiencies will still abound, supplies of goods and services will be restricted, and consumers will continue to pay high prices.

6. Infrastructure

Improvements to China's public capital, including highways, airports, water systems, and telecommunications, are an absolute prerequisite to sustainable regional development. Indeed, infrastructure is the fabric that will eventually knit together a unified, integrated national economy. However, improvements to transportation and telecommunications networks will also facilitate mobility among regions and make it more difficult to control labor movement.

7. Lowering Trade Barriers among Regions

At present, a host of direct and indirect impediments to the movement of raw materials, goods, and services among China's regions is retarding the process of economic integration. These barriers must be removed without delay.

8. Technology Policy

China has established several dozen industrial technology centers across the country. Careful analyses should be performed to assess how these centers can facilitate technology transfer and regional economic development.

9. Human Capital

Finally, China's policies on education and training will have significant impact on all provinces and municipalities. Perhaps the most important role the central government can play in fostering regional economic development over the long term will be to ensure that high school graduates have mastered the basic requirements for lifetime employment, namely literacy and numeracy. The experience of the West demonstrates strongly that a good system of secondary and vocational education is a more critical element in the regional development process than even higher education.

China's Future: Can a Socialist Market Economy Deliver the Goods?

A corollary to the infamous economic axiom that "there ain't no free lunch" should probably be "there ain't no economic miracles." Yes, China's growth has been spectacular in recent years, and the rapid pace of development may continue for some time. But the explanations for China's success are really quite simple: education, deregulation, and privatization.

China's economy today is perhaps best described as one of semicontrolled chaos. It is simultaneously entrepreneurial, anarchic, dynamic, and corrupt. Can the boom last? The answer is unknowable, as are most questions about China's future. The Chinese themselves, however, appear increasingly skeptical about their country's economic future, as shown by capital outflows of $10 billion to $15 billion annually in recent years. As a Western economist based in Beijing observed recently, "One wonders why foreigners are so desperate to invest here when the Chinese seem to be so desperate to invest overseas."

The next five years will be critical, what with the presumed passing of Deng Xiaoping, the takeover of Hong Kong, and the inevitable political intrigues that will follow these developments. But regardless of how the leadership struggle sorts itself out, absent the evolution of democratic institutions and a rule of law, the Chinese economy will eventually disintegrate.

Article 13

Current History, September 1996

China's Human Avalanche

"Jin [Xiulin] is one of 70 million to 100 million Chinese peasants who are on the road in search of jobs in towns and cities. The migrants are coaxed from their villages not only by the prospect of a better livelihood; they are compelled to leave." Ann and James Tyson paint a portrait of the hardships of those who move from country to city and those who are left behind "in one of the largest peacetime migrations in history."

Ann and James Tyson

Ann and James Tyson are correspondents for the Christian Science Monitor. *This article is excerpted with permission from their book,* Chinese Awakenings: Life Stories from the Unofficial China *(Boulder, Colo.: Westview/HarperCollins, 1995).*

Early on a winter morning, in the darkness before dawn, Jin Xiulin slips out from under a cotton quilt, dresses, tiptoes by her sleeping niece, and steals out of her huddled brick dwelling into a cold drizzle.* She climbs onto a public bus and wedges herself into the damp, odorous

*We have used pseudonyms to thwart official reprisal. The name of the home village has also been changed.

pack of passengers. Rows of apartment houses jostle by, four-story tenements slapped together from concrete slabs into gray cubicles dimly lit by lone lightbulbs. On the edge of the city of Shashi the bus rises onto the spine of a dike, rides a network of the earthen ramparts, and descends toward a power plant and textile mill built in a wide basin.

Jin steps from the bus in front of a sheet-metal hut. She removes the padlock on the tiny workshop and switches on a fluorescent lamp. As the cold wind rattles the metal around her, she cuts cloth to be sewn into dresses by her employees, her niece and a fellow peasant migrant. Under the cold fluorescent glare, Jin puts in a few hours of work before sunrise heralds the arrival of customers who stop on their way to work in nearby factories. Seven days a week she labors shoulder to shoulder with her seamstresses, bending over scissors or hunching over a foot-powered sewing machine.

Jin is one of 70 million to 100 million Chinese peasants who are on the road in search of jobs in towns and cities. The migrants are coaxed from their villages not only by the prospect of a better livelihood; they are compelled to leave. Their flight testifies to the poverty, hardship, and unrest in the countryside. They are running from corruption, high taxes, and strict state controls on childbirth. They are also fleeing the lack of economic opportunity and the severe slowdown in the rise of living standards in China's villages.

Like many peasants nationwide, one in every five laborers in Jin's village of Baihe has gone to the city in search of work. Usually they must accept the dangerous and dirty jobs shunned by city dwellers. The *mangliu* (blind drifters) toil at construction sites on rickety bamboo scaffolding. They haul flatbed carts of garbage and tanks of night soil through the streets. They crouch amid the dust of curbsides, repairing shoes or awaiting work as charwomen or day laborers.

The exodus of Jin and other peasants is a wrenching rite of passage for China as it evolves from an agrarian to an industrial society. In terms of humanity, the stakes are enormous. The "human avalanche" is one of the largest peacetime migrations in history. Never have so many people taken to the road at once in search of good fortune beyond the horizon. The migrants are restless forerunners of a vast army of idle laborers among China's 860 million peasants, the world's largest rural population. They began setting out from villages in large numbers in the early 1980s after the Communist Party eased its grip on their lives by dissolving Mao's communes. Family farms revived and dramatically raised productivity. Millions of the peasants left idle by the reform have quit the land in search of prosperity.

By the next century, the number of surplus workers in the countryside will probably increase to 200 million as every year 10 million Chinese born during the 1966–1976 baby boom come of age. Construction on arable land will annually push 4 million farmers from their fields. While rural industry, the most dynamic sector of the economy, has employed tens of millions of peasants, it can absorb only a small part of the vast reservoir of jobless farmers. Many of the redundant workers will seek jobs in cities despite government efforts to stem the exodus.

The migrants are a relentless, volatile force and a major worry for China's leaders. The "muddy legs" loiter in teeming cities across China. Many of the migrants are hungry, tired, poorly educated, and easily abused. They lack urban residence registration and the grain rations, housing, health care, and other benefits that often go with it. They labor with little or no legal protections. Because of the desperation and abundance of the itinerant workers, bosses fire many of them at will, pay them meager wages, and work them in hazardous sweatshops more than 14 hours a day. Overall, the migration is a symptom of the kind of turmoil and rural discontent that have sparked upheaval and government collapse throughout Chinese history.

Since moving to the city, Jin and millions of migrants have turned their backs on Maoist dogma and embraced modern values that could fuel the widespread unrest feared by the party leadership. By acting on their ambitions, the migrants are shunning the orthodox mores of self-sacrifice, shared struggle, and equal wealth. They have forsaken the traditional ideal of cooperation and embraced the modern market principle of competition much faster than the peasants back in their native villages.

City Mouse, Country Mouse

As her savings and confidence have grown in the city, Jin has become headstrong and fond of fashionable clothes. She has pushed aside the communitarian values of her home village. Jin has also exposed her two daughters and eldest son to a comparatively freewheeling, forward-looking urban lifestyle by sending them to college in the cities of Wuhan and Xian. In the eyes of Jin's husband and other villagers, Jin and her children seem to bristle with individualism and self-assertiveness when they return to the village. As in the households of other migrants, the younger, bolder, or more resourceful members of Jin's family were the first to break the bonds of ancient tradition and Communist edict. Their modern values have split the family, dividing wife from husband, father from son, and sister from brother.

The party has intensified the ethical strains afflicting millions of Chinese families moving from village to city, field to factory, and poverty to plenty. It still tries to control where Chinese live and what they think. Antiquated laws hinder the flow of people and ideas between urban and rural China. The party also bars private ownership of land, a rule that hampers investment between city and countryside and between the flourishing coast and the sleepy hinterland. The restrictions, many left over from the Maoist era, worsen the destabilizing disparity in wealth between urban and rural China and between the coast and the interior. The constraints inhibit a smooth integration of the country with the city and discourage a melding between traditional collectivist mores and modern individualistic values.

In Jin's native Hubei province and many parts of China's hinterland, the gap in living standards and beliefs between people in the city and countryside remains vast. Nationwide, peasants annually earn less than half the income of city dwellers. The government fails to provide peasants with medical care, schooling, and other services at the level enjoyed by urban Chinese. Rural residents lack the same opportunities for entrepreneurship that enable urbanites to prosper. A party ban on private ownership of land denies peasants the efficiencies and wealth that could come with the freedom of individuals to buy and sell land. So in most of China the transition from city to countryside is abrupt, as one ventures suddenly from paved roads to footpaths, from unruly hawkers in swarming markets to languishing clumps of peasants in torpid village crossroads, from robust hope to blank resignation.

For Jin, the clash in values between city and countryside is as jarring as the move from the comforts of Shashi to the hardships of her native Baihe. In a livelier economy and looser society, Jin and her family could more easily reconcile modern and traditional values. Along the comparatively prosperous and progressive coast, members of the same family who have found work in rural enterprises near their homes can cope with strains in values together. By remaining in their native homes, these families can harmonize conflicting values more easily than can inland migrants. They are attuning urban individualistic values to rural collectivist traditions and turning their coastal villages into suburbs. But both the location and outlook of Jin's native village are too remote for a smooth, rapid transition from old to new ideas. As Jin quickly prospers she, like many migrants and city dwellers, increasingly finds her village backward and oppressive.

Homecoming

Jin finds it difficult to return for a visit to her home village. Since moving to Shashi in 1986, she has gone back to Baihe only twice, for the lunar New Year, the holiday Chinese families cherish most. She quickly tires of the crude lifestyle and straitjacket values in the village. She especially feels the sting from inept, corrupt, and intrusive officials; they are closer at hand than in Shashi. Indeed, for Jin a trip back to Baihe affirms the wisdom of her bold migration. It makes her appreciate Shashi and its relative comfort, easier mores, and respite from constant government hectoring.

Returning home, Jin feels a mixture of pride and self-consciousness. Walking alongside a creek past thatched dwellings, she carries pastries, fruits, toys, cassette tapes, and other gifts that many of her fellow villagers will never afford. Her outfit is cleaner, more colorful, and more stylish than the tattered and dirty olive drab and blue clothes they wear. Some of her former neighbors greet her from their yards; others turn away from her into the darkness of their dwellings. Jin again sees the

poor, cramped life of those who submit to official restraints on residency and to strict customs that tie women to the home.

As Jin approaches the green double doors of her small dwelling, she must hold inside a storm of conflicting emotions. She can count on a warm, happy welcome from her daughter-in-law and two grandsons who live there. But the heavy doorway symbolizes her subservience to her husband, Peng Min, according to an ancient Confucian tradition. (Jin has retained her maiden name, following Chinese custom.)

Indeed, the return to Baihe for Jin is like a return to the values and lifestyle of preindustrial China. In Shashi, Jin has a steady supply of electricity; in Baihe electric light comes only in intermittent bursts. In Shashi she gets water from a tap; in Baihe she must carry two buckets on a yoke across a creek to a well. In the city she rides taxis, buses, and cars; in remote Baihe she must rely on water buffalo, bicycles, and horse-drawn carts.

For Jin and millions of villagers in China, the road to the city is the only way out of poverty.

For Jin and millions of villagers in China, the road to the city is the only way out of poverty. The moribund economy of Baihe offers few opportunities for seamstresses and other skilled laborers. Before going to Shashi, Jin worked throughout the year but was often paid only at harvest time when her customers were themselves paid by the state for grain. Craftsmen like Jin's youngest son, a carpenter, also watch their talents go to waste. He and his father tried to launch an enterprise making wooden crates for factories in the nearby city of Shishou. But they confronted myriad obstacles: uncertain transport and a dearth of management expertise, capital and raw materials. So the young man left his wife and two young sons behind in the village and took up a job with his uncle's roofing company in Shashi.

The villagers' only sure resources—land and labor—also fall short. Quoting a popular adage, villagers say that the land and profits from tilling are so limited that they could not get by even if they reaped gold. Each person in Baihe may lease no more than a third of an acre. Farmers' incomes have shrunk since 1987 because rising prices of plastic sheeting, pesticides, fertilizer, and other agricultural supplies have far outstripped increases in the state purchase price for grain and cotton. As a result, more than half the village households are in debt to one another, to collective enterprises, and to village governments.

Rising Above the Mire

Of all the symbols of the backwardness and hardship of rural life for Jin and her family, none is more powerful or inescapable than mud. By moving to Shashi, Jin has found refuge from the fickle and cruel shifts of the Yangtze River and its ancient, ever present legacy of mire. She has won a separate peace for her family from the epic contest between man and mud that has preoccupied her village for centuries.

Jin's family and other villagers expend much of their sweat, money, and time trying to keep the water and earth of the Yangtze in safe, fruitful proportion. Their efforts are often in vain. According to local lore, the Lotus Pond River on the western side of the village changes course and overruns the village every 30 years. The river is a tributary of the Yangtze, which flows by the village's eastern side. A 10-yard-high earthen dike encircling the village occasionally gives way to the swelling and capricious shifts of the rivers. At flood time in July, each of the village's 331 families must send out an able-bodied man to stand on the dike around the clock. If necessary, these men reinforce the embankment with a mixture of mud and straw hauled on yokes and baskets. The rivers routinely flood the only road leading to Baihe, turning the village into an island sunk far below water level behind its earthen bulwark. If the surging rivers are especially menacing, all 1,300 villagers mass on the dike with shovels, yokes, and baskets at hand.

Within the dike the villagers can usually control the balance of water and earth in their fields. Using ramshackle sluices, they regulate the water flow from the river into a creek, through the village, and into fields of jute, tangerines, plums, rice, cotton, and sweet potatoes. When heavy rains bring too much water, they pump out the fields.

To the villagers, mud symbolizes their penury and backwardness.

Outside their fields, however, the villagers throw up their hands and abandon all but the most critical efforts to keep the water at bay. Everything assumes a coat of mud, smeared, caked, swiped, or smudged. It covers children from heel to hair and chickens from feet to comb. It outfits man and beast in drab, impressing everything animate into a uniform army of the humble and the vulnerable. It seems to ooze up walls and across thresholds, reinforcing the siding and packed earth floors of the wattle and daub dwellings.

To the villagers, mud symbolizes their penury and backwardness. Not even the party, to say nothing of rural entrepreneurs, will build workshops or small factories on the vulnerable land of Baihe. So as many villages in China rush toward prosperity behind a vanguard of rural enterprises, Baihe remains destitute. The per capita annual income is just $130—20 percent less than that of the national average for peasants and about one-third the income for city dwellers. The mud holds villagers in poverty more than anything else. Its coming every year reminds them of their helplessness before nature. A flood in 1943 swept away the house of Jin's husband and forced his family to spend a sodden, bitter winter huddled on a dike. A surge of the Yangtze in 1954 that killed 33,000 people wiped out the duck flock that Jin's father tended for a living. It is no wonder then that Jin and other villagers measure progress by how far they have risen from the mire. They migrate to the city not just for higher pay but for higher ground, to go from muck to macadam.

The House that Jin Built

Jin ostentatiously proclaims her successful rise from the mud. Using her earnings and savings, her family built a new brick and tile house in 1987 for $1,300. The whitewashed structure, the only clean-looking dwelling in the village, gleams from among the surrounding brown mire and earthen homes like a shining, arrogant challenge. She enters the house and embraces her children, her crowning achievement.

Day to day, Jin's family cannot hope to maintain its snow-white home in Baihe as a symbol of transcendence over mud. Each morning, observing a friendly peasant custom, the family removes a heavy beam from the front doors and flings them open to the dawn. Dogs, cats, sparrows, roosters, hens, chicks, and bugs enter the three-room dwelling. Each brings its own distinctive track of mud. Like the neighbors who drop in, the creatures tend to gather in a large, central front room under a ceiling fretted by rough-hewn rafters 20 feet off the concrete floor. The creatures freely peck, gnaw, cluck, scratch, doze, roost, and defecate. At sunset the sparrows and chicks gradually stop chirping and peeping and stay the night. The sparrows perch on the rafters among the hung laundry; the chicks nest in a corner beneath a sawhorse and the butts of two 15-foot logs to be hewn by Jin's son. The other uninvited visitors file out unprompted before bedtime.

The house Jin built is an indication that in China's poorer villages even well-off peasants live crudely. The design of the 300-square-foot dwelling is basically the same as in peasant homes across most of China. Leading from one side of the front room are doorways to two bedrooms. Jin's second son and his wife sleep in one of the rooms on a bed canopied with mosquito netting. On a small dresser stand neon-colored plastic chrysanthemums, apples, and peaches, a black-and-white television, and a wardrobe. Their two young sons sleep in the other room. Jin's husband, Peng, eats and sleeps in the medical clinic at the village crossroads, a 10-minute walk away. He is one of the village's two doctors. On the other side of the front room is a dark and narrow kitchen with a sagging tarpaper ceiling and two woks fired with sticks and coal. Behind the kitchen lives a pig in a sty. Adjacent to him is the family privy, a crude open teepee made of jute stems partially shielding a hole in the dirt crossed by two parallel boards. The pig, with his grunts and acrid odor, is an eager, intimate companion to those in the kitchen and the privy.

Jin has decorated the house in a way that testifies to how migration mixes a bizarre brew of conflicting values within a family. In the front room, posters and scrolls either made in the village or bought in the city suggest a mélange of traditional, Maoist, and modern mores. "Big fortune upon opening the door; good luck when going out," declare couplets written in black on red paper and pasted on the front doors. Directly across from the doors hangs a colorful five-foot scroll from which the wizened and berobed gods of longevity, prosperity, and official prestige beam as they hug frolicking children on a golden horse-drawn cart. On either side are scrolls. One says, "With the blessings of the three gods, this land of intellect produces people of eminence." On the other side, another scroll says, "With the arrival of the five guarantees, the country is in harmony and the people in peace." (Mao mandated that his "people's communes" guarantee childless and infirm senior citizens five benefits: food, clothing, medical care, housing, and free burial.) Beneath the scrolls, in another tribute to Maoism, glares a poster of a female navy pilot wearing a life vest and helmet, a marine with an AK-47 assault rifle and gunbelt, and a woman in a naval dress uniform. Across the bottom of the large, neon-colored plastic poster are the words, "The cream rises together." Among the messages of antiquity and dour militarism are the coy, softly seductive images popular in China under reform. In one poster a dewy-eyed young woman cuddles a kitten against her cheek. In another, a smiling girl clinging to a guitar reclines in a hammock. In a third, a shapely female in a striped bathing suit dallies by the side of a pool.

For a few days during her rare visits, Jin enjoys the slow rhythm, neighborly warmth, and mud-between-the-toes feeling of the village. But villagers also give her an earful of complaints about the government. The widespread rancor toward officials, like the crude living standards, makes Jin appreciate her life in Shashi. Indeed, corruption is the biggest popular gripe in the countryside and a leading inducement for migration, according to comments by scores of peasants in dozens of villages in China.

In Baihe, village officials have capriciously raised a slew of levies on the peasants. They have set the price of electricity far above the state-suggested rate and pocketed the difference. Also, officials have more than doubled the tax on land since 1987, plunging many families deeper into debt. They frequently seize the grain of villagers who refuse to pay the tax. Jin's daughter-in-law has a large concrete bin for rice next to the back door but she keeps it empty. Instead, she stores rice in a large clay vessel next to her bed behind a wardrobe in a room with a locked door and barred windows.

Officials add insult to injury by brazenly engaging in petty abuses. They spend much of their time "building the Great Wall," a slang term for mahjongg, the gambling game in which players line up dozens of small tiles in a long row. The officials are also guilty of *chihe* (eat-drink), the use of public funds for wining and dining. The village's only eatery opened primarily to serve officials who regularly regale higher cadres touring Baihe. If the village officials have not exhausted their annual banquet budget at the end of the year, they spend the remainder on themselves, according to Peng, Jin's husband. Villagers have no surefire way to revoke unjust taxes or to unseat abusive officials.

"Even if someone points his finger at an official's face and says, 'You're corrupt,' the official will say, 'Okay, so go to Beijing and sue me,' " Jin's brother-in-law said. "Everyone knows there are bigger problems for the leaders to deal with than corruption in the countryside."

Every three years the villagers "elect" a seven-member village council from among eleven candidates selected by the Communist Party branch in the township. But the ballot serves mostly as an announcement. The first seven candidates listed on the slate always win, Peng said.

Birth Guerrillas and "Black Children"

Among state controls, family planning is the most intrusive, most infuriating, and potentially most abusive.

"Deal resolute blows against excess birth guerrillas!" implores an official slogan scrawled in large characters on a wall outside the village. When Jin's youngest son fathered a second child, in violation of the one-child-per-couple policy, he could not pay the fine. So village officials seized his black-and-white television, bed, table, bureau, and other furniture. The officials auctioned the possessions and compelled the son's wife to undergo sterilization. Often officials pocket part or all of the "excess birth" fine of $280, a figure more than twice the per capita annual income in the village, Peng said. Thousands of migrants have become birthing "guerrillas," leaving their villages to evade local birth control officials. The official press has labeled the more than 1 million children illicitly born on the road as "black children."

Peasant hostility toward officials extends beyond corruption and resentment over birth control to all kinds of contacts. The tension is palpable in Baihe. At daybreak a cuckoo begins to sing as the soft dawn light silhouettes the feathery leaves of a water cedar tree standing beside a still creek. It is Sunday, 5:15 A.M. Suddenly villagers are jolted awake as loudspeakers throughout the village growl with the sound of the local leader clearing his throat.

"Comrades, in some cotton fields farmers have not dug irrigation ditches. Those who have are diligent; those who haven't are lazy," blares the leader.

"Comrades, all work group leaders will meet this morning; the meeting will start on time regardless of wind and rain," the village leader says before delivering a long lecture on farming.

Later, 25 minutes after the scheduled start of the meeting, the village leader no longer speaks in a lordly tone but shouts in a high, cracking voice, "Group leaders come to the meeting right now!"

In Charge But Not in Control

It is more than the sleepiness of a Sunday sunrise that makes it hard to rouse the villagers of Baihe. Throughout rural China, party cadres have seen their power to marshal farmers erode in recent years. With the exception of taxation and birth control policy, the party has eased most day-to-day restrictions on farmers since the move to market-oriented reform. Baihe villagers and other Chinese are far less dependent on the party than before reform. Jin, Peng, and other rural Chinese see the party as irrelevant or as an outright impediment to their struggle for prosperity. The party has never been geared to giving material and moral support to a migrant woman like Jin or to other kinds of newly self-assertive Chinese. It is unequipped to ease the social tensions that flare from their gumption.

The party surrendered some of its authority in the early 1980s by making farming families rather than the commune the basic organizational force for agriculture. The "household responsibility system" prompted a surge in incomes and grain production in Baihe and villages across China. But by promoting such sweeping change, the party denied itself many day-to-day controls over the land and those who till it. For example, it can no longer coerce villagers by withholding remuneration for fieldwork as it did when it kept Chinese peasants strictly regimented in communes. In wealthy villages nearer the coast, many farmers have abandoned farming and prospered in commerce, services, rural enterprises, and other work outside immediate party control. As a result, the party is no longer the sole boss and benefactor for farmers; it is just the most powerful among society's several emerging interest groups.

Jin's brother, Jin Guosheng, has felt party power slip through his own fingers. He built a reputation for efficiency and rectitude during 11 years as party secretary in a village neighboring Baihe. Eight of those years he spent concurrently as village leader. He launched a small lumber mill and other lucrative collective enterprises, and he organized the funding for and construction of a $36,360 water tower and pipe system that provides the luxury of running water.

Although the 2,000 villagers respect Jin Guosheng, his authority steadily degenerated. He quit his official posts in 1992 because he felt he was becoming the local villain while coping with what he calls the "five difficulties" of the village cadre: land, birth, death, water, and high officials. He repeatedly had to dun his neighbors for tax payments, including an annual levy of $22.50 for every acre of land. He also had to collect $272 from couples who broke family-planning regulations. When villagers died, Jin had to compel grieving families to cremate the remains in Shishou rather than hold a traditional burial on scarce land. He was also responsible for rallying reluctant farmers to donate their labor and money to common efforts in ditch digging, dike building, and other water conservancy projects. Finally, like his neighbors, Jin grew exasperated with officials.

"Township officials don't do solid work; they just give orders and expect village cadres to do all the work," he said, strolling through his lush two-acre field of cotton, sweet potato, tangerines, medicinal herbs, red pepper, plums, green beans, and grapes. "The officials' orders keep us running around all the time and meanwhile the higher officials never come down to the grass roots."

Like many of his neighbors, Jin has forsaken public service in search of personal gain. He is trying to emulate Peng's brother and make a fortune selling and installing tar paper. To do so, he has followed his sister Jin to the city.

The Bridge to . . .

Jin's family and other villagers can largely blame the national leadership for poverty, corruption, and most other official abuses. The harm from craven party leaders is clear at Baihe. On most mornings Peng shoulders a bamboo yoke with two pails and sets off into the dawn mist across a crumbling stone bridge toward the village well. In recent years as Peng crossed the bridge, he has regarded the cracked structure as a symbol of China's faltering effort to bridge the gap between indigence and affluence.

"Everyone uses this bridge and some villagers have plenty of money, but still we let it go to ruin," Peng says, pointing at the mossy span and shaking his head. "During the years of reform, we've only worked for ourselves, not for each other," he says as he sweeps a finger toward the mud and thatch dwellings around him.

Peng's disgust underlines the failure of the government to carry out full economic reform in the villages of China. Overall, market-oriented change has helped many of China's 860 million rural residents to prosper more than ever before. The per capita income of farmers more than tripled in the decade after paramount leader Deng Xiaoping disbanded Mao Zedong's communes and condoned family farming. But as self-reliant peasants like Jin cross the bridge to prosperity, many Chinese who are more dependent on the rickety socialist economy remain behind. State investment in agriculture has sharply declined under reform. Meanwhile, in Baihe and most other villages nationwide, the steep rise in the rate of inflation has far outstripped the meager rise in farmers incomes. Consequently, village tax revenues are insufficient to pay for the maintenance of crucial public works like the bridge in Peng's village.

The bridge is crumbling in large part because of political cowardice in Beijing. China's leaders are too ideologically divided and afraid of unrest to finish the high-stakes task of reform. They shy away from carrying the economy completely from socialism to a market system. Conservative leaders have ruled out allowing Peng and other peasants to own or sell land. They shrink from completely removing controls on prices of agricultural goods and undertaking other reforms essential to invigo-

rate the economy. The political uncertainty and irresolute leadership have provoked fears among Peng's neighbors and other Chinese peasants about a return to collective tilling. The farmers refuse to invest in the common good, favoring their own short-term interests instead. The cash-strapped government has not filled in the financial gap as it formerly did. Therefore, vital public projects such as roads, irrigation systems, and the bridge in Peng's village have gone to ruin.

The party, like Jin's family, is shaky because it has not fully adjusted to the profound shift in popular values from collectivism to individualism. Chinese today tend to cooperate less and compete more than at any other time under Communist Party rule. Before the party eased its totalitarian grip in the early 1980s, Jin and other Chinese knew they had to pull together in order to survive. Now that economic reform has all but guaranteed subsistence, common citizens like Jin no longer scratch for mere survival while clinging to a credo of cooperation. They increasingly strive for riches by upholding the idea of competition. Still, the party tries to hold citizens to collectivist values even though they are increasingly living and working for themselves. Party leaders want the enriching benefits from individualism, but they do not want to give up the harsh autocratic powers of their Leninist state.

At the end of one of Jin's visits home, the Pengs and their kin followed an old Chinese custom and saw her off on her journey back to Shashi. The family trudged the two miles on the road to the bus stop in the nearest town. Jin occasionally glanced at Peng as they silently walked far apart. She climbed onto the bus and sat down. As the engine started up, she quickly turned back to look at Peng. He had already turned away heading back to the village. The engine roared and he disappeared behind a cloud of dust. As the bus jounced away, Jin tightly shut her eyes and pressed her forehead against the window.

Article 14   *The World & I,* December 1995

A Floating Population

Migration and Culture Shock in China

Julian M. Weiss

Julian M. Weiss is International Communications Fellow at the Heritage Foundation. He has traveled to the People's Republic of China several times since 1981, most recently this past summer. His articles in the mid-1980s forecast political and social tensions in that country.

In a crowded city street, two residents gaze at a group of new arrivals and shake their heads. "More crime on the way," grumbles one. "There's no room for them, and no jobs either," admonishes the other. The time is now and the scene commonplace. But this is not a U.S. border community swamped by illegal migrants, a French metropolis where North Africans now converge, nor a German industrial city facing ever-increasing numbers of Turkish immigrants. Such conversations are taking place in Canton, Guangdong, Beijing, Guanzhou, Shanghai, and every other city in the People's Republic of China (PRC). And the unwanted immigration is not foreign, it's Chinese.

As the populous Chinese mainland pursues modernization, economic reforms and increased living standards have been accompanied by profound social transformations, most notably a massive exodus: Rural China is on the move.

"The 'floating population' may be as high as one hundred million," says Dru Gladney, a specialist on urbanization at Hawaii's East-West Center. Even the lowest current estimate, seventy million, represents a staggering share of the country's population. In fact, the number is accelerating at a phenomenal rate and could reach two hundred million—approximately one-sixth of the PRC's population—within five years. "Every day, large groups of men and women abandon the rural areas," explains Kenneth Lieberthal, author of *Governing China* and a leading Western expert on the PRC.

The itinerant homeless are predominantly young, but their numbers span all age-groups. "They seek a better living standard, if not wealth," Gladney points out, "[but] they may be blamed for crime, housing shortages, and low wages that affect even long-term urban residents." So-

phia Woodward, an activist with New York-based Human Rights in China and editor of *China Rights Forum,* agrees that the influx is producing social tensions. "The migrants are blamed for crime and other ills," she says.

Efforts to clamp down on undocumented *mangliu* (migrant) workers have created discussions reminiscent of those

in California when Proposition 187, the ballot initiative designed to curb publicly funded services to illegal immigrants, was debated and approved. But what is occurring in the PRC—and in a remarkably short space of time—has no historical precedent. The exodus to urban China is causing several worlds to clash. Not only communist social and

A narrow and crowded street in Guangdong.

T. S. LAM/The World & I

T. S. Lam/The World & I

A thriving seaport in the southeast. The easing of trade and industrial regulations has created economic and social imbalances in the PRC.

economic authority but also centuries of authentic tradition, life-style, and attendant cultural values are being overwhelmed by the headlong rush toward the dream of a glitzy, high-tech postindustrial age. A mélange of consumerism, mercantilism, Confucianism, Marxism, nihilism, and a myriad other value systems is being woven into the fabric of China's twenty-first-century tapestry.

Profound political shifts are also taking place. Paramount leader Deng Xiaoping, whose twenty-year reign unleashed the economic forces that have given rise to the current diaspora, may soon pass from the scene, and, veteran China watchers realize, the subsequent political transition may be less tranquil than most wish. Many believe that the nomadic legions are a significant potential source of political, as well as social, instability. China has only been united for a relatively brief period in its history, and sharp ethnic, cultural, and linguistic differences remain between even neighboring provinces.

Soaring Urban Economy

The economic boom has been largely limited to a handful of provinces. Before 1980, rural areas were home to 80 percent of the PRC's population. During 1978–79, special economic zones (SEZs) were created and the first steps toward capitalism approved by the gov-

ernment. However, only a few areas of the country would be permitted to make reforms. Following decades of failed communist economic policies, these southeastern SEZs were to be test cases for a "one country, many systems" approach toward development.

Reform-minded Chinese officials announced an "open door" policy allowing foreign manufacturing investment in the SEZs. The southeast's proximity to Hong Kong, with its bustling port and transport links to Asian and Western markets, made for a rapid surge in Chinese exports. Those fortunate enough to be put on payrolls in the new textile mills, factories, and electronics plants saw their incomes rise tenfold above the PRC's national average (then the equivalent of U.S. $170 a year). In 1985, Hong Kong-based companies employed eight hundred thousand mainland Chinese; today, that figure exceeds three million.

Consequently, income levels in the southeast rose sharply during the 1980s, and the demand for services, housing, leisure goods, better food, and amenities increased. Tourism was permitted and hotels, office parks, and restaurants constructed. By the early 1990s, in a further attempt to free up the economy, Beijing relaxed rules governing *dainwa* (work gangs) and changed policies governing residence permits and mandatory assignments on local work brigades. These

changes opened the door and allowed the floating population to emerge.

Increasingly, power began shifting to the provinces and away from central authorities in Beijing. Economic reforms were permitted to spread to other areas, including Shanghai, the venerable city of ten million that had been the leading port commercial bastion, and financial center for pre-World War II China. Beijing also became a mecca for foreign business, as indicated by soaring rents that had reached London-level rates by 1993.

Bicycle ownership is one indicator of the economic boom. Between 1980 and 1994, ownership rose from 7 to 40 percent of the population. In 1980 the cost of a bicycle was the equivalent of four months' salary, but, even at inflated 1995 prices, an even better bicycle can now be purchased for seven weeks' salary. Television sets are also more commonplace than before. Nationally, a scant three households in a thousand owned a TV in 1980. Today, the figure is around 180 per thousand. The disparity between urban and rural living standards is even more pronounced. In the major cities, probably four of five households today have at least one color television set, three-fourths have VCRs, six in ten have refrigerators, and four in five have dishwashers. In the 1970s, the "three essentials" (considered basic if not obligatory wedding gifts) consisted of bicycles, watches, and radios. In the mid-1980s, to "keep up with the Chins [Joneses]," those approaching marriage preferred color TVs, VCRs, and refrigerators. Today, the celebrated three essentials are cars, houses, and working telephones.

The notion of getting rich was increasingly sanctioned by those in power. "Being rich is everybody's No. 1 dream," says Liu Wan Ching, a sociology professor at Beijing University. And Chairman Deng himself proclaimed in 1978 that "to get rich is glorious."

But increasing wealth and urbanization have been matched by changing outlooks on life. The question remains as to how these changes will affect China's many ethnic communities. Gladney hopes that the boom and its excesses may be tempered by traditional sensibilities. Among the Hul Muslims, for example, "people accept wealth as long as part is returned to the community," he says.

This is important because regional economic disparities are already creating frustration and tension. "Those left behind by the boom are frustrated and resentful," commented one Chinese journalist off the record.

Changing Cultural Order

Li-kai Shu, a Taiwanese agricultural expert who directed technical assistance projects in rural south-central China, tells of an event that reflects the siren lure of urban life-styles. One day, while he was instructing farmers in the Yellow River Province about crop-rotation techniques, a rumor circulated about a former villager who had gambled his way to riches after moving to Ningbo, a city on the eastern coast, and was now a factory manager. All this after moving to Ningbo only two months earlier! Over the next few days, Shu recalls, several farmers failed to show up for the training course because they had joined the exodus eastward.

These contemporary Chinese "Horatio Alger" fables are widespread, and the commercial boom is fueled by an unending supply of low-cost migrant labor from the hinterland. Beijing now counts 3.3 million migrants among its eleven million citizens, and nearly all of the new arrivals are former villagers. But it is no easy task "to provide services, sanitation, schools, and other facilities for them," says John Courtney, a specialist with the Institute for Urban and Regional Development at the University of California at Berkeley who has worked on Chinese urban planning for the World Bank. Courtney was one of the first experts to recognize the pitfalls of China's massive population movement. "It creates major demands and stresses," he comments. Many others now suggest that the nomadic legions are a significant potential force for instability.

Shantytowns and loose communities have sprung up to meet the housing demands, and informal markets, mayors police, and taxation systems have appeared to prevent total anarchy. The construction industry is accelerating through cycles of boom and superboom: There has been no slowdown. Round-the-clock construction is commonplace, and the constant noise has become a source of aggravation for many urban residents. Yet joblessness remains a problem in the cities, and unemployment among 18–45-year-old males can be as high as 40 percent.

Furthermore, inefficient state-owned corporations are under pressure to abandon "featherbedding," and the resulting layoffs only add to the ranks of those without work. Overnight, China's cities have become places where "the best of times, the worst of times" intertwine. The swarming numbers of migrants and homeless are matched by increasing

numbers of the *wanyuan hu* (wealthy) and privileged. At the same time, revered Chinese traditions of family loyalty, hard work, and filial piety are threatened by the prevalence of corruption, banditry, prostitution, and materialistic overindulgence.

The new materialism—coming on the heels of institutionalized self-criticism during the pre-Deng era—has changed views about responsibility to other people. What is occurring, at least among nouveau riche mandarins, is a preoccupation with self, status, and gratification. Those who cannot yet afford luxuries are bedazzled by the ostentatious life-styles that are now glamorized in local media and known to exist in Hong Kong.

Among the established urban classes, a new cadre of spoiled teenagers openly rejects the order of traditional society "Young people don't want to wait," says Ching. "They see a world on television and in the movies . . . and most wish to take part in that world." Having been pampered and doted on as they grew up, a growing number of youths from China's urban elites mock their parents and reject not only hard work but any work. Self-centered attitudes and a "see no evil" stance toward lawlessness are commonplace, clearly violating all norms of cultural tradition. The relaxation of Marxism's repressive tentacles has led to acceptance of an "if it feels good, do it" mentality among a large share of young men and women.

Most experts agree that communism's tanks, storm troopers, and indoctrination failed to crush the Cofucianist ethic. But the worship of crass materialism and the willingness to cut any corner in the quest to get rich quick are shaking the foundations of Chinese society.

Erosion of the Value Structure

Godwin Chu, an authority on East Asia's changing cultures, conducted a survey in 1994 for Fudan University in the southeast. Some two thousand people were surveyed, many from the teeming port of Shanghai and others from villages and rural communities in Qingpu County. Chu found the "danger of cultural disintegration" to be substantial. Unlike Japan, which is renowned for its rapid industrialization and increased wealth, China is sorely affected by the widespread "erosion of traditional Confucian concepts," he states.

In Japan, "traditional cultures remained intact" despite westernization and modernity, says Chu, but "thirty years of class struggle" and the disastrous Cultural

Revolution have had a profound impact on the Chinese masses. Curiously, in Japan, it is those out of sync with tradition who have difficulty adjusting to modern life. In China, the situation is reversed. "The minority follow traditional values," says Chu, "and they experience more social conflicts and psychological tension" than is true with the majority.

The Chinese majority who no longer accept the underlying tenets of Confucian society include the intelligentsia and decision makers who guide the nation. Chu asserts that the value system has been largely maintained in Taiwan. He identifies eighteen key elements of that system, including respect for traditions; support (including financial) for elders; generosity; preservation of "harmony" (even in the face of insult or poor treatment); respect for farmers and low esteem for moneymakers; frugality; large families; pleasing superiors; sexual restraint; and loyalty to the state.

The roots of this cultural decline may be traced to years of protracted turmoil during the infamous Cultural Revolution launched by Mao Zedong in 1976. Throughout the mainland, scholars, artists, and suspected dissidents were killed or sent to concentration camps. The communists vigorously tore down all vestiges of China's long-held belief systems.

Chu's data suggest the degree to which traditional beliefs have been eliminated. The concepts of "saving face" and self-pride have been retained, but this is not true of other traditions. For example, ancestor worship, a cornerstone of China's 5,000-year-old civilization, is adhered to by a mere 3 percent of the PRC's populace. Nearly a third of those Chu surveyed argued that ancestors deserve less respect than the living and are irrelevant. Two-thirds felt pilgrimages to temples were no longer needed and would not result in any blessings; only one in four maintained that religious faith was a necessary feature of contemporary life. The concepts of *fengshui* (literally "wind and water"), which traditionally governed many aspects of construction and design, were accepted by a scant 7 percent of the population.

In particular, understanding of family values is shifting rapidly. To guarantee a support system for the elderly and because of the dowry assured the families of prospective husbands, large families of predominantly male children were traditionally desired. Fears of overpopulation and the impact of the government's "One Child" policy (and consequently the frequent abortion of female fetuses) have created approval for smaller families and a gender imbalance of 85 females born to 100 males. In turn, changing relationships among family members influence the attitude toward communities, and the mangliu phenomenon is also accelerating the trend toward smaller families.

Although most marriages are still arranged, other changes are taking place. For example, women once were subordinate to men and obliged to depend on them exclusively. This has changed permanently. Women have new options as a result of gaining access to rising personal incomes and greater rights in divorce settlements. However, opportunity and insecurity often appear on the horizon side by side. How Chinese society ameliorates tensions that inevitably occur when women and men compete for leadership, status, and income will tell much about the country's cultural evolution.

One Nation, Many Cultures

To cope with the rural exodus, Beijing hopes that promoting jobs in the hinterland will do much to prevent the anticipated increase in numbers reaching the cities. An infrastructure program is planned in concert with efforts to build new cities. Some hope increasingly polluted and overcrowded conditions will keep quality-of-life-minded Chinese "back on the farm." In addition, changes in the tax system that favor commercial activity could add incentives to maintain agrarian-based life-styles.

But reversing the impact of urban-bound migration is difficult, even under the most optimistic projections. Courtney points out that rural areas have been drained of human and capital resources. However, revitalization of small towns may help the "diffusion of modern values and technology" to the hinterland. "Towns offer a new range of choices between extremes," he explains. Courtney also points to the rise of teahouses in smaller villages as a positive sign. Newcomers relying on teahouses can more easily integrate themselves into social networks. Thus they gain a renewed sense of identity, which is required to maintain social cohesion.

Indeed, the migrant issue is bringing to the fore one of China's long-overlooked realities. The Chinese are not a single, homogenous people. *Minzue tuanjie* (national unity) has eluded modern China, despite the central government's attempts—peaceful or otherwise—to build it.

The 1.2 billion population of the PRC consists of fifty-six nationalities (including Tibetans) and as many cultures, although the Han group constitutes an overwhelming 90 percent of the population. *Minzu tedian* (ethnic traits) vary greatly among the various *minzus* (national groups). The Han consider themselves culturally superior to the inhabitants of border regions, such as the Mongols and Tibetans, to the many minority tribes, and the mercantilistic Hui. Because they trace their cultural and philosophical roots to Confucianism, the Han have never reconciled the relationship between commerce, profit, and social responsibility Indeed, although they are often revered as traders and merchants by outsiders, the Chinese are largely nonentrepreneurial. This is a significant factor in understanding China's response to the tens of millions seeking their fortunes in the urban-bound exodus.

One demonstration of just how different these groups are comes through the sharp language differences that exist, often from one province to the next. "There's nothing worse on the earth," says one ancient proverb, "than a man from the north trying to speak to a southerner." Indeed, the freedoms sanctioned by authorities in Beijing during the past fifteen years have led to an explosion of ethnic consciousness on the part of minority groups. The Cantonese, Hakka, Min, and other southerners are reasserting themselves. In the past, they were considered barbarians by the dominant northerners, whose Mandarin tongue was a lingua franca across the vast mainland.

One factor challenging the long-reigning Han culture is the increasing income gap between the booming southland and other provinces. But as the lure of jobs and money draws the ever-expanding floating population into big cities, concessions to the arrivals' language and customs will be inevitable. This will not occur easily. However, among the groups crowding into apartment flats and setting up shantytowns, there are patterns emerging: Women from Anhui Province in the central PRC have become nannies and servants for the newly affluent class in Beijing. Residents of Hunan Province are known for their talents in woodworking, and, as a result, they take to carpentry in the newfound urban environments. In Zhejiang cities such as Hangzhou, some fifty miles southwest of Shanghai, onetime farmers now act as intermediaries and sell the vegetables they would have planted. In Fukian on the southeast coast, migrants

are readily absorbed into the burgeoning tailoring industry.

One group that is largely content to remain in its traditional rural communities is the Hui. These nine million people, descendants of Muslim traders who colonized neighboring Indonesia and Malaysia during the twelfth century, are bound together by Islamic and entrepreneurial traditions. They are staying at home in the southeast province of Fujian, where the economic boom continues to reverberate in factory towns and smaller communities. In Chendai, for example, a population of six hundred claims ownership of more than seven hundred cellular phones. Ostentatious behavior, flaunting of high-tech "bells and whistles," plus other traits of the nouveau riche are evident, says Gladney, but "the Hui regard market success as an opportunity for ethnic and religious advancement." The link between commerce and religious faith is strong: Hui donations to mosques are substantial, and some Communist Party officials have actually become *imams* (priests) to gain from *sifei* (mosque income).

Caught between Worlds

The question facing the country is whether a movement to return to traditional values might emerge as a response to the massive social diaspora and a protest against flamboyant materialism. Increasingly, Chinese scholars and intellectuals decry the loss of folk heroes. President Jiang Zemin made use of this in a recent anticorruption campaign that was aimed at malefactors obsessed by instant riches but also portrayed average Chinese in a favorable light.

Party apparatchiks are a major source of corruption and are both envied and cursed as stories of their exploits circulate. For example, in Hubei Province, midway between Shanghai and Beijing, a party official and his mistress profiteered after granting licenses to Japanese businessmen attempting to build warehouses and factories. Although reporting an income of only a thousand rembei (U.S. $500), the pair had a Ferrari roadster and a Mercedes-Benz. The woman's sister was a favorite escort of visiting Taiwanese businessmen, who gave bribes to the pair. Within a few months the sister returned to the hinterland, where she was considered a hero because she was rich.

A schism is developing between traditionalists and adherents of the new-money gods. Status-seeking youths are acting in an amoral way to secure wealth, and the relatively free press is encouraging excesses. One new monthly publication, *Car Fan*, profiled a real estate developer who owns seven high-priced autos, including a Rolls-Royce. However, the economic miracle is under duress, inflation is on the rise, and doubts persist about the political future. Even the legacy of Chairman Deng is being debated. Meanwhile, the gap between the PRC's glamorized ultrarich and its less affluent is growing and especially evident in the cities and in media images.

If mass media's negative images—and influences—are pronounced in the West, the same is increasingly true in China. TV portrays confusing images of the new Chinese monied class flaunting its wealth. Whether satisfied or disillusioned, migrants to the overcrowded cities are quickly overwhelmed by modernization's conflicting messages about wealth and status. Nonetheless, the floating population remains fascinated by the gadgetry of the modern world and the lure of a life-style until recently unimaginable and off limits.

Indeed, as the PRC's social, economic, and political systems are transformed by the massive redistribution of its population, the most dramatic force for social and cultural change may well be modern communications. "We're not talking about the Internet," says Woodward. "A working phone system and telecopier [can] do a lot to promote communications." Likely, the informal interactions between people displaced from their traditional communities and regions, rather than government decree or traditional authority, will shape the new Chinese cultural milieu.

Article 15   *The American Enterprise*, March/April 1996

China's War on Children

John S. Aird

John S. Aird, former U.S. Census Bureau senior research specialist on China, is the author of Slaughter of the Innocents: Coercive Birth Control in China, *published by the AEI Press.*

In June of 1995, Britain's Channel Four television aired a documentary called The Dying Rooms. In it, Kate Blewett, Brian Woods, and Peter Hugh recorded what they found when they surreptitiously filmed several orphanages run by the Chinese government. They found infants and children tied to their cots and left unattended without food or medical attention until they died. Some particularly haunting footage shows a little girl in the last stages of starvation, abandoned in one of the "dying rooms" that give the film its title. When the film-makers called later to inquire about the girl, the orphanage denied that she had ever existed.

Then in January 1996, a Chinese doctor who had been on staff at a Shanghai

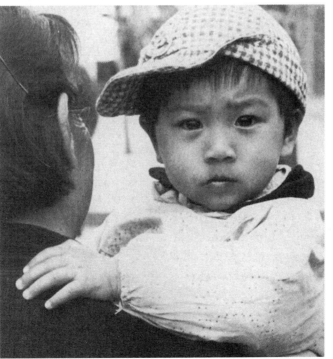

Photo Credit: UPI/Bettman

orphanage from 1988 to 1993, and is now living abroad, testified (with corroboration from medical reports and photographs she smuggled out) that at her one institution alone, 400 children were allowed to die, mostly by starvation, over a five-year period. (Orphanage personnel admit on camera in "The Dying Rooms" that as many as 90 percent of the children admitted to some institutions die there.) A January report on this subject from the group Human Rights Watch/Asia estimates from central government reports that deaths of children in China's state-run orphanages run in the thousands every year.

Some Chinese officials have denounced these revelations as "lies" and "malicious fraud" motivated by personal enmity. In January, Western reporters were taken by Chinese authorities on a tour of one model orphanage that had apparently been set up in some haste for their benefit. One journalist noted that its computers were so new their packing boxes were still in the building. Other Chinese officials admit that there are many deaths in state orphanages, but blame them on cold weather, lack of electricity, and a shortage of resources in a country where 80 million people live in poverty.

But poverty doesn't explain why Chinese orphans are given sleeping pills instead of food, tied to cribs and chairs, left unchanged when soiled, denied medical care, and allowed to die of neglect. According to press coverage of the Human Rights Watch/Asia report, state orphanages in China select out children for "summary resolution" (i.e. death by neglect) quite methodically. Typical state-run homes have become little more than "assembly lines" for the elimination of unwanted babies.

The basic problem is not that China can't afford to support these children. With the Chinese economy booming, living standards in the country are rising. Nor are the "dying rooms" just a matter of bad institutional management, as some Western observers have assumed. The real problem is the Chinese government's attitude toward the orphans. China's leaders consider these children "surplus" population. They try to prevent their birth by forced abortion (often so late in pregnancy as to amount to state-mandated infanticide), and they boast of the numbers of births averted by China's coercive family planning program. To these authorities, the death of orphans is nothing to regret, because it furthers their objective of reduced population growth.

The Chinese family planning program has a long history of coercion, dating back at least to the early 1970s. After peaking in 1983, the use of force eased somewhat because of a public backlash that caused "alienation of the masses from the Party." But the pressures escalated again by the late 1980s. Especially since 1993, reports by foreign journalists have detailed shocking human rights violations in the PRC's family planning program. Forced IUD insertions, forced abortions, and involuntary sterilizations are widely reported. Couples who refuse to abort unauthorized pregnancies face beatings, jailings, heavy fines, confiscations of all wealth and property, and the destruction of their houses as punishment.

Steven Mosher's 1993 book, *A Mother's Ordeal*, describes infanticide carried out by obstetricians working under orders not to permit unauthorized newborns to leave the hospital alive. In November 1995, a Chinese obstetrician now living in Melbourne, Australia, with whom I shared an interview conducted by Radio Australia, confirmed that this was official policy. Doctors in Chinese hospitals, she said, work under orders by the authorities to kill all babies born without government permission, or suffer severe penalties. The methods used include injecting formaldehyde into the infant's brain as it crowns, and crushing the emerging head with forceps. As long as the baby is killed while still partly in the womb, its death counts as an abortion, not as infant mortality. Unauthorized babies born before they could be destroyed have reportedly been suffocated or discarded alive in waste receptacles, from where their muffled cries are sometimes heard until they die.

In April 1993, *New York Times* correspondent Sheryl WuDunn reported that parents in Guizhou Province who had children without permission were punished by severe fines, confiscations of property, smashed houses, and physical beatings. That same month, *Washington Post* reporter Lena Sun described house smashing in Hebei and reported high forced-sterilization rates in 1991 and 1992. In April 1994, Sun told of two women in an Anhui village who were seized in the middle of the night and ordered to have abortions because their father-in-law had offended the local Party boss.

In August 1994, a Hong Kong journal described a midnight raid on the home of a pregnant woman in Fujian province:

With sticks, axes, iron bars, and big hammers in their hands, a dozen sturdy men stepped out of the commune building in the company of several members of the Family Planning Commission. Dogs began barking at that moment. Villagers here all say that the moment dogs begin barking, they know the Family Planning Commission has sent its men out again.

It took the group of men less than five minutes to reach the house . . . [They] forced their way into the house. While destroying everything in the house, they shouted out loudly: "The big-bellied woman, come out here immediately!" . . . However, the pregnant woman had already escaped into the dark night. Failing to capture her "hunting object," a female family planning propagandist gave the order to take away the old grandma of the family. To redeem the old lady, the family must either hand over the pregnant woman or pay a fine of 20,000 yuan to give birth to a child in excess of the plan.

According to the family planning policy currently in practice on the mainland . . . any attempt to give birth to children in excess of the plan will be crushed by the forced imposition of induced abortion . . . To this end, rural communes have set up special teams to search and capture pregnant women, and those who are caught will be sent immediately to nearby hospitals to have an abortion. . . . According to a nurse in Quanzhou City, forced abortions have left large numbers of pregnant women with uterine diseases, some of whom have even contracted cancer of the uterus while others have become sterile.

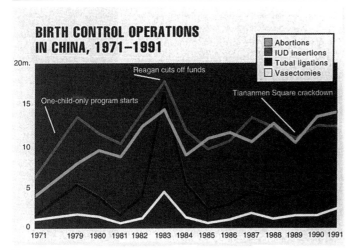

BIRTH CONTROL OPERATIONS IN CHINA, 1971–1991

One-child-only program starts
Reagan cuts off funds
Tiananmen Square crackdown

Abortions
IUD insertions
Tubal ligations
Vasectomies

20m.
15
10
5
0

1971 1979 1980 1981 1982 1983 1984 1985 1986 1987 1988 1989 1990 1991

Source: *Yearbook of Public Health in the People's Republic of China, Beijing, 1993.*

The results of these tactics show up clearly in official statistics. In the year 1991, according to the latest available government figures, the number of abortions carried out in China exceeded 14 million for the first time since 1983. The numbers of vasectomies and tubal ligations also were rising (*see* accompanying graph).

China's current birth control crackdown was launched on May 12, 1991, by a "decision" of the Chinese Communist Party Central Committee and the State Council that called for "stepping up family planning work and strictly controlling population growth." Chinese leaders claimed that the escalation was needed because without it the country's living standards, natural resources, ecology, and "the quality of the whole nation" would be threatened. The new directive demanded that local authorities "resolutely" implement existing policies "without any wavering, loosening, or changes." The intent was to tighten up on an already-established population control system under which birth quotas and other targets set by the central authorities are allocated to lower levels, and administrators at all levels are required to sign contracts guaranteeing their fulfillment. Any leader from the provincial level downward who fails to fulfill his targets is subject to penalties that range from loss of bonuses and promotions to loss of job. Authorities also adopted a rule that any leader who failed in family planning would be deemed a total failure regardless of his success in other aspects of his work.

The combination of mandatory targets and heavy penalties makes the Chinese program coercive. Quotas handed down to lower levels are reportedly often unattainable without using coercion, and central authorities excuse coercive measures so long as the quotas are met. Given the stringent population targets adopted through

the end of the century and beyond, it is clear that the Chinese leaders have no intention of abandoning forced family planning any time soon.

In fact, they regard the 1991 crackdown as highly successful. Early in 1992, Premier Li Peng announced that the 1991 birth rate had fallen seven percent from the year before. By 1994, the birth rate was down more than 16 percent from the 1990 level. Since 1992, Chinese fertility has actually been below the rate needed to keep the population constant over the long run. In October 1995, it was announced that population growth in China was actually below the state targets from 1991 through 1994 and could be as much as 15 million persons below target by the end of 1995. Still, the authorities warn the local cadres not to relax their family planning enforcement.

Chinese leaders now openly acknowledge in the domestic media that their present low birth rates have been attained by coercive means. In March 1994, Peng Peiyun, China's birth control chief, admitted that family planning in rural areas was being carried out "mainly through powerful executive measures," and that "if there was any relaxation in this sector, the birth rate would soon [rise] further." Other sources were even more forthright. In April 1993, an article in a Beijing law journal argued that in implementing China's family planning policies "it is impossible to totally avoid using forcible measures in practice" and that such measures needed to be explicitly provided for in Chinese law so that cadres implementing family planning policies would not be deterred by foreign human rights criticisms. In June 1993, an article in the official national family planning journal stated flatly that the reduction in China's rural fertility rate was due to "a coercion-based reduction mechanism." In September 1994, an article in the leading demographic journal said, "It cannot be denied that population control in China is a control model guided by administrative coercion."

Quite apart from human rights issues, the Chinese family planning program has had some distinctly adverse consequences for Chinese society. For one thing, the one-child policy has caused rising sex ratios in China—the 1990 census reportedly found 114 male infants for every 100 females. The source of this is extensive infanticide of female (or handicapped or otherwise "undesirable") babies, plus sex-selective abortion practiced on a massive scale. According to one Chinese estimate, 98 percent of fetuses currently aborted in China are female.

A sex ratio of 114 to 100 implies that some 800,000 girl babies are eliminated annually in China. According to a Hong Kong source, a 1992 survey found the sex ratio at birth was actually as high as 119 to 100, which would mean 1.1 million missing girls each year. Local sex ratios at birth can run much higher, especially in the cities. A Shanghai source worries that if today's sex ratios continue, China will soon have "an army of bachelors numbering some 70,000,000 strong," a potential cause of real social instability.

The rising incidence of involuntary abortion also has its own adverse consequences for Chinese society. Sources indicate that more than a third of all Chinese pregnancies end in abortion. Abortions are often carried out under unsanitary conditions, without anaesthetic, and by obstetricians who are sometimes abusive or cruel to the women in what seems a deliberate attempt to discourage further pregnancies. These experiences leave scars, both physical and psychological.

Another cause for concern is the rapid aging of the Chinese population, which will ensure that growing numbers of elderly persons must depend for care and financial support on a shrinking number of workers. Among other problems, social security systems may become insolvent.

Even a rise in Chinese fertility starting tomorrow would not compensate for the low birth cohorts of the past 20 years. In solving the supposed "problem" of high fertility, the Chinese authorities have thus created other serious social and economic problems for the future.

They have also generated more political trouble for themselves. One adverse consequence of using coercive family planning measures is a further alienation of the people from the government at a time when political authority is already waning and prospects for domestic order are uncertain. Forced birth control has hardened popular resistance to the point where family planning is now heavily dependent upon compulsory measures, warned a 1994 article in a Chinese demographic journal. It has also given rise to extensive bribery of local officials and falsification of documents and statistics, at a time when official corruption is already a major source of popular dissatisfaction with the current regime.

Despite the new candor in the domestic media about coercion in family planning, the Chinese government continues to insist to foreigners that its family planning program is voluntary. In August 1994, Peng Peiyun repeated in a Xinhua English-language dispatch the official line that "it is a firm policy of the Chinese government to prohibit any kind of coercive action in implementing family planning." In May 1995, she told the English-language *Beijing Review* that the program's success was due to the "understanding and support" of the Chinese people, and added, "we let families become conscious of their own immediate interests and that of the nation, and let them make wise choices according to their own will." In a "white paper" on family planning issued in August 1995, the authorities insisted that "the current family planning policy has won the understanding and support of the whole Chinese people as it is actually a combination of government guidance with the voluntary participation of the masses."

The Chinese leaders know these claims are untrue. Peng Peiyun herself virtually admitted as much to a domestic audience in March 1994, when she said that in rural areas there was "a big gap between the state family planning policy and the desire for having children." But when speaking to the outside world, Chinese officials pretend that popular support for the program is almost universal.

One reason they do this is the gullibility of many in the West. For a decade and a half, most Western demographers, family planners, and foreign aid officials seemed to take no notice of the inhumane aspects of the Chinese program. Before 1993, media reports on family planning in China often referred to the "alleged" coercion in the program as a "controversial" matter, implying that the charges were not proven. Only since 1993 has the international press begun to treat China's coercive population control plan and its utter disregard for human rights as undisputed fact.

Although the cruelty of the Chinese birth control program is now generally recognized, the reaction of foreign governments and non-government organizations has been incongruously mild. In 1993, the United Nations Fund for Population Activities (UNFPA)—which has been supporting the program since 1979, the year the one-child policy was adopted—was finally obliged to drop its pretense that birth control in China was "totally voluntary" and even talked briefly about possibly withdrawing from China. Instead, the organization stayed, ostensibly to exert a "moderating influence" on the program. The International Planned Parenthood Federation (IPPF) has been sending financial assistance to the Chinese program since 1983, the peak year for coercive birth control surgeries in China. It also steadfastly denied the program's coerciveness until that position became untenable, then quickly adopted the UNFPA's "moderating influence" posture.

In all the years of their involvement, however, there has been little moderation in the program for which these organizations could claim credit. If anything, the "influence" of foreign participants has been to encourage the Chinese authorities in the view that they can use coercive measures without risking worldwide condemnation. The Chinese interpret foreign participation in their program as evidence of approval, and officials of the UNFPA and the IPPF have confirmed that interpretation by lavishly praising its methods and results. If the UNFPA and the IPPF had been sincere in their claim to support only voluntary family planning, they would never have become involved in the Chinese program in the first place and would have condemned its excesses.

When the coercion in the program became undeniable in 1993, statements of protest were issued by the Clinton administration. Yet President Clinton then went on to restore U.S. funding for the UNFPA—withheld since 1985 by the Reagan and Bush administrations because of the UNFPA's support for the Chinese program. Clinton worked out a face-saving provision with the UNFPA under which no U.S. funds would go directly to China. Most European governments, meanwhile, have been even more eager than the Clinton White House to aid and abet the Chinese. Some increased their contributions to the UNFPA to compensate for the loss of U.S. funding during the Reagan-Bush years.

The insensitivity of world governments to the inhumane Chinese program is also evident in the cavalier treatment of Chinese nationals under threat of forced sterilization or abortion who seek asylum abroad. In the U.S., for example, a 1989 immigration board ruling known as *Matter of Chang* establishes as current policy the idea that coercive national family planning programs do not constitute "persecution" so long as they are enforced on everyone, not just particular ethnic, religious, or political groups. Therefore asylum is not granted to Chinese refugees facing forced abortion or sterilization if returned to China. *Matter of Chang* even argues that China's program is justified by the size of the Chinese population and because "China was encouraged by world opinion to take measures to control its population." Advisory documents issued by the U.S. Department of State for use by immigration judges ignore the overwhelming evidence of coercion in the Chinese family planning program.

Frustrated by the refusal of Clinton administration officials to consider the asylum applications of several Chinese women currently seeking protection in the U.S., the Subcommittee on International Relations and Human Rights of the House Committee on International Relations held hearings in May, June, and July of 1995. Testimony was taken from, among others, four asylum seekers, led into the hearing room in handcuffs by immigration police. They told in detail of being dragged from their homes to undergo mandatory abortions and sterilizations before fleeing their homeland. One couple had been threatened with forced sterilization because they had retrieved and kept alive a baby girl found abandoned in the street.

Recently, a group of Chinese women who have been imprisoned in California for two years since arriving in the U.S. as refugees conducted a 50-day hunger strike to protest their pending deportation back to China. Members of Congress have asked President Clinton to grant them asylum, but he has refused. Attempts by the Congress to overrule *Matter of Chang* with legislation have so far also been stymied; a House-passed legislation to grant asylum to refugees from the Chinese program is currently being blocked in the Senate. As a result, the U.S. continues to send Chinese refugees back home to be sterilized and undergo abortion against their will. Aside from making our government an accomplice of the Chinese program, such actions encourage the Chinese leaders to believe that the rest of the world doesn't really care what they do to their own people.

Strong words followed by weak actions sending a contrary signal have become the standard response of the Clinton administration to human rights offenses in China. Other countries seem to be following the same model, except that they often omit the strong words. There are at least two reasons for this. One is that the unsubstantiated but widely held belief in a world population crisis has dulled public outrage over violations of reproductive freedom in China. A second reason is that business interests intent on seeking profits by investing in China's booming economy do not want to risk strained relations with China over its human rights violations.

The result: most Western governments have done scandalously little to discourage coercive family planning in China. Observing their inaction, China's rulers apparently now feel free to expand tyrannical practices not only in birth control but also in the treatment of political dissidents. Although Chinese leaders say publicly that foreign criticism of China's human rights record is interference in their country's internal affairs that will not be accepted, China has in practice shown itself to be extremely sensitive to determined criticism backed by potential actions.

To show that our disapproval of Chinese human rights violations in China is serious, the U.S. should amend our immigration laws to recognize persecution under compulsory family planning programs as a basis for granting asylum. And we should withhold all funding from the UNFPA, IPPF, and any other organization that provides assistance to China's harsh birth control program.

Both provisions are contained in a bill passed last spring by the U.S. House of Representatives, H. R. 1561. The corresponding Senate bill (S. 908) does not contain these measures at the moment, but they may be reinstated in the conference version of the legislation. The two bills go to conference in February. If Americans who feel strongly about this issue demand action from their representatives, a new law placing the U.S. government on the side of China's victims could be in place in a matter of weeks.

Article 16

World Press Review, August 1996

When China went mad

Mao's Frenzy of Mass Violence

In May, 1966, Lu Chen, Yao Zhongyong, and Li Jiang were 12-year-old schoolboys in Beijing. Today, like people in their early 40s all over China, they have at least one thing in common: The defining experience of their lives began that month and, three decades later, remains vivid. For Lu Chen, it is still almost too painful to talk about. "It happened a long time ago," he says—and starts to sob.

From 1966 to 1968, his father was detained as a "Capitalist Roader." Lu's mother was away at the time, and Lu was left to fend for himself. "I just ate noodles," he remembers. "But one day, I had a meat sausage. The Red Guards saw me eating it in the courtyard." Not long afterward, his father was allowed home for a brief visit. "One night, father came and knelt down by my bed," Lu recalls. "He begged me not to eat in front of other people any longer. It was so shocking. For a very long time, when I picked up a bowl of food, I felt scared."

Yao Zhongyong remembers how he and his brother wandered the streets of Beijing. "We could go to Houhai Lake to see people committing suicide. Some wrote their wills in chalk on the ground. One could often see corpses in the lake."

> *"I thought that to prove we were revolutionary we must beat people."*

Li Jiang is haunted by one particular afternoon. "Near our school, there was a wife of a landlord," he says. The Red Guards went to the house to take the property. "But the old lady was quite tough. At first she screamed and tried to push the Red Guards out of the house. . . . We pushed the old lady on the ground and beat her for one hour with our belts. And she died. I was one of the beaters."

Thirty years ago, Chairman Mao launched China's Cultural Revolution. The "16 May Circular" called for the unrestrained mobilization of the masses against the "bourgeoisie" who had "sneaked" into the Communist Party as "counterrevolutionary revisionists." Ostensibly, Mao's aim was to purify the revolution; in reality, his goal was to reassert control over the party and purge his political rivals.

To this end, he unleashed a decade of savagery and chaos, encouraging a whole generation of teenagers to run riot in a frenzy of mass violence so fanatical as to be scarcely credible. Soon schools and universities had suspended all classes, and Red Guards were taking to the city streets in an uncontrolled fury of righteousness. Teachers were often the first victims, locked up in schools and in many cases tortured. "Bad elements" were beaten to death by teenagers wielding metal-buckled belts. No one knew who would be targeted next as neighbors and work mates turned on each other in vicious denunciations and "criticism sessions." Over the next decade, hundreds of thousands—probably more than 1 million—died.

Yao's most vivid memory is of the scene in the garden of an old Qing Dynasty palace where a group of Red Guards was dumping belongings ransacked from people's homes: "At the back door was a pile of books, all very precious. There was a line of 'bad factor' people, also known as 'cow ghosts' and 'snake spirits.' They were beaten by the Red Guards along the way and forced to carry the ransacked things. Pages from these books were blowing in the wind."

What was going on in the minds of these teenagers? "There were two kinds of feeling," says Li, whose parents were party officials. "I thought that the beatings were correct, and in order to express that we were revolutionary, we must beat other people. But this kind of thinking contradicted the moral education I had previously been given. In our hearts we also felt frightened. Because of this fear we were eager to take part in the revolution. The main feeling then was fear."

Fear was compounded by confusion as the Cultural Revolution spread through society. No one could be sure they were safe. Toward the end of 1966, Li's parents fell from grace and were attacked as rightists, and he could no longer be officially classified as a Red Guard. This was common; of the 100 youths in his Red Guard group, he says, 80 saw their families turned upon. Such teenagers then formed their own gangs.

The chaos gave free rein to personal vendettas and settling of old grudges. Standard humiliation rituals evolved for the public criticism sessions. Li's father was forced to stand for hours in the crippling "airplane position," bent over with arms stretched out behind, and made to wear a dunce's hat and a placard detailing his crimes around his neck. "In 1968, after a criticism meeting, my father had heart failure and died," says Li. Women often had half their heads shaved.

By this time, the whole country was engulfed in violence. Armed battles between Red Guard factions took place in major cities across China. Many factories had closed, and foreign trade collapsed. Food was in short supply.

In mid-1968, alarmed that he was losing control of the situation, Mao disbanded the Red Guards. Over the next year or so, 16 million urban teenagers were sent into the countryside for "reeducation" by the peasants. This highly organized logistical feat illustrates one of the most striking aspects of the Cultural Revolution. The rule of law had completely broken down, yet the Communist Party apparatus could still exert complete control over the population.

Among those who boarded trains were Lu, Li, and Yao. "We were very happy because we thought we were responding to appeals from Mao," says Lu, who was dispatched to Shuangyashan village in the far northeastern province of Heilongjiang. His group included 12 boys and 12 girls from Beijing. "We were sent in equal numbers, with the idea that we could build a family there."

On arrival, the urban teenagers were shocked at the living conditions and physical work. Lu was set to work planting vast acreages of wheat and corn by hand, herding cattle, and laboring. "The psychological hardship was worse than the physical pain," Lu says. "There was only work, no schooling. But we had to read Mao's works every day."

The persecutions continued, Lu says: "We used to be called on by local party officials to join in criticism sessions against local 'bad factors.' I remember one engineer, Ye Tingchang. The group planned to hold a criticism meeting against him and went looking for him. We found him and beat him. Ye said: 'I should be beaten. I deserve that.' I can never forget this incident."

Li and Yao were dispatched, separately, to the opposite corner of China, an impoverished Yunnan province town called Ruili on the border with Burma (now Myanmar). "Living conditions were very poor, quite different from what the propaganda had taught us," says Li.

Li's first doubts about Mao started in September, 1971, when, on a visit to Beijing, he heard about the downfall and death of Lin Biao, Mao's second in command. He recalls, "In the past, I had adored Mao without limit. But by that time I had lived in the countryside, and I found the difference between the reality and what we had learned in school was enormous. So the death of Lin Biao aroused all my feelings and suspicions and made me think."

As the years passed, the Cultural Revolution started to wind down. In 1974, Lu and Li were allowed to return to Beijing. After Mao's death in 1976 and the subsequent arrest of the Gang of Four, China finally set about a process of material and spiritual repair. Lu now works as a private investigator and is trying to qualify as a lawyer. He married one of the 12 girls in his reeducation group: "One good thing to come out of the experience," he smiles.

When the universities reopened in 1978, Li studied history in Beijing, went on to be a journalist and publisher and is now in property development. Yao, at that point still in Yunnan, passed the exams for teachers' training college, where he met his wife. He did not return to live in Beijing until 1990. He now works for the *City Environment Paper*. Lu and Yao joined the Communist Party; Li did not.

Lu is the one most visibly still pained by his family's experiences. As we sit in his office, he expresses sadness about lost opportunity. Li, on the other hand, sits poised and confident in his book-lined study, an intellectual trying to make the most of business opportunities in modern China. But he reflects: "I feel that there is no real authority in the world. In that period, all the teachers, officials, parents whom I respected, all lost their dignity. My respect for humanity was totally smashed."

Yao, who spent by far the longest time out of Beijing, is the most tense and serious on first meeting. He says: "I can face any cruel reality without being astonished. But that does not mean I am numb to life. It also wasted a lot of time and made me miss a lot of chances. . . . Most of my generation is not very successful."

Just as significant to them is the legacy of the Cultural Revolution to Chinese society as a whole. "The wound on the heart of my generation is too deep," says Lu. He points out how everyone had to mouth slogans to have any chance of surviving. "Everybody learned how to lie," he says.

During the turbulent years the persecutors often became the persecuted, and there were no easy divisions between the guilty and the innocent. Few are honest enough to recall publicly their roles as protagonists or victims. Do the three men feel that more people should have been punished for their crimes? Lu says: "The influence of the Cultural Revolution was too wide. Almost everybody has some black mark in their history. It is not possible to punish them all." Yao agrees. "The crimes were witnessed by a lot of people, but it is not practical to punish all the murderers." With Mao still lying in state in Tiananmen Square, the history of that period is still politically sensitive. Even in private, people do not usually talk very openly about their experiences. Lu says, "That period is a kind of scar on Chinese history. Like a scar on somebody's body, they do not want to expose it."

In Beijing's curio markets, foreign tourists browse through Cultural Revolution memorabilia, bargaining over old copies of Mao's Little Red Book or kitsch statuettes of revolutionary opera characters. These are not mementos locals want to buy.

—*Teresa Poole, "Independent on Sunday" (centrist), London, May 12, 1996.*

Article 17

Natural History, July 1996

The Long River's Journey Ends

China's Three Gorges Dam will soon transform the Yangtze

Erling Hoh

China, with its diverse river systems, extreme fluctuations in rainfall, and wet-rice agriculture, has long looked to hydraulic works to solve problems of transportation, irrigation, and flood prevention. The classical Chinese term for hydraulic engineering, *shuili*, means "benefit of water," and the question of how to harness water resources has been crucial throughout the country's history. Taoist engineers argued that rivers should be managed by dredging and channeling; while Confucians favored reliance on dikes, either low and far apart, or high and near one another. The modern Chinese government has followed in this latter tradition by building some 86,000 dams and reservoirs during the past forty-seven years.

Now the biggest hydroelectric dam in the world—606 feet high and 7,640 feet wide—will tame the Yangtze (Chang Jiang, or Long River) in the Three Gorges, a 125-mile-long string of canyons. Construction is well under way, with the river scheduled to be partly cut off by September 1997. At its completion in 2009, the dam will raise the water level about 330 feet higher than the current normal level, impounding 31 million acre-feet of water in a snakelike lake stretching 370 miles upstream to Chongqing. The reservoir will not only diminish a scenic treasure but also submerge sites of historical, archaeological, paleontological, and biological interest. On a re-

cent trip on the Yangtze, I embarked at Chongqing, well upstream of the Three Gorges, and traveled down past the dam site. Along the way, I sampled the region's rich heritage, meeting people who are working to preserve it before the impending changes.

My first stop was Fuling, a gray, bustling city renowned for spicy, crisp pickled cabbage cores. Situated on the terraced banks of the Yangtze, 300 miles upstream from the dam site, the city will be partly inundated when the reservoir is full. There I met Huang Dejian, head of Fuling's Cultural Relics Office and one of the many scientists taking part in the biggest salvage operation since the one that preceded the building of Egypt's Aswan Dam.

On the wall in Huang's spartan office was a map showing the scores of known archaeological sites around the city. Too many Han Dynasty (206 B.C.–A.D. 220) graves for them even to be remarkable, he said. More notably, Fuling was a burial ground for the kings of Ba, a people who controlled salt production in the Three Gorges during the Xia Dynasty (ca. twenty-first to sixteenth centuries B.C.) and who slowly migrated upstream along the Yangtze. In 316 B.C. they were subjugated by the Qin, who went on to unify China in 221 B.C.

Huang was also eager to talk about his latest project, a book about White Crane Ridge, a mile-long sandstone formation that only appears when the water recedes to its lowest level, in February and March. "At Fuling there are stone fish, engraved beneath the waves," wrote the prefect Xiao Xinggong in the late seventeenth century. "Their appearance portends a good harvest." Numerous inscriptions on White Crane Ridge mark low-water levels. The oldest entry is a fish, carved no later than 763. Its belly line corresponds to the river's present average low-water level. Although the dam will render these historic records irrelevant, they will be kept on view in an underwater museum.

Thirty miles downriver from Fuling lies Fengdu, the first capital of Ba, where, according to Chinese folklore, departed souls go to await their transition to heaven or hell. There are several Buddhist and Taoist temples in the "ghost city" above the town, as well as a somewhat gaudy exhibition of the tortures awaiting those who are sent to hell. People come on certain days of the lunar calendar and burn paper money, paper boats, and joss sticks to expedite their ancestors' transition to the afterlife.

One morning, as I stood outside the gates of the temple precincts above the city, I spotted a sign that read 175M (175 meters, or 575 feet), one of many that are preparing people for the coming flood. When the residents of Fengdu are resettled on higher ground across the river, their abandoned buildings will become an underwater ghost town, mirroring the ghost city above it.

Not far from Fengdu, in the little town of Gaojia, Professor Wei Qi, of the Institute of Vertebrate Paleontology and Paleoanthropology at the Academia Sinica in Beijing, was supervising the excavation of one of the most bounteous paleolithic sites in south China. By the time I paid a visit, the thirty young archeologists in Wei's training class, working their way down through the three layers of the 645-square-foot locale, had unearthed more than 1,000 stone tools made from cobbles and boulders. According to Wei, the artifacts are the remains of a tool workshop, situated on the banks of the Yangtze 100,000 years ago. The tools were probably used to collect roots, unlike the smaller tools of northern China, which paleontologists believe were used for hunting.

After returning to Fengdu, I boarded a passenger boat headed downstream toward the Three Gorges. In the evening we arrived in the city of Wanxian, where the muddy river makes a sharp turn and heads due east. The steep hillsides were largely planted with rows of pine trees to prevent landslides and erosion—major worries for the dam builders. Geologists have identified 263 historic landslides in the Three Gorges reservoir area. One, in 1030, cut off river navigation for twenty-one years; another, in 1542, for eighty-two. On June 12, 1985, the town of Xintan, fifteen miles upstream from the dam site, was obliterated when more than 70 million cubic feet of earth came sliding down a nearby hill, creating a 128-foot-high surge wave on the river. Fortunately, the town had been evacuated a few days earlier.

One of the difficulties with reforestation is that soil degradation is already so severe that only coniferous trees can be introduced easily. These trees acidify the soil, reduce its fertility, and increase the risk for plant diseases and insect pests, thereby knocking out the surviving indigenous broad-leafed forest. Another problem is that the hundreds of thousands of farmers displaced by the rising reservoir will need new land for cultivation.

Despite the concentration of agriculture, the Three Gorges reservoir area actually boasts a diverse flora. Little affected by the Pleistocene glaciations and enjoying varied topography, mild climate, and abundant rainfall, the region is home to many ancient species of plants and trees, such as dawn redwood, dove tree, magnolia, and gingko. The Chinese Academy of Sciences lists forty-seven species as rare and endangered. One that is threatened by the dam is lotus leaf maidenhair, a fern found near the river's banks. It is used in Chinese herbal medicine to treat kidney stones. Botanists have succeeded in propagating it artificially by cultivating the spores in test tubes before planting them.

My next stop along the river was Yunyang. Approaching it and the Three Gorges also meant stepping into an era, the Three Kingdoms, treasured by both teahouse storytellers and television producers. After the dissolution of the Han Dynasty in A.D. 220, three separate kingdoms became established—Shu in the west; Wu, east of the gorges; and Wei in the north. They fought a series of wars that immortalized such heroes as the Shu general Zhang Fei, whose temple stands on a hill opposite Yunyang. At 460 feet, the temple falls well below the new water level and will be moved farther up the hill. To find out more about what had befallen Zhang Fei, I paid half a yuan for the river crossing and climbed the steep slope.

It all started when Sun Quan, the ruler of Wu, beheaded the Shu proconsul Guanyu, the sworn brother of both Zhang Fei and the Shu king Liu Bei. The impetuous Zhang Fei obtained Liu Bei's permission to exact immediate revenge. As recounted in *The Romance of the Three Kingdoms,* a popular fictional account of the events, Zhang gave his two commanders only three days to equip the army with white flags and whitened arms in mourning for Guanyu. Faced with this impossible task, the two commanders decapitated their general and set off to present his head to Sun Quan.

Legend has it that while traveling down the Yangtze past Yunyang, the two commanders, haunted by their hideous act of treason, threw their general's head into the water, where it became caught in a whirlpool around an old fisherman's boat. At night, the old man dreamed that the head belonged to Zhang Fei, and that he was asked to save it and bury it. He did, and that is where the temple now stands.

Following the deaths of his two sworn brothers, Liu Bei himself set out with an army of 25,000 men to wreak vengeance on Wu. He was routed, however, and retreated to Baidi Cheng (White Emperor City), where he died in A.D. 223. Baidi Cheng stands on a hilltop at the entrance to Qutang Gorge, the most upstream of the Three Gorges. When the dam is completed, the hilltop will become a small island and an important villa on the side of the hill—the Western Pavilion—will be moved to higher ground.

In the eighth century, the Western Pavilion witnessed what American sinologist D. R. McCraw calls the "greatest lyrical outpouring in Chinese literary history." Having traveled down the Yangtze with his family, the poet Du Fu arrived in Baidi Cheng in the spring of 766. The local warlord, an old acquaintance, set him up with a house, a fruit garden, a rice paddy, and a few servants. For perhaps the first time in his peripatetic life, the fifty-five-year-old Du Fu did not have to worry about the basic necessities.

Although debilitated by malaria, tuberculosis, diabetes, and arthritis, Du Fu had a burst of creativity. During his twenty-one months in the area, he wrote a third of his life's work, 429 poems, many of them in the highly demanding five- or seven-character regulated octaves called *lushi*. One is "From the Highest Building in White Emperor City" (translation by Paul Rouzer of Columbia University):

The walls are sharp, the paths steep—the banners droop in grief
Alone I stand in the misty void, here in this lofty hall.
Through cloven gorges, the clouds shadow the tigers and dragons in their sleep;
On the bright river, the sunlight enfolds the water lizards at play.
Western limbs of the Tree of Dawn face these broken crags;
Eastern sparkle of the Sunset River follows the Yangtze's flow.
Leaning on staff, lamenting the times—who am I after all?
As bloody tears splash the sky, I turn my gray head home.

In this poem, "cloven gorges" evokes the legendary Yu, founder of China's first hereditary dynasty, who supposedly opened the cliffs at Qutang to let the Yangtze through. How these 3,000-foot-high, vertical, thick-bedded limestone gates were formed, along with the gorges that lead eastward to the lake-studded Hubei plains, has since been investigated by modern-day geologists. According to the British scientist G. B. Barbour, who surveyed the region in the 1930s, the Yangtze formerly flowed on an extensive eroded surface (a peneplain) that developed after the main folding of the underlying rock. Subsequently, the land was uplifted and the river carved through it to create the gorges. J. S. Lee, the founder of modern geology in China, offered another theory: What is now the middle Yangtze was once two rivers flowing in opposite directions, eastward and westward, divided by an anticline (an arched fold of rock). Erosion of this divider allowed the east-flowing river to capture the west-flowing one, unifying them in an eastward flow.

Walking on the path along the north side of Qutang Gorge, which is five miles long and at most 500 feet wide, I saw the heavily folded rock up close—towering slabs of limestone tilted at sharp angles. About halfway through, I passed Wind Box Gorge, where the path cut into the cliff's vertical wall. Until a few decades ago, this was a "tracker's gallery," used by gangs of up to 300 men whose job it was to tow junks, sampans, and other boats through rapids flowing against them with a speed of up to ten knots.

The innumerable crevices, caves, and shelters in this rugged limestone region led archeologist N. C. Nelson, of the American Museum of Natural History, to speculate that they contained "perhaps the whole story of the Old Man of Asia." In 1925, as part of the Museum's Central Asiatic Expedition, he traveled to the Three Gorges, "trying to see the entire environmental setting from the point of view of an imaginary primitive man; to guess which of the caves and shelters he would most likely have occupied." Instead, he found many of them inhabited by modern humans. "In the end," he wrote, "after scanning more than two hundred miles of the Yangtze trough proper and traversing in more hasty fashion a similar distance in the back country, mainly to the south of the river, we were in possession of only the faintest suggestions that prehistoric man had ever been near the caves!"

Although Nelson failed to find the "Old Man of Asia," his intuition seems to have been correct. Ten years ago, paleoanthropologists found a fragment of a mandible and a single tooth at Dragon Hill Cave, about fifteen miles south of Qutang Gorge. These are now being hailed as evidence of the earliest Asians yet (see *Natural History*, December 1995).

In Wushan, a city situated just before the entrance of the next gorge, I met Zhuang Kongshao and Liu Mingxin, two anthropologists from the Central University for Nationalities in Beijing. Traveling upstream from Yichang, they had been meeting with local writers, archeologists, and historians, pursuing several projects—among them a study of the Tujia minority who claim descent from the Ba people. Zhuang and Liu invited me along to their next destination, Wuxi, a little town fifty miles up the Daning River, a northern tributary of the Yangtze.

The Daning, with its Three Little Gorges, offers a popular side excursion for tourists. We left early in the morning with a motorized sampan whose shady operator soon abandoned us in favor of something more profitable—a stranded tourist group. Despite our protests, we were transferred to a wooden cargo sampan to continue our journey. I sat beside a case of goods imprinted with the characters for "amusement tiles," a common euphemism for mah-jongg, which, despite being frowned upon officially, is played everywhere. As the sampan sputtered peacefully along, we saw plentiful bird life along the banks, and once even spotted a group of golden monkeys. The clear, shallow water and narrow passage made the perpendicular limestone cliffs along the pristine Daning even more dramatic than those of the monumental Yangtze gorges. High up all along the western wall, spaced four to six feet apart, ran a single row of square holes. These were what remained of the bamboo pipeline for brine and the plank road that once served as an important military, commercial, and cultural conduit between northern and central China. During the Tang Dynasty (A.D. 618–906) the concubine Yang Guifei had her favorite lichees sent fresh from Fuling along this route. We stopped to eat lunch in Dachang, and reached Wuxi, above the Three Little Gorges, late in the evening.

The ultimate goal of our excursion was the cliff graves at Jingzhu Gorge. Li Ming, from Wuxi's Cultural Relics Office, took us there the next morning. With binoculars, we spotted twenty-four wooden coffins wedged into horizontal crevices in the cliff wall, about 1,000 feet above the river. According to archeologists from Sichuan University, who "excavated" one coffin in 1980 and another in 1988, they date from as far back as the Warring States period (403–321 B.C.) and were a burial form used by a people called Pu. Exactly how they got there remains a mystery, as is the reason for this peculiar manner of burial—although Li Ming suggests it may simply have been a way to display wealth.

On our way back to Wuxi we passed by the desolate salt-producing town of Ning Chang and saw some pensioners playing mah-jongg in the sun. An old lady greeted us. "This used to be a very good place," she said with tears in her eyes. A year or so before, the salt factory had finally been shut down after some 2,000 years. In times gone by, Ning Chang had flourished as the center of the region's economy, teeming with inhabitants from every province in China. Produced in only a limited number of places, salt held a position in the country's economic life commensurate with its indispensability to humans. Merchants accumulated fortunes trading the commodity; while the taxes levied upon it provided the imperial government with a major source of revenue.

East of the Three Gorges, the whole Yangtze Valley received its supplies from factories in Jiangsu Province. Be-

cause of the distance and the difficulty of navigating up the river, however, Sichuan produced its own salt from brine wells drilled as much as 3,000 feet deep. Ning Chang's prosperity arose from the fluke that it possessed a saltwater spring. Furnaces were used to extract the salt, and since wood fuel produced the best salt, the forest around Ning Chang had been chopped down until no trees remained; then coal, which made the salt blackish and slightly bitter, had to be used instead.

Back in Wushan, on a chilly morning I boarded the *Double Dragon*, one of the hundreds of passenger boats that ply the Yangtze from Chongqing to Shanghai. The rising sun cast shafts of light across the deep, shadowed ravine. In a few hours, the boat passed through the twenty-five miles of Wu Gorge and down the next thirty miles of river, making stops along the way. At the entrance to the last and longest gorge, forty-seven-mile-long Xiling Gorge, I went for a walk uphill. I met a lucky orange farmer whose house and groves were situated just above the coming high-water level. "We're going to buy a boat," he told me.

The trip down Xiling Gorge the following day took about eight hours. As the boat neared the end of the Three Gorges, I viewed the immense earth-moving activity at the dam site, which has been transformed into a lunarlike dust bowl. On the northern bank, the bedrock was being blasted to accommodate the five shiplocks that will raise and lower vessels 330 feet.

Treacherous rapids in the Xiling Gorge have already been tamed by dredging and by the low-level Gezhouba Dam, twenty-seven miles downstream from the Three Gorges Dam site. Completed in 1989, Gezhouba is a hydroelectric dam that will also serve as a regulating dam when the new project is complete.

In the fast-flowing waters below the Gezhouba Dam, the Chinese sturgeon—whose fossil record extends back at least 140 million years—is trying to adapt to the new obstacle. The sturgeon's old spawning grounds were more than 600 miles farther upstream. Mature fish returned there as often as every three years from the China and Yellow Seas. Efforts have been made to capture fish below the dam and get them to release their eggs by treating them with hormones. The artificially raised hatchlings can then be returned to the river. Research also shows that some fish are now spawning at sites below Gezhouba Dam. If the sturgeon is adjusting to its new situation, one reason could be that it is not so new. Since the sturgeon is probably older than the gorges, this part of the river just might have been the place where it spawned before Yu clove the gorge.

Article 18   *U.S. News & World Report,* September 9, 1996

China Takes a Deep Breath

After decades of breakneck economic growth, Beijing confronts an environmental disaster

In 1956, to the astonishment of his personal physician and provincial officials, Mao Zedong declared his intention to swim in three of China's greatest rivers—the Pearl, the Xiang and the Chang (Yangtze). Serenely braving the dangerous currents, Mao transformed his dips into a powerful metaphor for his bold leadership. Today, China's churning rivers are testament to a far different message: the staggering environmental costs of a monolithic preoccupation with economic growth.

Nearly half of China's seven river systems are severely polluted. An estimated 80 percent of the country's industrial and domestic waste is discharged, untreated, into rivers. According to a top Chinese environmental official, no more than five of China's more than 500 cities have clean air. Respiratory disease occurs at five times the rate in the United States and is the leading cause of death in China's urban areas. Such grim statistics would be alarming in any country, but in vast China, they portend a potential disaster of global proportions.

Most of China's 1.2 billion people—22 percent of the world's total—live along the country's eastern and southern coasts in an area about the size of the United States east of the Mississippi River. China's population could hit 2 billion by 2050 if already strict population-control programs fail to further reduce fertility.

The Chinese economy has quadrupled in size since 1980. If that pace continues, China will overtake the United States as the world's largest economy by 2010. China already consumes more grain, red meat and fertilizer and produces more steel than the United States. But the rapid loss of croplands due to urbanization, just as China's increasingly well paid populace is gaining an appetite for more consumer goods and a richer diet, already is straining the country's ability to feed itself.

A hint of green. Apparently sobered by the worsening situation, China's leadership finally is taking on a noticeable, if belated, tinge of green. Western concerns are no longer dismissed out of hand as a hypocritical invasion of China's sovereignty by wealthy, already industrialized nations, or as a malign attempt to put the brakes on China's increasingly competitive economy. In recent years, China has produced a number of environmental action plans. And during China's Fourth Environmental Protection Conference in July, Premier Li Peng dryly admonished a stiff assemblage of Communist Party officials to do more to fight pollution and promote sustainable development.

Yet Beijing's bureaucrats will have to bring more revolutionary zeal to bear if the greening party line is to have any real impact. In Inner Mongolia's Boatou, huge state-owned industries have for decades pumped colorless hydrogen fluoride into the air—leaving the local population with brittle bones and brittle teeth. Shanghai's 13 million residents rely on drinking-water supplies that are contaminated with oil, ammonia, nitrogen and an assortment of other potentially dangerous organic compounds. Worst of all in most cities is the soot and smoke from the widespread burning of coal. It seeps through ramshackle window frames, settling on furniture, appliances and books. It streaks any laundry that is hung out to dry. It makes grit-covered teeth and stinging eyes as much a part of the Chinese urban winter as the sweet potatoes cooked by street vendors in converted oil-drum ovens.

China's polluting ways increasingly are being felt beyond its borders. One Japanese study indicates that as much as 30 percent of the acid rain that falls on western Japan can be traced to sulfur dioxide emissions from coal burning in China. And by one Western estimate, Chinese sulfur dioxide emissions will exceed those of the industrial world by 2035. China ranks second in the world, after the United States, in industrial emissions of carbon dioxide. Production of ozone-eating substances, such as the chlorofluorocarbons used in refrigerators and aerosols, could more than double 1991 levels by the end of the decade.

A broad social consensus in China remains in favor of continued economic growth, but popular enthusiasm for a fledgling "green foods" industry, a rash of angry lawsuits against dirty industries and the increasingly obvious toll of pollution are prompting national leaders to contemplate unprecedented restrictions on industry.

Capital offense. The fate of Lotus Flower, the world's fourth-largest producer of monosodium glutamate and a Deng Xiaoping-era success story, could be a lesson for other polluters. Until recently, Lotus Flower's factory in Henan province spewed out 3,500 tons a day of a noxious, yellowish-green effluent that helped make the Huai River in east central China one of the country's dirtiest. When controlled flooding of the river in 1994 revealed the extent of the pollution by wiping out croplands and fish stocks downstream, Zhu Rongji, the most nononsense of China's top leaders, barely flinched. "The [Lotus Flower] MSG plant only has 10,000-plus workers. If it can't fix its pollution problems, close it down." Lotus Flower hurriedly cleaned up its act, but it used an experimental treatment program that involves introducing bacteria into the water that could have other, as yet unknown, health consequences.

Beijing recently shut down nearly 1,000 paper mills on the Huai and intends to do the same to small polluting industries nationwide. "We are determined to make a shift from extensive economic development to intensive economic development," says Zie Zhenhua, the administrator of China's National Environmental Protection Agency (NEPA). In its growing zeal to respond to China's environmental problems, the leadership in April made "jeopardizing the environment" a capital offense.

Yet economic growth remains the last word. As China's 1994 environmental action plan puts it: "The precondition for sustainable development is development." NEPA lacks the clout to enforce environmental regulations in many sectors of the economy and often finds itself trumped by more powerful ministries, which remain preoccupied with production totals. "If the environment needs to be bypassed for something that is perceived to be for the greater good, it just gets bypassed," says a Western environ-

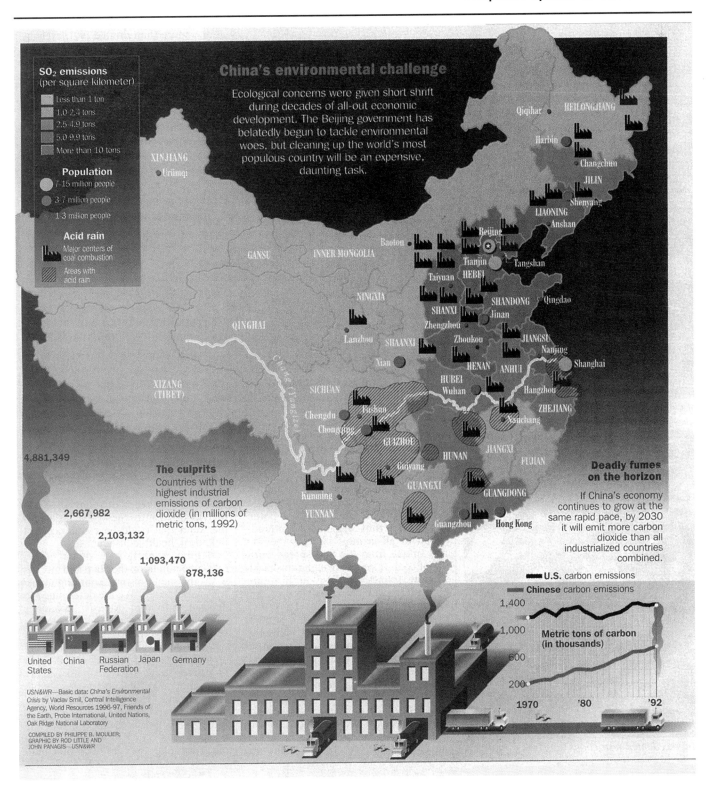

China's environmental challenge

Ecological concerns were given short shrift during decades of all-out economic development. The Beijing government has belatedly begun to tackle environmental woes, but cleaning up the world's most populous country will be an expensive, daunting task.

SO₂ emissions
(per square kilometer)
- Less than 1 ton
- 1.0-2.4 tons
- 2.5-4.9 tons
- 5.0-9.9 tons
- More than 10 tons

Population
- 7-15 million people
- 3-7 million people
- 1-3 million people

Acid rain
- Major centers of coal combustion
- Areas with acid rain

The culprits
Countries with the highest industrial emissions of carbon dioxide (in millions of metric tons, 1992)

4,881,349
2,667,982
2,103,132
1,093,470
878,136

United States | China | Russian Federation | Japan | Germany

Deadly fumes on the horizon

If China's economy continues to grow at the same rapid pace, by 2030 it will emit more carbon dioxide than all industrialized countries combined.

■ **U.S.** carbon emissions
■ **Chinese** carbon emissions

1,400
1,000
600
200

Metric tons of carbon (in thousands)

1970   '80   '92

USN&WR—Basic data: China's Environmental Crisis by Vaclav Smil, Central Intelligence Agency, World Resources 1996-97, Friends of the Earth, Probe International, United Nations, Oak Ridge National Laboratory

COMPILED BY PHILIPPE B. MOULIER;
GRAPHIC BY ROD LITTLE AND
JOHN PANAGIS—USN&WR

mentalist working in China. In fact, U.S. government analysts expect that the Chinese leadership will defer a vigorous attack on pollution until after 2010, when the current phase of industrialization is scheduled to end.

Understandably, money is also a problem. Beijing plans to increase annual spending on the environment from 0.7 percent of GDP (about $17 billion) to 1.5 percent of GDP (about $40 billion) by 2000. But to make a real difference, says Husayn Anwar, an environmental engineer working in China, the government would need to commit at least 5 to 10 percent of GDP—a level of funding that many Chinese officials say is simply beyond reach until China grows richer.

The World's Largest Dam

Building the Next Great Wall of China

A pile of red bricks is all that remains of the Du family's house. Struggling to keep her balance, Du Kaiyin navigates a wooden vat of water through the dusty rubble and begins to prepare supper on a small table amid the debris. "They forced us to tear everything down and move away," explains the 55-year-old grandmother. She has spent her entire life on this farm in Zxiangjiadian, a village on the banks of the Chang (Yangtze). But soon she will leave to join her son in Yichang, the main city of the district, three hours downstream by boat.

Sinking cities. The reason is "Da Ba"—the "Big Dam," as locals call China's largest engineering project since the Great Wall. The Three Gorges Dam—named after the majestic valley where it is being built—will be the largest dam in the world, 600 feet tall and 1.4 miles long. Behind it, the waters of the Chang will form a reservoir over 400 miles long and covering an area as large as Los Angeles. Some 140 cities and villages—including Xiangjiadin—1,600 factories and at least 80,000 acres of arable land will be submerged.

The purpose of the mammoth project is twofold. More than 300,000 people have died in this century in floods along the Chang. "The dam," maintains chief engineer Lu Youmei, "will protect 15 million people from flooding." And the economic advantages are plain: Twenty-six huge generators will produce the equivalent of one ninth of China's entire power production today, energy needed to industrialize China's heartland.

But the costs will be high as well. To clear the area to be flooded, Beijing has initiated the largest forced resettlement in Chinese history: 1.3 million residents of the area must leave. New cities are being planned and built for them, and a five-person family is supposed to get 29,000 yuan (about $400) in compensation for the loss of its home.

An invaluable cultural topography also will sink. According to legend, the ancient hero Yu conquered the torrents of the mighty Chang with the help of the goddess Yao Ji and created the cornerstone of the first dynasty. Since then, countless poets and artists have paid homage to the beauty of the Three Gorges. Inscriptions line the cliff faces and fill temples on the water's edge.

According to environmentalists, completion of the dam could mean extinction for endangered species including Yangtze river dolphins and Chinese alligators. Other experts consider the monumental undertaking downright dangerous. As the reservoir fills with sediment, the river behind the dam will grow increasingly torrential. There are fears that lifesaving dikes could burst under the strain. The area around the dam site also is earthquake prone.

Concerned by such risks, international sponsors such as U.S. agencies and the World Bank have withdrawn their support. But Beijing is forging on. If all goes according to plan, next year will be diverted into a concrete riverbed. Six years later, engineers will set in motion the first electric generator. The dam is scheduled to be completed by 2009, forever altering what poet Du Fu described 1,200 years ago as "the river of heaven."

By Harald Maass in Xiangjiadian

Power and water and sanitation infrastructure alone will require more than $300 billion in investment by 2004, making dollars for environmental projects scarce. "It's really kind of a pinprick approach," says a U.S. official of Beijing's environmental spending plans.

Even if China's top party leaders remain ambivalent about investing in the environment, many people and businesses across China are not. In Zhoukou, in Henan province, 70 percent of the city's drinking water comes from the polluted Sha River. That is a potential market opening that the Huacheng Science and Technology Development Co. finds hard to ignore. A manufacturer of handcuffs, thumb cuffs and electric batons—technologies with an entirely different purpose—Huacheng is now trying to boost its income through the sale of water-purification equipment. On the wall of its headquarters hangs a warning. "A siren call," it reads. "People have already discovered, or are discovering, that we are playing a cruel and terrible joke on ourselves.... Our drinking water is leaving a legacy of pain and sorrow for our descendants." The question now is whether China can begin to practice that kind of preaching before it is too late.

By Tim Zimmermann in Washington and Susan V. Lawrence and Brian Palmer in China, with Philippe B. Moulier

Article 19   *The Wall Street Journal,* August 5, 1996

Old Folks in Beijing Dance in the Streets, Annoying the Young

Yang Ge Folk Dance Liberates Thousands, While Others Try to Work and Study

Craig S. Smith

Staff Reporter of the Wall Street Journal

BEIJING—As Wang Guirong hammers away on his bright-red drum, shattering the quiet evening, dancers hop and strut to the beat on the sidewalk around him. But not everyone is in the groove.

"I hate it," mutters Zhang Gun as the racket reverberates through her tiny fourth-floor apartment in Beijing's Peace Bridge neighborhood, a collection of drab brick apartment blocks. The 13-year-old glares down at a group of more than 70 elderly women gyrating around gray-haired Mr. Wang.

Beijing is in the throes of a classic generational upheaval—but this time it is the old folks who are the upstarts. Freed by recent economic reforms from 40 years of political campaigns and material deprivation, throngs of oldsters are dancing up a storm in the streets, with many in the younger crowd looking on sourly. The dancers are reviving *yang ge* (pronounced "YONG-gehr"), a northeastern folk dance first brought to the city by the Communist People's Liberation Army in 1949.

Beijing officials estimate that as many as 60,000 senior citizens fill the streets each night, clad in lime-green or magenta silk tunics and hoofing to the cacophonous clash of cymbals and drums. Police measurements put the close-up decibel level of the average yang-ge band at about that of a freight train at 25 yards. One local hotline registered 1,652 noise complaints in just four days. "It's the young people who complain," a Peace Bridge neighborhood official says.

Originally, yang ge was a harvest dance. Mao Tse-tung's soldiers learned it from peasants in the 1940s, then took it with them as the civil war against Chiang Kai-shek's army moved south.

In a remarkably effective public-relations campaign, they taught it to the masses. Then Mao's policies brought famine and the 10-year Cultural Revolution, and the party was over.

Looking For Fun

No longer. The generation that came of age "eating bitterness" is out to have a little fun. "We went through so much, now we want to enjoy the rest of our lives," says Pan Jiying, a grandmother squeezed into a T-shirt emblazoned with the name Umbro, a British soccer-shoe maker. Besides, she argues, dancing boosts circulation, cuts medical costs and unkinks family disputes by separating cranky elders from their children for a few hours each night.

"We're contributing to the stability of the state," she says, and a dozen gray heads around her nod in agreement.

Nowadays, with socialist sinecures going the way of Mao suits and Marxism, many of China's youths spend evenings mastering economics or English. Young parents work longer hours and go to bed early. "Old people should enjoy themselves," grumbles Miss Zhang's mother, a schoolteacher, "but not by sacrificing those of us who are serving society."

She and her daughter sit uneasily in their sitting room, a cramped concrete box, eyeing a plastic clock on the wall. Miss Zhang's father pokes his head into the room. "They haven't started yet," he says, his voice edged with feeble hope. But at 7:28, Mr. Wang's drums are throbbing.

The Zhangs know every turn in the music by heart. A sudden rise in volume means the dancers are nearing their break, halfway through their nightly three-hour session. The worst, they say, is the *suo-na,* a many-piped wind instrument that sounds like a squealing pig.

The city fathers have tried to muffle Mr. Wang and friends. Dancing is banned near hospitals, schools and, of course, government offices. The mayor signed a regulation ordering dancers to stay at least 200 yards from residential buildings.

Enforcement is another matter: On this night, Mr. Wang drums a scant 100 yards from Ms. Zhang's sitting-room window. "What are we going to do," an exasperated police officer asks, "arrest all of them?"

Beating Out Boomboxes

Beijing's Cultural Bureau did try handing out boomboxes and recorded cassettes—hoping they would be quieter than the live music—but to no avail. Mr. Wang breaks into a big grin as he points out a huge, black Japanese tape player displayed in the neighborhood committee's meeting room. "It doesn't excite people enough, the sound doesn't carry," he says. The drum, he says, "echoes in your heart."

Old people can't sit still when they hear it, he says. Before helping organize the group in his neighborhood, the 72-year-old Mr. Wang bicycled 10 miles to dance near the ruins of a Qing Dynasty palace north of the city. His children tried to keep him home but couldn't, he says.

As he begins beating his drum, senior citizens appear from all directions, many toting pink fans trimmed with white fluff and tinsel. Doing a dance that looks like a cross between the stroll and the bunny-hop, they march in a circle, form rows, strut forward together, then back. The dance has endless variations.

The nightly floor-dusting has split this neighborhood, as it has many others across the capital. Mr. Wang and Ms. Pan, who grew up farming the land where apartment blocks now stand, organized the Peace Bridge dance group. They drew on memories of what Mao's soldiers taught them when they were young.

Drumming Forever

Like them, most of the old folks who come to dance are former peasants living in the western half of the neighborhood. But it's crowded there, so they rally in the east, where most residents are white-collar workers like Miss Zhang's parents. "They should find someplace in their own half of the neighborhood to dance, not bother us over here," says Miss Zhang, tugging at the ends of her red kerchief—neckwear of the Young Pioneers, China's Communist Party youth organization.

But the older generation says it intends to keep raising the roof every night of the year, weather permitting. "I'll play this drum until I die," vows Mr. Wang.

Even then, the beat will go on. Mr. Wang is training a 50-year-old apprentice to take up his drumsticks when he is gone.

Article 20

The New York Times, June 25, 1996

As a Pampered Generation Grows Up, Chinese Worry

Patrick E. Tyler

BEIJING—It was just another school day for Liu Huamin when the father of one of her students burst through the classroom door and said his teen-age son was threatening to commit suicide by jumping off the fourth-floor balcony of the family's apartment building.

Why? asked Mrs. Liu, a chemistry teacher at Waluji Middle School here.

Because, the man replied, the boy's mother would not cook his favorite meat dumplings for breakfast.

He did not jump, but the story of his breathtaking display of willfulness incites a look of instant recognition across the faces of many Chinese teachers today.

Indeed, it seems at times as if the willfulness of China's generation of "little emperors"—children growing up without siblings under China's one-child population control policy—knows no bounds.

In Guangdong Province a power failure prevented a housewife from cooking dinner for her 14-year-old son, who flew into a rage and went out to watch television with a friend. When the boy returned, there was still no dinner, so he seized a meat cleaver and killed his mother with 10 blows to the head. Then he hanged himself.

An extreme case, but the fact that China's Government-run news organizations gave it prominent display last year also illustrates the concern of many

Chinese that its first generation of only children is rapidly maturing into a generation of spoiled, self-absorbed tyrants.

After decades of famine and political turmoil in China, parents who grew up in troubled and often violent times under Mao, suffering long periods of deprivation in the countryside and interrupted schooling are now rearing—in many cases doting on—a generation of only children.

And these new parents are filled with anxiety about whether they are doing it right.

"This is a fixation," said James L. Watson, an anthropologist at Harvard University who has studied the Chinese family. "I would call it kind of a compensation complex. The generation of parents that we are dealing with now, many of them are Cultural Revolution veterans who themselves did not have much of a childhood, and I think that many of them are trying hard to make sure that their own children get all the benefits and more that they missed out on."

But they are doing it with little cultural guidance. The current generation of parents has been cut adrift from both the traditional Confucian values emphasizing reverence for elders that were once the foundation of China's extended families and from the Communist values imposed for three decades under Mao.

Neither has much credibility in China today.

Specialists say it is too early to say whether China's "little emperors" are growing up to be a generation of self-centered autocrats, whose politics may be more aggressive than the generation that grew up under Mao, or whether they are so overindulged at home that they will be ill prepared for the competitive pressures and harsh realities of China's market economy.

Off to Bad Start, Teachers Say

"Seems like it could go either way," said David Y. H. Wu, an anthropologist at Chinese University of Hong Kong. "You could either raise a generation of rebels against the controls of the Communist Party or you could raise a generation that would feel more nationalistic and assertive as Chinese.

"Talking about personality traits and trying to project to the whole nation is very difficult, but I can see a whole generation perhaps more independent and willing to challenge authority, or simply more authoritative because of their intensified relationships with their parents, and the symbol of parents is government."

Either way, if today's teachers are any judge, the "little emperor" generation is off to an inauspicious start.

"As life and economic conditions get better and better, the moral principles of students and their sense of responsibility to society and family get worse and worse," said Mrs. Liu, the chemistry teacher, who has an 18-year-old son. "We teachers often wonder how these students can take up their social responsibility when they get older."

Teachers around the world have long complained about the quality of the next generation. But in China, a generation of children is growing up in the midst of a profound economic revolution, where social and political values seem suspended in time as the country waits for the death of Deng Xiaoping, the 91-year-old paramount leader, not knowing whether that event will usher in a new era with a new value system.

"My most terrifying concern," said Zhang Xiaoyun, 33, who teaches literature at the China Youth Political College in Beijing, a former Communist Party school, "is that you must raise a child within some system of beliefs, but our generation has no beliefs, so how can we educate our children?"

The demographic shift from multi-child families under strong patriarchs to small, nuclear families centered on only children "is going to have a profound effect" on Chinese society, Professor Watson said.

Increased Spending on Toys and Books

One of the ways that Chinese are overcompensating in bringing up the country's only children is by spending the greatest portion of family income ever on toys, books, educational materials, personal computers and food.

The national obsession with children is fostering multibillion-dollar opportunities for business.

Baby food, which barely existed in China a decade ago, is now a staple of family life and a major item in family budgets.

China's "little emperors" are the single greatest force in determining consumer decisions today, experts say.

"I met a woman who took her daughter to McDonald's in Beijing twice a week to give her modern nutrition," said Yan Yunxiang, a Chinese-born anthropologist at Johns Hopkins University, who frequently returns to examine the culture he grew up in.

When he asked the woman why she was spending as much as half a normal worker's income each month on

McDonald's, she replied: "I want my daughter to learn more about American culture. She is taking English typing classes now, and next year I will buy her a computer."

Professor Watson said: "It turns out that most Chinese don't even like the food, but what they are buying is culture. They are buying connectedness to the world system.

"The idea is that if these kids can connect with McDonald's, they are going to end up at Harvard Law School."

One of China's most popular amusement parks, Window on the World, has no rides and no arcades. Chinese come from all over the country to pay, in some cases a week's wages, to show their children miniatures of Manhattan Island, the Statue of Liberty, the Eiffel Tower and the Taj Mahal.

A Generation Driven by Rewards

"Most of our time and money are spent on this child," said Wen Geli, the mother of a 2-year-old boy who seems less attentive to the park's attractions than to gorging himself on ice cream. "We want to give him an introduction to the world and expand his outlook."

"My generation grew up with hardship," said her husband, Zhang Xinwen, a communications officer in the Chinese Army, "We were born in the 1960's, and that was a period of bitter shortage, but this generation is growing up in richer times and we want to take advantage of this better environment."

Not far away, a retired sports teacher, Cai Kunling, 59, was squiring his 5-year-old granddaughter, Fu Hua, past the wonders of the world. "She should be in kindergarten today," he said, "but she wanted to take me to this place," he added in a tone that reflected who was in charge.

The two of them sat for their photo in front of a miniature of Niagara Falls and then strolled over to the little Manhattan.

To Mr. Cai, who lived through the Mao period, it was like a dream world.

"My generation made a lot of sacrifices and had a lot of devotion to the country," he said. "But this generation needs a reward if you want them to do something. If there is no compensation, they don't want to do it."

Sitting around a dinner of baked carp with three other teachers one evening,

Mrs. Liu and some of her colleagues vented their anxieties.

Free-for-All Future Worries the Parents

Li Shunmei, 31, a high school teacher with a 3-year-old daughter, said: "I worry a lot about my daughter's future, because I have doubts about whether she can survive under the harsher and harsher competition of Chinese society.

"Nowadays, there are many children who commit suicide. I think it is because parents obey their children's every demand, so they are not able to endure any reversals or hard times."

This strain of anxiety is very prominent in Chinese families.

The old "iron rice bowl" society of cradle-to-grave social welfare protection is giving way year by year to the new market economy, where life is beginning to look like a terrifying free-for-all to many Chinese used to something more secure.

"The home can be very sweet and gentle for these toddlers, but the world out there is a cruel world," said Jing Jun, a Beijing native who now teaches anthropology at City College in New York. "When we were growing up, the state arranged everything for you, but now parents know the state is not going to do anything for them and the job market is pretty grim."

Mr. Jing said he believed that China's "little emperors" would have to pass through a tough period of adjustment. "They are under so much pressure," he said, "and their parents have such great expectations for them. Whether they are psychologically prepared for that, I cannot say."

Professor Watson said, "A lot of people, including Chinese psychologists, are concerned whether the next generation is going to be able to 'eat bitterness,' whether they are going to be able to work hard or whether they will be willing to sacrifice themselves as was true under socialism."

Some Chinese feel that the "little emperors" will adjust.

"I'm optimistic," said Wang Xujin, a teacher at Beijing Business College with a 9-year-old son.

But, he confessed, "although the students each year are smarter and smarter, I like them less and less."

Article 21   *Archaeology*, September/October 1996

Buddhas of Cloud Hill

China's earliest cave-temples reflect the imperial ambitions, religious sentiments, and sculptural artistry of a fledgling dynasty.

James O. Caswell

James O. Caswell, a professor in the department of fine arts at the University of British Columbia is author of Written and Unwritten. A New History of the Buddhist Caves at Yungang *(Vancouver: University of British Columbia Press, 1988).*

Larry Gartenstein

Scores of Buddhas, Bodhisattvas (savior-like figures), apsaras (angel-like figures), celestial musicians, and other images adorn the walls and ceilings of cave 12's anteroom.

About A.D. 460 Tanyao, the head of the Buddhist church in the court of the Northern Wei dynasty, petitioned the emperor Wencheng to "open up five caves and carve a Buddha image in each of them, the tallest to be 70 feet high, the next tallest 60 feet high, with superb carvings and decorations, a crowning glory to the world" ("Treatise on Buddhism and Daoism," *History of the Northern Wei*). Skilled artisans flocked to the one-half mile of porous sandstone cliffs at Yungang, or "Cloud Hill," in northern Shanxi Province. There they carved out five caves, each with a central colossal Buddha or Bodhisattva (a savior-like figure), representing the power and authority of the first five Northern Wei emperors. Scholars believe there was a precedent for such an effort in the casting of five bronze Buddha images honoring the emperors at a temple in the nearby capital of Pingcheng. The head of the church at the founding of the dynasty in 386 was reported to have said, "I am not worshiping the emperor, I am only paying respect to the Buddha." The later collaboration between Tanyao and the court indicates a relationship had been established between the power of the Buddha and Northern Wei rulers.

Today these five imperial caves are numbered 16–20. Other caves (5–13) in the central area of the site are of almost equal size and sculptural richness but, though stylistically related to the imperial five, are quite distinct. The 14 caves (there are also minor grottoes and niches) constitute the earliest extant Buddhist site of major significance in China, and are comparable in importance to India's magnificent Buddhist cave shrines at Ajanta (see ARCHAEOLOGY, November/December 1992).

When I first visited Yungang nine years ago, I was intrigued by the carved images of Buddhas and Bodhisattvas as well as other figures and decorative motifs on the cave walls. The calculated austerity and programmatic coherence of the carvings in the imperial caves contrasted sharply with the florid, even joyful exuberance of those in caves 5 through 13. It was difficult for me to imagine that these images were as close and sequential in date as other scholars said they were, that they were products of the same religious vision, or that they served the same ends. I felt that the caves must have been built for different reasons, using Buddhist imagery in different ways, perhaps at different times.

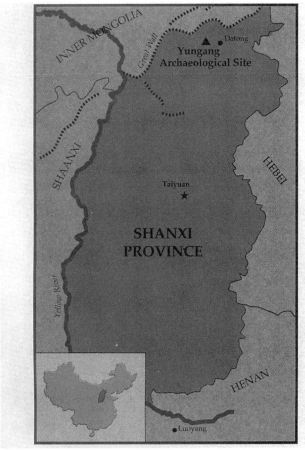

Lynda D'Amico

the same territory some 150 years earlier, they took advantage of China's political weakness in the aftermath of the collapse of the Han dynasty (206 B.C.–A.D. 220), establishing an empire that extended across northern China, mostly south of the Great Wall, from Gansu Province in the west to the Yellow Sea in the east. Seeking to legitimate their rule and at the same time maintain their identity, they adopted Buddhism as a state religion. By doing so, they could claim they were culturally distinct from Chinese subjects who practiced ancestor worship, while using the organization of the Buddhist monastery as a model for their administrative bureaucracy.

Buddhism was at first an uncomfortable fit for the Chinese. The Indic languages of its texts were alien, as were many of its ideas; for example, believers were asked to sever their connections with the world and even give up their surnames. In A.D. 446, in an effort to dislodge the religion, two Chinese ministers employed by the Northern Wei court deceived the emperor Taiwu (reigned 423–452) into believing that Buddhists were planning an armed revolt. To counter such sedition, the emperor ordered the killing or defrocking of monks and nuns and the destruction of monasteries and their contents. The persecution lasted until Taiwu's death in 452. "His body had scarcely cooled," as one contemporary historian wrote, before Buddhism was restored. Wencheng's decision to build the five imperial caves at Yungang may have been an act of atonement for the persecutions carried out by his predecessor.

After the last visit of a Northern Wei emperor to the site in 483, the court appears to have lost interest in Yungang, focusing its attention instead on beautifying the capital of Pingcheng with splendid structures. At the same time both lay and clerical Buddhists with no attachment to the court were building their own monuments throughout the countryside. A census of 477 reports that there were 6,478 temples with 77,258 monks and nuns. Another, in 513, lists 13,727 monasteries. By the end of the dynasty there were some 30,000 temples housing roughly two million monks and nuns. The growing number of Buddhists, with their voracious appetite for new temples and the consequent waste of both human and financial resources, was lamented by a court officer in a memorial written toward the end of the dynasty. In spite of regular court edicts prohibiting temple construction, the officer concluded that "the [imperial] restrictions of earlier days were given no heed." The court itself joined in this building frenzy when it moved the capital to Luoyang. According to a nearly contemporary account known as the *Luoyang qielan ji (Record of the Monasteries in Luoyang)*, the building program at Luoyang was probably the most profligate waste of resources on the most splendid buildings ever known in

There are only scant references to Yungang in the mid-sixth century imperial annals known as *History of the Northern Wei*. Two of Wencheng's successors are said to have visited the site, Xianwen in 467, possibly to dedicate the finished imperial caves, and the boy-emperor Xiaowen, in 480, 482, and 483. Thereafter the imperial record says nothing about the caves until the early sixth century, when they are cited as a precedent for the Longmen grottoes near the new capital at Luoyang where the court moved in 494. Only two inscriptions survive from before 494, one dated 483 and the other 489. The earlier one reports the donation of a large wall composition by 54 villagers, and the latter indicates the support of a nun for a smaller one. Both may represent gifts from nonimperial Buddhists hoping to gain divine merit. There were clearly two distinct major cave building phases at Yungang: the imperial caves, ca. 460–467, and after a hiatus of some 16 years nonimperial caves, from ca. 483 to no later than 494.

The Northern Wei dynasty was established by the Tuoba Tartars, a people of Turkic stock from central Asia who had invaded China in A.D. 386. Adopting the name Wei from a Chinese dynasty that had ruled over roughly

An Endangered Sanctuary

Over the centuries wind erosion, rock fractures, water seepage, and the depredations of thieves have taken their toll on the Yungang cave-temples. So have coal mines from the nearby city of Datong, source of the soot that covers much of the statuary. In 1988 the Chinese State Bureau of Cultural Relics invited the Getty Conservation Institute to suggest strategies for preserving the sculpture. Most of the carvings exposed to the elements, such as those on pillars outside caves 9 and 10, had been destroyed by weathering, and much of the remaining paint was in danger of flaking. Restorations beginning in the seventh century had mainly addressed cosmetic problems; eroded or flaking surfaces, for example, were plastered over with mud, then decorated with paint and gilding.

The Getty's first task was to assess the extent and impact of weathering caused by pollution, wind, and rain. It determined that the deterioration of paint on carved surfaces had been aggravated by the presence of coal dust. It also found that regular dustings by maintenance workers were inadvertently removing paint. Studies by the Environmental Laboratory of the California Institute of Technology in Pasadena revealed that a great deal of soot had accumulated on the sculpture, in some cases forming a layer several millimeters thick. The lab estimated that reducing the amount of soot in the air could limit dust in the caves by 38 percent. It suggested covering loaded trucks to prevent coal from spilling onto roads, paving streets in the village of Yungang, and paving or spray-washing dirt roads in front of the caves.

The Chinese plan to install shelters in front of some of the cave entrances to reduce the soot problem. Caves 5 and 6 still retain ancient wooden pagoda facades mounted against the cliff to provide the interiors a measure of protection against the elements. The new shelters will be constructed of fabric and mimic the

Courtesy The J. Paul Getty Trust

Severe weathering has eroded carvings on pillars of cave 10.

the history of Chinese cities. The account listed some 1,367 temples in the city of Luoyang alone.

Caves 5 through 13 are probably evidence of the construction boom that began after the court had abandoned Yungang and lasted until the capital was moved. They were the work of nonimperial patrons who dug cave-temples for religious rather than political reasons. While the art of the imperial caves is solemn, the carvings in the later caves reflect greater thematic and artistic variety. Some of the Buddhas in the later group, particularly in cave 6, are clad in Chinese dress, making them more comprehensible to native Chinese. Visitors to the imperial caves probably

kept a deferential distance from the colossi. The later caves were more spacious, afforded more intimate viewing, and paid greater attention to religious themes and iconography. Cave 6 is full of scenes from the life of the Buddha, while carvings in caves 7 and 8 show multiarmed and multiheaded figures derived from Indian images, though direct formal precedents are lacking. Chinese motifs such as dragons and phoenixes also appear in the later caves.

Thus what began at Yungang as political statements exalting imperial authority by equating the emperor with the Buddha became, in the second phase, statements of religious devotion. Concurrent with this transformation

Courtesy The J. Paul Getty Trust
California Institute of Technology professor Glen Cass takes a reading from a particle analyzer monitoring concentrations of soot in cave 9.

Courtesy The J. Paul Getty Trust
Restorers examine the eroded remnants of small niches carved into the wall between caves 19-B, left, and 19.

design of the traditional wooden ones. Miguel Angel Corzo, director of the Getty Conservation Institute, says the site is also threatened by the remains of a Ming fortress on the plateau above it. "The walled perimeter of the fort acts as a catchment basin," he says. "When it rains the walls create a pond and the water filters down. Salt in the rock is dissolved by water and then crystallizes on the stone surface, promoting the exfoliation of the painted layer of the statues and the exfoliation of the stone itself."

The Getty team studied the site's drainage in an effort to control the spread of damaging salts. In the past 30 years the Chinese have installed surface drainage channels above the grottoes to alleviate the problem, but their effectiveness has not been monitored. In a successful experiment, the Getty buried drainage pipes to collect and channel the runoff. According to Corzo,

"Several drains need to be installed to divert water from the fort and away from the caves. Unfortunately the Chinese are having problems obtaining government funds, so installation may be delayed."

Perhaps the Getty's most important service was to cosponsor a program with the Australian Heritage Commission advising the site's caretakers on the nuts and bolts of site conservation. The team offered a series of on-site lectures "trying to instill a clearer sense of site management at Yungang," says Corzo. "The Chinese have to figure out the best way for tourists to visit the site." Tourism is a growing factor in China's economy, and conservation of the Yungang caves serves not only cultural interests but those of China's pocketbook as well.

Spencer P. M. Harrington *is an associate editor of* ARCHAEOLOGY.

was the explosion of Buddhist temple-building throughout the empire. The human and financial investments in Buddhist buildings, the worship commitment required by Buddhist practice, and friction between the court and the landed gentry, who gradually withdrew from official

life and refused to pay taxes, contributed to the collapse of the Northern Wei in 535. Almost forgotten after the dynasty's fall, the caves at Yungang remain a silent witness to the exercise of both political authority and uncontrolled religious enthusiasm.

Article 22   *Archaeology,* January/February 1996

The First Asians

A cave in China yields evidence of the earliest migration out of Africa.

Roy Larick and Russell Ciochon

Roy Larick of the University of Massachusetts and Russell Ciochon of the University of Iowa, in collaboration with Vietnamese scientists, are writing a monograph on the excavation of the Lang Trang Caves southwest of Hanoi, the first Vietnamese-American paleoanthropological field project.

Hominid remains and stone tools from Longgupo (Dragon Bone Cave) in south-central China have been dated to nearly two million years ago, suggesting that humans from East Africa arrived in Asia much earlier than previously thought. The fossils resemble specimens of *Homo habilis* and *Homo ergaster,* species that appeared little more than two million years ago in East Africa, and the artifacts recall the simple stone tools closely linked with them. The Longgupo finds suggest that soon after evolving in Africa a primitive hominid migrated to Asia with the aid of an elementary technology. They also confirm scattered and ambiguous evidence that *Homo erectus,* once believed to have been the first hominid to colonize Asia, may instead have developed there from an earlier form.

Located 12 miles south of the Three Gorges area of the Yangtze River in eastern Sichuan Province, Longgupo was first investigated in 1985 by Beijing's Institute of Vertebrate Paleontology and Paleoanthropology in an effort to recover fossil mammals. A middle layer of sediments yielded more than 10,000 fossils including teeth of an extinct giant ape (*Gigantopithecus blacki*). In 1987 and 1988 a hominid jaw fragment, with a fourth premolar and a first molar, and an isolated incisor were found within the middle layer along with two artifacts. In 1990 excavation leaders Huang Wanpo and Gu Yumin asked us to assemble a collaborative team to date and analyze the finds. Joining us were geochronologist Henry Schwarcz, geologist Charles Yonge, and paleontologist John de Vos, among others.

The presence of extinct species of mastodon, horse, and pygmy giant panda dates the cave's hominid-bearing middle deposits to about 1.5 to 2.0 million years ago. Paleomagnetic dating, based on the periodic reversal of the earth's magnetic poles, allows a more precise dating of the deposits to 1.78 to 1.96 million years ago. We have confirmed this estimate using electron spin resonance spectroscopy, which determines age by counting elec-

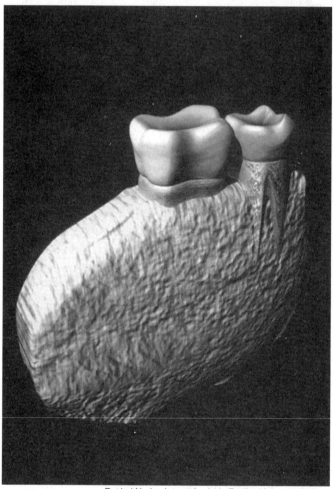

Rachel Nador, Image Analysis Facility, University of Iowa
Molar and premolar of Longgupo jaw, shown in this computer model, have cusps typical of the earliest species of Homo.

trons trapped in the calcium phosphate of tooth enamel. A mammal tooth from more than 12 feet above the hominid deposits yielded an age of more than one million years, a result fully consistent with the paleomagnetic interpretation for this and the lower, hominid-bearing level.

The link between hominid type and tool technology is a key to understanding early dispersal. The earliest members of our genus, currently known as *Homo rudolfensis,* appear slightly more than 2.5 million years ago in the Rift Valley of East Africa, having evolved from

Russell L. Ciochon

Retaining wall protects the collapsed entrance and fossil-bearing deposits of Longgupo (Dragon Bone Cave) in Sichuan, China.

an australopithecine forebear. The earliest technology, known as Oldowan and consisting of cobblestone battering tools and simple flakes for cutting, appears nearly simultaneously. By 2.0 to 1.8 million years ago, however, there are at least two more hominid species in the Rift Valley associated with simple stone tools: small-bodied *Homo habilis* and much larger *Homo ergaster*. Early dispersals of hominids to Eurasia began during the transition from the Pliocene to the Pleistocene, from about 2.0 to 1.6 million years ago, and new finds and dates suggest that the early hominids with simple tools had migrated extensively by 1.6 million years ago. Shortly after this date, African populations began using the more advanced Acheulean technology based on bifacial cutting and chopping implements, tools not found in Early Pleistocene Eurasia.

The hominid teeth found at Longgupo exhibit similarities with *Homo habilis* and *Homo ergaster* that distinguish them from those of classic Asian *Homo erectus* found at Zhoukoudian in northern China and Java in Indonesia. The Longgupo fourth premolar or bicuspid, for example, has small principal cusps located well forward as does

Homo habilis. The much larger cusps of *Homo erectus* fourth premolars, by contrast, have migrated rearward to the middle of the tooth. Moreover, like those of some African hominids, the Longgupo fourth premolar has two roots, whereas *Homo erectus* fourth premolars always have just one root. The Longgupo first molar, like those of the African hominids, has five cusps and smooth enamel surfaces, whereas *Homo erectus* first molars have six cusps and highly wrinkled enamel. The Longgupo jaw fragment is not robust, and the cheek teeth are smaller than any known for *Homo erectus*. Finally, the Longgupo incisor is indistinguishable in size and shape from those known for *Homo habilis,* but rather small for *Homo erectus.* Given the incomplete nature of the Longgupo dentition, we can only say that it is an early form of the genus *Homo* with similarities to *Homo habilis* and *Homo ergaster.*

The two artifacts from Longgupo are tantalizing evidence for an early stone technology in East Asia. Both are river cobbles of porphyritic andesite, a volcanic stone that does not occur locally. They must have been brought to the cave. One is a nearly spherical cobble with crushing and pitting marks in three separate areas. The other cobble, split to form a rather large flake, has signs of battering around its periphery. The Longgupo finds indicate that an early population of *Homo* left Africa with very primitive features, at least in their dentition. The critical factor in colonizing Asian subtropical areas may have been simple stone tools.

This early Asian hominid may have given rise to the classic *Homo erectus* of China and Java. Recently, Huang Pelhua of the Chinese University of Science and Technology has redated the Zhoukoudian deposits to between 585,000 and 250,000 years ago, more than 100,000 years younger than previously thought. With Longgupo significantly older than Zhoukoudian, there was ample time to develop the classic *Homo erectus* dentition from the earlier form. For the past decade *Homo erectus* fossils on Java have been thought to be no more than one million years old. Recently, geological deposits at two Javanese *Homo erectus* sites have been dated surprisingly early: 1.6 million years ago at Sangiran and 1.8 million at Mojokerto. However, questions of erosion and redeposition render these dates dubious for the fossils, and the significance of archaic features in the hominid remains from Sangiran will not be evident until the geology is understood. The Javanese sites are also puzzling in that they contain numerous remains of classic *Homo erectus* but never stone tools. Although the report on the new dating argued that early *Homo* must have departed Africa before inventing Acheulean tools, it never explained the absence of tools from these sites. Longgupo proves the existence of a Plio-Pleistocene Asian technology consistent with Oldowan African origins.

Until quite recently, Europe seemed to have been colonized very late. Cranial remains from sites such as Mauer (Germany) and Tautavel (France) are very similar to African fossils from Elandsfontein (South Africa) and Bodo (Ethiopia), all of which may be called *Homo heidelbergensis*, after the Mauer jaw, found near Heidelberg. New analyses indicate that the earliest of these fossils date to about 600,000 years ago on both continents, which is also the age of the oldest European Acheulean. Within the last few years, however, a few sites have yielded possibly more primitive specimens of *Homo* associated with simple tools at Plio-Pleistocene dates. A small jaw and associated core flakes have been found at Dmanisi, Georgia, on the border between western Asia and eastern Europe. The jaw, with a mixture of primitive and evolved features, is best described as an early species of *Homo* with some resemblance to *Homo erectus*. If the paleomagnetic date of 1.8 million years ago is valid, Dmanisi may represent a population related to the Longgupo hominid in age, morphology, and technology. At the Gran Dolina site at Atapuerca, in northern Spain, core-flake tools accom-

Russell L. Ciochon

Cobblestone artifact from Longgupo, an Oldowan-type tool, shows signs of battering in three places.

pany an early representative of *Homo* more than 780,000 years old. Similar tools in a lower level of this site may be significantly older. At Orce, a controversial site in south-central Spain, core-flake tools as well as purported hominid remains have a paleomagnetic age of as much as 1.6 to 1.8 million years. While the identity of the Early Pleistocene European colonizers awaits discovery of more complete specimens, it most likely derived from an African species closely related to the earliest forms of the genus *Homo* that most successfully employed the simplest of stone tools.

Longgupo Cave demonstrates how paleoanthropology and archaeology, too often pursued independently, should converge in the study of human evolution. The genus *Homo* and stone tools appear to arise simultaneously slightly more than 2.5 million years ago in East Africa; the relationship of biology and technology must have been complex. Longgupo shows that *Homo* dispersed from Africa within 500,000 years of evolving from an australopithecine forebear and developing stone tools. We may imagine this as a first "biotechnological" revolution foreshadowing the dispersal of early African hominids throughout the Old World. Longgupo also exemplifies the east-west collaborative nature of evolutionary studies in Asia, where cave sites generally have different and more difficult local geologies than their open-air counterparts in Africa. As Asia becomes critical for understanding the early development of the genus *Homo*, international teams will provide the needed technical expertise and resources.

Article 23

The World & I, October 1989

Script Reform in China

Victor H. Mair

Victor H. Mair is professor of Chinese in the Department of Oriental Studies at the University of Pennsylvania. He is a specialist on early vernacular texts and Sino-Indian cultural relations. Among his publications are Tung-huang Popular Narratives *(Cambridge, 1983).* Painting and Performance: Chinese Picture Recitation and Its Indian Genesis *(Hawaii, 1988), and* T'ang Transformation Texts: A Study of the Buddhist Contribution to the Rise of Vernacular Fiction and Drama in China *(Harvard, 1989).*

| | | | | | Disaster |
| Battle | Solitary | Dragon | Old | Nation | or Difficulty |

Samples of complicated or full forms of the tetragraphs on the top line, with the simplified modern forms on the bottom line.

Nearly everyone who has seen Chinese characters is deeply impressed by them. Even without being able to read a single graph, one is struck by their longevity, beauty, complexity, and numerousness. Indeed, all these qualities are true of the Chinese writing system and account for the strong feelings it evokes. These emotions are particularly intense for those who consider the script to be one of the primary symbols of Chinese cultural identity. There is a great fear that, without this distinctive set of graphs, Chinese civilization as such would cease to exist.

Yet, during the past century, there have been persistent and equally urgent calls for radical changes in the script—including its abolition—from other segments of society. The traditionalists strive to maintain a proud and unique heritage that goes back over three millennia. The reformers worry that, unless their country modernizes its cumbersome, out-of-date script, everything—including the script itself—will be lost in an unsuccessful race to keep up with the rest of the world. A dispassionate look at the history and nature of writing in China may help to reconcile these two contradictory attitudes.

The Chinese writing system first occurs in virtually full-blown form around 1200 B.C. in the oracle bone inscriptions of the Shang dynasty. Scholars are perplexed by the suddenness with which the script appears; prior to the oracle bone inscriptions, there were only a few isolated and still undecipherable marks on pottery and occasionally on other objects. Hence the origins of the Chinese script remain a mystery. Its basic characteristics, however, do not. From its very inception as a tool for re-

cording facts and ideas, the same fundamental principles have governed both the shape and the function of the individual graphs. In spite of widespread belief to the contrary, there seems never to have been a purely pictographic or ideographic state of full writing in China. The earliest connected texts contain sizable proportions of signs that communicate meaning through sound (the so-called "cyclical stems and branches," the graph for "all" [*xian*], the graph for "come" [*lai*], and so forth).

John DeFrancis and others have convincingly shown that it is actually impossible to record all the nuances of speech without substantial recourse to phonetic indicators. Certainly, for at least the last twenty-five hundred years, by far the largest proportion of Chinese characters was made up of a component that conveys meaning and another component that conveys sound, though neither does so with precision alone. Since these components are gathered together in a consistently quadrilateral configuration, Chinese refer to them as tetragraphs (*fangkuaizi,* literally "square graphs" [a cluster of four successive letters in cryptography]).

REASONS FOR LANGUAGE REFORM

Perhaps the single most outstanding dissimilarity between the Chinese writing

system and alphabets is the vast quantity of separate units in the former compared to the strictly limited elements of the latter. In contrast to the 26 letters of the English alphabet, for example, there are over 60,000 discrete tetragraphs in the Chinese script, and new ones are being added continually. Mastery of such an enormous assemblage of individual shapes is beyond the ability of any mortal. For practical purposes, literacy in Chinese requires the passive recognition of approximately 2,000 tetragraphs and the active ability to write about 1,000 of them. Even the most learned persons are rarely able to read more than 5,000 tetragraphs and can reproduce only about half that amount without the aid of a dictionary. The other 50,000-plus tetragraphs consist largely of obscure variants, shapes whose sound or meaning (or both) is not known, and classical terms seldom or never used in modern parlance. Unfortunately, once a tetragraph has entered the lexicon, it becomes embedded there permanently. Typesetters, teachers, and translators must be prepared to cope with all 60,000 of them when the occasion demands.

Such large figures immediately lead to one of the most difficult questions about the tetragraphs: how to order them. It is easy to store and retrieve information in languages using an alphabetical script. The systematic nature of straightforward alphabetical ordering is one of the hallmarks of modern civilization. The case is entirely different with the tetragraphs. There is a large variety of traditional ways for arranging them, and they are very hard to control. The most common method is to break down each of the tetragraphs into a semantic classifier (also popularly called a radical or key) and a number of residual strokes. There are still several problems: The semantic cluster is not always readily identifiable, counting the residual strokes is both time-consuming and fraught with error, and the exact sequence of the semantic classifiers (usually 214) can be memorized only with tremendous effort.

Another complaint of the script reform advocates is the excessive amount of time and energy students have to spend in their early years to acquire minimum reading and writing skills. Several steps have already been taken to alleviate the burden placed upon young schoolchildren during the first few grades of their studies. In Taiwan, the National Phonetic Alphabet is used as an auxiliary to help beginners remember the sounds of the tetragraphs, and in the People's Republic of China, the initial lessons are given in Pinyin (romanized spelling). An increasing number of children's books written entirely in the National Phonetic Alphabet or in Pinyin are made available for students in elementary grades. Wide-scale experimental projects in Pinyin only or Pinyin mixed with tetragraphs for elementary education have been initiated in China. Results thus far show unmistakably that students learn to read much more quickly through Pinyin than when they are exposed to the tetragraphs alone.

Even more dramatic is the drastic reduction of the strokes in many tetragraphs and the limitations on the total number of tetragraphs officially accepted by the government of the People's Republic. These steps, particularly the former, fall under the rubric of "simplification." By 1964, altogether 2,238 tetragraphs, most of those that are frequently used, had been simplified. Nearly another 900 were scheduled for simplification in 1977, but the scheme was withdrawn when it met with stiff opposition from those who asserted that it would lead to intolerable confusion. Because of the disparity between the original, complicated forms used in Taiwan and the simplified forms employed on the mainland, there now exist, in essence, two sets of tetragraphs. This has caused some obstacles to communication between peoples from the two areas.

Another very important sphere of language reform activity in China centers on efforts to increase familiarity with the national language, Modern Standard Mandarin, and to diminish reliance upon regional languages such as Cantonese, Taiwanese, and Shanghainese. The latter are often referred to erroneously as "dialects," but this is due to misinterpretation of the Chinese term *fangyan* ("topolect" [speech pattern of a place]) as well as to certain nonlinguistic, political constraints. Even within the Han or Sinitic group, there are dozens of mutually unintelligible tongues, most of which have never been written down. This is not to mention the non-Sinitic languages such as Mongolian, Tibetan, Uighur, Zhuang, Yi, and the like, many of which have their own alphabets or syllabaries. The linguistic map of China is thus quite complicated. Statements to the effect that there are a billion speakers of "Chinese" are therefore as misleading as to say that there are a billion speakers of "European" worldwide or a billion speakers of "Indic." Pinyin has played a vital role in attempts to unify the pronunciation, vocabulary, and grammar of the various Han languages, but there is still a tremendous amount of work that needs to be done before someone from Peking will be able to converse with someone from Amoy, Swatow, or Fuchow.

The governmental organ charged with overseeing language reform in China is the Script Reform Committee (Wenzi Gaige Weiyuanhui), whose name, significantly, has recently been changed to the State Language Committee (Guojia Yuyan Wenzi Gongzuo Weiyuanhui). The new name may be interpreted as reflecting either decreasing government involvement in script reform or a resolve to broaden the committee's work. Judging from discussions with ranking members, it would seem that the chief aim of the reconstituted body is to transfer reform initiatives to the private sector, leaving the committee to act merely in an oversight capacity.

RESISTANCE TO TAMPERING WITH THE SCRIPT

The government was prompted to downplay its championing of language reform because of the strong opposition to it from certain circles of society. Particularly during the period of liberalization that began after the close of the Cultural Revolution, the hostility toward officially sponsored changes in the script

This is the cover of volume eleven of the Mandarin language text used in the six-year elementary school curriculum of the People's Republic of China. Note the use of Pinyin.

became more vociferous and more determined. It is curious that the most outspoken adversaries of language reform are to be found among the overseas communities. Living in countries where they are a minority, these émigrés keenly feel the need to assert their cultural identity. The tetragraphic script, as one of the most remarkable attributes of Chinese civilization, makes an excellent vehicle for the expression of nationalistic sentiments. Overseas spokesmen against language reform have contributed sizable sums of money toward the campaign to prevent further erosion of their cherished script. They are regularly given ample opportunity to express their opinions in such prominent newspapers as the *Peoples' Daily* and the *Guangming Daily*. By contrast, proponents of additional modifications of the script no longer have a nationwide forum in which to air their views. Instead, they work in small semiofficial or unofficial groups at the city or, at best, provincial level.

Echoing the overseas opponents to script reform are classicists and other conservative factions within China proper. They decry the publication of ancient texts in simplified characters, pointing out that such practices often lead to ambiguity and distortion. There are, as well, those who propose a return to more ancient styles of writing and the

The Vertical message in Canton is an exhortation to the people in Canton to remember those who worked hard and overcame many struggles in the oil fields. For political messages, the Chinese prefer simplified characters, which ably lend themselves to the horizontal widening that has become commonplace for such purposes. The first and fourth characters are the same as in the past; the remaining ones are simplified and originally contained from six to twelve additional character strokes. Although one of the reasons for using these simplified characters was to save ink (and paint) and to ease comprehension, many Chinese actually have greater difficulty in distinguishing the meaning of look-alike character sets or their elements. Note, for example, the similarities between the fourth and fifth character.

reintroduction of more classical materials in the curriculum. The nearest parallel that can be imagined for the West would be the restitution of Greek and Latin as a requirement for all pupils.

Whether living abroad or within the homeland, critics of language reform declare that further adjustments to the script will only serve to cut young Chinese off from their past even more decisively than they already are. Although all middle and high school students are minimally acquainted with ancient Chinese through exposure to set passages, much as we might learn a few lines of *Beowulf* or Chaucer in the original, only highly trained specialists can read the Confucian *Analects* or a T'ang essay with any degree of facility. The gap between Classical Chinese and Modern Standard Mandarin is at least as great as that between Sanskrit and Hindi or between Latin and Italian. If additional changes are imposed upon the Chinese script, traditionalists argue that it will be impossible for all but paleographers to make any sense whatsoever of the old texts.

The antireformers are also alarmed by the flood of vernacular translations of classical texts issued in Taiwan, China, Hong Kong, and Singapore. This tendency is tantamount to admission that Chinese can no longer read the original texts anyway and only adds fuel to the fires of those who demand a complete revamping of the script. In truth, the trend toward greater use of the written vernacular at the expense of the classical

goes back over one thousand years and would appear to be irreversible. With the final collapse of the imperial structure of government in 1911 and the abandonment of the examination system that went hand in hand with it, the demise of Classical Chinese as the officially sanctioned written medium was inevitable. This has naturally had a huge impact on the status of the tetragraphs, which are so perfectly well suited to Classical Chinese but are demonstrably less congenial to the vernaculars.

PROSPECTS FOR THE FUTURE

The principles governing the operation of the Chinese tetragraphs are almost identical to those on which the ancient Sumerian, Egyptian, and Hittite scripts were based. All four writing systems relied heavily on a mixture of phonophoric (i.e., "sound-bearing") components and semantic classifiers to convey meaning. It is no wonder that the Chinese people are experiencing hardship in trying to make their archaic writing system compatible with modern information procession technology, which is geared to phonetic scripts. Here lies the real source of the debate over the future of the tetragraphs: Can technology bend to accommodate the tetragraphs, or must the tetragraphs make concessions to technology?

Their affection for the beloved tetragraphs notwithstanding, the Chinese people as a whole have already permitted Pinyin to displace the traditional script in many applications, simply because it is more convenient and efficient. Hotel and hospital registration, Chinese braille and semaphore, book indices, library catalogs, and dozens of other instances could be cited. It is particularly revealing that both the Modern Standard Mandarin translation of the *Encyclopaedia Britannica* and the new *Great Chinese Encyclopedia (Zhongguo Da Baikequanshu)* have selected the Pinyin alphabetic order for their entries. This choice is sure to have a deep influence on the way Chinese view Pinyin vis-à-vis the characters. Above all, it is the computer that is pushing China further and further down the path to phoneticization. For modern word processing, the most user-friendly inputting methods, such as those devised by Tianma, Great Wall, and Xerox, all use Pinyin entry by word (not by syllable) and automatic conversion to tetragraphs. The danger, of course, is that there is but a short step from Pinyin in and tetragraphs out to Pinyin in and Pinyin out.

It is highly unlikely that China will ever legislate the romanization of its national language in the sweeping manner

子貢問 曰有一言而終身行之者乎子曰其恕乎
己所不欲勿施於人

Original Classical Chinese text written in the full (i.e., complicated) forms of the tetragraphs.

子贡问,"有可以一辈子奉行的一句话吗?"
孔子说,"就是宽大吧!自己不喜欢的事儿,
也不加在别人的身上."

Translation of the above into Modern Standard Mandarin and written in simplified tetragraphs.

Zigong wen, "You keyi yi beizi fengxing de yi ju hua ma?" Kongzi shuo, "Jiushi 'kuanda' ba! Ziji bu xihuan de shir, ye bu jiazai bieren shen shang." Romanized Modern Standard Mandarin.

[The disciple] Zigong asked, "Is there a motto which one can follow all one's life?" Confucius said, "How about 'generosity?' Do not do unto others what you yourself do not like." English translation.

---

adopted by the Turks on January 1, 1929. Instead, there will undoubtedly be a gradual spread of Pinyin in those areas where it is warranted for strictly economic reasons. For example, international Chinese telegraphy is largely carried out in Pinyin because it is much cheaper than paying operators to memorize and transmit accurately the arbitrary code consisting of 10,000 numbers that has hitherto been used to send tetragraphic telegrams within China. Alphabetic telegraphy has already begun to make inroads in China proper. Pinyin has also been used for more than twenty years in experimental attempts at machine translation.

At present, there in only one romanized journal, *Xin Tang*, published in China. Yet nearly all Chinese journals give their titles in Pinyin and in tetragraphs. Barring unforeseen political upheavals, it will not be long before other scattered Pinyin magazines spring up in various parts of China. A few mostly independent, locally financed newspapers employing a mixture of Pinyin and tetragraphs have begun to appear in the past few years. Educational authorities in the province of Honan have stressed Pinyin heavily in grade schools, and many parents, along with their children, are learning it enthusiastically.

A momentous step toward romanization was quietly taken in August 1988 when the rules for Pinyin orthography were promulgated without fanfare in *Language Construction*, the official organ of the State Language Commission. With these rules, word boundaries were established, punctuation was regularized, and grammatical usage defined. Pinyin now has the potential to become a fully functioning alphabetical script. Whether it does or not depends on many factors, including the extent to which English is used instead of Pinyin Mandarin in international networks and other instances where an alphabetical script is deemed superior to the tetragraphs. The most likely scenario is a long period, at least fifty to a hundred years, of digraphs in which the tetragraphic script and Pinyin coexist. During this period of digraphs, use of the tetragraphs and Pinyin will probably be restricted to those applications for which they are best suited—Pinyin for science, technology, commerce, and industry; the tetragraphs for calligraphy, classical studies, and literature.

The fate of Chinese characters has yet to be decided. Vietnam and North Korea have outlawed them, South Korea spurns them for most general purposes, and Japan restricts their number severely in favor of its two syllabaries

(*katakana, hiragana*) and *romaji* (romanization). Only in the land of their birth, China, do the tetragraphs still hold sway. Even there, however, these extraordinary signs have come under attack. They have been simplified, reduced in number, phonetically annotated, analyzed, decomposed, put in sequence according to hundreds of different finding methods, and otherwise abused by reformers whose sole purpose is to make them more amenable to the needs of modern society. However, the tetragraphs will not fade from the scene without a struggle. Regarded even by illiterates with utmost veneration, their disappearance would constitute a mortal blow against what many hold to be the very soul of Chinese civilization. It is a gross understatement to say that traditional Chinese intellectuals have a large stake in maintaining their tetragraphic writing system intact for as long as possible. On the other hand, China's most celebrated writer of the twentieth century, Lu Hsün, is reported to have declared that "if Chinese characters are not annihilated, China will perish."

Where the tetragraphs are concerned, emotions run high both among those who want to reform them out of existence and among those who wish to preserve them eternally. Both sides are earnestly committed to their cause and honestly believe they have China's best interest at heart. Ultimately though, one side will lose. Regardless of the outcome, China is undergoing a painful process of self-discovery. The tumultuous events that have recently wrecked China are part of a continuous adjustment to modernity. At the vortex of these struggles may be found the Chinese script and all that it represents.

ADDITIONAL READING

John DeFrancis, The Chinese Language: Fact and Fantasy, University of Hawaii Press, Honolulu, 1984.

—-, Nationalism and Language Reform in China, Princeton University Press, Princeton, 1950; reprint: Octagon, New York, 1972.

——, Visible Speech: The Diverse Oneness of Writing Systems, University of Hawaii Press, Honolulu, 1989.

I. J. Gelb, A Study of Writing, University of Chicago Press, Chicago, 1963, revised edition.

William Hannas, The Simplification of Chinese Character-Based Writing, University of Pennsylvania Ph.D. dissertation, 1988.

Robert K. Logan, The Alphabet Effect: The Impact of the Phonetic Alphabet on the Development of Western Civilization, William Morrow, New York, 1986.

Tom McArthur, Worlds of Reference: Lexicography, Learning and Language from the Clay

Tablet to the Computer, Cambridge University Press, Cambridge, 1986.

Victor H. Mair, "The Need for an Alphabetically Arranged General Usage Dictionary of Mandarin Chinese: A Review Article of Some Recent Dictionaries and Current Lexicographical Projects," Sino-Platonic Papers, 1 (November 1986).

Jerry Norman, Chinese, Cambridge University Press, Cambridge, 1988.

S. Robert Ramsey, The Languages of China, Princeton University Press, Princeton, 1987.

Robert Sanders, "The Four Languages of 'Mandarin,'" Sino-Platonic Papers, 4 (November 1987).

James Unger, The Fifth Generation Fallacy: Why Japan Is Betting Its Future on Artificial Intelligence, Oxford University Press, Oxford, 1987.

Article 24   *Sinorama*, January 1992

Red Envelopes: It's the Thought that Counts

Melody Hsieh

Past or present, in China or abroad, it is unlikely you could find a gift like the "red envelope," which in Chinese society has the capability of ascending to heaven or plumbing the depths of hell.

To attach a piece of red paper to a sacrificial offering depicts sending a red envelope to the deity, symbolizing a request for expelling evil or granting of good fortune. On Ghost Festival (the fifteenth day of the seventh month on the lunar calendar), you may burn some paper money wrapped in red paper to bribe the "good brothers" (ghosts), in hopes that they will be satiated and do no more mischief.

In the corporeal world, the red envelope is even more versatile: as a congratulatory gift for all manner of auspicious events, as a New Year's gift given by adults to children, as a "small consideration to the doctor before surgery or the birth of a child, as an expression of a boss's appreciation to his employees. . . . For whatever the giver may desire, the red envelope is just the thing to build up personal sentiment in the receiver.

In fairy tales, the fairy godmother can wave her magic wand and turn stone into gold or a pumpkin into a luxurious carriage. But calling it a magic wand is not so good as seeing it as a wand of hope for all mankind.

The red envelope is like the Chinese wand of hope, and it often carries limitless desires. To give a red envelope at a happy occasion is like embroidering a flower on a quilt; when meeting misfortune, to receive a red envelope is a psychological palliative which just might change your luck.

Whether it be congratulations, encouragement, sympathy, gratitude, compensation . . . just give a red envelope, and not only will the sentiment be expressed, substantive help will also have arrived.

The fact that the red envelope opens so many doors and is so versatile today also naturally has practical advantages. For marriages, funerals, birthdays and illness, send a gift. But choosing a gift is an art in itself, and you can wrack your brains and spend a whole day shopping, and you still won't know if the other person will like it or need it. That's not nearly as good as wrapping money in red paper, which on the one hand saves work and on the other is useful, so everybody's happy. Compared with the way Westerners give gifts, giving a red envelope may be lacking in commemorative sentiment, but it's a lot more practical.

Nevertheless, Chinese haven't always been so substantive." In fact, it is only in the last few decades that red envelopes have become so commonly used.

A Brilliant Fire Neutralizing the Year: Kuo Licheng, a specialist in popular culture who is today an advisor to *ECHO* magazine, points out that traditionally Chinese did not present gifts of money. For example, when a child reached one month old, friends and family would send a gold locket; when visiting a sick person, people would bring Chinese medicine; upon meeting for the first time, people would exchange rings or jade from their person as a greeting gift. . . . None of these carry, as the Chinese say, the "unpleasant odor of brass," implying penny-pinching greed.

No one knows when money began to replace these traditional gifts. The only certain continuous tradition of using money to express sentiment—perhaps the origin of the practice of combining usefulness and sentiment, material and spiritual—is the tradition of the "age neutralizing money" (cash given on New Year's day to children), which has been carried down to this day.

"In the past, the New Year's money was simply a piece of red paper attached to a gold yuan, or the use of a red twine to string together cash. When eating New Year's dinner, the money would be pressed beneath the stove, representing 'a brilliant fire, abundant wealth;' only after dinner would it be pulled out and handed out to the small children. The meaning is that, after undergoing a baptism of fire, it was hoped that it could expel evil and resolve dangers, so that the children could put the past behind them ("neutralize" the past) and grow up strong and healthy," says Juan Chang-juei, director of the Anthropology Committee of the Provincial Museum, laughing that in fact "age neutralizing money" should be called "age extension money."

The writer Hsiao Min lived in Peking before 1938. At that time she was just a little sprite of less than ten years old, but because the New Year is quite different today from what it was in the past, she has a very deep impression of the New Year's money.

She recalls that it was not easy to get the "age neutralizing money" in those days. The children had to kneel on the floor and kowtow, and your forehead had to touch the floor, and it would only count if it was hard enough to make a sound. "In the past, floors were made of rough concrete, and we kids often had to kneel until our knees hurt and knock our heads until we were dizzy, before we could get our New Year's money."

It was only with the spread of paper currency that the New Year's money became paper cash wrapped in red envelopes. The reason why the paper is red, or why in early days red thread was used, rather than white, green, or black, is from religious rituals.

Better Red Than Dread: Juan Chang-juei suggests that in primitive times, when man would see a bright red flower in a green field, he would find it quite eye-catching and delightful. so maybe this is why red is an "auspicious" color.

Further, red is the same as the color of blood, and since a sacrifice of blood has a lucky effect, red came to be ordained as having the meaning of avoiding ill-fortune.

"Before the red envelope form appeared, people 'carried red' to represent auspiciousness and evading evil," says Juan. He says that in previous generations people would attach a piece of red paper to a religious offering or to a wedding dress, in both cases having this meaning. It was only after cut-paper techniques had been invented that the red piece of paper was changed to the "double-happiness" character. Before paper was invented, perhaps they used red cloth or painted on some red pigment instead.

Juan Chang-juei reminds us that because red symbolizes the vitality of life, and all mankind in early times had their magic ways to expel evil, it was by no means unique to China, and in the distant past Westerners also considered red to represent auspiciousness.

For example, shortly after Columbus landed in America, he gave the local natives red cloth to wrap around their heads to show celebration. For this reason, in the past red was always the color used to wrap presents in the West, and only later did it evolve that many colors were used.

But Chinese are relatively more concerned about colors, as Confucius has said: "I hate the way purple spoils vermilion," Colors are divided into "appropriate" colors and "deviant" colors. Red

in this sense is the orthodox representation for good fortune, which cannot be altered lightly.

A Not Unreasonable Perquisite: As for using red envelopes as a small consideration in order to get the other person to do something on your behalf, very early on there was the "gratuity" for servants.

Kuo Li-cheng indicates that in novels like *The Golden Lotus*, you can often see in old style banquets that when the chef serves the main course the guest of honor must give the cook a "gratuity," using silver wrapped in red paper, to express appreciation to the host.

Or, family or friends might dispatch a servant to deliver a gift to your door. For the person giving the gift, it's only natural that they would send a servant, but for the person receiving the gift, the emissary is performing an unusual service, "so the recipient always had to ask the servant to bring back a letter of thanks, and to give a red envelope, which was called a *li* [strength] or *ching-shih* [respect for the emissary], to express gratitude for his legwork and provide transportation expenses." Kuo Li-cheng adds that the *ching-shih* was usually about 1/20th the value of the original gift, so this kind of red envelope was a reasonable perk as far as the servant was concerned.

"The ching-shih was originally a gift of money replete with sentiment, and it's only because modern people use it erroneously that the significance of the red envelope has become muddled," notes Kuo, who cannot help but lament that today "sending a red envelope" is synonymous with giving a bribe.

Some Chinese have adapted to circumstances, and since a red envelope can bribe a living, breathing human being, the effect should be no less in sucking up to the ghosts of the nether world. Today, in some rural townships in south and central Taiwan, especially at Ghost Festival, people wrap up the spirit money in red paper and burn it as an offering to the "good brothers" (spirits), hoping that after they get a red envelope and become a local god of wealth, they will no longer tamper with the affairs of men.

Juan Chang-juei says that in the past there was by no means the custom of sending red envelopes to ghosts, and this is a product of circumstance invented by Chinese in recent years.

Evangelical Red Envelopes: "The red envelope in and of itself is not to blame, and originally it was just to express a friendly intent, a symbol of sentiment," states Juan. Those who can afford to give red envelopes are always the older generation or the boss or the leader. He raises an example, noting that over the New Year's holiday in 1991, the Provincial Museum sponsored an opera appreciation activity for children. The day work began, the museum curator gave every one of the people who worked on it with him a red envelope, to thank his colleagues for giving up their holiday to work for the museum.

Hsiao Min also believes that there have also been some positive changes in the red envelope as it has evolved.

"In the past, the red envelope was just a simple red packet, without any characters printed on it. Today a lot of organizations, like restaurants or hotels, will imprint relevant auspicious phrases, and will give a set of red stationery to customers as a small gift at New Year's, to add a little more human feeling." For example, the Lai Lai Sheraton prints "May good fortune come, May wealth come, May happiness come" on its red envelopes, a play on the word lai (to come) in its name; steakhouses may print a golden bull, to make a deeper impression on their customers.

It's worth noting that even evangelical organizations cannot underestimate the attraction of a red envelope. Hsiao Min, a Christian, says that every time the passage to a new year approaches, churches will print their own red envelopes, which congregants can use at no charge. Because propitious proverbs from the Bible have been imprinted on the set, they are very popular among the congregants, so that supply can't keep up with demand. Since they integrate traditional customs, they can also help the evangelical church spread and adapt to local conditions.

"However, no matter how much money is in the red packet, how can a few pieces of paper currency take the place of or outweigh the feeling in one's heart?" says Hsiao Min. She concluded, that a small gift given with a big heart, the act of giving and receiving, and mutual affection are the real meanings of giving a red envelope.

TAIWAN ARTICLES

Article 25   *The New York Review of Books*, May 23, 1996

How China Lost Taiwan

Jonathan Mirsky

1.

For foreign correspondents who had been present in Peking's Tiananmen Square in June 1989, the events of the night of March 17, 1996, in the plaza in front of the Taipei city hall, showed more clearly than any other what the China-Taiwan crisis is about.

With the first truly democratic election in history for a Chinese president only a few days away, 20,000 supporters of the Democratic Progressive Party (DPP), which stands for full Taiwanese independence, were holding a rally in which the burning of an effigy of Deng Xiaoping was only a sideshow. Since 1989 none of us who have been reporting for years from the mainland had heard so many thousands of voices demanding that the national leader himself, in this case Taiwan President Lee Teng-hui, "get off the stage," or resign; they were also shouting, "Down with the Kuomintang" (KMT), the ruling party. These cries were only an amplification of what we heard nightly on Taipei's radio talk shows when callers described the KMT leaders as "hoodlums"—*liumang*—and President Lee Teng-hui, who was soon to be reelected, as the chief hoodlum.

Also reminiscent of Tiananmen Square seven years ago were the professors and young intellectuals who conducted seminars on the history of Taiwan with hundreds of young people squatting on the ground, while excited demonstrators buttonholed every foreign journalist in sight to tell them of the iniquities of the president and the KMT, and to explain that while Taiwanese were ethnic Chinese, politically they were independent. They wanted, the professors said, nothing to do with the Republic of China, an alien, defeated regime that had fled to Taiwan in 1949, uninvited by the original inhabitants, who today make up 85 percent of the population, and who have long been tired of rule by the heirs of Chiang Kai-shek's mainlanders.

There were armed police in and around Taipei's central square that eve-

ning, and for those who remembered how in Peking in 1989 the People's Liberation Army and the People's Armed Police smashed their way into Tiananmen Square, it was astounding to watch the Taipei police briskly directing traffic through the tumultuous throng as if it were no more than a crowd leaving a football match.

Peking would have called what was being declaimed in that square subversive, but it was something else. It was the kind of energetic, frantic, and occasionally libelous political discourse that one can still hear on Hyde Park Corner. It ranged from insistence on alternative views of Taiwan's status to charges that had a McCarthyist tinge, directed mostly against President Lee by militants from the DPP and his other main adversaries. Some said that Lee had been a Communist in his university days in Taipei. In fact he had probably belonged to left-wing groups that were anti-KMT. But listening to the excited crowds during that warm Taipei night, I wondered for a moment if Peking was not making a big mistake in attacking Lee so fiercely. Very few people in the crowd that was calling for independence as soon as possible said that they thought of Lee as what Peking calls a "splittist," someone who wants to permanently sever Taiwan from the mainland. But, as will become clear, Peking is right about Lee.

So far as I could see, the Taiwanese, who only ten years ago risked jail for having outspoken anti-KMT views, were now uninhibited about expressing every sort of opinion. The slogan painted on a bed sheet draped across the front of a van put it directly: "F— China."

The owner of a photography shop said, "Lee thinks that Taiwan is part of China. The KMT has controlled Taiwan for forty years, and we still don't even have a name, and we're not part of the United Nations. We are not Chinese, we are Taiwanese."

"Singaporeans are ethnic Chinese, too, but 98 percent of them say they are Singaporean, not Chinese," said a professor at the National University. "If Chinese come here, I'll fight."

A mild-mannered Taiwan-born law professor in his sixties, educated in Göttingen, and whose German was better than his Mandarin or English, came through the crowd on March 17 listening to one of the weekly "underground seminars" being broadcast on an unlicensed radio station. "Taiwan is Taiwan, not part of China," he said. "There is no evidence or law to show it's part of China. Lee wants to unify, but that would be death." He made a pistol with his hand. "And we don't want to be dead."

The entire event surged with the same political euphoria that we saw in Tiananmen Square, but without any bloody consequences whatever, and this seemed to underline the challenge that the Taiwan elections pose for Peking.

The Chinese Communist state in recent decades has had to deal with "splittists" in Tibet, Xinjiang, and Mongolia, but the peoples involved, although called Chinese by the regime, both linguistically and in other basic respects, come from non-Chinese cultures. The men and women demanding independence in Taiwan, however, speak a Chinese dialect, read Chinese characters, and come from an unquestionably Chinese Confucian, Buddhist, and Taoist background. Their island had been under rulers from the Chinese mainland until 1895, when the Japanese took it over. Only after the defeated Japanese left in 1945 did Chiang Kai-shek's government take control of Taiwan.

When the people I talked to said, "We are Taiwanese, not Chinese," they were making a political statement; they were not much different from the American colonists of the eighteenth century who demanded freedom from the Britain where many of them had originated. Here lies China's danger. Although for 2000 years there were long periods of disunity when the country fell into independent or semi-independent kingdoms or warlord territories, most regional potentates were pretenders to the imperial throne and advocates of unity. In Taiwan, the marching men, women, and children were demanding something much more limited: an independent island. But the demand was limited only with respect to physical size. The banner that said "F— China" and the signs saying "One China, One Taiwan" posed a threat to Peking. So did the steady renaming of streets and parks which now have local, even aboriginal names, like Katagelan, the name of a tribe, replacing KMT names like Reunification Road; the disgusted older people originally from the mainland, steadily declining in proportional numbers and influence, resolutely refuse to learn the new names.

Except for a few firebrands from the DPP advocating total independence, no one I met anywhere on Taiwan, including its outer islands, bragged about beating back the mainland invaders. A war, it was generally agreed, would be horrible. But Taiwan has shown itself well able to resist Chinese pressure. Unlike Hong Kong it is guarded from immediate mainland assault by an excellent army, by the Taiwan Strait, and by the possibility of American defense. Nor is it encumbered, as Hong Kong is, by an unbreachable treaty which makes reunification inevitable on a certain day. Whatever Taipei and Peking may say about ultimate reunification, the last real military collision between them came in 1958, when mainland shore batteries bombarded Quemoy and Matsu.

What happened to interrupt this seeming coexistence, and in so spectacular a fashion that 620 international journalists came to a small island with a population of about 21 million to watch 14 million of them vote? Part of the attraction was the possibility of an accident which could transform Peking's war games into some sort of battle, possibly involving what US Defense Secretary Perry called "the best damn navy in the world."

The new crisis over Taiwan began last spring when President Lee announced he would attend, in June, a college reunion at Cornell, where he had received his doctorate in agricultural economics in 1968. Peking demanded that this leading opponent of its claim to Taiwan should not be given a visa for this trip and, in May, Warren Christopher assured Chinese Foreign Minister Qian Qichen that he would not. When the Republican Congress insisted that Lee receive a visa after all, Christopher had to explain to the Chinese that under American democracy there were limitations on presidential power. This was an embarrassment for Qian, and something which China's leaders did not want to believe,

although they have experts on America who could have explained it to them if they had been willing to listen.

Peking's leaders are convinced anyway that in its policy toward China the US is waging "smokeless warfare" and that it favors a "peaceful evolution" of Chinese communism into something else. They believe that Washington was secretly encouraging Taiwan to proclaim de jure independence. Lee had already offered the United Nations $1 billion in exchange for membership in June 1995. It looked, in Peking, as if Lee was spurning a reasonable-sounding offer of a deal made the year before by President Jiang Zemin. Under that deal Taiwan would accept a long-term plan for reunification—but for how long a term no one can say. By making this offer, and then being thwarted by Taiwan and the US when Lee made his fateful trip to Cornell, Jiang put himself at the mercy of the saber rattlers in the army.

The apparent collaboration between Lee and the US in administering a snub to the Peking leaders has been repeatedly mentioned in the Chinese press for a year, as if to justify Peking's subsequent show of force in the Taiwan Strait, the cancellations of high-level meetings with the US, the recall of the Chinese ambassador from Washington, and cessation of discussions with Taiwan on shipping and trade guarantees.

Throughout July and August of 1995, with only mild protests from Washington, China fired missiles into the waters near Taiwan and conducted war games that included mock landings and the use of live ammunition. There was a brief lull in December, when candidates favoring eventual reunification did well in elections for Taiwan's legislature. Meanwhile Peking was concentrating what eventually amounted to 150,000 soldiers along the coast directly facing Taiwan, and menacing the islands of Quemoy, Little Quemoy, and Matsu, from which one can easily see the mainland. In March, with the presidential election a few weeks away, Chinese missiles again began landing in the ocean near Taiwan. To express the army's often stated conviction that its "holy task" was to maintain Chinese unity, the big war games began, with thousands of troops charging ashore on mainland beaches resembling Taiwan's. The US dispatched two naval battle groups to the western Pacific, the largest such force seen in those waters since the Vietnam war. Much cited in Peking was Deng Xiaoping's statement of a few years ago that China would use force if Taiwan attempted to go independent.

2.

The plain fact is that Taiwan *is* independent, with a few anomalous limitations. It has a flag, a national anthem, an army, and a government which now includes a democratically elected president. Few governments recognize it, although it is one of the world's major traders. But no matter how many billions President Lee offers, the United Nations is not going to enrage China by even considering some sort of recognition for Taiwan.

Taiwan, moreover, has abandoned since the 1980s any claim that it has the right to assert by force its status as the legitimate government of all of China, including Tibet and Mongolia. And this comes close to abandoning as well the concept of One China, including Taiwan, to which Richard Nixon agreed in the early Seventies. The idea of One China was reasserted in 1979 when the Carter administration gave full recognition to Peking and broke its defense treaty with Taiwan, while continuing to assert that the US continued to oppose "any resort to force or other forms of coercion that would jeopardize the security of the people of Taiwan." This promise lay behind the "constructive ambiguity" of American statements made this past March, as the *Independence* and the *Nimitz* cruised closer and closer to the Taiwan Strait. The White House and the State Department insist that Peking was repeatedly warned that its military threats were being viewed very seriously.

Such ambiguity, creative or not, explains why no country, including the United States, has accused China of breaking international law with its war games and missile firing, which, after all, were conducted in the vicinity of what most countries officially say is a Chinese province. All the US has been able to claim is that the games and missiles are violent threats that disturb the peace of the region, which is true enough. What no American official will say out loud is that Taiwan has been increasingly independent since 1949, and that, as Lee Teng-hui likes to say, the Communist regime in Peking has not ruled the island for a single minute. Even the Taiwanese presidential candidates urging reunification became vague when asked when it might take place. They said it would take perhaps decades, even centuries, and then only when "the system changed" on the mainland.

Until Lee announced this election, a genuinely popular one, Peking was able to swallow a good deal of Taiwanese independence because it was informal. At international meetings delegates from the island sat behind little signs with such formulas on them as "China-Taipei," and Taiwan's athletes competed at the Olympics and Asian Games with similar words on their banners. Like the CCP, which it historically preceded, the exiled KMT is a Leninist structure, although it is now barely a skeleton. Its presidents, Chiang Kai-shek, his son Chiang Ching-kuo, and Lee Teng-hui, were chosen by KMT conclaves. When democratic elections were allowed during the 1980s for county and provincial legislatures, and for mayors and governors, these could be dismissed by Peking as local activities peculiar to Taiwan Province. But the president who was elected in March uses the word "national." Independence is bad enough; real elections for a government spat in Peking's face by undermining the increasingly dubious myth of "China-Taiwan."

Taiwan also poses a second traditional problem for Chinese rulers: an unreliable frontier region could be a base, or entry point, for foreign invaders. This explains a particular form of abuse. Taiwan's President Lee, Hong Kong's Governor Chris Patten, and Tibet's Dalai Lama have been singled out for personal insults—"criminal," "splittist," "whore"—which would never be directed at Bill Clinton, no matter how much he were disliked in Peking. This abuse helps to maintain the Big Lie: that the inhabitants of what is in fact an estranged region long for reunion with the motherland, from which ill-intentioned leaders keep them divided.

Peking has made a demon of Lee Teng-hui. He is particularly irritating because he is not an easy man to pin down. He insists he is not creating an independent Taiwan, yet during the campaign he would shout, "We are going to be masters of our own country. Since the beginning of Chinese history this is the greatest year." He maintains—just barely—the central dogma that Taiwan is a part of China—but he says that reunification must wait for a change in the system on the mainland. He will, in short, only settle for an independent nation-province that will retain its independence until the Communist Party vanishes.

Lee was born in 1923 near Taipei when Taiwan was a Japanese colony, which it had been since 1895, when China lost the island in the Sino-Japanese war. He had an early Japanese education, as well as a period in an elite Japanese university during World War II. His brother was killed fighting in the Im-

perial Japanese Army. Lee's most fluent second language, after Taiwanese, a southern Chinese dialect, is Japanese, and his Mandarin Chinese is awkward. In interviews which have caused him difficulty in Taiwan and in China, Lee told Japanese journalists how close he still felt to Japan. But he maintains he is an ardent Presbyterian, while also comparing himself to Moses, who led his people to freedom, and to the goddess Matsu, the traditional protectress of Taiwan. He claims, too, that he is a thoroughly modern man and he gives his traditionalist KMT colleagues lectures on science and technology. But he also runs a traditionally corrupt political machine.

Lee has been a minister in KMT governments since 1972. He takes credit, along with his predecessor, Chiang Kai-shek's son President Chiang Ching-kuo, who died in 1988, for turning Taiwan into a democratic state. He also gave up Taiwan's claim to retake the mainland, and encouraged trade, negotiations over investment, and communications with Peking, where some Taiwanese politicians have had talks with President Jiang Zemin. He made it clear that pro-Taiwanese plane hijackers on the mainland, who at one point were seizing a passenger jet every week or so and diverting it to Taiwan, would be returned across the strait. While Taiwan businesses have invested hundreds of millions in the mainland, no one really thinks Lee was moving closer to Peking politically. Whatever he did made Taiwan seem strong and its President statesmanlike. He said recently that in the present crisis "cutting off talks is them; missiles is them; objections to our elections is them."

Lee's main adversary in the presidential race, Peng Ming-min of the DPP, got 20 percent of the vote and certainly would have won more if Peking's threats had not frightened voters into supporting President Lee and the status quo. Peng also had an elite Japanese education, and he says his missing arm is the result of an American bombing raid. His Democratic Progressive Party opposes unification at any time: "All we have to do is affirm we are already independent," he says. For years Peng was either a political prisoner of the KMT or in political exile, and he disputes Lee's claim to be a political messiah. Just before the election, asked whether the KMT deserved credit for Taiwan's democracy, Peng said, "For fifty years Taiwanese paid an enormous price in execution, torture, prison, and exile. We have thousands of martyrs. The KMT couldn't resist the pressure."

It is hard to know where to assign the main credit for the transformation. Antonio Chiang, for years Taiwan's most interesting independent journalist, told me, "We used to have 10,000 political prisoners here, many of them on our own little gulag, Green Island. Their sentences amounted to seven thousand years. All the leaders of the DPP have been in prison. Not many governments would open up a system like that without there having been violence or the threat of violence." (I remember from my own student days in Taipei that it seemed to foreigners a daring act even to utter the name "Green Island.")

Peking sees clearly what Lee Teng-hui has been doing. The time is not far off, perhaps only a few years, when Taiwan's independence could move from de facto to de jure, when President Lee and his successors would no longer have to use university reunions or international sports meetings as excuses for foreign appearances, and threats of force against Taiwan would be regarded as threats to world peace.

An invasion now, except of one of the offshore islands, would be impossible. In two or three years; although at great cost, the people's Liberation Army will be able to crash ashore on Taiwan's beaches, but what it would do then with a population in which millions of men have received military training no one can say. It is true, too, that it can bring all kinds of other pressures to bear on Taiwan, attempting to strangle it economically—although this would damage its own economy, in which Taiwan has been a major investor—and to isolate it from international contact. This threat of isolation lies behind the constant attempts by President Lee to put the island on the international map.

And here lies Peking's great failure this past March. President Jiang is lucky that he does not preside over a democratic government. By now, a British-style government would have fallen. An American-style government would have been subject to major upheaval, with many political resignations and a reshuffling among military officials.

Without the Chinese threats, Lee Teng-hui would probably have received 40 percent of the vote and won the presidency with a shaky mandate. Instead he got 54 percent, a percentage referred to even by Lee's supporters as "Jiang's gift" to them. Taiwan's voters did not stay away from the polls; upward of 70 percent voted. Those who had been hankering after some sort of rapprochement with the mainland, even if a very distant one, are thinking again. It will be hard now for the exponents of the barren notions of "Asian" or "Confucian" values—championed by authoritarians in China, Singapore, Indonesia, Burma, and Hong Kong—to assert convincingly that what Asians prefer is stern but just government which satisfies their material needs and that they distrust democracy, which they fear leads to what Peking calls *luan,* or "chaos." In Hong Kong, Peking's war games and missiles accelerated fears of what what will happen when Peking takes charge in 1997. Conversely, it can no longer be said that Peking will never behave really badly in Hong Kong because that would upset Taiwan about its future.

Finally, not only did Peking's threats install Taiwan on the mental map of millions of international newspaper readers and television watchers. They made Taiwan an important election-year issue in the US and forced Bill Clinton to make a difficult military decision when he moved the two aircraft carriers, although he was probably also receiving Chinese assurances that there would be no immediate invasion.

What is dangerous about this outcome is that China has a weak polity; it is beset by huge official corruption, and peasant and industrial-worker unrest, and it is encumbered by useless state industrial enterprises which devour much of its internal budget but cannot be dismantled because they employ hundreds of thousands of workers. Ambitious and uninspiring leaders maneuver within this unstable environment, attempting to look tough abroad while Deng Xiaoping slips from the scene. This means that the coercive tactics toward Taiwan will continue, even though China is defying what might look like common sense, risking international obloquy, isolation, and pariah status. Hence Deng's willingness to order the Tiananmen crackdown in full view of the international press; he did so because the survival of the Party was at stake. Hence the continued Chinese practice of stealing foreign intellectual property, although this keeps China out of the World Trade Organization; the fact is that the army runs many of the factories which pirate compact discs and software. Hence the imprisoning of virtually all political dissidents; it causes considerable irritation in diplomatic dealings, but the regime still sees any fundamental criticism as a dangerous virus. And hence the threats to Taiwan; for no territory, from Tibet to Hong Kong, can be allowed to harbor thoughts of

genuine semi-autonomy, except economically. The danger for Peking is that such hopes could spread to rich regions around Shanghai and Canton, which already display a degree of defiance of the central government.

Until this spring there were usually some reporters from the mainland stationed on Taiwan, although what they published was limited largely to economic matters. There were none there this spring, although if they had been there and seen what was actually happening they could not have written about it for their papers. During the elections in Taipei and on Quemoy I watched, on local stations, up to half an hour of more or less straightforward news from Peking, with plenty of statements attacking Taiwan. There was no news from Taiwan on mainland TV during the same period, although there was editorial commentary attacking Lee and a little coverage of the elections. After Lee won, official spokesmen in Peking said the elections were a defeat for the pro-independence forces, but they did not note that Lee and Peng, the two candidates who one way or another represented keeping Taiwan as it is, took well over 70 percent of the vote. The pro-unification candidates did very badly.

Andrew Nathan of Columbia University thinks Peking will resume its military pressure on Taiwan, apply economic pressure, and perhaps impose some sort of blockade. "By acting decisively, Beijing believes it can isolate Taiwan, impose unbearable pain, and force capitulation. China's strategy is therefore to escalate military pressure in order to test US resolve and locate Taiwan's breaking point."

Taiwan officials say they hope the US will provide military defense but the people I talked to have little expectation of this. On a visit to Quemoy, I cycled up to a farmer raking his garden and asked him what he expected from the US. "Nothing. They will suit themselves. Look what happened in Iraq. They actually defeated the Iraqi army, right? Then what did the Americans do? They went home. Saddam is still there, right? Forget the Americans." He gestured toward the Fukien coast, clearly visible across the water. "We definitely don't want a war with them."

3.

During its conflict with the mainland, Taiwan itself should not be idealized. It is indeed a doughty island democracy defying the world's biggest dragon. Its citizens are

wildly enthusiastic about having an open politics and they genuinely seem to believe in the principle of live and let live. Foreign correspondents used to living in cities on the mainland appreciated the courtesy, friendliness, and the intensity of Taiwanese political discourse; no one first looks over his shoulder when he denounces Taiwanese leaders.

But one of the reasons that Jiang Zemin's "gift" to Lee Teng-hui—the gift of issuing a challenge that rallied people to Lee's side—was so valuable was that it blunted the debate about the island's official corruption. By bringing into political life more than twenty years ago the long-excluded Taiwanese, who since 1949 have had most of the money in Taiwan, the KMT, itself always a corrupt party, also introduced into the heart of government the Taiwanese "black societies," Mafia-style gangster syndicates with strong clan and territorial power. "We have a saying," said Yang Taishuenn, an academic and member of the Taiwan provincial assembly. "If you don't get elected you go to jail." Many of these gangsters were appointed heads of county governments by the KMT. Some 140 members of the 175-strong provincial assembly have been indicted for buying votes and almost all of them were found guilty. They will probably never be sentenced.

The same holds true for Taiwan's county and city councils and for their speakers. At the recent gigantic funeral of the *capo di tutti capi* of these gangs, shot dead while eating in a restaurant, most of the important political figures and parties, including the KMT, sent wreaths and representatives. "Black" candidates even ran in the elections on explicit gangster-protecting platforms.

Several members of the overseas Chinese democratic groups who have been in exile since Tiananmen, including Chai Ling, the "commander-in-chief" of the protesters, the brilliant journalist Liu Binyan, and Su Shaozhi, once the director of the State Council's Marxism-Leninism-Mao Zedong Thought Institute, came to Taiwan to observe the elections. All agreed that something astonishing had happened there politically, something for which many on the mainland are yearning. But several also said, not for the record, that they were horrified by the omnipresence of official corruption. If President Lee, who leads the corrupt KMT, which also owns the main newspapers and television stations, fails to control and cut back this corruption during the next four years, Taiwan will come to resemble Japan: democratic and deeply corrupt. In Japan this combination has badly corroded democracy.

Just before the voting I discussed the election's significance with Liu Binyan and Su Shaozhi. They have been condemned as two of the "Black Hands" behind the Tiananmen uprising in the spring of 1989 and now live in exile in Princeton. Liu was twice expelled from the Party and spent years in detention until he left China in 1987.

"What Peking fears here is independence," he said. "If Taiwan became a real country it would be an obvious, concrete loss by the Party, something they couldn't hide or explain away. They can get plenty of support for their Taiwan policy in China, except among high-level intellectuals. Most Chinese know nothing about what happens in Taiwan, and they were so brainwashed for years that words like 'Chiang Kaishek' and 'Kuomintang' still make them

anxious. There is also a kind of ignorant superficial nationalism in China, which has nothing to do with making the country better. Its believers insist that Taiwan like Tibet must not be torn away from China."

It is ignorant to blame Jiang Zemin alone, Liu said. "The whole Central Committee agreed on the military pressure, too. It's not like 1979, when it was Deng Xiaoping personally who ordered the invasion of Vietnam against the advice of the Army, and he was powerful enough not to get blamed for the defeat."

Su Shaozhi, once one of the Party's leading intellectuals, was expelled for pressing for ideological reform in the direction of Western-style democracy. He escaped from Peking to Holland immediately after June 4, 1989.

"I just telephoned a friend in Peking," he said, "and asked him what the Party really feared in Taiwan. He said it was

Mr. De." Mr. De was the code word for Democracy used in 1919 by university students insisting that to save itself from imperialism China needed democracy.

"At first the Party got a lot of support for this action near Taiwan because many Chinese," he said, "including democrats in the exile community, believe in reunification more than they believe in democracy."

According to Su, the leaders in Peking made two mistakes in their expectations of what would happen. "Taiwan hasn't surrendered and the US came to help. They never expected Clinton to do something so decisive. So they have a problem now: a rebellious province with an army. They have lost the emotional tie with the people of Taiwan; I have friends in Taiwan who were in favor of some sort of reunification. No longer."

—April 25, 1996

Article 26

Free China Review, January 1988

Vibrant, Popular Pantheon

Tong Fung-wan

Dr. Tong Fung-wan is academic dean and an associate professor in the history of religion at Taiwan Theological Seminary.

Traditionally every agricultural society has a polytheistic view of God, and this is seen as well in the Taiwanese religious experience. The Taiwanese pantheon originated in Southern China, especially the provinces of Fukien and Kwangtung, and came to the island with Chinese immigrant believers over a 300 year period. Today, it is clear that different members of the pantheon have taken root in different localities throughout Taiwan.

Nowadays, the Taiwanese, 85 percent of whom are descendants of those original immigrants from Fukien and Kwangtung, rely on this pantheon as they seek secular security, set their ideals, and earn their living. Such religious phenomena are an integral part of Chinese tradition and culture. As such, the pantheon offers an insight into the thought and activity of contemporary Chinese on Taiwan.

The Taiwanese pantheon exhibits the characteristics of anthropomorphism, geographical relatedness, efficacy, and laissez-faire.

Anthropomorphism

All kinds of objects can be anthropomorphized as personal gods or goddesses. For instance, there are the gods or goddesses of *heaven*, such as the heavens themselves, the five directions of the firmament, and those of the sun, moon, and stars, and of lightning, thunder, rain, and wind; of *earth*, including the earth itself, the five directions of the earth's foundation, the seas, waters (rivers, lakes), mountains, stones, and plants; of *animals*, especially the dragon, phoenix, turtle, snake, tiger, lion, pig, dog, and cat; plus *fetishes*, such as bones of the dead, packages of incense, idols, icons, written spells, and magic tools; and *spirits of the dead*, including those of ancestors, sages and heroes, wandering spirits, and fierce ghosts.

Moreover, there are social levels in the kingdom of the pantheon, just as there are in human society, and the members must have their needs provided for; this

is made easier by assigning them titles like those in the mundane world.

Titles fall into two general categories, official and familial. The former include the following: Emperor (or more specifically, the Jade Emperor); King (King Hsieh); General (General Fan); and Commander-in-Chief (Commander-in-Chief Kang). These are all gods.

There are also high-ranking goddesses: Queen (Queen Tien); Princess (The Princess of the Jade Emperor); and Madam (Madam Cheng Huang).

The latter category of family includes the male god, Grandfather (Grandfather Earth), and Grandmother (Grandmother Wenchou, who is a local Matsu); and Maiden (Maiden Seven Stars).

Gods, like humans, require a home. Thus, geographical positioning and maintenance of temples is a key part of Taiwanese folk religion.

Temples are the houses of gods and goddesses. More correctly stated, they are actually their palaces or courts.

Birthdays for the gods or goddesses are an explicit result of anthropomorphism. Examples are the 9th day of the 1st month for Grandfather Tien, the 23rd day of the 3rd month for Matsu,

Ching Shui Tsu Shih—Protective God of Anshi people from Fukien Province.

Geographical Relatedness

Taiwanese people have a strong sense of being related to their own locality. Such a tendency also expresses itself in worship objects, especially the so-called local protective pantheon. Generally the local protective gods are connected with the immigrants' homelands in Fukien and Kwangtung. People worship them as an expression of community identity as they seek to earn their living. Some especially popular local protective gods are as follows:

People and their locality
Chuanchou people, Fukien
Changchou people, Fukien
Anshi people, Fukien
Hakka people, Kwangtung

Protective gods
Kuang Tse Tsun Wang
Kai Chang Sheng Wang
Ching Shui Tsu Shih
San Shan Kuo Wang

Efficacy

Taiwanese go to temples looking for security. They explicitly require efficacy from their gods. Any god that gives people the blessings they want earns great quantities of "burning incense." On the other hand, if the god they approach cannot help them (or so the worshippers feel), he is left alone so that only a spider's web keeps him company in his temple.

To such a tendency as this, Max Mueller gave the term "kathenotheism," for people choose their worship objects according to their own likes and dislikes. "Matsu could not help me, so I went to ask Grandfather Earth, but when I doubted his efficacy I prayed to the Tiger God." Everyone seeks his gods or goddesses according to how he feels at the time. So this kind of kathenotheistic current causes people to fall into superstition—the members of the pantheon are their servants, seemingly like the genie in the Arabian Nights whom people urge to do what they want. Obviously, the relationship between gods and men is upside down: the gods are the servants and men are the lords of the pantheon.

Laissez-Faire or "Doing Your Own Thing"

There is a Taiwanese saying: "It is better to believe in something than not to believe in anything." This attitude makes Taiwanese believe in all kinds of gods. For instance: Buddhas, bodhisattvas,

the double 7th for Maiden Seven Stars, and the double 9th for King Chung Yang. Almost every day of the year as reckoned by the lunar calendar is the birthday of some member of the Taiwanese pantheon.

Offerings are important to the pantheonic society. Like humans, the gods and goddesses need food, clothing, and money for their daily existence. Generally people offer pigs and goats to the pantheon when the most important festivals are underway. Considerable quantities of delicious Chinese food are first offered to the pantheon, then the worshippers eat what remains. Moreover, large amounts of paper money are burned for their use; sometimes there are even offerings of new clothes decorated with old-fashioned gold medals for the gods.

Family, according to tradition, is also a key heavenly institution. The gods may have their wives and children living together in a joyful family atmosphere. People give their children the

titles of princes or princesses, and call their wives "madam." Unfortunately a god always has many wives, such as Madam Cheng Huang No. 1 and No. 4. It is unclear whether or not family quarrels and divorce often occur in the polygamous society of the gods.

Clearly, pantheonic society is a copy of human society. People follow their own ideals when constructing their pantheonic kingdom. And people's needs and customs are reflected in the pantheon as well. Nevertheless, the traditional ideology still remains in place. So far the gods of the pantheon have not become Westernized to the extent of wearing Western jackets and neckties; they continue wearing the old-fashioned robes of officials. In addition, worshippers do not offer Western food or U.S. dollars to the Taiwanese pantheon—they are as much strangers to the intricacies of knives and forks as they are to the customs of George Washington and Abraham Lincoln.

and arhats in Buddhism; Confucius in Confucianism; Lao Tzu and the pantheon in Taoism; even Jesus and Mohammed have been accepted as their protective gods.

In olden times, people talked about three religions (Confucianism, Taoism and Buddhism) in one, but today it is five or six (the previous three, plus Christianity, Islam, and Shintoism) in one. Even now, new gods or goddesses are freely coming into being all the time. All divine beings, even dead spirits or demons, may be worshipped if they can help people live in peace.

About 15 years ago a serious flood occurred in the central part of Taiwan, causing many deaths. Among the dead was a young girl, whose body was washed down Chuohsui River and found by villagers. They were afraid that her spirit would harm them, because according to traditional beliefs, it was thought that due to her unnatural death her spirit would be exceptionally malevolent. So they began worshipping her as a goddess called Chang Yu Koo. Through the propaganda of shamans and sorcerers, the place suddenly became a sacred spot and attracted many pilgrims from all over the island. This extraordinary religious phenomenon lasted for several years until it finally ended in police intervention.

Furthermore, people in Taiwan also believe in the pantheon that comes from Chinese classical histories and fiction. This includes figures from *The Legend of Deification, Pilgrims to the West* also known as *The Adventures of Monkey,* and *The Romance of the Three Kingdoms.*

So far, for example, the Prince of No Cha in *The Legend of Deification,* Sun Wu Kung or the Great Monkey in *Pilgrims to the West,* and Kuan Kung in *The Romance of the Three Kingdoms* are among the most important gods in Taiwan. No Cha and Sun Wu Kung are both fictional characters, only Kuan Kung is an historical figure from the Three Kingdoms era (220–265 A.D.).

From these examples we can clearly see how Taiwanese do as they please in religious beliefs.

Social Structures in the Taiwanese Pantheon

Before considering the social structures in the Taiwanese pantheon, it would be useful to examine two diagrams that illustrate the external expression of Taiwanese folk beliefs. These will help put

Lin Bor-liang

Kuanyin, Goddess of Mercy, is immensely popular in Taiwan, with over 450 temples in her honor.

the following analysis into more understandable form:

Diagram One

Diagram One. The inner circle represents the three major religions found in Taiwan: Taoism, Confucianism, and Buddhism. these make up the core of folk

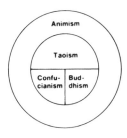

belief, but Taoism occupies half of the circle to demonstrate its stronger influence on folk religion generally speaking.

The outer circle in the first diagram is labeled "animism." This represents an operational hypothesis to describe folk

beliefs, including all the elements of primitive religious phenomena. These include, for example, nature worship, ancestor worship, fetishism, and magic.

Diagram Two

Diagram Two. The innermost circle has five key objects of worship:
  A. Grandfather Heaven
  B. Grandfather Earth
  C. The Sea Goddess, Matsu
  D. The Healing God, Ta Tao Kung
  E. The Pestilence God, Wang Yeh
The second circle from the center in Diagram Two represents the next eche-

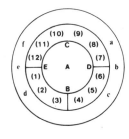

lon of 12 important gods and goddesses in Taiwan:

The Gods of Confucianism: (1) Confucius, (2) Kuan Kung, and (3) Koxinga;

The Gods of Buddhism: (4) Buddhas (Trinity Buddhas), (5) Bodhisattvas (Kuanyin and Ti Tsang), (6) Ching Shui Tsu Shih (who is the protective god of Anshi people in Fukien Province) and 18 Arhats;

The Gods of Taoism: (7) Lu Tung Pin, (8) San Chieh Kung, (9) Hsuan Tien Shang Ti, (10) Shen Nung Ta Ti, (11) Prince No Cha, and (12) Wang Mu Niang Niang.

The third, outer circle of the second diagram represents various categories of popular worship in Taiwan;

(a) Ancestor worship or filial piety;

(b) Animism, which includes the four major sub-categories of: Nature worship (sun, moon, stars; the five directions of both heaven and earth; thunder, lightning, storm, and wind; mountains and the waters of the four seas; and animals, vegetables, stones, and the earth); Worship of the Dead (demons, unnatural dead, hungry ghosts, malevolent spirits, dead relatives, historical heroes, and sages); Fetishism (natural fetishes such as dead bones and turtle shells, and artificial fetishes such as idols and magic tools); and Magic (shamans, exorcists, spells, and charms);

(c) Local protecting gods and goddesses;

(d) Gods and goddesses protecting various occupations;

(e) Gods and goddesses from myths and legends; and

(f) Foreign gods and goddesses.

Both diagrams present a summary of Taiwanese folk beliefs. The first indicates their syncretic religious content; the second expresses the totality of worshipped objects.

The latter diagram has especially deep implications for Taiwanese religious life. The innermost circle represents the core of folk beliefs. Grandfather Heaven is

Tong Fung-wan

Tai Tzu Yeh belongs to the third level of military command in the pantheon.

the highest god, expressing Taiwanese dependence upon Heaven for earning a living. Grandfather Earth is a production god, for Taiwanese work very hard and have an intimate relationship with the soil. The Sea Goddess, Matsu, is a sacred Mother of the Taiwanese people, reflecting the adventurous spirit of their ancestors who crossed the terrible Taiwan Straits. The Healing God, Ta Tao Kung, is a Preserver of the Taiwanese, reflecting the need of the people for security. The Pestilence God, Wang Yeh, is a Destroyer—so people hold a great festival every there years to humor him and prevent pestilence.

The second circle contains 12 gods and goddesses in three groups belonging to Confucianism, Buddhism and Taoism. Among them, the members of the Taoist pantheon are greater in number than those of the other two. It is easy to find very strong sectarian Taoist influence in Taiwanese folk religion.

The outer circle shows the popular pantheon in Taiwan. Clearly the pantheon in this circle has religious phenomena which are psychologically primitive, traditional, and syncretic. It may even be called a new pantheon in the making, for today Jesus, Mohammed, Sun Yat-sen, and Chiang Kai-shek are all accepted as new gods in Taiwanese folk beliefs. This shows the unrestricted laissez-faire nature of local religious attitudes.

Tong Fung-wan

The Ti Tsang Bodhisattva is a civil administrator commanding 10 courts in hell.

The Military Organization of the Taiwanese Pantheon

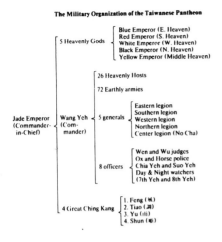

Jade Emperor (Commander-in-Chief)			
	5 Heavenly Gods		Blue Emperor (E. Heaven)
			Red Emperor (S. Heaven)
			White Emperor (W. Heaven)
			Black Emperor (N. Heaven)
			Yellow Emperor (Middle Heaven)
	Wang Yeh (Commander)	26 Heavenly Hosts	
		72 Earthly armies	
		5 generals	Eastern legion
			Southern legion
			Western legion
			Northern legion
			Center legion (No Cha)
		8 officers	Wen and Wu judges
			Ox and Horse police
			Chia Yeh and Suo Yeh
			Day & Night watchers
			(7th Yeh and 8th Yeh)
	4 Great Ching Kang		1. Feng (風)
			2. Tiao (調)
			3. Yu (雨)
			4. Shun (順)

Tong Fung-wan

King Hsieh (left) and General Fan (right) serve as adjuncts to Commander Cheng Huang.

The Hierarchy of the Taiwanese Pantheon

At the apex of the Taiwanese pantheon is Grandfather Heaven, also known as the Jade Emperor. Next in power and importance are two gods who sit at either hand, the God of Life (The Southern Star God) who is Left Prime Minister of Heaven, and the God of Death (The Northern Star God) who is Right Prime Minister of Heaven.

Next there is a trinity of officials (San Chieh Kung): the God of Blessing (Shang Yuan or Heaven Official), the God of Forgiving (Chung Yuan or Earth Official), and the God of Saving (Hsia Yuan or Water Official).

On a lower level of power and importance come the *Gods judging certain localities*. These include Cheng Huang, who is the city god; the Lord of Area, Grandfather Earth, and Wang Yeh.

Next come *Gods protecting various occupations and special groups,* who are so important to the daily life of Taiwanese:

Other categories of gods are listed below to give a sense of the diversity of the Taiwanese pantheon. These are still but a portion of the virtually uncounted total:

The gods judging in hell are the Ti Tsang Bodhisattva, Tung Yueh Ta Ti, and an additional Ten Gods of the Courts in Hell. These are served by various other gods, such as the Assistant gods (one who holds the seal on the left side, and another who holds the sword on the right side); Assistants to the judge gods (the secretary god who sits on the left side, and the god of punishment on the right side; and Matsu's assistant gods (the god with thousand mile eyes, and the god with radio-like ears).

The civil organization of the gods is matched with a military one that is once again a copy of the organization found in the mundane world:

These social and military structures in the Taiwanese pantheon are copied from ancient Chinese society, and therefore their organized systems can never be changed. Today Taiwanese still keep this traditional ideology as part of their beliefs, for they satisfy such areas as mysticism.

In spite of scientific developments, Taiwanese steadfastly believe in a trichotomous view of the cosmos: the Heavenly World, the Earthly World, and the World of Dead Spirits. Each world has its ruler and officers, and its organization and specific activities, but the whole cosmos is controlled by the highest God, the Heavenly Grandfather. The kingdom of the pantheon always faces its rivals—demons, evil spirits, malevolent ghosts, and wandering devils, for example, so it needs military forces to exorcize them and keep the people at peace.

Conclusion

It may be wondered why Taiwanese people still worship such a pantheon in this civilized era. The answers lie in the realization that folk beliefs have their cultural essence and also their historical background. It is unjust to call this re-

ligious phenomenon superstition, for it is a true religious experience among Taiwanese people. For example, though many people are converted in their hearts to more institutionalized religions such as Christianity, and appear to have forsaken traditional worship, they still cannot forsake the old ideology. As a result, some Taiwanese Christians may be described as "folk religion Christians" because they seek security in Jesus Christ and the Holy Spirit and look to God the Creator as a benevolent old man—an Earthly Grandpa—while praying to Jesus as a healing god.

This can be illustrated by the Christian church elder who asked his dying father to protect his family during the funeral. How natural Christian ancestor worship is! If every kind of religious experience is true, it is very difficult to say these kinds of religious expression are superstitious.

Polytheistic beliefs are a necessary tendency of an agricultural society because the cultural situation supports people in this way of thinking. Obviously it cannot be denied that folk beliefs include superstitions, especially laissez-faire religious attitudes such as living in fear of demons, believing in shamanic therapy, and control by unknown divine beings. But these beliefs are the contemporary manifestations of a lengthy, and continuing, tradition.

Article 27

Sinorama, November 1992

Every Number an Omen—Chinese Lucky Numbers

Congratulations! Mr. Chang, today is your 80th birthday, and is also a good day to bring a daughter-in-law into the house. Let me calculate for a minute here and get you a good expression. To celebrate: Living in harmony as one group, The coming of two happinesses to your door, The Mutual support among three generations, All as you wish for the four seasons, The approach of the five fortunes, Six-six everything goes smoothly, Seven sons and eight sons-in-law, Many things through the nine wishes, and Perfection ten times over.

There is a set of famous streets in Kaohsiung City in Taiwan, which all begin with numbers. They are Yihsin (One Heart), Ersheng (Two Sacreds), Santo (Three Mores), Ssuwei (Four Upholds), Wufu (Five Fortunes), Liuho (Six Realms), Chihsien (Seven Virtues), Pateh (Eight Moral Precepts), Chiuju (Nine Wishes), and Shihchuan (Perfect Ten) Streets. This sequence of auspicious street names gives people a warm feeling when they hear it, and brings more than a little luck to the residents.

Many foreign visitors can't help but exclaim that the Chinese are really creative, and can line numbers up so "auspiciously."

Chinese not only use numbers to appeal for good fortune, they also bring them out to chew people out: "You 250 [fool], you do things neither three nor four [without any order or out of touch], and still you dare to say that I'm 13 points [stupid] and 3–8 [scatterbrained]."

Although it isn't really possible to know where these came from, one thing is for sure: numbers are intimately related to the daily life of Chinese!

Origins in the *Book of Changes*: In antiquity, people kept tallies by tying knots in ropes, and only employed numbers and words later on.

From natural phenomena and life experience, people gradually came to recognize the signs of change in a particular matter. For example, there was the ancients' saying that "If the moon has a halo it will be windy, and a damp plinth foretells rain." It is inevitable that there will be misfortune in life, so people began to adopt ways to attract the auspicious and expel the malicious. Add to this that people have psychological activity and the ability to link things together in their minds, and a whole set of auspiciousness-attracting and evil-expelling habits took shape.

The *I Ching* or *Book of Changes* is a compilation which records the experience of people in ancient times with luck and divination. In the *Book of Changes*, each number has some significance: one is the *tai-chi* or "great supreme," two is the "two rituals," three is for the "three powers," four for the "four directions," five is for the "five pathways," six stands for the "six realms," seven for the "seven rules of government," eight means the "eight trigrams," nine is for the "nine chains," and ten is the "ten depictions."

We often say "three *yang* make good fortune" to describe the hope that misfortune will be held at bay and good luck will follow. It is a saying often used at the New Year and symbolizes a new beginning and finds its origins in the *Book of Changes*. *Yang* is the positive force in the universe, and there is enormous *yang* and very weak *yin* (negative force) in the first, second, and third of the ninth trigrams. So the three *yang* are very positive.

Li Heng-lih, chairman of the International Taoism Scholarly Foundation, who feels that numbers have no connection with fortune good or ill, says that the only significance numbers have is what people ascribe to them. Trying to say that a given number is either auspicious or ominous is mere superstition.

Still, unlike the western sensitivity to the number 13, Chinese have a whole philosophy built up around numbers, which is spread or experienced in real life.

Yuan Chang-rue, head of the Anthropology Section at the Taiwan Provincial Museum, raises the theory of "identity supernaturalism." He states that Chinese people believe that similar sounds can produce similar outcomes, so that "identity of pronunciation" has become the foundation of many allegedly beneficent numbers.

The vast influence of identical pronunciation: For example, in Cantonese the pronunciations of "eight" and "success" are very close, which makes the number significant for Cantonese. But for Fukienese it has no function.

Taiwanese have many taboos around the similarity of the sounds for "four" and "death," but Hakkanese couldn't seem to care less.

The study of names and the nine-boxed-paper, a very widespread belief among ordinary people, involves surmising a person's personality and fate according to the number of strokes of the pen in the three characters of the name. In the West and Japan, a type of fortunetelling has been developed based on adding together the numbers of the year, month, and day of one's birth, and using it to assess the person's fate. Others are able to roughly guess a person's personality from their favorite numbers.

The popularity of auspicious or lucky numbers is related to the idea of the pursuit of harmony in names by, for instance, using the radical or character for "metal" to compensate for apparent lack of "metal" in the person, or using the "water" radical to make up for a deficiency of same. Li Heng-lih points out that numbers can be divided into *sheng* and *cheng* types, the former being one through five and the latter being six through ten. In this scheme, one and six are for water; two and seven are for fire; three and eight belong to wood; four and nine signify metal; and five and ten are for earth. If you divide them up by *yin* and *yang*, the negative and positive forces, one, three, five, seven, and nine are all *yang,* and two, four, six, eight, and ten are *yin.*

If a person's celestial branch or stem as determined by their date and time of birth (the *pa-tzu* or "eight character horoscope") come under "wood," then it is necessary to add "water" to feed the wood. So one could choose one or six as lucky numbers. Which one would be better? If the person comes under *yin* wood, then it would be better to choose the number one, which symbolizes both *yang* and water.

Gods can be alone, but people cannot: One is the number marking the beginning, and also has the meaning of "independent" or "alone."

Tong Fung-wan, a professor of theology at Taiwan Theological Seminary, points out that in Taiwan people prefer even numbers which symbolize "fortune comes in pairs." They are more wary of one, three, five, seven, and nine. Because the character for "odd" in Chinese (*tan*) also means "alone," people are not very fond of it. But although people like even numbers, the gods can be alone. Thus in odd-numbered months holidays have been stipulated to help people get by, from New Years (first day of the first month on the lunar calendar) and Tomb Sweeping Day (third day of the third month) to Dragon Boat Festival (fifth of the fifth), Chinese Valentine's Day (seventh of the seventh), and Old People's Day (ninth day of the ninth month in the lunar calendar).

At weddings, when Chinese people give "red envelopes" with gifts of cash, they only send even amounts, like 1,200 or 3,600. Because the pronunciation of "four" is close to that of "death" in Taiwanese, if you send 4,400 to the bride and groom, people won't be grateful and might even criticize you behind your back for failing to understand basic manners. At funerals, on the other hand, people usually give offerings with the last digit being odd, so as to avoid ill fortune not coming "alone."

Happiness comes in pairs: In the book *Popular Chinese Customs* Professor Lou Tzu-kuang notes that when people got married in ancient times, betrothal gifts would include a document recording all the details of the accompanying gifts. The writing style was rather meticulous. Thus, for example, chickens or ducks would be written as "Four wings of poultry." Gold bracelets would be written "Gold bracelets becoming a pair." Candles would be written as "Festive candles with double glow." No place would odd numbers be allowed.

年畫「三陽開泰」
New Year's painting: "Three *yang* bring good fortune."

年畫「一團和氣」
New Year's painting: "Harmonious as one unit."

年畫「五福迎春」
New Year's painting: "Five fortunes welcome the coming of spring."

年畫「百子千孫」
New Year's painting: "One hundred sons and one thousand grandsons."

Courtesy of the Council for Cultural Planning and Development

When inquiring into the other's name and the "eight character horoscope" of the other party, it would be written for instance: "The groom [or bride] is in the beginning of the sixth month of his [her] twentieth year, having been born at such-and-such an hour...." The number of characters in the Chinese text would always have to add up to an even number; if they were short one then an "auspicious" character would be added.

The writer Hsiao Min adds that because the character for "odd" also means "incomplete," when she was in her old home in Peking, they would always make sure that the number of steamed rolls made for New Year's was even in order to make a good beginning.

Chuang Po-ho, a scholar of folk traditions, argues that Chinese have always been rather inclined to the number three. Just open up a Chinese dictionary and there are sayings using three or multiples thereof sprinkled everywhere. They are even more numerous in local sayings and slang.

He points out that one reason Chinese like three is that it stands for "many." In *Lao Tzu* it is said that "Tao gave birth to the one, the one gave birth to the two, two gave birth to three, and three gave birth to the ten thousand things." From nothing to something, or something to infinity, "three" plays a critical role.

Huai Nan Tzu points out that in making offerings to the dead, three bowls of rice was considered in accordance with ritual; and in expressing an offering three gestures were appropriate.

"In the hopes of Chinese people in their lives, 'more' is considered to have an auspicious meaning, so the term 'three mores' naturally arose," says Chuang Po-ho. In widespread folk depictions, the "three mores" are the three fruits including the bergamot orange, the peach, and the pomegranate, signifying "more fortune, more years of life, and more sons." Buddhists, on the other hand, describe the three mores as "more closely associating with friends who will be good for you," "more inhaling of mild fragrance from prayer incense," and "more self-cultivation to correct bad habits."

Elevators without fourth floors: The scholar Su Hsueh-lin has written that in ancient China the numbers four and 72 were perhaps both mysterious numbers, and moreover that "four" was a symbol for the great earth.

But in Taiwan four is not especially well looked-upon. Hospitals and hotels normally have no fourth floor, and the numbers in the elevator just skip right

from three to five. It's probably only in places where Chinese people live that this type of facility is necessary. Also, the price of an apartment on the fourth floor is usually cheaper.

In general, Chinese assign little good or bad significance to "five."

"May the five fortunes approach your door" is a saying often seen at festive occasions. The five fortunes are long life, wealth, health, an ethical life, and a peaceful death.

Besides this, the five elements (metal, wood, water, fire, earth) provided a framework for people at former times to classify natural phenomena. Confucianism also says that five implies the concept of "the mean."

The writer on geomancy Li Jen-kuei points out that Confucians believe that five is very close to the path of the golden mean of "adopting the middle between two extremes," and also promotes the thought of the "five pathways." As a number, five has two at the front and two behind, with one in the middle. "This middle figure has two assistants on each side, and is unbiased in the middle. Thus five fits in well with the idea of the 'mean' always promoted by Confucian scholars," he has written.

Leaving aside for the moment the question of how accurate this is, few people ever suspect anything bad about the number five. The only exception is that in playing the Taiwan drinking game of guess-fingers, the probability of five coming up is higher than for any other number, so there is a slight "taboo" that rules that one cannot call out this number.

One six eight, on the way to success: Where did "66 everything goes smoothly" come from? Lin Mao-hsien, executive secretary of the Chinese Customs and Handicrafts Foundation, contends that it might have something to do with playing dice. Six is the largest number on a die, so wouldn't one win by coming up with two sixes?

According to informal statistics, not many people take seven to be a lucky number. According to the old text *Yu Hsiao Ling Yin*, when someone first dies the mourning period should be seven days. "Doing the sevens" is the custom at funerals in Fukienese areas. For the first seven days after someone passes away, to the seventh seven days, there are appropriate rituals for each. Some people, because the number seven can easily bring to mind "doing the sevens," plus the fact that the seventh month of the lunar year is "ghost month," don't like it. In Taiwanese "3–7" refers to the

30–70 division of money between a prostitute and her pimp, so it cannot be lightly employed.

The fondness for "eight" comes, most people would say, from the Cantonese. In Cantonese, eight and "success" are similar in sound. And in North China, there is the saying that "if you want to succeed, don't stray from eight."

Hongkong, where most of the population is Cantonese, is perhaps the place where faith in numbers is strongest. Li Heng-lih analyzes that it is a very crowded, very competitive industrial metropolis. Businessmen are especially obsessed with success or failure, so they have to include auspiciousness in consideration of any affair like opening a factory or signing a contract. If they can choose a day with eight in it, then they have a "successful" beginning. Nine symbolizes smoothness and endurance, while six, as noted, is for "66 everything goes smoothly."

In the 1980's, lucky numbers went from Hongkong into Kwangtung Province in mainland China, as this trend began to spread from south to north.

Liu Cheng-feng, columnist for the *China Times*, noted in one report that the last four digits of the phone number of the Canton Hotel were 8168, a homophone for "success and yet more success." Most of the shoe stores in the Lungfu Building in Peking use "auspicious" prices on their tags. One of the fastest movers is one whose tag is 168, which symbolizes "the road to success." And when businessmen stay in hotels, they like to stay in rooms 518, 688, or 816. One hotel in Canton even has a higher price on rooms with lucky numbers.

Mainland numbers fever in Taiwan: When the stock market was all the rage, the Jihsheng Securities Company spent NT$600,000 (over US$23,000)to buy the license plate ending in "8888." Now that the stock market is bullish no longer, during bidding for license plates for personal cars this fall, the highest price fetched by "8888" and "6666" was only NT$55,000.

In mainland China, the first time the city of Chungking auctioned off telephone numbers, a mobile phone number of 900-8888 drew a bid of RMB50,000. In the auction held in Shanghai in March of this year, the starting price of numbers ending in 8888 was RMB30,000, and one sold for RMB46,000. A number ending in 2222 was bought for RMB37,000, because in Shanghai dialect it sounds like "come, come, come, come." The record was set on May 18 (the numerical date of which, 5-18, is a homophone for "I will succeed"), when a Hangchow mobile phone number 901-688 was sold for RMB129,000 (over US$25,000).

At the auction of telephone numbers in Peking in August of this year, in just one morning 48 numbers were auctioned off for a total amount of RMB1.04 million. That's about 400 years' salary for the average worker earning about RMB200 a month.

Believe it or not, its up to you: Nine generally refers to a great majority or large number. In former times people often used nine to say "a great many."

Because nine is an extreme number, Chinese have the saying that it is inauspicious to run across nine. Especially for older men, the 69th and 79th birthdays are celebrated as the 70th and 80th instead. Many people also believe that a young man of 29 is at the decisive point in life.

When people use lucky numbers to symbolize wealth and fortune, or peace and benevolence, any number can be explained in such a way as to make it fit. Aren't "everything starts with one and comes around again," "seven generations living together," and "wealth flowing across the four seas" all pleasing to the ears?

Although that's easy enough for us to say, there are still plenty of people who play the lotteries or play the ponies, running near and far, burning incense to the gods, looking for a lucky number that belongs only to them!

Sunny Hsiao/photos courtesy of the Council for Cultural Planning and Development/tr. by Phil Newell)

HONG KONG ARTICLES

Article 28 • *The World Today, June 1996*

At midnight on 30 June 1997, Hong Kong will revert to Chinese sovereignty. The intervening twelve months are bound to be full of uncertainty as the practicalities of the handover and the new government become clearer. In forthcoming issues, The World Today will carry a number of articles reflecting a range of concerns about Hong Kong, China and the region. In April the Gaiko Forum held an international colloquium in association with Chatham House. The two articles which follow are based on the views of Japanese analysts.

Hard and Soft Policies and the Future of Hong Kong

Akio Takahara

Akio Takahara is Associate Professor at the Faculty of Law and Politics, Rikkyo University, Japan.

It is an intriguing historical coincidence that Hong Kong's transfer of sovereignty coincides with significant political developments in China and Taiwan. In Beijing, the ongoing succession contest is approaching its climax. This year and next, the power struggle will inevitably intensify. Meanwhile in Taipei, a democratically elected president has emerged, seeking Taiwan's international recognition. This has produced tension between Beijing, Taipei and Washington. Besides investigating the 'local' issues of Hong Kong, it is worth contemplating how these developments in the wider context may or may not affect the stability and prosperity of the territory. The China factor, the Hong Kong factor and the international factor are all relevant to Hong Kong's future.

What happens in China will, of course, affect Hong Kong in various ways and in varying degrees. Among the numerous variables, such as China's economic performance or the development in its central-local relations, I will focus on the question of future policy tendencies—that is, the kind of policy orientation likely to be dominant in the next few years. This naturally entails a discussion of the future of the Jiang Zemin administration and its power structure.

Let me first give a brief summary of the current power structure in Beijing. In the centre of the political spectrum is the mainstream group, led formerly by Deng Xiaoping and now by General Secretary Jiang Zemin. It advocates policies that are 'hard' on politics but 'soft' on economics; in other words, it is not supportive of further political reform—thus 'hard' on politics—but does support economic reform—thus 'soft' on economics.

This mainstream thinking is flanked by leftist and rightist groups. The leftists are those who are 'hard' on both politics and economics, being unsupportive of reforms in either area; while the rightists are 'soft' in both areas and support political as well as economic reform. The leftists have strongholds in the Party Propaganda Department and the Party Organisation Department, which both have their raison d'être in supporting Party ideology. The rightists, on the other hand, are based in the law-making and consultative bodies, that is, the National People's Congress and the Chinese People's Political Consultative Conference.

As long as mainstream thinking prevails, this structure will be reproduced. If you are 'hard' on politics, you will inevitably activate the leftists, while if you are 'soft' on economics, you cannot avoid the rise of rightist thinking. This is because reliance on the market, which is the essence of economic reform, pluralises interests at the societal level. This creates the need for a political system to express these interests.

Deng Xiaoping has repeatedly emphasised the danger of the left, and if the leftists prevail, this may well have grave implications for Hong Kong. Even now, it is not clear what kind of ideas and policy about Hong Kong the Propaganda and the Organisation Departments have. If the rightists prevail, Hong Kong may be able to follow a smoother transition path.

Third-Generation Leadership

But the likelihood is that Jiang Zemin will be able to keep both leftists and rightists on the sidelines, at least for the time being. To establish his authority as the core of the third-generation leadership, Jiang has to be reselected by his colleagues of the same generation at the Fifteenth Party Congress in late 1997. To achieve this, it is essential for Jiang to secure the support of the military, which traditionally enjoys considerable political clout.

Winning the backing of the military could cause other problems, to which I shall turn later. Jiang is likely to maintain the current power structure in Beijing and continue with the mainstream line of policy, although at times he will lean to the left, or to the right, to keep the balance of power within his administration.

Preserving Charm, Prosperity and Stability

Assuming that there will be no major change in Beijing's general policy orientation and its policy towards Hong Kong, can we say that Hong Kong will manage to retain its charm, prosperity and stability?

First, let me give some indication of what the Japanese business world thinks about it. In recent years, it has been popular to compare the development potential of the Shanghai area with that of the Hong Kong-Guangdong area, or

Greater Shanghai and Greater Hong Kong.

It is safe to say that, in the long run, many Japanese now see more potential in Greater Shanghai. They point to the large area and purchasing power of its hinterland, the firm basis of industrial technology, particularly heavy industry, the high quality of the labour force, the support of the central government in policy and resources, and so on.

However, that is a long-term consideration. The competition between Greater Hong Kong and Greater Shanghai is certainly not a zero-sum game. A good illustration is the Shanghai-based Baoshan Iron and Steel Corporation, which plans to invest in Zhanjiang in Guangdong province, adjacent to Hong Kong.

The Japanese View

The Japanese businessman's view of the future of Hong Kong is reflected in an interesting survey conducted last year by the Japanese Chamber of Commerce in Hong Kong.[1] Of the 449 Japanese firms surveyed, only 15 failed to report a bright future for Hong Kong in the next five years—partly because of the rise in their operational costs. Seventy-seven per cent saw the prospects as good, while eight per cent reported very good prospects.

What Japanese businessmen value most is the low degree of control and regulation of business activities, the well-established system of laws and regulations, and political stability.

Among their concerns about the 1997 transition are the effects of pegging the Hong Kong dollar to the US dollar, possible changes in tax rates, and self-censorship in the media. Their greatest concern by far is the possible erosion of security and an increase in crime—a situation which Japanese firms face in mainland China.

Keeping the Mandarins Clean

Will people in Hong Kong and the Chinese authorities be able to safeguard its advantages and prevent social confusion after the transition? Judging by the views of Japanese businessmen, one of the prerequisites for Hong Kong, if it is to maintain its present charm, is to retain a clean and efficient administration, including, of course, the tax authorities and the police.

It is widely agreed that an institution which has played a crucial role in keeping the mandarins clean is the Inde-

pendent Commission Against Corruption (ICAC), a powerful institution reporting directly to the Governor. Hong Kong's Basic Law stipulates that the ICAC will remain after 1997.

However, in 1993 a Beijing journal intended for internal circulation carried an article by the Chinese Procuratorial Institute of Theory, criticising the ICAC as 'a political tool of the British authorities in their struggle against the Chinese'. It said the ICAC had targeted Chinese enterprises, spreading the view that corruption was increasing with the approach of 1997 and growing contacts with Chinese businessmen.[2]

This small article was alarming, not because of its anti-British tone but because it criticised the special power, organisational status and perks enjoyed by the ICAC and its staff. These are the conditions that are widely regarded as the basis for its effectiveness. Although the ICAC cannot be perfect, I hope the Chinese authorities will assess its merits and drawbacks objectively and support the SAR government in making the most of its fine traditions.

Tense Times

China says it needs a peaceful international environment for its economic development, but it is clear that Hong Kong, too, needs a peaceful environment to sustain and develop its economy. The recent heightening of tension between Beijing, Taipei and Washington hardly bodes well for Hong Kong.

According to Taiwanese statistics, the island's investment in the mainland at the end of last year amounted to $5.6 billion, while figures issued by China are almost double this.[3] Some 30,000 Taiwanese firms have already crossed the Taiwan Strait, and over 100,000 Taiwanese people are working in China.

What is important for Hong Kong is that most of the investment and trade between China and Taiwan is conducted through Hong Kong. However, a survey published by Taiwan's National Association of Industry indicates that 70 per cent of the 45 Taiwanese firms questioned had their confidence in mainland investment shaken by the recent military manoeuvres of the People's Liberation Army (PLA).[4]

Still Most-Favoured?

More worrying from Hong Kong's point of view is the rift between Beijing and Washington. It seems that the Taiwan problem has revived the argument in the

United States for a withdrawal of China's Most-Favoured Nation (MFN) status, a nightmare for Hong Kong which had been forgotten since 1994, when President Clinton decided to de-link MFN from human rights issues.

Unfortunately, the conflict over Taiwan is unlikely to fade in the near future. The basic cause of this lies in the deeply rooted—and reasonable—desire of Taiwanese people not to be treated as second-class citizens in the global community. It was this growing sense of national identity and pride—which was perhaps related to but not necessarily caused by the rise of the middle class—that moved the leadership towards democratisation. It drives them now to pursue international recognition for Taiwan.

On the other side of the Pacific Ocean, an increasing number of Americans have discovered a fledgling democracy resisting the military threat of a communist giant newly arisen from under the ruins of the Soviet Union. The US President is facing an election he needs to win. The military-industrial complex does not mind at all if he sends a couple of aircraft carriers into the seas of China. However, in Beijing, unification with Taiwan is a highly emotional, not necessarily a logical, issue.

Ready for an Arms Race

The doveish foreign-policy initiatives pursued by China in early 1995 failed to contain Taiwan's external activities, which culminated in President Li Denghui's visit to the United States in June last year. This failure apparently provided the PLA with an irresistible opportunity to force the pace of its modernisation and prepare for all sorts of operations across the Taiwan Strait. The results of the Taiwanese presidential election March clearly indicate that China's muscle-flexing can only harden Taiwanese attitudes, although it may to some extent restrict the external activities of President Li.

Thus we can identify a growing vicious circle which is dragging the region into an ominous arms race. For the sake of the prosperity and stability of the region—and not only that of Hong Kong—we must think of ways to break it.

The industrialised countries should, without fanfare and without formally recognising the Republic of China, give first-class treatment to Taiwan citizens. They should abolish whatever comparative inconvenience there is for Taiwanese to travel or conduct economic and cultural activities.

We need not view China as another evil empire because of its military exercises. If we were to do that, what would we think of a Taiwan that planned to conduct manoeuvres on the Mazu Islands just off the coast of mainland Fujian?

On the other hand, Beijing should try to understand the feelings of those who live on the periphery of the former Middle Kingdom. I understand the historical reasons why China is obsessed with the fear that it might be hurt by other powers. However, I also sense a lack of understanding in Beijing about what people in Taiwan and Hong Kong really think and care about.

Of course, it is understandable that China cannot accept Hong Kong becoming a base for subversive activities. But in Hong Kong the major pattern of conflict over the transition is reportedly no longer that between Britain and China; it is now between the local, long-time underground communists and the newcomer communists recently sent from the mainland.

For a smoother transition process, we can only hope that due respect will be paid to the experience, wisdom and judgment of the long-time residents of Hong Kong, and that the principle of 'Hong Kong people rule Hong Kong' will be upheld even within the Chinese Communist Party.

Notes

1. Nihon Keizai Shinbun, 27 November 1995, p. 10.

2. 'Another Aspect of the Hong Kong ICAC', Chinese Procuratorial Institute of Theory, Neibu Wengao, No. 24, 1993.

3. Asahi Shimbun, 24 March 1996.

4. Nihon Keizai Shimbun, 23 March 1996.

Article 29   *The World Today, June 1996*

Learning to Survive with 'Gulliver'

Tatsumi Okabe

Tatsumi Okabe is Professor of International Politics and Asian Studies at Senshu University, Japan, and Professor Emeritus, Tokyo Metropolitan University.

Since the nineteenth century, China has regarded Hong Kong and Taiwan as symbols of its humiliation, and recovering sovereignty over Hong Kong has been one of Beijing's most cherished desires. China attaches so much importance to sovereignty that some of its people are ready to sacrifice economic development for it—especially with regard to Taiwan. China's modern history is also made up of a series of efforts to achieve equality with other powers—including the Western powers and Japan. The problem is: what degree of equality does China require?

The ambiguity of degree is one of the sources of the view that China will present an increasing threat in the future.

It goes without saying that it is better for China to promote the economic development and prosperity of Hong Kong after 1997. In this respect, there is a wide area of common ground between Britain and China. For that matter, most neighbouring countries share the same view. This encourages China to maintain the status quo as far as possible in that territory. What is unfortunate is that China and Britain define the status quo differently.

Whose Status Quo?

The 'one state, two systems' formula is the maximum compromise China is willing to make to maintain the status quo. In this sense, China wants to replace British rule with its own. That is why it has opposed all the reforms carried out by Britain in the run-up to 1997: China seems to think that these reforms are destroying the status quo.

I presume that, on the British side, these reforms are considered indispensable in order to guarantee the rule of law and maintain the status quo without a British presence. The rule of law is a prerequisite for the prosperity of Hong Kong and most other economies. The problem is, therefore, whether China, under the 'one state, two systems' formula, can keep the rule of law rather than the type of rule prevailing on the mainland.

China, being unaccustomed to running a capitalist city, cannot understand the need for political reforms. Besides, these reforms might appeal to elements in mainland China—and there is a 'spiritual pollution' and 'peaceful evolution' spreading through Hong Kong. This might range from exposure to democracy to pornography. I do not agree with China's reaction, but given its historical, domestic and psychological situation, such an attitude is understandable.

Some people in the West are concerned with possible policy changes in China and their international impact. A case in point is the question of whether the reform and open-door policy will continue after Deng Xiaoping. There are many other concerns of this kind. What matters here, however, is not policy intentions but policy effects. I believe China's economic reform policy cannot be changed after Deng Xiaoping. A tighter line, both economically and politically, may be feasible, but the general approach is now impossible to change.

Too Much Competition?

What, then, will happen in Hong Kong after 1997? No one can say exactly, but I believe that the biggest problem will be economic rather than political. Can Hong Kong withstand the economic pressure from the mainland? Many factors are involved, one of which is the fu-

ture of Pudong-Shanghai. Some people believe that Shanghai is trying to replace Hong Kong, although I do not find this convincing.

There are shortfalls of grain production and energy supply. In 1994 the Director of the Worldwatch Institute in Washington, Lester Brown, raised the problem of grain production, and there followed a heated controversy both inside and outside China.[1] At first the Chinese government denied the possibility of such shortages, but in September 1995 a government agricultural research institute, in a joint project with the Japanese Overseas Economic Cooperation Fund, forecast that by the year 2010 the grain shortage might amount to 136 million tons. This could push up the international price of grain. The same considerations apply to the supply of energy. On top of this there are environmental problems and surplus labour in both rural and urban areas. There is mass migration towards the coastal areas, causing confusion and insecurity.

> *Without doubt, China will become a superpower in the middle of the twenty-first century, but until then there will be ups and downs.*

Another very important issue, raised by Paul Krugman of Stanford University in late 1994, is provoking intense debate.[2] He argues that the economic development of East Asia was made possible by increasing input, not by improving productivity. He views East Asia's development as comparable to that of the Soviet Union in the 1960s.

At the Fifth Plenum of the Central Committee of the Communist Party of China in September last year two key issues were emphasised as future tasks in economic development. One, which has been repeated since the beginning of the reform and open-door policies, is the transformation from a planned to a market economy. The other is the transition from extensive to intensive production. This, too, has been discussed for years, but it was not until September last

year that it achieved this degree of importance. I think this reflects the influence of Professor Krugman's argument. Failing to carry out this transformation would produce a stagnant economy, and Hong Kong would be one of the biggest victims of any economic breakdown in China.

Without doubt, China will become a superpower in the middle of the twenty-first century, but until then there will be ups and downs. For the next ten to twenty years, the fluctuations in economic development will probably be the biggest problem for Hong Kong and China's other neighbours. In the years to come, neighbouring countries must anticipate adverse effects from any Chinese economic panic, or even social and political confusion.

Independence or Collusion

There are two possible ways for Hong Kong to survive under these circumstances. One is to unify with Guangdong Province and turn the area into a semi-independent economic unit. The conflict between central and local forces is strong in China, and if decentralisation proceeds, even federalism might move onto the agenda.

The second approach is to behave like typical Chinese merchants and become a kind of parasite of the biggest government in the world. The best way to make money in the Chinese world, both at home and abroad, is to collude with the authorities and use their power. In this case, the prosperity of the region would apparently be maintained, but China, whatever the government, would be exploited by Hong Kong, not vice versa.

The impact of the Hong Kong problem on neighbouring areas and countries, including Taiwan, is clear. Hong Kong's fate, together with the recent military operations in the Taiwan Strait, intended to disrupt Taiwan's presidential election, has made Taiwan more reluctant to unify, although a confederation or some other nominal measures might be possible in future.

Japan and other developed countries have accepted the return of Hong Kong as a *fait accompli*. Their investment is increasing, especially as a door to the Chinese market, but if things go wrong on the Chinese mainland they are ready to switch to Southeast Asia or to other developing countries, such as India.

The 'China Threat'

Southeast Asia's policies of 'engagement' are more political than economic.

The countries of the region have close economic ties with China through Hong Kong. It is, in essence, a kind of Lilliputian strategy 'to tie up Gulliver'. Southeast Asian states see the fate of Hong Kong as a test of China's ability to adapt to international society. If Hong Kong were to become a military base for operations in the Spratly Islands, then the situation would become more serious for Southeast Asian countries.

As for the 'China threat', I am rather cautiously optimistic. When China becomes a big power, the increasing vulnerability of its developing coastal areas to possible retaliatory military attacks will prohibit the use of force by Beijing. But no one knows in which direction China will go or whether Beijing understands the situation well. My belief is that a more liberal policy towards Hong Kong would be advantageous for China and the people of Hong Kong and the region.

Notes

1. Lester Brown, *Who Will Feed China?*, Worldwatch Institute, October 1994.
2. Paul Krugman, 'The Myth of Asia's Miracle', *Foreign Affairs*, Nov./Dec. 1994.

Article 30   *Harvard International Review,* Summer 1996

China's Golden Goose

The Economic Integration of Hong Kong

Charlotte Chui

Charlotte Chui is a Staff Writer for the Harvard International Review.

At midnight on July 1, 1997, Great Britain's 99-year lease on Hong Kong will expire, and jurisdiction over one of the most modern capitalist cities in the world will officially pass into the hands of the People's Republic of China (PRC). Hong Kong presents China with a great economic opportunity. Hong Kong is the world's eighth largest trading entity and the sixth busiest foreign exchange market. Its growth has been exceptional. In the 1990s, Hong Kong's real GDP has grown by approximately five percent per year. With a 1993 per capita GDP of US$18,800, Hong Kong ranks alongside Great Britain and Australia in income—an impressive accomplishment for an island only 75 square kilometers in size.

This spectacular growth has occurred despite the fact that, since 1984, Hong Kong's economy has been shadowed by the impending change in government. In 1984, China denied Great Britain's efforts to renew its lease on the colony. The only agreement that Britain could attain was the Sino-British Joint Declaration. In this statement, Britain agreed to give up its colony on July 1, 1997, on the conditions that Hong Kong would maintain a high degree of autonomy and that its lifestyle would continue unchanged for the next 50 years. After July 1, 1997, Hong Kong would become a special administrative region (SAR) within the PRC. This policy is known as "one nation, two systems."

At the time, this news was greeted with great enthusiasm by the residents of Hong Kong. They were thrilled at finally throwing off the yoke of British colonialism. However, the Tiananmen Square massacre of 1989 turned their joy to apprehension. People wondered how the Beijing government, willing to treat its own people so brutally, would treat its new province.

The Hong Kong Dilemma

China has two alternatives concerning the treatment of Hong Kong. It can destroy Hong Kong's civil liberties, or it can adhere to its promise to leave the island alone for 50 years and allow Hong Kong's economy to grow freely. There is a precedent for the latter approach in Beijing's policies toward five other largely autonomous regions within China. In fact, two of these regions, Guangdong and Shenzhen, are Hong Kong's nearest mainland neighbors. Guangdong is largely self-financing, sets its own economic policy, pays little of its tax revenue to Beijing, and generally ignores central power. Hong Kong could wind up in a similar situation.

Such a hands-off approach is in the PRC's interest. China needs an economically strong Hong Kong to help finance badly-needed infrastructure projects. Shortages of power and poor transportation continue to plague the PRC; China must build more dams, power plants, highways, and railways. Its antiquated telecommunications system also needs an overhaul. All of these projects are projected to cost over US$1 trillion by the year 2000. Investment from Hong Kong would facilitate China's modernization.

Hong Kong has a number of other economic advantages as well. It occupies a key geographic location; it has often been called the gateway to China. It has the largest container port in the world, handling 70 percent of the mainland's export shipments. Furthermore, 91 percent of Hong Kong's re-exports either originate from or are bound for China, and it currently acts as a trade buffer between the estranged nations China and

Taiwan. In 1993, US$8.7 billion worth of trade passed between the PRC and Taiwan through Hong Kong. Thus, Hong Kong plays a crucial role in linking Chinese trade with the rest of the globe.

However, from China's perspective, the Hong Kong issue is not merely economic. If China were to take a completely hands-off approach, it would have to leave in place all the legal structures created by Great Britain, including a popularly elected legislature and a Bill of Rights that was implemented just last year. Such an arrangement would make Hong Kong a hotbed of democracy in China. Beijing cannot afford this situation.

Democratic tendencies aside, Beijing also cannot afford to continue to foster the economic disparity between northern and southern China. Highly industrialized southeastern China, with its Special Economic Zones where investors receive lucrative tax breaks, is already considerably more prosperous than the north. In recent years, the World Bank estimates that as many as 100 to 150 million immigrants have flooded areas such as Guangdong in search of work. The Chinese Labor Ministry puts this number at 214 million. Crime is on the rise, and the government is too weak to fight back. The Communist Party, worried about rising discontent and possible insurrection, has sent out urgent pleas for stability and patience. It could be that, instead of boosting the national economy, the addition of wealthy Hong Kong might destroy it by furthering this destabilizing disparity in wealth. Beijing may not wish to take such a risk.

Finally, Hong Kong's long-term benefit for the Chinese economy is also questionable. At this point in time, Hong Kong does indeed have many resources. However, as China's economy grows larger and stronger, Hong Kong will diminish in importance. Indeed, many in the Chinese central government believe that Hong Kong's importance has already been exaggerated. The acquisition of Hong Kong, they say, is important to south China, but not to China as a whole. With costs in the south rising, businesses are beginning to move north. Shanghai is now being touted as the new gateway to China, and container ports are being built all along the northern coast. Also, several countries, including South Korea and Japan, have indicated that they would be willing to help finance China's modernization projects. Despite the perceived risk of dealing with China, international companies are flocking to invest in the vast resources there as well. In addition, Tai-

wan and China are currently negotiating a direct trade agreement. Thus, China may not be as desperate for the aid of Hong Kong as it seems.

Has China Decided?

In the Sino-British Joint Declaration of 1984, Beijing promised that Hong Kong's capitalist system would remain until at least the year 2047. Furthermore, since the terms of the Joint Declaration were vague, China has, with the aid of numerous prominent Hong Kong citizens, drafted the Basic Law as the future constitution of Chinese Hong Kong. While this document does not give Hong Kong the freedom that had been implied in the Joint Declaration—only one-third of the legislature will be directly elected, and the powerful chief executive will be appointed by Beijing—it does ensure that all contracts, rights, and laws made under British rule would continue to be valid after 1997. Moreover, the Chinese have also been investing heavily in Hong Kong. Over US$20 billion worth of Hong Kong property and stocks are now Chinese-owned.

However, it is not Beijing which is pumping money into the colony, but local governments and officials. Beijing appears to believe that Hong Kong is only important to southern China and not to China as a whole. Hong Kong's economy has already suffered because of Chinese policies. For example, in December of 1992, the Hong Kong stock market, the Hang Seng, plummeted after Beijing threatened to dismantle the government structure of the island. Though the Hang Seng recovered, the damage had been done. Investors began to see Hong Kong as a risk and to look for larger returns on their investments. Soon after Beijing made its announcement, a major investment firm downgraded the status of Hong Kong from a good investment to a risky one. With the prevailing uncertainty about Hong Kong's future, China itself has become a more attractive alternative for investors. China might well have connived for and counted on this situation. This way, Beijing is promoting the economic welfare of the entire nation rather than just one region of the country.

Furthermore, China seems very interested in making Hong Kong into a tractable province, even at the expense of Hong Kong's economy. Already, the inhabitants of Hong Kong are busy learning Mandarin, the official language of the PRC. More significantly, Hong Kong residents will probably not have much

more freedom than their fellow citizens across the harbor. Beijing has already reneged on the terms of its own Basic Law. In 1991, British governor Christopher Patten opened nearly one third of the seats in Hong Kong's Legislative Council to direct elections. The unofficial Chinese embassy in Hong Kong, Xinhua (which doubles as a news agency), campaigned hard for the Beijing-backed candidates. Despite its efforts, though, pro-democracy nominees swept the elections, defeating pro-PRC candidates by humiliating margins. Beijing promptly announced that the new legislature would not be allowed to sit after 1997, and that all the judges would also have to be reappointed. The Patten-sponsored Bill of Rights, which would have allowed individual citizens to sue the government for violations of civil rights, met the same fate. China has stated that the bill will be revoked. It appears that after 1997 China will take over Hong Kong's entire government structure—executive, legislative, and judicial.

Law, Beijing style, has already moved into Hong Kong. In January 1995, a local entrepreneur was abducted in broad daylight. After a long chase, Hong Kong police finally caught up with the kidnappers in Victoria Harbor. The businessman was found tied and gagged on a boat, otherwise unharmed. He had been abducted simply because his Chinese partner wanted to withdraw from a contract. He was lucky to be rescued; he could easily have become one of the many businessmen, embroiled in commercial disputes, who have simply disappeared.

Such occurrences are common on the mainland. Even short of such extreme cases, cronyism and influence-peddling are ways of life there. Those with *guanxi*, or connections, are powerful enough to oust any foreigner. Richard Grosling, a British businessman, had entered a joint venture with a municipal government, but once his money had been invested, he was forced to leave. He is now trying to seize the assets of the government-run corporation which he helped finance. Even large US firms are getting mired down in such disputes. McDonald's in Beijing, for example, had a contract for a 20 year lease on a highly desirable site, but it was recently forced to move. Lehman Brothers, a New York investment firm, is suing two Chinese companies for reneging on $100 million dollars worth of trading losses.

China's looming shadow is further demonstrated by the widespread corruption that has taken root in Hong Kong. Political payoffs, kickbacks, and other such practices are on the rise. Law enforcement is weakening, especially as many British-employed civil servants have requested early retirement before 1997. All this has undermined the stability of the legal institutions which are the foundation of Hong Kong's economic performance. If Hong Kong law becomes just as volatile and inconsistently enforced as Chinese law, economic growth will certainly stagnate.

Hong Kong's Options

The people and businesses of Hong Kong, however, are not entirely subject to the whims of Beijing. They can always leave. Some investors, worried that arbitrary justice could sweep away the legal system after the turnover, have already begun to pull out of Hong Kong. Jardines, a major British-owned corporation, has quietly moved its registered office to Bermuda, delisted from the Hong Kong stock market, and switched share trading in its main subsidiaries to Singapore. Alasdair Matheson, the head of the Hong Kong branch of Jardines, claims its behavior is like that of the hundreds of thousands of Hong Kong residents who have acquired foreign passports. They do this "not because they want to leave Hong Kong, but because they want to be comfortable about staying on."

Other firms, though, are not so reserved in their fears. They worry that property could be seized in 1997. "What matters," explains one businessman, "is where the assets are. If they are in Hong Kong, the Chinese can seize them, whether your corporate headquarters are in Bermuda or Timbuktu." There is indeed precedent for such action. The Chinese government did this in Shanghai in the 1950s; and Jardines was one of the companies which lost all its holdings there. Nevertheless, not everybody is scared. A few corporations, such as Swire Pacific, believe that Chinese policy has changed in the past few decades and are actually deepening their involvement in Hong Kong.

As far as Hong Kong residents are concerned, confidence in Beijing's promises is low. In light of the overwhelmingly pro-democracy, anti-Communist results of Hong Kong's last free election, jittery Hong Kong residents believe that there may very well be a crackdown after the PRC takes over. As a result, they are scrambling to obtain foreign passports. Approximately 65,000 people, lucky enough to be either well-connected or rich, emigrate per year. Although the number of immigrants from China compensates somewhat for the emigrants, there has been a significant brain drain. Those who leave are generally well-educated, middle-level managers, while those who arrive are mostly laborers. To further exacerbate the situation, wealthier residents are pulling their money out of Hong Kong and investing elsewhere in Asia. If the brain and capital drain continues, when China takes over in 1997, the Hong Kong it inherits may well be as worthless as the barren piece of rock it ceded to the United Kingdom in 1842.

In the end, it may not be Beijing which decides Hong Kong's fate at all. With the loss of talented entrepreneurs and managers, Hong Kong's economy may not remain viable, even if China decides to leave it alone. Furthermore, the early retirement of a large number of civil servants may create a legal vacuum which the mainland will be quick to fill. Thus, even if sufficient capital were to be invested, without the ingenuity and skills of a well-educated work force and a strong legal system, Hong Kong's economy cannot prosper.

The hope is that Beijing will prove to be reasonable, capital will once again flow into the city, and the brain shortage will disappear as those who have fled will return home and rebuild Hong Kong under the new system. Unfortunately, reality appears to dictate an entirely different outcome. Hong Kong appears to be relatively insignificant to the long-run welfare of the Chinese economy, and thus China has little incentive to preserve the island's political and economic systems. Without any assurances of democracy, and with the legal system disintegrating, there would be little motive for new investments or for Hong Kong's expatriates to return. Should such a scenerio unfold, in a few years, today's vibrant, dynamic Hong Kong may be little more than a memory.

Credits

PEOPLE'S REPUBLIC OF CHINA

Page 94 Article 1. This article appeared in *The World & I,* April 1996. Reprinted by permission from *The World & I,* a publication of The Washington Times Corporation. © 1996.

Page 98 Article 2. Reprinted with permission from *Current History* magazine, September 1996. © 1996, Current History, Inc.

Page 103 Article 3. Reprinted by permission of *Harvard International Review.*

Page 107 Article 4. © 1996 by Review Publishing Company, Ltd. Reprinted by permission from *Far Eastern Economic Review,* Hong Kong.

Page 108 Article 5. © 1996, The Washington Post. Reprinted by permission.

Page 112 Article 6. Reprinted with permission. © 1996 *The National Interest,* No. 45, Fall 1996, Washington, DC.

Page 119 Article 7. This article appeared in *The World & I,* April 1996. Reprinted by permission from *The World & I,* a publication of The Washington Times Corporation. © 1996.

Page 124 Article 8. Reprinted by permission of The Bulletin of the Atomic Scientists. © 1996 by the Educational Foundation for Nuclear Science, 6042 South Kimbark Avenue, Chicago, Illinois 60637, USA. A one-year subscription is $36.

Page 128 Article 9. © 1996 by The New York Times Company. Reprinted by permission.

Page 130 Article 10. © 1996 by The Economist, Ltd. Distributed by The New York Special Features.

Page 132 Article 11. Reprinted with permission from The World Future Society, Bethesda, Maryland.

Page 136 Article 12. Reprinted by permission from M. E. Sharpe, Inc., Armonk, NY 10504.

Page 140 Article 13. Reprinted with permission from *Current History* magazine, September 1996. © 1996, Current History, Inc.

Page 147 Article 14. This article appeared in *The World & I,* December 1995. Reprinted by permission from *The World & I,* a publication of The Washington Times Corporation. © 1995.

Page 151 Article 15. Reprinted from *The American Enterprise,* a Washington-based magazine of politics, business, and culture.

Page 156 Article 16. Reprinted from *World Press Review,* August 1996, first published in *The Independent.* © 1996 by The Independent. Reprinted by permission.

Page 158 Article 17. With permission from *Natural History,* July 1996. © 1996 by the American Museum of Natural History.

Page 162 Article 18. © September 9, 1996, U.S. News & World Report. Reprinted by permission.

Page 165 Article 19. Reprinted by permission of *The Wall Street Journal,* August 5, 1996. © 1996 by Dow Jones & Company, Inc. All rights reserved worldwide.

Page 166 Article 20. © 1996 by The New York Times Company. Reprinted by permission.

Page 168 Article 21. Reprinted with the permission of *Archaeology* Magazine, September/October 1996. © 1996 by the Archaeological Institute of America.

Page 172 Article 22. Reprinted with the permission of *Archaeology* Magazine, January/February 1996. © 1996 by the Archaeological Institute of America.

Page 175 Article 23. This article appeared in *The World & I,* October 1989. Reprinted by permission from *The World & I,* a publication of The Washington Times Corporation. © 1989.

Page 179 Article 24. Reprinted by permission of *Sinorama Magazine.*

TAIWAN

Page 181 Article 25. Reprinted with permission from *The New York Review of Books.* © 1996 Nyrev, Inc.

Page 185 Article 26. Reprinted from *Free China Review,* January 1988.

Page 190 Article 27. Reprinted by permission of *Sinorama Magazine.*

HONG KONG

Page 193 Article 28. © 1996 by The Royal Institute of International Affairs. Reprinted by permission.

Page 195 Article 29. © 1996 by The Royal Institute of International Affairs. Reprinted by permission.

Page 197 Article 30. Reprinted by permission of *Harvard International Review.*

Sources for Statistical Reports

U.S. State Department, *Background Notes* (1996).

C.I.A. *World Factbook* (1996–1997).

World Bank, *World Development Report* (1996).

UN *Population and Vital Statistics Report* (January 1997).

World Statistics in Brief (1996).

Statistical Yearbook (1996).

The Statesman's Yearbook (1996–1997).

Population Reference Bureau, *World Population Data Sheet* (1996).

World Almanac (1997).

Demographic Yearbook (1996).

Glossary of Terms and Abbreviations

Ancestor Worship   Ancient religious practices still followed in Taiwan, Hong Kong, and the People's Republic of China. Ancestor worship is based on the belief that the living can communicate with the dead and that the dead spirits to whom sacrifices are ritually made can bring about a better life for the living.

Brain Drain   A migration of professional people (such as scientists, professors, and physicians) from one country to another, usually in search of higher salaries or better living conditions.

Buddhism   A religion of East and Central Asia founded on the teachings of Siddhartha Guatama (the Buddha). Its followers believe that suffering is inherent in life and that one can be liberated from it by mental and moral self-purification.

Capitalist   A person who has capital invested in business, or someone who favors an economic system characterized by private or corporate ownership of capital goods.

Chinese Communist Party (CCP)   Founded in 1921 by a small Marxist study group, its members initially worked with the Kuomintang under Chiang Kai-shek to unify China and, later, to fight off Japanese invaders. Despite Chiang's repeated efforts to destroy the CCP, it eventually ousted the KMT and took control of the Chinese mainland in 1949.

Cold War   A conflict carried on without overt military action and without breaking off diplomatic relations.

Communism   Theoretically, a system in which most goods are collectively owned and are available to all as needed; in reality, a system of government in which a single authoritarian party controls the political, legal, educational, and economic systems, supposedly in order to establish a more egalitarian society.

Confucianism   Often referred to as a religion, actually a system of ethics for governing human relationships and for ruling. It was established during the fifth century B.C. by the Chinese philosopher Confucius.

Contract Responsibility System   A system of rural production in which the land is contracted by the village to individual peasant households. These households are then responsible for managing the production on their contracted land and, after fulfilling their production contracts with the state, are free to use what they produce or to sell it and pocket the proceeds. Such a system has been in place in China since the late 1970s and has replaced the communes established during the Maoist era.

Cultural Revolution   Formally, the Great Proletarian Cultural Revolution. In an attempt to rid China of its repressive bureaucracy and to restore a revolutionary spirit to the Chinese people, Mao Zedong (Tse-tung) called on the youth of China to "challenge authority" and "make revolution" by rooting out the "reactionary" elements in Chinese society. The Cultural Revolution lasted from 1966 until 1976. It seriously undermined the Chinese people's faith in the Chinese Communist Party's ability to rule and led to major setbacks in the economy.

De-Maoification   The rooting-out of the philosophies and programs of Mao Zedong in Chinese society.

Democratic Centralism   The participation of the people in discussions of policy at lower levels. Their ideas are to be passed up to the central leadership; but once the central leadership makes a decision, it is to be implemented by the people.

Exco   The Executive Council of Hong Kong, consisting of top civil servants and civilian appointees chosen to represent the community. Except in times of emergency, the governor must consult with the Exco before initiating any program.

Feudal   In Chinese Communist parlance, a patriarchal bureaucratic system in which bureaucrats administer policy on the basis of personal relationships.

Four Cardinal Principles   The Chinese Communists' term for their commitment to socialism; the leadership of the Chinese Communist Party; the dictatorship of the proletariat; and the ideologies of Karl Marx, Vladimir Lenin, and Mao Zedong.

Four Modernizations   A program of reforms begun in 1978 in China that seeks to modernize agriculture, industry, science and technology, and defense by the year 2000.

Gang of Four   The label applied to the four "radicals" or "leftists" who dominated first the cultural and then the political events during the Cultural Revolution. The four members of the Gang were Jiang Qing, Mao's wife; Zhang Chunqiao, former deputy secretary of the Shanghai municipal committee and head of its propaganda department; Yao Wenyuan, former editor-in-chief of the *Shanghai Liberation Daily*; and Wang Hongwen, a worker in a textile factory in Shanghai.

Great Leap Forward   Mao Zedong's alternative to the Soviet model of development, this was a plan calling for the establishment of communes and for an increase in industrial production in both the cities and the communes. The increased production was to come largely from greater human effort rather than from more investment or improved technology. This policy, begun in 1958, was abandoned by 1959.

Great Proletarian Cultural Revolution   See *Cultural Revolution*.

Gross Domestic Product (GDP)   A measure of the total flow of and services produced by the economy of a country over a certain period of time, normally a year. GDP equals gross national product (GNP) minus the income of the country's residents earned on investments abroad.

Guerrilla A member of a small force of "irregular" soldiers. Generally, guerrilla forces are used against numerically and technologically superior enemies in jungles or mountainous terrain.

Han Of "pure" Chinese extraction. Refers to the dominant ethnic group in the P.R.C.

Ideograph A character of Chinese writing. Originally, each ideograph represented a picture and/or a sound of a word.

Islam The religious faith founded by Muhammad in the sixth and seventh centuries A.D. Its followers believe that Allah is the sole deity and that Muhammad is his prophet.

Kuomintang (KMT) The Chinese Nationalist Party, founded by Sun Yat-sen in 1912. Currently the ruling party on Taiwan. See also *Nationalists*.

Legco Hong Kong's Legislative Council, which reviews policies proposed by the governor and formulates legislation.

Long March The 1934–1935 retreat of the Chinese Communist Party, in which thousands died while journeying to the plains of Yan'an in northern China in order to escape annihilation by the KMT.

Mainlanders Those Chinese in Taiwan who immigrated from the Chinese mainland during the flight of the Nationalist Party in 1949.

Mandarin A northern Chinese dialect chosen by the Chinese Communist Party to be the official language of China. It is also the official language of Taiwan.

Mao Thought In the post-1949 period, originally described as "the thoughts of Mao Zedong." Mao's "thoughts" were considered important because he took the theory of Marxism-Leninism and applied it to the concrete conditions existing in China. But since Mao's death in 1976 and the subsequent reevaluation of his policies, Mao Thought is no longer conceived of as the thoughts of Mao alone but as the "collective wisdom" of the party leadership.

May Fourth Period A period of intellectual ferment in China, which officially began on May 4, 1919, and concerned the Versailles Peace Conference. On that day, the Chinese protested what was considered an unfair secret settlement regarding German-held territory in China. The result was what was termed a "new cultural movement," which lasted into the mid-1920s.

Nationalists The KMT (Kuomintang) Party. The ruling party of the Republic of China, now in "exile" on Taiwan.

Newly Industrialized Country (NIC) A term used to refer to those developing countries of the Third World that have enjoyed rapid economic growth. Most commonly applied to the East Asian economies of South Korea, Taiwan, Hong Kong, and Singapore.

Offshore Islands The small islands in the Formosa Strait that are just a few miles off the Chinese mainland but are controlled by Taiwan, nearly 90 miles away.

Opium A bitter, addictive drug made from the dried juice of the opium poppy.

Opium War The 1839–1842 conflict between Britain and China, sparked by the British import of opium into China. After the British victory, Europeans were allowed into China and trading posts were established on the mainland. The Treaty of Nanking, which ended the Opium War, also gave Britain its first control over part of Hong Kong.

People's Procuracy The investigative branch of China's legal system. It determines whether an accused person is guilty and should be brought to trial.

People's Republic of China (P.R.C.) Established in 1949 by the Chinese Communists under the leadership of Mao Zedong after defeating Chiang Kai-shek and his Nationalist supporters.

Pinyin A new system of spelling Chinese words and names, using a Latin alphabet of 26 letters, created by the Chinese Communist leadership.

Proletariat The industrial working class, which for Marx was the political force that would overthrow capitalism and lead the way in the building of socialism.

Republic of China (R.O.C.) The government established as a result of the 1911 Revolution. It was ousted by the Chinese Communist Party in 1949, when its leaders fled to Taiwan.

Second Convention of Peking The 1898 agreement leasing the New Territories of Hong Kong to the British until 1997.

Shanghai Communique A joint statement of the Chinese and American viewpoints on a range of issues in which each has an interest. It was signed during U.S. President Richard Nixon's historic visit to China in 1971.

Socialism A transitional period between the fall of capitalism and the establishment of "true" communism. Socialism is characterized by the public ownership of the major means of production. Some private economic activity and private property are still allowed, but increased attention is given to a more equal distribution of wealth and income.

Special Administrative Region (SAR) A political subdivision of the People's Republic of China that will be used to describe Hong Kong's status after it comes under Chinese sovereignty in 1997. The SAR will have much greater political, economic, and cultural autonomy from the central government in Beijing than do the provinces of the P.R.C.

Special Economic Zone (SEZ) An area within China that has been allowed a great deal of freedom to experiment with different economic policies, especially efforts to attract foreign investment. Shenzhen, near Hong Kong, is the largest of China's Special Economic Zones.

Taiwanese Independence Movement An organization of native Taiwanese who want to overthrow the Mainlander KMT government and establish an independent state of Taiwan.

Taoism A Chinese mystical philosophy founded in the sixth century B.C. Its followers renounce the secular world and lead lives characterized by unassertiveness and simplicity.

United Nations (UN) An international organization established on June 26, 1945, through official approval of the charter by delegates of 50 nations at a conference in San Francisco. The charter went into effect on October 24, 1945.

Yuan Literally, "branch"; the different departments of the government of Taiwan, including the Executive, Legislative, Judicial, Control, and Examination Yuans.

Bibliography

PEOPLE'S REPUBLIC OF CHINA

Periodicals and Newspapers

The following periodicals and newspapers are excellent sources for coverage of Chinese affairs:

Asian Survey
Australian Journal of Chinese Affairs
Beijing Review
China Business Review
China Daily
China Quarterly
Far Eastern Economic Review
Foreign Broadcasts Information Service (FBIS)
The Free China Journal
Free China Review
Joint Publications Research Service (JPRS)
Journal of Asian Studies
Modern China
Pacific Affairs

General

Jung Chang, *Wild Swans: Three Daughters of China* (New York: Simon and Shuster, 1992).
   A superb autobiographical/biographical account that illuminates what China was like for one family for three generations.
Kwang-chih Chang, *The Archeology of China,* 4th ed. (New Haven: Yale University Press, 1986).
_____, *Shang Civilization* (New Haven: Yale University Press, 1980).
   Two works by an eminent archaeologist on the origins of Chinese civilization.
Nicholas D. Kristof and Sheryl WuDunn, *China Wakes* (New York: Times Books, 1994).
   The authors, who won the Pulitzer Prize in journalism for their reporting on the Tiananmen crisis of 1989, have written a highly readable composite of their memories and perspectives on China since the late 1980s.
Mark Salzman, *Iron and Silk* (New York: Random House, 1987).
   A written account of the experiences of a young American teacher in China in the early 1980s that provides a perspective on life in post-Mao China.

History

Patricia Buckley Ebrey, *The Cambridge Illustrated History of China* (New York: Cambridge University Press, 1996).
   Beautifully illustrated book on Chinese history from the Neolithic Period through to the People's Republic of China.

John King Fairbank, *China: A New History* (Cambridge: Harvard University Press, 1992).
   Examines motivating forces in China's history that define it as a coherent culture from its earliest recorded history to 1991. Looks at the multifaceted, often contradictory aspects of Chinese civilization that have been the source of both its unity and its internal conflicts.
Tony Saich and Hans Van de Ven, eds., *New Perspectives on the Chinese Communist Revolution* (Armonk, NY: M. E. Sharpe, Inc., 1995).
   Articles provide new perspectives on the CCP's rise to power from its founding in 1921 to its victory in the civil war in 1949. Looks at how the CCP operated, the role of intellectuals and women in the Communist movement, the peasants' responses to the CCP's efforts at mobilization, and other topics related to the ultimate success of the CCP.
Edgar Snow, *Red Star Over China* (New York: Grove Press, 1973).
   This book, which first appeared in 1938, is the author's account of the months he spent with the Communists' Red Army in Yan'an in 1936, in the midst of the Chinese civil war. It is a thrilling story about the Chinese revolution in action, and includes Mao's own story (as told to Snow) of his early life and his decision to become a Communist.
Jonathan D. Spence, *The Search for Modern China* (New York: W. W. Norton & Co., 1990).
   A lively and comprehensive history of China from the seventeenth century to 1989. Looks at the cyclical patterns of collapse and regeneration, revolution and consolidation, growth and decay.
Denis Twitchett and John K. Fairbank, *The Cambridge History of China*, Vols. 1–15 (New York: Cambridge University Press, 1978–1992).
   The most authoritative general history of China from Vol. I (the Chin and Han Empires dating back to 221 B.C. through 220 A.D.) through Vol. 15, (the People's Republic of China through 1982).

Politics, Economics, Society, and Culture

Julia F. Andrews, *Painters and Politics in the People's Republic of China, 1949–1979* (Berkeley: University of California Press, 1994).
   A fascinating presentation of the relationship between politics and art from the beginning of the Communist period until the eve of major liberalization in 1979.
Robert Barnett, ed., *Resistance and Reform in Tibet* (Bloomington: Indiana University Press, 1994).
   An informative and quite balanced collection of articles on the highly emotional and politicized topic of Tibet.
Ma Bo, *Blood Red Sunset* (New York: Viking, 1995).
   Perhaps the most compelling autobiographical account by a Red Guard during the Cultural Revolution. Responding to Mao Zedong's call to youth to "make revolution," the

author captures the intense emotions of exhilaration, fear, despair, and loneliness. Takes place in the wilds of Inner Mongolia.

Nien Cheng, *Life and Death in Shanghai* (New York: Grove Press, 1987).
A gripping autobiographical account of a woman persecuted during the Cultural Revolution because of her earlier connections with a Western company, her elitist attitudes, and her luxurious lifestyle in a period when the Chinese people thought the rich had been dispossessed.

Qing Dai, *Yangtze! Yangtze!* (Toronto: Probe International, 1994).
Collection of documents concerning the debate over building the Three Gorges Dam on the upper Yangtze River in order to harness energy for China. Among opponents are many scientists, committed Communists who argue the dam will lead to environmental disaster. The book itself was banned in China in 1989.

Michael S. Duke, ed., *World of Modern Chinese Fiction: Short Stories & Novellas from the People's Republic, Taiwan & Hong Kong* (Armonk, NY: M. E. Sharpe, Inc., 1991).
Collection of short stories written by Chinese authors from China, Taiwan, and Hong Kong during the 1980s. The 25 stories are grouped by subject matter and narrative style.

B. Michael Frolic, *Mao's People: Sixteen Portraits of Life in Revolutionary China* (Cambridge: Harvard University Press, 1980).
A must read. Through composite biographies of 16 different types of people in China, the author offers a humorous but penetrating view of "unofficial" Chinese society and politics. Biographical sketches reflect political life during the Maoist era, but the book has enduring value for understanding China.

David S. G. Goodman, *Beijing Street Voices: The Poetry and Politics of China's Democracy Movement* (London: Marion Boyars, 1981).
An analysis of the 1978–1979 "democracy movement" and its participants. Includes translations from wall posters posted on "democracy wall" in Beijing, the first prodemocracy movement to occur in the P.R.C.

David S. G. Goodman and Beverly Hooper, eds., *China's Quiet Revolution: New Interactions between State and Society* (New York: St. Martin's Press, 1994).
Articles examine the impact of economic reforms since early 1980s on the social structure and society generally, with focus on changes in wealth, status, power, and newly emerging social forces.

Ruth Hayhoe, ed., *Education and Modernization: The Chinese Experience* (New York: Pergamon Press, 1992).
Examines the role that education has played in China's modernization, from Confucian education in imperial China to Marxist education in the Communist period. Looks at pedagogical issues and how women and minority groups are treated in the educational system.

Alan Hunter and Kim-kwong Chan, *Protestantism in Contemporary China* (New York: Cambridge University Press, 1993).
Examines historical and political conditions that have affected the development of Protestantism in China. Chinese cultural beliefs and religious practices, which are an eclectic mix of Shamanism, Buddhism, Daoism, animism, and ancestral worship, have shaped Protestantism, as have the government's policies toward religion.

William R. Jankowiak, *Sex, Death, and Hierarchy in a Chinese City* (New York: Columbia University Press, 1993).
Written by an anthropologist with a discerning eye, this is one of the most fascinating accounts of daily life in China. Particularly strong on rituals of death, romantic life, and the on-site mediation of disputes by strangers (e.g., with bicycle accidents).

Maria Jaschok and Suzanne Miers, eds., *Women and Chinese Patriarchy: Submission, Servitude and Escape* (New York: Zen Books, 1994).
Examines Chinese women's roles, the sale of children, prostitution, Chinese patriarchy, Christianity, and feminism, as well as social remedies and avenues of escape for women.

Zhisui Li, *The Private Life of Chairman Mao* (New York: Random House, 1994).
A credible biography of the Chinese Communist Party's leader Mao Zedong written by his physician from the mid-1950s to his death in 1976. Wonderful details about Mao's daily life and his relationship to those around him.

James T. Myers, *Enemies without Guns: The Catholic Church in China* (New York: Paragon House, 1991).
Interrelates history of the Chinese Catholic Church with the course of Chinese domestic politics, with an emphasis on persecution and oppression of Chinese Catholics.

Suzanne Ogden, *China's Unresolved Issues: Politics, Development, and Culture,* 3rd ed., (Englewood Cliffs: Prentice Hall, 1995).
A thematic and issue-oriented approach to Chinese politics. Presents the ongoing issues in Chinese politics in terms of the interaction between Chinese culture, politics/ideology, and development.

Suzanne Ogden, Kathleen Hartford, Lawrence Sullivan, and David Zweig, eds., *China's Search for Democracy: The Student and Mass Movement of 1989* (Armonk, NY: M. E. Sharpe, 1992).
An excellent collection of wall posters, handbills, and speeches of the prodemocracy movement of 1989. These documents capture the passionate feelings of the student, intellectual, and worker participants.

Michel Oksenberg, Lawrence R. Sullivan, and Marc Lambert, eds., *Beijing Spring, 1989: Confrontation and Conflict: The Basic Documents* (Armonk, NY: M. E. Sharpe, 1990).
Collection of the major official documents of the Chinese government and Communist Party in the period immedi-

ately preceding and during the prodemocracy movement in the spring of 1989.

Tony Saich, ed., *The Chinese People's Movement: Perspectives on Spring 1989* (Armonk, NY: M. E. Sharpe, 1990).

A collection of essays on the prodemocracy movement of 1989. Topics include the Chinese tradition of student protests, the political economy, the lack of organization in the student leadership of the movement, the emergence of civil society, and the changing role of the Chinese media.

Martin Schoenhals, *The Paradox of Power in a People's Republic of China Middle School* (Armonk, NY: M. E. Sharpe, 1993).

An in-depth study of aspects of Chinese culture as revealed in the educational system.

Ronald D. Schwartz, *Circle of Protest: Political Ritual in the Tibetan Uprising* (New York: Columbia University Press, 1994).

Focuses on demonstrations in Tibet against Chinese rule from 1987 to 1992. Author argues that Chinese policy, which encouraged the revival of religion and culture in the 1980s, unexpectedly provided the basis for the revival of Chinese nationalism.

James and Ann Tyson, *Chinese Awakening: Life Stories from Unofficial China* (Boulder: Westview Press, 1995).

Lively verbal portraits of the lives of Chinese people from diverse backgrounds (for example, "Muddy Legs: The Peasant Migrant"; "Turning Iron to Gold: The Entrepreneur"; "Bad Element: The Shanghai Cosmopolite").

Ezra F. Vogel, *One Step Ahead in China: Guangdong under Reform* (Cambridge: Harvard University Press, 1989).

A case study of Guangdong Province, which abuts the "Special Economic Zones" and Hong Kong. Demonstrates how Guangdong has raced ahead of the rest of China through economic liberalization, and the problems and opportunities created by a mixed (planned and free market) economy.

Robert P. Weller, *Resistance, Chaos and Control in China: Taiping Rebels, Taiwanese Ghosts, and Tiananmen* (Seattle: University of Washington Press, 1994).

Addresses issues of tacit cultural resistance, which may or may not become a political movement or armed rebellion. Uses three cases to illustrate forms that cultural resistance may take: the Taiping Rebels in the nineteenth century; ghost worship in Taiwan; and efforts of the Chinese people to resist cultural control after the Tiananmen crisis of 1989 led to cultural repression.

Chihua Wen, *The Red Mirror: Children of China's Cultural Revolution* (Boulder: Westview Press, 1995).

A former editor and reporter for New China News Agency in Beijing presents the heartrending stories of a dozen individuals who were children at the time the cultural Revolution started. It shows how rapidly changing policies of the period shattered lives of its participants and left them cynical adults 20 years later.

Mayfair Mei-hui Yang, *Gifts, Favors, and Banquets: The Art of Social Relationships in China* (Ithaca: Cornell University Press, 1994).

Investigates the social grease of relationships in China through an analysis of how, why, and to whom gifts, favors, and bequests are given in China. Looks at the etiquette, tactics, and ethics of developing relationships that are the basis for getting anything done in China.

Jianying Zha, *China Pop: How Soap Operas, Tabloids, and Bestsellers Are Transforming a Culture* (New York: W. W. Norton, 1995).

A Chinese mainlander examines the impact of television, film, weekend tabloids, and best-selling novels on today's culture. Some of the material is based on remarkably revealing interviews with some of China's leading film directors, singers, novelists, artists, and cultural moguls.

Foreign Policy

Harry Harding, *A Fragile Relationship: The United States and China since 1972* (Washington, D.C.: The Brookings Institution, 1992).

Traces U.S.–China relations from President Richard M. Nixon's historic visit to China in 1972 to the 1990s. Takes a U.S. perspective to interweave commentary on issues of U.S.–China relations with the corollary issue of U.S.–Taiwan relations.

Richard Madsen, *China and the American Dream: A Moral Inquiry* (Berkeley: University of California Press, 1995).

Looks at the emotional and unpredictable relationship the United States has had with China from the nineteenth century to the present.

Thomas Robinson and David Shambaugh, eds., *Chinese Foreign Policy: Theory and Practice* (New York: Oxford University Press, 1994).

Provides the most comprehensive study of China's foreign policy since 1949 to date. Carefully documents the historical, cultural, domestic, perceptual, economic, ideological, geopolitical, and strategic issues influencing China's formulation of foreign policy.

Robert S. Ross, *Negotiating Cooperation: The United States and China, 1969–1989* (Stanford: Stanford University Press, 1995).

The difficulties of engineering a cooperative relationship between the United Sates and China are presented from a "realist" framework that assumes the primary concern of both sides is with national security and the "strategic balance." The Soviet threat is considered critical to Sino-American efforts to cooperate.

Jonathan Unger, ed., *Chinese Nationalism* (Armonk, NY: M. E. Sharpe, 1996).

An excellent collection of articles about Chinese nationalism today, how this nationalism has developed, and how nationalism might be used to pursue China's domestic and foreign policies.

TAIWAN

Politics, Economics, Society, and Culture

Joel Aberbach et al., eds., *The Role of the State in Taiwan's Development* (Armonk, NY: M. E. Sharpe, 1994).
Articles address technology, international trade, state policy toward the development of local industries, and the effect of economic development on society, including women and farmers.

Hsiao-shih Cheng, *Party-Military Relations in the PRC and Taiwan* (Boulder: Westview Special Studies on China and East Asia, 1990).
Argues that military participation in government, not the control of the military through the political commissar system, is the key stabilizing factor in both the P.R.C. and Taiwan.

Bih-er Chou, Clark Cal, and Janet Clark, *Women in Taiwan Politics: Overcoming Barriers to Women's Participation in a Modernizing Society* (Boulder: Lynne Rienner Publishers, 1990).
Examines the political underrepresentation of women in Taiwan and how Chinese culture on the one hand and modernization and development on the other are affecting women's status.

Hill Gates, *Chinese Working Class Lives: Getting By in Taiwan* (Ithaca: Cornell University Press, 1987).
An in-depth, well-written account of the culture of Taiwan's working people. Includes nine individual histories. Particularly strong on Taiwan's culture, religious traditions, family relations, status of women, and the political economy of working-class people.

Stevan Harrell and Chun-chieh Huang, eds., *Cultural Change in Postwar Taiwan* (Boulder, Co: Westview Press, 1994).
A collection of essays that analyzes the tensions in Taiwan's society as modernization erodes many of its old values and traditions.

Steven J. Hood, *The Kuomintang and the Democratization of Taiwan* (Boulder: Westview, 1997).
Looks at the controversial role of the ruling Kuomintang (Nationalist Party) in Taiwan's development. Examines role of Kuomintang in democratization of Taiwan.

David K. Jordan, *Gods, Ghosts, and Ancestors: The Folk Religion of a Taiwanese Village* (Berkeley: University of California Press, 1972).
A fascinating analysis by an anthropologist of folk religion in Taiwan, based on field study. Essential work for understanding how folk religion affects the everyday life of people in Taiwan.

Chin-chuan Lee, "Sparking a Fire: The Press and the Ferment of Democratic Change in Taiwan," in Chin-chuan Lee (ed.), *China's Media, Media China* (Boulder: Westview Press, 1994), pp. 179–193.

Tse-kang Leng, *The Taiwan–China Connection: Democracy and Development across the Taiwan Straits* (Boulder: Westview Press, 1996).
A case study of Taiwan's policies toward the China mainland. Includes analysis of institutional conflicts and power struggles in Taiwan over policies toward China, as well as the role of the business community in developing these relations.

Robert M. Marsh, *The Great Transformation: Social Change in Taipei, Taiwan, since the 1960s* (Armonk, NY: M. E. Sharpe, 1996).
An investigation of how Taiwan's society has changed since the 1960s when its economic transformation began.

Murray Rubinstein, ed., *The Other Taiwan: 1945 to the Present* (Armonk, NY: M. E. Sharpe, 1994).
Articles focus on those groups within Taiwan whose views of Taiwan differ from those of the establishment. Critical perspectives on the "Taiwan miracle."

N. T. Wang, ed., *Taiwan's Enterprises in Global Perspective* (Armonk, NY: M. E. Sharpe, Inc., 1992).
A series of articles on Taiwan's economy, including such topics as Taiwan's personal computer industry, the internationalization of Taiwan's toy industry, liberalization and globalization of the financial market, and Taiwan's economic relationship with mainland China.

Mayside H. Yang, ed., *Taiwan's Expanding Role in the International Arena* (Armonk, NY: M. E. Sharpe, 1997).
This book, edited by the director of Taiwan's main opposition party, presents the perspectives of a number of governments (including Taiwan, Australia, the United States, Hong Kong, China, and the governments of Germany and divided Korea) on Taiwan's role in the international arena.

Foreign Policy

Dennis Hickey, *United States–Taiwan Security Ties: From Cold War to Beyond Containment* (Westport: Praeger, 1994).
Examines U.S.–Taiwan security ties from the cold war to the present and what Taiwan is doing to ensure its own military preparedness.

Martin L. Lasater, *The Changing of the Guard: President Clinton and the Security of Taiwan* (Boulder: Westview, 1995).
A policy-oriented book concerning how the Clinton administration can manage Taiwan's security within the context of the U.S. relationship with China. Focuses on the changing aspects of American interests due to the changed conditions in the international security environment of the 1990s.

Robert G. Sutter and William R. Johnson, *Taiwan in World Affairs* (Boulder: Westview Press, 1994).
Articles give comprehensive coverage of Taiwan's involvement in foreign affairs. Topics covered include Tai-

wan's role in the economic development of East Asia; Taiwan in the international arms market; Taiwan's efforts to gain legitimacy as an international actor; Taiwan's relations with the P.R.C.; and the implications of Taiwan's international role for U.S. foreign policy.

Nancy Bernkopf Tucker, *Patterns in the Dust: Chinese–American Relations and the Recognition Controversy, 1949–1950* (New York: Columbia University Press, 1983).

An excellent account of the Truman government's efforts to make the right decision about how to treat both the Chinese Communists when they gained control of China's government, and the Chinese Nationalists who had fled to Taiwan.

HONG KONG

Politics, Economics, Society, and Culture

"Basic Law of Hong Kong Special Administrative Region of the People's Republic of China," *Beijing Review*, Vol. 33, No. 18 (April 30–May 6, 1990), supplement.

Bruce Bueno de Mesquita, David Newman, and Alvin Rabushka, *Red Flag over China* (Chatham: Chatham House Publishers, Inc., 1996).

The author argues that Hong Kong is going to suffer greatly once it is returned to Chinese rule. Negative about virtually everything China does, but positive about virtually everything Hong Kong has achieved under colonial rule.

Ming K. Chan and Gerard A. Postiglione, *The Hong Kong Reader: Passage to Chinese Sovereignty* (Armonk, NY: M. E. Sharpe, 1996).

A first-rate collection of articles about the issues facing Hong Kong during the transition to Chinese rule, by these authors who live and work in Hong Kong. Also examines how the issues may he addressed after July 1, 1997, as well.

Stephen Y. L. Cheung and Stephen M. H. Sze, *The Other Hong Kong Report, 1995* (Hong Kong: Chinese University Press, 1995).

An annual publication with timely articles of the time of Hong Kong's transition to Chinese rule on topics such as Hong Kong's legal system, the Basic Law (constitution), elections, the civil service, anticorruption, and women.

John Gordon Davis, *Hong Kong through the Looking Glass* (Hong Kong: Kelly & Walsh Ltd., 1977).

A humorous, informed, and insightful presentation of life in Hong Kong, through narrative and photographs. Gives readers a feel for life in Hong Kong.

Berry Hsu, ed., *The Common Law in Chinese Context* in the series entitled *Hong Kong Becoming China: The Transition to 1997* (Armonk, NY: M. E. Sharpe, Inc., 1992).

Examines common law aspects of the "Basic Law," the mini-constitution that will govern Hong Kong after 1997.

Benjamin K. P. Leung, ed., *Social Issues in Hong Kong* (New York: Oxford University Press, 1990).

Collection of essays on select issues in Hong Kong such as aging, poverty, women, pornography, and mental illness.

William McGurn, *Perfidious Albion: The Abandonment of Hong Kong 1997* (Washington, D.C.: Ethics and Public Policy Center, 1992).

A condemnation of the British selling out of the interests of the people of Hong Kong, beginning in 1984, in the interests of strengthening Sino-British ties.

Jan Morris, *Hong Kong: Epilogue to an Empire* (New York: Vintage, 1997).

Witty and detailed first-hand portrait of Hong Kong by one of its long-term residents. Gives the reader the sense of actually being on the scene in a vibrant Hong Kong.

Foreign Policy

Ming K. Chan, ed., *Precarious Balance: Hong Kong between China and Britain, 1842–1942* (Armonk, NY: M. E. Sharpe, 1994).

Collection of essays concerning Hong Kong's efforts to balance its relations with China and Great Britain from the time it became a British colony in 1842 to 1942.

Robert Cottrell, *The End of Hong Kong: The Secret Diplomacy of Imperial Retreat* (London: John Murray, 1993).

Exposes the secret diplomacy that led to signing of the "Joint Declaration on Question of Hong Kong" in 1984, the agreement to end 150 years of British colonial rule over Hong Kong and return it to Chinese rule.

Mark Roberti, *The Fall of Hong Kong: China's Triumph and Britain's Betrayal* (New York: John Wiley & Sons, Inc., 1994).

A fast-paced, drama-filled account of the decisions Britain and China made about Hong Kong's fate since the early 1980s. Based on interviews with 150 key players in the secret negotiations between China and Great Britain.

Frank Welsh, *A Borrowed Place: The History of Hong Kong* (New York: Kodansha International, 1996).

Best single book on Hong Kong's history from the time of the British East India Company in the eighteenth century through the Opium Wars of the nineteenth century to the present.

MISCELLANEOUS

Johan Bjorksten, *Learn to Write Chinese Characters* (New Haven: Yale University Press, 1994).

A delightful introductory book for writing Chinese characters with many anecdotes about calligraphy.

Index